FANNY KEMBLE

THE MACMILLAN COMPANY
NEW YORK · BOSTON · CHICAGO · DALLAS
ATLANTA · SAN FRANCISCO

MACMILLAN AND CO., Limited
LONDON · BOMBAY · CALCUTTA · MADRAS
MELBOURNE

THE MACMILLAN COMPANY
OF CANADA, Limited
TORONTO

FANNY KEMBLE
From the portrait by Thomas Sully
In the Pennsylvania Academy of Fine Arts

FANNY KEMBLE

A

Passionate Victorian

—•—

By Margaret Armstrong

—•—

*"The death I should prefer would be
to break my neck off the back of a good
horse at a full gallop on a fine day."*

F. K.

THE MACMILLAN COMPANY

NEW YORK

1938

PRINTED IN THE UNITED STATES OF AMERICA
BY H. WOLFF BOOK MFG. CO., NEW YORK

CONTENTS

FANNY KEMBLE

CHAPTER I

Warp and Woof

"The web of our life is of a mingled yarn."
—SHAKESPEARE.

THE STORY begins a long way back, on an August morning in the year of Our Lord 1676 and in Hereford gaol where John Kemble, a priest of the old religion, sat waiting for the cart that was to carry him to Widmarsh and the gallows. Of an ancient Wiltshire family and nephew of that George Kemble who had saved the life of Charles II after the battle of Worcester, Father John had been wont to think rather well of his family in general and of Uncle George in particular. But now, in common with other Roman Catholic subjects of King Charles, he was beginning to wonder whether George Kemble's noble deed had been worth doing; for Father John was a victim of the Popish Plot. He had nothing to hope for from the King. At best, the Stuart memory was conveniently short and with England in hysterics Charles was too distracted to remember such unimportant friends as the Kembles.

As everybody knows, the Popish Plot was an imaginary conspiracy invented by Oates and developed by Bedloe, whose tales of vast armies mustering in Spain and Flanders to invade Great Britain filled English gaols, kept the hangman busy and, incidentally, added several names to Rome's list of martyrs. Why Father John Kemble should have been singled out remains a mystery; he was an inconspicuous old man, living in retirement in Pembridge Castle. But if the offer of a martyr's crown came as a surprise, it was accepted with alacrity. According to his chronicler: "When Mr. Kemble was apprised of some being come to take him, he replied that he had but a few years to live, and that it would be an advantage to

1

him to suffer for his religion, and therefore he would not abscond." So he offered no resistance when he was arrested by Captain Scudamore and lodged in Hereford gaol where, being of a kindly disposition, he made friends with his gaoler and the Scudamore children, "who he treated with whatever he had that was good sent him by his friends."

But the months dragged. He was glad when he was sentenced to death, still gladder when the morning of the twenty-second of August came at last. He asked for a cup of sack and a pipe of tobacco and proceeded to enjoy these refreshments with his gaoler, never dreaming that the incident, omitted by his chronicler as unsuitable for a martyr's last moments, would so take the popular fancy that to this day a "Kemble cup" and a "Kemble pipe" are rustic terms for a pledge at parting. Then the cart arrived; he drove cheerfully to Widmarsh, made a little speech, and turned to the executioner. "He took him by the hand," the chronicle goes on, "and calling him by name, Honest Anthony, said he, my friend Anthony, be not afraid, do thine office, I forgive thee with all my heart, thou wilt do me a greater kindness than discourtesy. Then drawing the cap over his eyes, and after a little meditation upon his knees, he told them they might do their office when they pleased. The cart was drawn away, and he hanged at the least half an hour before he was dead, the knot of the rope not being properly applied; though this, it is believed, happened rather by accident than by design. The Protestants that were spectators of his exit acknowledged that they never saw one die so like a gentleman and a Christian. His head was cut off, his body being begged by his nephew Captain Richard Kemble, who put it in a coffin, carried it to Welsh Newton, buried it in the churchyard there, and erected a tomb over it."

But it seems that death could not end the old man's affection for the Scudamore children. Soon after his execution, the rope that had hanged him being applied to the neck of one of Captain Scudamore's daughters afflicted with a sore throat she was instantly cured, and when a prayer at his tomb restored the hearing of another the miracles were reported far and wide and Welsh Newton churchyard became an object of pilgrimage.

The years went by. Charles II left the stage; Stuarts less picturesque such as Queen Mary and Queen Anne followed him; the first Georges went their way; but the name of Father John Kemble was still remembered in Hereford. For over a hundred years the cathedral chimes had kept toll of the hours since old John had enjoyed that last cup and last pipe, and still the feet of pilgrims trod a path across Welsh Newton churchyard. A humble procession for the most part, uninteresting except from the clerical standpoint. If Heaven permitted old John to keep watch over his shrine it must have been gratifying to see two stately figures approach the low green mound one summer's day in the early nineteenth century, and stand gazing at it with reverence although they neither prayed nor crossed themselves. For the names and faces of this couple were known from one end of England to the other; moreover, any contempt a priest might feel for their calling would, with Father John, be offset by the claims of family. They were Kembles: Sarah and Charles, eldest and youngest of the twelve children of Roger—perhaps belonging to the same branch as Father John and perhaps not. Anyway, they were Kembles, and Sarah Siddons, known as the "Tragic Muse," was the greatest actress the world had ever seen, and Charles was "Shakespeare's ideal gentleman and hero of romance."

In all probability it was Charles who had suggested this visit to the ancestral shrine—a matter of history, commemorated by a minor poet—for he had been educated at the martyr's own college of Douai in the hope that he might take holy orders, and would have heard the story of the cup and pipe. However that may be, if Heaven allowed Father John a glimpse of his young kinsman his feelings must have been mixed. Charles was a fine figure of a man, in his claret-colored coat, brass buttons, tight-strapped trousers and voluminous neck-cloth, but in spite of a pious education Charles was Catholic in name only. As for Sarah—Sarah was not even that. Roger had shared his children with his Protestant wife; all the boys had been started safely in the old religion but all the girls were Protestant. However, there was no denying that Sarah was a magnificent creature, as she stood there, beautiful head a little bent, reading the martyr's name on the stone, her full silk skirts falling to her feet in classic folds. But too serious-minded; of the two, Charles would prove the merrier company. For Charles was smiling—perhaps recalling his narrow escape from Douai and the tonsure as he gave his arm to his sister and they turned away, crossed the grass, reached the gate, and were lost in the shadow of its guardian yews.

A trivial incident? Not altogether; few families can boast of a martyr in the background, a martyr who died *like a gentleman;* and it must have been this solemn tradition that enabled the Kembles, root and branch, to feel themselves just a little better than anybody else, and to win respect for their name at a time when their trade was still considered shady if not wicked. In France, an actor might not receive the last sacraments or be buried in consecrated ground; even Talma could sigh: *"Pour moi, je serai heureux si les prêtres me laissent enterrer dans un coin de mon jardin!"* But their contemporaries speak of the "Kemble dynasty," the "Kemble manner," the "Kemble jaw and the Kemble nose," and compare the "Kemble line to the line of Banquo." To be sure, the "six generations of Kembles that adorned the stage" worked hard to elevate their profession, but they could never have succeeded—as they most certainly did succeed—if they had not been sustained by a belief in the superior quality of the Kemble brains, birth and breeding. It was family pride that gave the Kembles their mannerisms and tricks of speech, their measured diction and erect carriage, and that took them serenely through waves of misfortune where a less self-satisfied tribe would have been engulfed.

One finds them moving majestically across the pages of almost every English diary and memoir from 1750 to 1900. Charles Greville and Sir Thomas Lawrence, Emerson and Longfellow, Henry James and the Brownings, all had a word, a respectful word, for the Kembles. The elder group were very tall, very handsome, heads well up, aloof, a trifle condescending like aristocrats with a kindly tolerance for the failings of the peasantry. And one marvels at the fate that turned these splendid, slightly pompous creatures towards the stage. Their "properties" were not masks and buskins, but the crozier and the woolsack. Roger's sons should have been bishops and judges. Mrs. Siddons should have been an empress of Byzantium. Thackeray's daughter Anne summed it up: "The Kembles," she wrote, "strike one somehow as a race apart. They seem divided from the rest of us by more dominant natures, by more expressive ways and looks; one is reminded of those deities who once visited the earth in the guise of shepherds, as wanderers clad in lion skins, as muses and huntresses; not as Kembles only."

In this family Olympus Mrs. Siddons reigned supreme; while Charles, "whose looks Apollo might have envied," being possessed of an ungodlike sense of humor, took a lower place than John Philip, known as "Glorious John," the Jove of the group, who only smiled complacently when Byron called him "supernatural," or Scott brought him an eagle's feather from the Highlands for his helmet in 'Macbeth.' The portraits of all three, as well as half a dozen lesser Kembles of their time, were painted and copied and engraved and caricatured. Anecdotes of them were told and retold. Reynolds, Gainsborough and Lawrence felt honored in being allowed to paint Mrs. Siddons; no one thought it odd that the "Tragic Muse" should bear Sir Joshua's signature on the hem of her robe in order that "his name might thus be preserved to posterity." Even the caricatures and anecdotes were tinged with awe. It was said that "Glorious John" had a rival in his retirement at Lausanne; he was jealous of Mont Blanc. Mrs. Siddons was compared to the ocean with only the East India Company grand enough for a lover. When Talleyrand asked Brougham whether Fox had not been *"très occupé de madame Siddons?"* *"Oh, que non,"* said Brougham, *"je ne conçois pas comment on pouverait être; on serait tout aussi bien occupé de la mer que de madame Siddons. Elle était trop grande dans son genre pour inspirer l'amour. La Compagnie des Indes, par exemple, pourroit oser l'aimer—rien moins que cela!"*

As for Charles, the debonair, "his comedy had high spirits and high breeding, and was the very embodiment of graceful well-bred wit." Long after his time, an admirer reproved a young actor who had ventured to suspect that Charles Kemble had not been anything very wonderful, with: "Young sir, if you were to dream tonight that you saw Charles Kemble as he was in his prime, when you woke in the morning you would cut your throat!" Brander Matthews wrote: "As Faulconbridge, he came into Angiers with the indolent grace of a tawny lion."

This graceful, well-bred young man was Fanny Kemble's father.

The story on the mother's side is very different; no sombre tradition to add dignity to the family tree, no gallant rescuer of royal lives, no martyr dying for the faith. From the world's standpoint, the De Camps were as devoid of ancestors as Melchisedek himself. Victorian writers remark with simple directness that Mrs. Charles Kemble was "of vulgar origin"; but they used the term in an old-fashioned sense; we should say today that she "came of plain people." The record begins with a French captain and a young Swiss girl who met and married while the French army was invading Switzerland. Captain De Camp was penniless and the bride's father too poor to afford a *dot*. But the range of the Jungfrau dominated her childish horizons, and in her blood was a love of nature in its wilder aspects of mountain and waterfall that, handed down, was to console more than one of her grandchildren and great-grandchildren in the darkest moments of their lives.

For the Swiss girl herself the Alps soon became a memory. Captain De Camp brought his family to London hoping to find an opening there—he had a turn for the arts; but fog and cold were too much for him, he coughed his life out and left his wife and five children to follow his example unless one of his offspring turned out better equipped than himself for the battle of life. One of them did. Marie Thérèse De Camp, the oldest child, born in Vienna on the birthday of the empress, was scarcely more than a baby when the family began to depend on her; the little creature could dance and sing and act —dance like a butterfly, sing like a nightingale and act better than most full-grown actresses of the time—and from the night of her début as Cupid in an opera of Novelle's she helped to support her still smaller brothers and sisters. She was twelve when her father died and she became her family's sole support. Luckily she was courageous as well as clever, and passionately fond of the stage; she might arrive at the opera house half starved and shivering but once dressed in her fairy frock she could wave her wand and point her satin slippers as if she had not a care in the world. Very soon the grace and spirit of the "little French fairy" made friends for her outside the theatre; Lady Perceval instructed her in reading, writing and ciphering; Miss Buchanan gave her music lessons, corrected her English pronunciation and taught her Italian; "the delightful dark-eyed girl, whose every motion was music e'er her voice was heard," became the fashion.

For in Regency London art was at a premium; painters, musicians and poets were well paid and admired; even actors were tolerated, and the Prince Regent's architects were encouraged to turn London into a modern metropolis. In Marie Thérèse's childhood Londoners of middle age could remember seeing foxes killed in Cavendish Square, and recalled the site of Berkeley Square as "a capital place for snipe"; the streets she hurried through at night were nearly as dark as a medieval town and plumbing usually began and ended at the pump, until a row of gaslights made their appearance in front of Carleton House and the Prince built himself a bathroom of pure white marble. The British public instinctively distrusted a prince with "an exquisite ear for music," who admired Raeburn's pictures, read Jane Austen's novels, made a friend of Sheridan because he was so witty and of Brummell because he was so well dressed; they disapproved of everything George said or did, with one exception; they approved his alliance with Maria Fitzherbert and liked to believe that she was his wife.

George and Maria were just back from their honeymoon when the "little French fairy," Marie Thérèse De Camp, was brought to Mrs. Fitzherbert's house in Park Street to entertain them. Not quite so gorgeous as Carleton House, it was large enough for theatricals and concerts and gay with looking-glass and gilding; from the high ceilings crystal chandeliers sprouted hundreds of wax candles, enormous fires roared up the chimneys, flowering shrubs scented the air, insuring the hot-house atmosphere the Prince enjoyed and his guests found so oppressive that strong men panted for breath and ladies fainted dead away upon the polished floors.

But one may be sure that little Marie Thérèse found no fault with warmth and light and glitter when she made her first appearance there as a dancer in Le Texier's troupe of performing children; she was half starved, the refreshments handed about by attendants in green and gold tasted like manna from heaven. And a very friendly heaven it must have seemed to her, for the Prince was devoted to children. The pleasantest anecdotes of George IV are connected with children. He meets the child Victoria with a jolly, "Give us your little paw!" and rewards her with a jewel for her compliance; he takes small Minney Seymour, Mrs. Fitzherbert's adopted daughter, on one plump satin knee and small George Keppel on the other, and makes them laugh with jokes about "Minney and Prinny." But the earliest and prettiest of these anecdotes is the story of the Prince and "the little French fairy."

For Marie Thérèse was too individual to remain in any background; after a few appearances she was singled out from the group of children and soon made a special place for herself in the household. Perched on that plump satin knee of "Prince Charming"—at twenty-four he deserved the name— the little thing was encouraged to display her accomplishments until her head would have been turned if it had not been level as well as pretty, and rewarded with more sweets than she could manage. When in after life Marie Thérèse described, as she liked to do, "the extraordinary beauty and charm of manner of the Prince of Wales," she was apt also to recall his enormous capacity for food; no matter how many sugar-plums she made away with he would always exclaim: "My poor child, Heaven has not blessed you with an appetite!" Another scene is pretty enough for *toile de Jouy:* "One of the Prince's favorite jokes was to place the child under a huge glass bell made to cover some large group of precious Dresden china, where her tiny figure and flashing face produced an even more beautiful effect than the costly work of art whose crystal covering was her momentary cage."

A pretty scene, and worth remembering; for this picture of the laughing child imprisoned under a glass bell is the companion piece to that other picture in the family gallery, Charles Kemble standing beside the tomb of his martyred kinsman. And the contrast is significant. Marie Thérèse had no dignity or family pride to bequeath, but her charm and sensitiveness to beauty in art and nature were handed down in full measure, and if some of her children inherited their mother's passionate likes and dislikes and lack of self-control, one of the four also received a high courage and the power to laugh and keep on laughing even when she found herself in prison. This child, whose life was made and marred by her inheritance from the "little French fairy," was Marie Thérèse's eldest daughter, Fanny Kemble.

CHAPTER II

Birth

"By all thy dower of lights and fires,
By all the eagle in thee, all the dove."

—CRASHAW.

IT WAS the year 1809. In Europe, a year of battles; Corunna and Wagram and a dozen other hard knots snarled into the skein that Napoleon and his enemies were dragging back and forth across the Continent. In England, a year of quarrels in politics; Canning and Castlereagh fighting it out at last with pistols for two on Putney Heath. At court, Mrs. Fitzherbert encountering her last rival, Lady Hertford, with disastrous results and departing for the botany and gardening of Parson's Green. All these disturbances could no doubt be traced to their sources by historians and economists. But no chart has yet been plotted that can tell why this was also a year of memorable birthdays, and whether heredity or environment played the part of fairy godmother in the matter of gifts.

The distribution was dispassionate enough. The baby who came to the Poes one bleak January day in Boston had little in either his ancestry or his surroundings to warrant expectations, yet he received a remarkably pretty gift. On the other hand, young Felix Mendelssohn, who made his appearance in Hamburg that February, had a right to what he got; there was music in the family past and present. But was it heredity or environment that played fairy godmother a few days later, crossed the Atlantic, lighted on a Kentucky farm and dropped into the cradle of Nancy Lincoln's lean long-limbed boy a gift more magnificent than poetry or music? And if this birthday seems to prove that genius owes "nothing to nobody," what about two other birthdays that same February?—Charles

10

Darwin inherited straight from grandfather Erasmus, and
Cyrus McCormick's reaper was half his father's. As for Edward Fitzgerald, who came into the world just as spring was
brightening Suffolk copses with her last violets, there can be
little doubt that a godparent brought a blessing, a Persian
godparent by the name of Omar; and it must have been the
wolds of Lincolnshire that turned Tennyson into a poet and
London that made Dicky Milnes into Lord Houghton. But
why should cool New England ancestry and environment
have produced that genial soul Oliver Wendell Holmes, and
which variety of fairy was in attendance at the Gladstones
when Highland Anne presented her Lowland husband with a
fourth son just as the old year was making way for the new?

Anyhow, that old year must have slipped into the past with
a smile of satisfaction, for no year before or since can boast
of so many gifted children. Indeed a whole century might be
proud of the richness and variety of the list, and that without
counting still another birthday of 1809 which is marked with
a star, one that to the Kemble family was worth all the others
put together. Spring, summer and winter all made their mark.
It was in the autumn, on the twenty-seventh of November,
that Mrs. Charles Kemble gave birth to her second child, a
girl. The child's heredity was a blend of France and England;
her environment was to be a blend of Europe and America.

It was not a propitious moment for another Kemble to
come into the world. The preceding year had been marked
by turmoil and anxiety for the whole family connection;
every Kemble to the remotest cousin was interested in the
success of John Kemble's venture, a part purchase of Covent
Garden theatre. And for a time "Glorious John" had the
sympathy of the public, everybody approved the purchase,
lamented when the theatre was burned down, applauded the
Duke of Northumberland's contribution of ten thousand
pounds to rebuild it, and admired the larger handsomer structure that rose on the ruins of the old. Everybody compli-
mented John on his pluck and compared him to the phoenix,

and shook hands with Charles—and would have shaken hands with Mrs. Siddons if they had dared—and with all London buzzing praise and congratulation John set about his preparations for the opening night.

London expected great things of him and John determined that London should not be disappointed. No expense must be spared, scenery and costumes down to the smallest architectural and archeological detail must be absolutely perfect. John proceeded to let himself go; turned a deaf ear to Sarah Siddons's remonstrances—Sarah's economy was a family joke—insisting that a slight rise in the price of tickets—a mere seven shillings instead of six in the boxes, and a corresponding extra shilling in the pit—would make everything all right. The public would understand.

The great night came. John's optimism as to that extra shilling a ticket had not been entirely justified, and the box-office reported the public in a fretful mood; but the house was sold out and at an early hour a vast audience was on its way to the new theatre. An audience of the utmost respectability; just that agreeable mingling of the world of fashion, country gentlemen and notables of the professional classes necessary to make an opening night a success, enlivened by a sprinkling of artists who recognized John Kemble as the first great producer of the English stage and felt it their duty to encourage him.

Among the latter was Sir Thomas Lawrence, a lifelong admirer of Mrs. Siddons and her family. Though he and his party arrived long before the hour the streets were already crowded with a turbulent mob, and having made their way in with some difficulty they found the theatre nearly full. Lawrence observed that few women had ventured to be present; but the rise of the green curtain brought applause and everyone joined so heartily in 'God Save the King' that misgivings were forgotten until John Kemble entered for the opening speech. And then, to the horror of his friends, a volley of hisses came pelting down from the gallery! The Kemble faction clapped their loudest; in vain. As Lawrence wrote later to a friend: "The effect of a lawless, hir'd, determin'd and persevering Minority continued sensibly to tell, while the Majority wearied out with opposition and disappointment (for not one word, from the first scene of the Play to the last of the Farce, was heard) sat in silent chagrin, thinning gradually in their numbers, and every vacant place immediately occupied by blackguards, evidently marshalled for the purpose. At intervals a Fellow attempting some outrage was dragged out, but all attempts to check the general Tumult was totally in vain. The cries were 'Off! off!'—'No raised prices!' " When the performance was over, the mob swarmed up on the stage, and held it until dispersed by the magistrates.

All London agreed that it was a shocking affair, and all London at once took sides. Duchesses and charwomen, cabinet ministers and costermongers, bishops and chimney sweeps, fell to arguing; meanwhile, night after night, the street mobs grew larger and the audiences smaller. For the Kembles— royalty slapped in the face—refused to give in. At length Mrs. Siddons and her brothers found themselves acting to empty boxes; for their firmest adherents could not face the "O.P. dance" on the seats of the pit, the tin horns, catcalls and yells of *Old Prices! Old Prices!* "reiterated in shouts, thrown upon the stage in letters, written upon papers four feet long and hoisted upon poles."

The "O.P. Riots" had begun early in September. October found the deadlock as hopeless as ever. Neither John Kemble nor the mob would yield an inch. From the first Mrs. Charles Kemble had been in the thick of the fight. The Kemble wives were courageous and not given to sparing themselves even when their babies were well on the way. Mrs. Roger Kemble —the "old lioness of them all"—had taken the part of Prospero to oblige her husband, acted it to the public's satisfaction, and only a few days later, at the Leg o' Mutton Tavern in Brecon, produced her most famous child, the future Mrs. Siddons!

With this example to encourage her, Mrs. Charles Kemble had done her share of acting during the preceding winter and made herself useful with the costumes and scenery for the new theatre. Her love of beauty and elegance was gratified by its magnificence and the events of the opening night came as a shattering blow. She shared her husband's fears in the months of anxiety that followed and no Kemble of them all felt more keenly the misery of defeat when at last "Glorious John" put his pride in his pocket—by now entirely empty of cash—and announced a return to the old prices.

The riots had reached their height during the month before the baby Fanny's birth. A mob's catcalls were not the sort of lullaby a mother would choose, and one need not be a superstitious believer in prenatal influences to admit that such experiences might leave a mark and that the "O.P. Riots" were probably responsible for the nervous horror of crowds and noise that was one of the few weak spots in Fanny's character. Indeed, to a sensitive ear, the echoes of those cries, "Off! Off! Old prices! Old prices!" can be heard reverberating in her life from beginning to end. However this may be, there is no doubt that Covent Garden theatre, in failure and in triumph, was the pivot around which the family fortunes turned all through Fanny's babyhood and childhood and, when the final crisis came, her girlhood was sacrificed to Covent Garden in much the same matter-of-course fashion that St. George's princess was thrown to the dragon.

The room was quiet at last. Mrs. Charles Kemble lifted a wavering hand and let it come to rest on the minute bundle of flannel that the nurse was smoothing to a cocoon on the farther side of the bed. It was bliss to lie still; Covent Garden forgotten, "O.P. Riots" unimportant now. Nothing important but the baby . . . The whole house was quiet: Charles gone to the theatre; little John, the older child, asleep upstairs. Only an occasional sound came from outside, for the rattle of wheels from Oxford Road was muffled by the fog that, to the nurse's horror, was drifting into the room through an open window, an abnormal liking for fresh air being one of Mrs. Charles Kemble's peculiarities. Even the bed-curtains were not permitted to make a warm nest for mother and child; they were looped back so that Mrs. Kemble could superintend the nurse, as she moved softly about tidying the room, and direct the placing of footstool, fire-screen and work-box. For another of Mrs. Kemble's peculiarities was a passionate interest in furniture and everything connected with the decoration of a house. Of course this house in New-man Street was too old-fashioned to suit a lady of taste in 1809 when a classic revival was strewing Europe with *objets* of bronze and marble, but Mrs. Kemble had done her best and as difficulties always stimulated her she had contrived, with little money and no leisure, to give a modern effect to her bedroom, in spite of the ruffled chintzes that she hoped soon to replace with curtains of sarsenet hanging straight, such as the fashion papers reported were to be seen in Lord Palmerston's countryhouse.

And now the room was in order. The nurse departed, murmuring of Scotch broth. As the door closed Theresa Kemble moved herself nearer to the sleeping baby and lifting the blanket gazed consideringly at the small face. A pretty face, remarkably pretty for so young a child. Brunette or blonde? The eyes were shut, but the very long thick eyelashes were dark and so was the tuft of hair that showed under the tight cap. But dark baby hair often turned light later on, and not all the Kembles were dark; Mrs. Siddons's hair was auburn. A pretty little nose, not the usual baby retroussé; naturally enough, the "Kemble nose" was admired and caricatured across two continents. And the mouth was exquisite. That also was a matter of course; all the Kembles had beautiful mouths. Mrs. Siddons's mouth was as celebrated as her nose. Charles's mouth was considered to be the handsomest feature of the handsomest man in London. It was to be hoped that the baby had inherited the Kemble figure as well as . . . Kemble—Kemble—Kemble— Why should the child be *all* Kemble? She let the blanket fall.

Lying there staring up at the ceiling, Theresa sent her thoughts back to the days before she had met any member of the Kemble family—there had never been a time when the name was unfamiliar—long before she had acted with John Kemble, fallen in love with Charles, married him, and became annexed by the tribe. Back to her childhood. What a childhood! Her hand groped for and found the sleeping child, and rested on it with a gesture of protection. Tears stood in her eyes; then, as suddenly, she smiled. There had been bright spots in the past, and kind people. Some figures stood out. The Prince in brocade and lace, laughing, clapping his hands as the "little French fairy" came dancing towards him the length of the polished floor . . . Five years later. The Prince was Regent now, splendid still, but with a double chin; and still kind, he had spoken for her at the Haymarket. And the fairy, wings outgrown, had become Edward the Blind Boy, Prince Arthur, a *vivandière* in a short red jacket singing 'The Soldier's Return' . . .

The door opened; Theresa stretched out a welcoming hand to her husband. He stooped and kissed her; she lifted the cover from the sleeping baby and he looked down at it with a smile, remarking that the little thing had, by gad, a look of the Kembles—in fact, she was the image of his mother, Mrs. Roger Kemble. Theresa murmured that Mrs. Roger had been a Ward, not a Kemble; but Charles brushed that aside and went on to hope that his daughter might also have inherited the family brains and the family talent. Though he nodded agreement when his wife exclaimed that she did not want a second Mrs. Siddons, another "Tragic Muse," in the family— imagine hearing a baby ask for pap with a "Give me the daggers!" inflection! Charles laughed, the baby stirred, the nurse came in. Charles gave his wife a hasty kiss and turned away.

But in the doorway he paused and looked back, his figure drawn to its full six feet, a smile illuminating his beautiful face, one hand raised in farewell. It was a perfect exit. Even on a domestic occasion with only two spectators, Charles Kemble never failed to make a perfect exit.

CHAPTER III

Childhood

"Oh born in days when wits were fresh and clear."
—MATTHEW ARNOLD.

EVERYONE AGREED that Fanny was a charming child. But the more observant agreed that she was also very naughty and that this was her father's fault. Charles was proud of his boy—little John would be a judge or a bishop some day—but this second baby with her laughing eyes, red cheeks and dancing feet, was a plaything. Charles bought her toys, fed her with sweets, tossed her to the ceiling till she shrieked with delight, teased her till she cried, and showed off her parlor tricks to every visitor. He had a cap made for these occasions, a cap with feathers and a wide lace brim that set off the cherub face like a halo and was considered vastly becoming by masculine admirers, but deprecated by the ladies who quoted the poet's advice:

" 'Tis better to wear a sweet smile on the face,
  Than to wear a rich frock with an elegant lace;
  For the good-natured girl is loved best in the main,
  If her dress is but decent, though ever so plain."

But Charles's experience with the fair sex having led him to an opposite conclusion, he went on amusing himself with his pretty Fanny, aided and abetted by his men friends, especially Charles Young whose love for children always took him straight to the nursery when he came to the Kembles'. The great actor would make the baby Fanny "do Lady Macbeth;" fold her arms, pucker her forehead in a frown, and respond to the cues he gave with a lisp that could turn even the line, "My hands are of your color!" into farce.

18

Charles had of course soon shortened the Frances Anne of the baby's christening to the crisp and playful Fanny that not only suited his daughter but happened to be the latest thing in nicknames. Whether it was Fanny Burney or some other lady of fashion who first brought it into vogue, Fanny Kemble came midway in a long list of Fannies; Fanny Trollope, Fanny Elssler and Fanny Wright, Miss Austen's Fanny Price and Dickens's Fanny Dorrit, down to Louisa Alcott's Fanny Shaw.

And Fanny justified her frivolous name. At a very early age she became interested in dress. Her favorite plaything was a paper-doll, but it was the pasteboard frocks, cloaks and bonnets that gave her pleasure. She never played with her wax doll, Philippa; her esthetic sense was shocked by its mimicry of babyhood. Already, at the age of four, Fanny Kemble hated make-believe.

In any case, she was too lively for quiet amusements. She was, it is recorded, a child who "never cried, never resented, lamented, or repented either her ill-doings or their consequences"; a combination of contempt for authority and indifference to punishment so exasperating to her family that at length Mrs. Siddons was appealed to. Surely the "Tragic Muse", who could throw an audience into convulsions and in private life curdle the blood of her servants with a simple: "Bring me the beer!" would be able to quell a child. So the child was placed upon the stately knee and encircled by the stately arm while that wonderful voice discoursed of sin and judgment to come, until a chirp from Fanny: "What beautiful eyes you have, Aunt Sarah!" brought the sermon to a laughing conclusion. When an attempt of Mrs. Siddons's friend, Mrs. Fitzhugh, along the same lines: "Fanny, why don't you pray to God to make you better?" was answered: "So I do, and He makes me worse and worse!" matters came to a head.

Aunt Sarah Siddons had failed. Aunt Frances Twiss, Fanny's godmother, was appealed to. Mrs. Twiss kept a fashionable

school in the fashionable town of Bath and to this establishment Fanny was despatched at the age of five. She soon justified her reputation. Having brought with her a dozen story
books outgrown by her brother John who already preferred
history to fiction, and read them with the speed that characterized her, Fanny decided to make them give a more material thrill. She piled the books together, stole a match and
lighted a bonfire that attracted so much attention it made
up for the scolding that followed. Her next scrape was
even more alarming. Leaning out over the banisters of an
upper story to see what was going on in the hall where gaily
dressed ladies were arriving for a dinner party, she stood on
tiptoe, lost her balance and turned over the rail; hung like
Quasimodo for a horrible moment and then dropped straight
to the marble pavement far below. She was not killed, not
even seriously injured. Her family were not particularly surprised. It was felt that Fanny had as many lives as a cat.

But on the whole the atmosphere of Camden Place was
soothing. Her cousins were kind. If Fanny had been older she
would have enjoyed the fashionable life of Bath, for the
Twisses, though they kept a school, were in society; as relations of Mrs. Siddons they shone in a reflected glory. Bath was
at the height of its popularity. It was the Bath of Miss Austen.
A dozen counterparts of Catherine Morland and Anne Elliot
tripped along the sidewalks on their way to the bazaars in
search of pastry or millinery; dressed in the latest fashion, the
scant, high-waisted, sprigged India muslins, the pelisses, tiny
parasols and monstrous hats of Hugh Thomson's illustrations.
Innumerable Mr. Thorpes dashed over the cobblestones in
gigs as smart as his fifty-guinea vehicle, "town built, curricle-
hung, trunk, swordcase, splashing-board, lamps, silver mould-
ings all complete, ironwork as good as new, or better." A
town all glitter and gaiety. Any child would have been happy
in Bath.

So a year passed pleasantly, and then Fanny returned to

London. Her family had moved to Covent Garden Chambers (later known as Evans's) and here the youngest child was born —the fourth, a little Henry had arrived not very long before— and christened Adelaide after her aunt, Adelaide De Camp.

Aunt Dall—her name had been shortened by the children— filled an essential place in the Kemble household; serene and unself-conscious, few would have guessed that she had been "crossed in love." It is a strange little story; she and her bosom friend, Stephen Kemble's daughter Fanny, became engaged at the same time to two young army officers whose families disapproved because the girls were on the stage. One affair prospered; after all, the girl was a Kemble and her fiancé, Robert Arkwright, was the grandson of a barber (a barber clever enough to invent the spinning frame and make millions); the marriage took place, and Fanny Arkwright betook herself to Stoke, a charming country place in Derbyshire, and lived happy ever after. Unluckily, Adelaide was not a Kemble. Her lover did his best; he stood by her, until his father, a Yorkshire squire, carrying determination to lengths unusual even in Yorkshire, called his neighbors together and declared that the young man supposed to be his heir was illegitimate. Disowned and disinherited, Adelaide's lover sailed away to the colonies. They never met again. She took refuge with her sister Theresa and became the good angel of Charles Kemble's household.

Fanny took Aunt Dall as a matter of course; you didn't think about Aunt Dall any more than you thought about sunshine or fresh air. She was there when you wanted her, that was all. There were other aunts, not in any way essential but pleasant enough. There was Aunt Victoire De Camp, who was a governess in a school in an old house at Lea shaded by cedars of Lebanon. Fanny loved the dim drawing-room fragrant with pot-pourri and plum cake, but its chief fascination was a picture that hung on the faded wall; a black sea, a black sky, a black boat, two pale figures, Prospero and his poor lit-

tle daughter Miranda cast forth by wicked relations to drown.
She shuddered whenever she looked at that picture, but she
enjoyed its mysterious sadness.

There was not much mystery at home. There were too
many children and too little money, and the house was too
near Covent Garden theatre for that family bugbear ever to
be forgotten. But it was a pleasant house; distinguished foreign actors always found their way to Covent Garden Chambers. Talma, coming to call one day and being told that no
one was at home, made friends with pretty Fanny peeping
round-eyed from behind the parlormaid's skirts, and told the
child to remember his name: it was Talma who had come to
call, Talma, the great French tragedian. Fanny, always ready
for conversation, at once poured out fluent assurance; she
wouldn't forget and she understood perfectly. Her father was
a great tragedian and her uncle John was a great tragedian
and, as it happened, they had still another great tragedian in
the family—baby Adelaide upstairs cried a great deal, and
wasn't anybody who cried a great tragedian? Talma laughed,
and made a good story out of it. All the best people in the
theatrical world came to the Kembles; Charles and Theresa
were young and agreeable; Mrs. Kemble was celebrated both
for her wit and her French cooking; they would have entertained more, if they could have afforded it.

But whether he could afford it or not, Charles was determined that his children should have a good education.
John was going to Dr. Malkin's school at Bury St. Edmund's.
What about sending Fanny abroad? Several of the Kembles
had been educated in France. A good French accent was most
important. Theresa agreed—though she remarked that she
had never known a Kemble yet who had a good French accent—and Fanny was despatched to Boulogne, to a school in
the *Rue tant Perd tant Paie* presided over by Madame Faudier. Here Fanny was taught to speak French with fluent perfection—De Camp ancestry being in this case stronger than
Kemble—and learned enough dancing, music and Italian to

bring her plenty of prizes when the great day came. Prize-days were magnificent; the courtyard floored over and draped with awnings; a stage built for the mayor and the bishop seated at the top of a long flight of red-carpeted steps; pupils in rows below, all trembling with expectation. Fanny, the *cadette* of the establishment, looked very small as she marched up the steps, and very pretty—head erect, cheeks scarlet, eyes flashing—to receive a book or a medal.

But such days came seldom. Fanny was not happy at Madame Faudier's. That lady's experience with docile French *demoiselles* had not prepared her for Fanny. Lock Fanny up in the garret, and a ring would come at the front door and a passer-by would report a child in danger on the roof: *"Ah, ce ne peut être que cette diable de Kemble!"* Madame would cry, and there was Fanny, perched on the coping blandly sur-veying the landscape, enjoying the warning cries from below. So they put her in the cellar. Fanny never forgot her hour in the dark cellar, huddled on the top step of the stairs, cheek pressed against the door; for her imagination told her those stairs ended in an oubliette. In ten minutes she was ready to cry like Esmeralda; *"Oh, laissez moi sortir! J'ai froid! J'ai peur! Et des bêtes me montent le long du corps!"* She came out so limp that Madame Faudier was satisfied; this naughty English miss could be tamed through the imagination.

It was the day of "shocking examples." Children's stories all ended in a moral; their poems told of agonizing brass meat-hooks that accidentally but inevitably penetrated the jaws of boys that fished on Sunday; or reminded the young sinner:

> "Thou art not so healthy and gay,
>   So young, so active and bright,
>   That Death cannot snatch thee away
>   Or some terrible pestilence smite."

Lord Grey at the age of six was taken by his nurse to see a batch of Jews hanged for forgery at Tyburn; mounted on the shoulders of an obliging grenadier he watched the contortions of the wretches as they were one by one turned off the cart, and, years after, the great statesman would wake sweating at night from a vision of Tyburn. As late as 1813 Fanny's little friend Julian Young was taken to the Haymarket to see a man pilloried; "placed on a parapet the man was exposed to the merciless peltings of the mob," and Julian was supposed to profit by the sight. So Madame Faudier had ample precedent for the "shocking example" she planned for Fanny. Fanny was sent with a governess to see the guillotine at work. Perhaps the governess was squeamish, for they arrived at the *Grande Place* after the actual beheading was over, so Fanny did not derive the full benefit of the scene; but the gutter still ran with blood which was pointed out to her, and she was told that a sad-looking boy busy about the scaffold was the executioner's son, and though she said nothing her pallor showed that some impression had been made.

But there was balm in Gilead. A long country walk could make Fanny forget even the guillotine; sometimes the school girls would be taken to the cliff top strewn with the remains of the triumphal pillar that Napoleon had ordered to be built pointing the finger of scorn at perfidious Albion, and allowed to play hide and seek among the blocks of stone; or, still farther, to La Garenne with its sand dunes and scampering wild rabbits. But in spite of these agreeable interludes Fanny had had enough of Boulogne long before her two years came to an end, and returned thankfully to London. She got home in time to enjoy a notable family event.

When Fanny recited the list of family celebrities for Talma's benefit she had overlooked the greatest name. Talma would have included Mrs. Siddons and put her far ahead of John or Charles; she "filled his idea of tragic acting; the union of grandeur without pomp, and nature without triviality." But Fanny had been born too late; to her, Aunt Sarah was merely a rather dreary elderly relation, so restless, so oppressed with ennui, after her retirement from the stage, that even a child could see she was weary of life. So no one was surprised when, in 1819, Mrs. Siddons decided to appear for one night only as Lady Randolph in a performance of 'Douglas' given for Charles's benefit. Her family received the news with a sort of trembling elation. There was no doubt of her success financially, Covent Garden would overflow and Charles, Heaven knew, needed the money; but there were misgivings, misgivings shared by the family friends. Macready heard the news with consternation. He had acted Norval to Mrs. Siddons's Lady Randolph at its peak of perfection. He was not sure that he could bear to see her in her old age, but he knew he could not keep away.

Hearing the affair discussed in every aspect Fanny began to take an interest in Aunt Sarah and with her usual determination never to be left out when anything exciting was going on, teased her father until he nearly went out of his mind. "Why couldn't a little girl go to see 'Douglas'? She had seen 'Hyppolita Queen of the Amazons', why couldn't she see Aunt Sarah? Why? Why? Why? . . ." The great night came; Charles, knowing Fanny's fear of crowds, took her up in his arms and walked out into the street hoping that she would be satisfied by the sight of the mob filling the square and pressed against the doors of the theatre. Fanny hid her face on his shoulder, but she would not give in; Charles did, and Fanny was taken to see Mrs. Siddons act for the first and last time. But it was disappointing; just a tall lady in a black dress, very far off, very solemn. The roar like a hundred thunderstorms that came bursting out all over the theatre whenever the tall lady came in or walked away, was frightening, but rather splendid. Everybody stood up, some people even stood on the seats, clapping and calling and shouting and waving their handkerchiefs. That was indeed something to remember.

But Macready went home and wrote in his diary: "Only the last flicker of a dying flame, a glimpse of the grand force and simplicity of her style." And Hazlitt asked himself: "Who shall make tragedy stand once more with its feet upon the earth, and its head above the stars, weeping tears and blood!"

Not long after Fanny's return from Boulogne her family moved again, out of town this time for Mrs. Kemble detested smoke and crowds and noise and in Bayswater she found a sort of half country. Between the Edgeware Road and Bayswater stretched open fields sparsely dotted with cottages and traversed by the canal; on the farther side of Bayswater Road lay Hyde Park, an untidy space innocent of paths, flower beds and railings. The Kembles' house stood on the gentle rise known as Craven Hill, one of a pretty flowery row that included Lord Ferrar's and Harley House; their front windows looked out on a large quiet green meadow and beyond to a nursery garden where the children bought pots of violets, flower seeds, and roots of future fragrance for their own small plots. At the back lay a still wider stretch of meadow with more elms and scarcely a building in sight in any direction. A peaceful place; life went smoothly at Craven Hill.

But the neighborhood still kept one reminder of a turbulent past: Tyburn turnpike, a spot of wicked memories peopled by Fanny with romantic figures made vivid by a story of her mother's girlhood. One afternoon Uncle Victor had brought a friend to the De Camps' cottage at Finchley, whom he introduced as Captain Clayton, come to try his hand at pigeon shooting on the common, a quiet, gentlemanly man with nothing remarkable about him except his handsome white hands and an uncanny skill at bringing down the birds. Of course no one connected the Captain with recent highway robberies in the neighborhood. Then one night Moody, the actor, was held up and robbed by a "gentleman of the road;" and a few days later Victor De Camp and Moody, hearing that a famous highwayman had been caught went to Bow-street police station to have a look at him and recognized— Victor, his agreeable, white-handed, pigeon-shooting friend— Moody, the fellow who had relieved him of his watch!

There were other stories of the past that held the Kemble

children spellbound as they sat around the fire on winter evenings, curtains drawn and chestnuts roasting in the coals; tales of adventure on the other side of the world. Aunt Eliza Whitelock sometimes came to stay at Craven Hill, and in her actress youth she had toured the States. A coarse edition of her sister Mrs. Siddons, wearing an auburn wig and a monstrous Pamela cap always on one side, Mrs. Whitelock possessed the sonorous Kemble voice but none of the family dignity; as she talked, she would slap her thigh in enforcement of some incredible statement and fling out an "I declare to God!" that would send the children into fits of stifled laughter. But how Fanny envied Aunt Eliza! Not because she had met General Washington, whose favorite "bespeak" was the School for Scandal, and Talleyrand—Fanny and her mother would exchange amused glances at his name, for Aunt Eliza had the usual Kemble difficulties with French pronunciation; celebrities meant nothing to Fanny. She longed to see flocks of wild pigeons so vast that they clouded the sun; to travel over forest roads so deep in mud that one's carriage sank in to the axle-tree; to visit a town called Philadelphia where Red Indians roamed the streets. One night, coming home alone from the theatre, Aunt Eliza had heard soft footsteps padding along the pavement, had looked over her shoulder, had seen a Red Indian following close behind! The end of the story was tame; Aunt Eliza and her scalp got home all right. But Fanny's imagination could supply another ending, one that would dreadfully account for that auburn wig.

With or without Mrs. Whitelock's enlivening presence the children and their mother were contented at Craven Hill and would willingly have lived there all the year round. Unfortunately, Charles disliked the country as heartily as his wife loved it, and Bayswater was inconvenient for a man who spent half his time in town. It was before the days of omnibuses and a hackney coach was too expensive; so when he was acting Charles usually walked the five miles in to Covent Garden.

But the return trip at night became too much for even his superb physique; he took lodgings in an old house in Gerard Street, Soho, and his family vacillated between town and suburb.

It was a fine old house, belonging originally to the "wicked Lord Lynton," now owned by a picture dealer whose works of art covering every wall space gave an air of mystery to the halls and staircases that Fanny found fascinating. Often she would stop on her way to the Kemble part of the house for a long look at a story-telling picture, or some dim canvas that brought shuddering memories of the red gutters of the guillotine, until a horror of the "wicked Lord," whose ghost was known to revisit the scene of his excesses, sent her hurrying on to the warmth and light of her mother's rooms.

There was always warmth and light and prettiness in whatever house Theresa Kemble chanced to live. Here in this fine old house her talent for furnishing found a magnificent background. Dining-room with fluted pillars; drawing-room, oval in shape, lighted by a skylight; boudoir lined with looking-glasses framed in the delicate scrolls and garlands of Louis-Quinze, all encouraged a passion unusual in her generation, a passion for antiques. She never tired of searching the shops of second-hand dealers for some piece worthy of the old house. And if her pocket-book were empty she had her own way of consoling herself; she would bring about a change in the appearance of her rooms by moving the furniture. The panacea was disconcerting to her family and when Charles came home from the theatre at night, tired out, and found chairs, tables and sofas playing puss-in-the-corner, good natured though he was he could not always resist an impatient: "God bless my soul, you're not changing the room *again!*" But this was the only flaw in Theresa as a housewife. Her potted gravies, sauces, game jellies and meat jellies were famous; in Dr. Kitchener's celebrated cookbook she appears as the "accomplished lady" responsible for some of the most alluring recipes.

Among the intimate friends of the house were several great actors—Liston, Charles Mathews and Charles Young—who carried friendship so far as to provide audience and applause for the young Kembles' theatricals. Beginning with the puppets of a toy theatre, the children became ambitious and decided to try a real play. 'Amoroso King of Little Britain' was given to a crowded nursery audience and Fanny made her first bow on any stage.

A greater actor than even Young or Mathews may have been present on this occasion for John Philip Kemble was in London, come from Lausanne, where he had taken refuge from creditors, to enjoy a last glimpse of England and to persuade Charles to take over the Covent Garden property that had already lost "Glorious John" some eight thousand pounds. Fanny for the first time heard Covent Garden affairs openly discussed. As long as she could remember, the family atmosphere had become clouded whenever the name was mentioned; now she was old enough to realize that her father and mother did not agree about taking over the theatre. Her mother seemed to be afraid of Covent Garden and, as they argued, Covent Garden became for Fanny a sort of monster, a monster that you admired but that you were obliged to propitiate because it might at any moment decide to eat you up. But Charles had no such feeling; he accepted the responsibility with his usual off-hand optimism, convinced that if anybody could make the damn thing pay he could. "Glorious John" returned to Lausanne, and Fanny never saw him again.

She was eleven now, and Charles, again recalling the Kemble tradition of education, decided that Aunt Dall's primer had been outgrown. He himself had educated Fanny's poetic sense; he had read aloud to her for hours that seemed like minutes to Fanny, listening chin on hand, dark eyes fixed on her father's face, as his voice rang with the clash of steel in 'Marmion' or deepened in the solemn measures of 'Paradise Lost;' already Milton and Scott were her demi-gods. And she was taking music lessons; but she did not seem to be learning very much although her teacher used an instrument called a chiroplast, a complication of brass rods that held every finger of his pupils in the correct position while they labored over 'O Dolce Concerto' and 'Sul Margine d'un Rio.' Anyhow poetry and music were not enough; at least not enough for a Kemble. Fanny must go to boarding-school. Not to Boulogne this time, but to Paris.

CHAPTER IV

School

"How I do love a well-educated little girl of twelve."
—THE ETTRICK SHEPHERD.

THE JOURNEY from London to Paris in 1821 was no light undertaking. But Mrs. Charles Kemble and her daughter Fanny, accompanied by Mrs. Charles Mathews and her small son, would have found the trip pleasant enough except for an incident—or rather, an accompaniment—that happened to be peculiarly annoying to Mrs. Kemble whose sense of smell, like all her other faculties, was too acute. The party travelled by the *malle-poste* and as the carriage rolled on in the August weather along the dusty white roads past files of poplars and fields speckled with poppy red, Mrs. Kemble was the first to comment on a whiff suggestive of a beach at low tide. Demanding an explanation from the coachman, she was told that a hamper fastened behind the carriage contained a fish on its way from the coast to the banquet of a nobleman in Paris, whose title, to the coachman's surprise, did not appear to console the unreasonable Englishwoman for the smell of his fish. The heat increased. The smell became insupportable. Mrs. Kemble was in a frenzy, holding her handkerchief over her nose and breathing in gasps until, reaching a *bureau de poste,* her passionate appeal to the officials, the flash of her splendid eyes, the tragic tones of her glorious voice, and the magnificent gesture with which she indicated the offensive hamper were convincing. The corpse was left by the roadside, the party went on its way triumphant, and arrived without further misadventure in Paris.

Fanny's school was in the Rue d'Angoulême, Champs Elyseés. Mrs. Rowden, the head-mistress, had a great reputation, having come from a school in London where she had had the honor of educating Miss Mitford, as well as the more doubtful privilege of doing her best for Lady Caroline Ponsonby, whose poetic talent was often praised by Mrs. Rowden while her eccentricities were ignored. But one may be sure the school girls were less reticent. Many stories about Lady Caroline Lamb—she was married now—were flying about; even unsophisticated little Fanny could contribute an anecdote.

During a visit in Paris, Mr. and Mrs. Charles Kemble had dined at Lord Holland's with the Lambs. It so happened that as Mr. Lamb spoke of leaving Paris next day somebody else mentioned Byron's approaching arrival, and a suppressed smile went around the table for Lady Caroline instantly contradicted her husband—they were *not* leaving, they were staying on indefinitely. The sequel was amusing. Returning to their hotel, Meurice's, where the Lambs were also stopping, the Kembles arrived in time to see Mr. Lamb gallantly pick his wife up in his arms as she emerged from her carriage, and carry her across the wet pavement; and a few minutes later had a full view of what followed in the Lambs' brightly lighted apartment across the courtyard for their windows faced the Kembles' and the curtains were not drawn. The first scene showed Lady Caroline and her husband side by side on the sofa, her arm around his neck, cheek pressed to his. Next came an even more touching display of affection; Caroline kneeling on the floor gazing up at him in tearful supplication. And then—a sudden spring—she was on her feet, dashing back and forth, snatching at vases, clocks and candlesticks and sending them smashing to the ground; while William Lamb raced after her, she eluding him and he trying to catch her, until an unseen hand pulled down the curtain and shut out the finale.

But gossip of this quality would never have been whispered within reach of Mrs. Rowden's immaculate ears. She was far too proper. Propriety came first with her, and then piety. A deeply religious atmosphere pervaded the school.

Her young ladies not only read the Bible aloud every evening, committed chapters to memory, were taken to church three times on Sunday and wrote out an abstract of the sermon; they were occasionally required to hand in sermons of their own composition. Fanny did not mind. She could learn anything by heart in a marvelously short time, and she liked reading aloud; she liked the sound of her own voice and she liked the Bible—there were bits as exciting as 'Marmion.' As for sermon writing, writing was as easy as breathing; laughing at the other girl's despair she would reel off sermon after sermon at lightning speed until every pupil had been supplied.

It was a time when fashion was permitted to walk hand in hand with piety. All the fashionable accomplishments were taught by experts at Mrs. Rowden's. Fanny's contralto voice was well trained. She acquired enough Italian to let her read 'Inferno,' a little Latin, even a little Greek. Her Parisian accent soon became the envy of the other English girls; for she had inherited from her mother that sort of mocking-bird faculty that can mimic the sounds of a foreign language apart from the sense and chatter along in happy disregard of moods and tenses. From her mother she had also inherited a turn for dancing; she possessed an "eye" that could memorize every step, pirouette and gesture of a ballet once seen, no matter how intricate, as people with an ear for music can pick up and recall an air. In the school dancing-class she was of course the star pupil. Wearing the prunella shoes and white cotton gloves considered necessary for dancing, Fanny was guided around the room by M. Guillet's aloof fingertips, outwardly demure, inwardly on fire. For with her, dancing was more than an art, it was a passion; even the prim gyrations of the school dancing-class could transport her into another world. Not a Kemble world. When Fanny danced she was no longer a Kemble and a Christian and a pupil in Mrs. Rowden's school. She was a pagan, she was Marie Thérèse, the "little French fairy," dancing down the length of Mrs. Fitzherbert's drawing-room while the Prince stood laughing and clapping his hands.

Once, only once, she was allowed a special excitement, a party at the boys' school in the Rue de Clichy. It was her first ball, memorable not only for that reason; a magnificent *ponçeau* sash enlivened her school-girl muslin, and one of her partners, an English boy named Augustus Craven, was so flatteringly attentive that she hoped they might meet again.

But at best dancing could be only an interlude, and free hours at school would have dragged if Fanny had not possessed another taste verging on passion. She read every book that she could lay her hands on, even 'L'Anthologie Française à l'Usage des Demoiselles'. No book was too dull for her; she was so stirred by Voltaire's 'Henriade' that she waked the dormitory one night by sitting bolt upright in bed, sound asleep, declaiming at the top of her voice:

"Je chante ce héros qui régna sur la France,
　　Et par droit de conquête et par droit de naissance!"

The few novels she was allowed were read from cover to cover. 'Mathilde', 'Atala', even the foolish romances of Madame de Genlis, seemed thrilling, until the "Wizard of the North" exerted his magic. The day that brought her 'Guy Mannering', was marked in memory by a stone of superlative whiteness. Reading Scott, she came as near perfect happiness as she could ever attain sitting still, indoors.

For any *out* was always better than any *in,* for Fanny. The daily promenade was dull enough, and she envied the freedom of a little boy living in the same street who used to stand watching the "crocodile" as it emerged from the school gates; a little boy whom she knew slightly for their families were friends; his name was Edward Fitzgerald. But sometimes the girls were allowed to stroll in the Luxembourg Gardens, ending with a visit to the picture gallery so that they might learn to like modern art. The subjects of these canvases, the Didos and Phèdres and Atalas that David and Gérard were giving to

the world, might not always be *comme il faut* but they were
historical, which made *such* a difference, and as the best fruits
of the classic revival could not, in Mrs. Rowden's opinion, be
ignored—the poor lady, being elderly, was unaware that the
classic had not only ceased to revive but was trembling before
the onslaught of the advancing romantic movement. But
though Fanny liked pictures another treat was far better; on
a very fine day the girls would be taken for a ramble through
the lovely wilderness of the Parc Monçeaux, a shady *jardin
anglais* belonging to the Orléans family, with winding walks
and running brooks fed from springs cradled in moss-grown
rock-work. Fanny loved every inch of the Parc Monçeaux.
Especially the brooks. Dabbling her fingers in clear water,
watching her reflection come and go, she felt a longing to slip
in, become an Undine, lose herself in that limpid coolness.

But the Parc Monçeaux soon faded to a memory; Mrs.
Rowden moved to a still larger and finer house at the top of
the Champs Elysées. Robespierre was said to have lived there
and a well in a corner of the cheerful playground, shaded by a
quincunx of lindens, lent a touch of romance to the girls'
games, for in its dark water "the seagreen incorruptible" was
said to have enjoyed *noyades* of his own. But the walks in the
new neighborhood were commonplace. There were no good
streets, no gardens or villas, between the school and Chaillot;
the highroad that led to the Bois de Boulogne was dusty, and
the Bois a mere stretch of tangled copse criss crossed by sandy
paths singularly unalluring.

For most of the English pupils Paris was limited by these
narrow horizons. Fanny was more fortunate. As the expense
and fatigue of the journey made home holidays impossible, it
was arranged that she should spend them with a French family belonging to the *petite bourgeoisie* living in a sunny little
maisonette in the suburbs, whose garden overflowed with car-
nations, Reine Claude plums, and warm golden apricots;
Fanny expanded in the freedom of her holidays in that kindly
household. Still more delightful were her father's occasional

visits. Then indeed she saw Paris! Whenever her father could
escape from his work at Covent Garden he would appear at
Mrs. Rowden's, borrow his little girl and give her a few perfect hours. The day would begin with a ramble in the rue de
Rivoli, or the Tuileries, and *déjeuner à la fourchette* at the
Café Riche, and end with a dinner at the Trois Frères or the
Cadran Bleu and a play in one of the theatres on the Boule-
vard where Philippe, Fay, and Poitier and Brunet had developed a school of dramatic art. Taken to see Bigottini in the
ballet of 'Folle par Amour,' sitting red-cheeked, round-eyed,
hands clasped tight in her white tarlatan lap, while Charles
glanced at her now and then in affectionate amusement,
Fanny touched bliss; lost in pity and wonder, marvelling at
the pathos of Bigottini's acting and the grace and dignity of
her dancing. As for Poitier in 'Les Danaides,' a burlesque
of a spectacle at the Académie Royale de Musique, Fanny and
Charles both laughed till they cried at the wicked King Dan-
aus and his fifty daughters and still had laughter left for that
triumph of farce, 'Les Anglaises pour Rire', in which Poitier
and Brunet took women's parts. The travelling English, now
that Europe was thrown open to them by the downfall of
Napoleon, were becoming celebrated from the Channel to
the Mediterranean for their riches, insolence, ignorance and
cleanliness. In 'Les Anglaises pour Rire,' the English Miss ex-
ploring foreign lands was caricatured to perfection. How
Fanny and Charles laughed at the two gaunt females, with
their flat figures, protruding teeth and huge splay feet, their
coal-scuttle bonnets, monstrous shoes and short-waisted, tight-
fitting spencers—the short skirtless coats brought into fashion
by Lord Spencer's bet that he could make the public wear
anything, no matter how absurd. How they clapped the two
actors' imitation of the English lady's terrible French, her
grotesque playfulness and equally grotesque bashfulness suspicious of improprieties; her angular strides, her kittenish
frolics and her sharp shrill squeals. Fanny and Charles, exhausted with laughter, decided that 'Les Anglaises pour Rire'

was the funniest farce they had ever seen or were ever likely to see, and all Paris agreed with them.

When the school doors shut behind her father, shutting Paris out and shutting Fanny in, everyday life became drab and school activities insignificant. With Poitier's antics fresh in one's mind, it was difficult to take school theatricals with the seriousness that Mrs. Rowden demanded, and Fanny, always cast for a prominent part, could scarcely keep her face straight as she stood posed in a graceful attitude, one arm indicating Mrs. Rowden for fear some guest might appropriate the apostrophe, and sang:

> "C'est une mère!
> Qui a les premiers droits sur nos coeurs?
> Qui partage, d'une ardeur sincère,
> Et nos plaisirs et nos douleurs?
> C'est une mère!"

Madame de Genlis' 'L'Isle Heureuse' was more amusing. 'Roxelane' promised well, but never came off. Fanny as the French heroine, *"dont le nez en l'air semble narguer l'amour,"* was almost word-perfect when Mrs. Rowden happened to pick up a book of the play. She was shocked. *"May, commang!"* she cried. *"Permettay may demoiselles être les filles d'un seraglio? Je vous défang!"* The girls wept; mademoiselle protested that the moral was excellent for the heroine disposed of the harem and got married in the most orthodox fashion possible in the Ottoman empire. But Mrs. Rowden was firm.

The bitterest prude could not object to the next choice, Racine's 'Andromaque,' for the plot was safely obscured by the antique setting. The girls studied and rehearsed and cut out gold paper crowns and turned white petticoats into Greek garments. The great night came; the girls all felt a little sick, partly from fright, partly from the number of raw eggs they had consumed to soothe their throats. Oreste knew her part, Pyrrhus was excellent, everyone agreed that Andromaque looked very handsome. But—to the astonishment of teachers

and pupils—it was Fanny's Hermione that brought down the
house! The audience clapped and clapped and clapped. The
girls stared at each other—Fanny hadn't been like this at the
rehearsals! It was really very strange. As Fanny stepped on the
stage something seemed to happen. It was as if a fairy had
waved her wand and, all of a sudden, Fanny wasn't Fanny
any more! She was Hermione. Not a school girl reciting poetry, but a woman, a beautiful woman—Fanny wasn't even
very pretty in real life—telling you about sad things that had
happened in a voice—not Fanny's voice at all—a voice that
made you want to cry and cry. And then the next minute flying into such a rage that you were scared to death. It was as if
Hermione hadn't, after all, died in Greece hundreds and hundreds of years ago but was alive, and here in Paris, in Mrs.
Rowden's school!

In the audience, the murmured: "Who is it? Who is Hermione?" and the exclamations: "Really? You don't say so:
just a *jeune fille* like any of the others? Amazing!" had been
followed by understanding nods: "Really? A Kemble? Ah,
that accounts for it! Not so strange after all. Now *my* little
Marie—and *my* little Jane—and *my* little Léontine—has had
no such advantages, and yet . . ."

Fanny was as surprised as anybody. It was true, what the
girls were saying; as she stepped on the stage, something happened. A voice seemed to say: "Now, you aren't Fanny any
more, you are Hermione. You don't have to do anything—just
let yourself go. Hermione will do it all!" And Hermione *had*
done it all. Hermione had moved and paused and wrung her
hands, while Fanny looked on. Hermione, not Fanny, had
spoken and wept and suffered, torn by those lightning changes
from hate to love, from joy to fury. When Hermione had
wailed, mourning the faithless Pyrrhus:

> "Lui qui me fut si cher, et qui m'a pu trahir!
> Ah! je l'ai trop aimé, pour ne le point haïr!"

Fanny had been only a mouthpiece. It was all very strange!

And the teachers too agreed that Fanny had come out in a new light, a light not altogether approved by Mrs. Rowden. As Fanny—still dazed and wondering—was emerging from Hermione's white robe and untwining the gold fillet from her hair, Mrs. Rowden appeared behind the scenes for a word of warning: "You were very nice, my dear, very nice indeed. But don't let yourself get thinking of the stage as a career; I assure you, you weren't a bit better than the other girls." Fanny smiled politely but she knew that Mrs. Rowden was only talking; she, Fanny, knew good acting when she saw it, and Hermione had been good, very good!

'Andromaque' made Racine and Corneille appetizing. They satisfied her until, one never-to-be-forgotten day, she experienced a new sensation.

She had been taking tea in the drawing room with the "parlor boarders," with whom the small fry were allowed to associate as a reward for a week's *bonne conduite*. The room was quiet; all the others had gone upstairs except one of these older girls sitting beside her on the sofa bent over a book. From the opposite wall a portrait of "Glorious John," for whom Mrs. Rowden had a great admiration, as Coriolanus, stared reproachfully at his niece's lazy figure; Fanny sat leaning back among the cushions, drowsy after many cups of hot tea and innumerable *petits fours* and *brioches*. Coriolanus was fading to a dream, she was almost asleep, when suddenly the big girl turned, laid her book in Fanny's lap and pointed to a line:

> "It is the hour when from the boughs
> The nightingale's high note is heard."

Fanny read, sat bolt upright, wide awake now, snatching at the book as it was withdrawn, with a cry:

"It's Byron!"—she had seen the page heading. "It's Byron! Oh, let me have it—do, do let me read just a little more!"

But the big girl only smiled teasingly, holding the book out of reach, as Fanny went on pleading—the little thing was too absurd, it was like dangling a mouse in front of a kitten! Then at the sound of an approaching footstep she surrendered, and let Fanny run off upstairs to hide the book under her pillow—the first thing in the morning, at the earliest crack of dawn, she would find out what came next!

But the secret was too exciting to keep to herself—Fanny was never much good at keeping anything to herself. As soon as the teacher had left the dormitory Fanny confided in her next-door neighbor; she, Fanny, had a copy of Lord Byron's works under her pillow. She had expected an excited response, but the return whisper was more shrill with horror than she had bargained for. Aware that a mysterious wickedness hovered about Byron, that his poetry was not supposed to be reading for the *jeune fille,* it was news to Fanny that this wickedness was contagious. It was, it appeared, dangerous to so much as turn a page of Byron, and as for sleeping with a book under her pillow—what spirits of darkness might assault the sleep of a young person so rash as to allow her head to rest, with only a few feathers between, on that concentrated essence of iniquity! When her friend went on to dilate on the risk of being caught, Mrs. Rowden's anger and the mortification of fond parents, and made a complete job of it by bursting into tears, Fanny's nerve broke. She jumped out of bed, went tiptoeing across the dark floor and hid the book under the *paillasse* of an empty couch.

But she could not sleep. The nightingale would not let her. All night long she seemed to hear his sweet high call; vaguely sensuous; a note that Milton, Scott, Racine (Shakespeare was still a sealed book) never touched. Lying huddled under the bedclothes, Fanny became aware of a tumult in herself that tossed her about between opposing forces; the nightingale's warm song clashed with another voice—a cool Kemble voice—that said: "Be good! Be careful!" said it over and over. Towards dawn the Kemble voice won, and the nightingale stopped singing. In the morning the big girl got back her book, and, like Francesca, Fanny "read no more that day."

During her last year at school, she was summoned to Mrs. Rowden's sanctum to be told with due solemnity that her uncle, "Glorious John," had passed away at Lausanne. She managed to express enough regret to satisfy the school-mistress, but in reality Uncle John's death left her unmoved. It was a very different matter when, a few months later, she heard of Byron's death at Missolonghi. Dead! *Byron* dead! Fanny felt as if her heart would break. Like young Alfred Tennyson, at that moment carving "Byron is dead" on the bark of a tree with tears in his eyes, she experienced a sense of irreparable loss. Yet she had never seen Byron, and knew nothing of his poetry but those two nightingale lines.

CHAPTER V

Friendship

"J'aime l'amitié à la folie."
—MADAME DU DEFFAND.

MRS. ROWDEN had done well by his little daughter, Charles decided, giving Fanny a considering glance as she stood at the rail of the packet-boat, scant skirts fluttering in the breeze, turning her face up to the sun and greeting the salty air on her lips with exclamations of delight and a fresh shriek of joy for every gull that wheeled overhead and every sail on the horizon. A very pleasing young creature, Charles said to himself; she had a pretty French accent, pretty manners and a pretty face. Pretty because of her brilliant coloring and animation; a little like Sarah Siddons but lacking Sarah's classic perfection and, thank God, Sarah's tiresome dignity—it wasn't from the Kemble side of the house that the child got all that shine and sparkle and verve. And Fanny's eyes were not quite Kemble eyes. Fanny's had an added warm light, a hint of passion, that she got straight from her mother. A pity she was so small; it would be a handicap if she ever wanted to go on the stage, which God forbid! The stage had eaten up too many Kembles, the stage shouldn't get little Fan if her father had anything to say about it. But the child's figure was neat and promised something of her mother's exquisite grace—people used to come all the way from London for a glimpse of Miss De Camp walking along the Brighton pier or promenading in the streets of Bath. Charles sighed, feeling old, regretting his wife's vanished slimness. Then his handsome chin settled itself complacently into the folds of his high black stock, and his cane stroked a well-turned calf encased in skin-tight nankeen pantaloons; a consoling thought came to him—Theresa

42

could not make the same criticism of her husband's figure! No double chin as yet, no hint of a "corporation"—Charles pulled down his flowered waistcoat . . . There, Fanny had lost her bonnet! Fanny, it seemed, had forgotten all about her bonnet when that pale blur in the distance turned out to be the cliffs of Dover; bonnet only a bunch of straw and ribbon now, bobbing up and down on the water and far astern already. It didn't matter, nothing to look so tragic about. They would buy another bonnet, and a prettier one, in London.

Fanny at the milliner's now. Trying on hat after hat—bonnets were out of fashion—each one larger and more ornate than the last. The hat that finally took her fancy was a leghorn flat of cartwheel size blooming with bows of green ribbon; Fanny's small face peeped out from under the brim like a fairy's from the shade of a plantain leaf. Charles laughed. Couldn't she satisfy herself with a more modest affair? She would lose it from the coach just as she had lost the other from the boat. "But large hats, dear Papa, are the fashion," Fanny pleaded. "And it ties under the chin. It can't blow off." Such a pretty little chin, round and white; Charles gave in.

Delicious to be back in England again, bowling along behind four spanking horses; Fanny loved horses, and it was good to watch these glossy bays pick up their feet and toss the foam from their bits, after suffering from the shambling nags of the French *diligences;* and the English countryside seemed unbelievably green and flowery after the pale French landscape. Delicious to be going home at last. And not, *grâce à Dieu,* to London, but to the country! For Mamma had her wish; she was living in the very heart of the country; at Weybridge, three hours' drive from town.

A beautiful wild sort of country too, Fanny decided, as they approached their destination; a moorland country, all golden gorse and purple heather sometimes aromatic with pine trees, sometimes giving a glimpse of the sea. Fanny exclaimed and admired; until at dusk she became silent and Charles asked: Was she cold? Was she tired? She shook her head. As was

Fanny's way, imagination was getting the best of common sense. It was three years since she had seen her mother. Three years was a long time. Suppose Mamma had changed. Suppose she, Fanny, didn't know her and kissed some other lady waiting there in the dark street when they got to the Weybridge inn? How dreadful, how utterly and unspeakably dreadful not to recognize one's own mother! . . . The coachman reined in his horses, the coach stopped, lights shone out, a voice asked: "Is there anyone here for Mrs. Kemble?" and Fanny went scrambling down over the wheel and flung herself, hat and all, into her mother's arms.

Morning light showed an agreeable prospect. The cottage that Mrs. Kemble had rented from the baker sat aloof from the little red and white village, on the edge of country as wild as the most ardent "lover of Nature" could desire even in this year of 1825 with the romantic movement in full swing. Not Rousseau's "Nature," of course; his bland guardian of fields and vineyards had given way to Byron's. Nature was now *picturesque*—brand-new word coined by the ultra-modern to describe the blasted oaks, foaming waterfalls, peaks and precipices viewed with abhorrence by Queen Anne's generation, admired by the ultra-modern who could perceive beauty in decay. As they had also discovered the exquisite enjoyment of "making your flesh creep," haunted towers were in demand, ghosts were encouraged to walk, spectres to gibber; an erlking might be encountered in any wood, and every fountain held an Undine.

Even from this exacting standpoint the Weybridge neighborhood was satisfactory. Fanny, fifteen and romantic, pronounced it picturesque. In one direction lay the desolate domain of Portmore Park, with its fine old mansion falling to decay; walking the other way you came to Oatlands, lately the seat of the Duke of York. But this house too stood empty now, and the Kembles had the place to themselves. They could stroll across the meadow that had seen Queen Elizabeth practice with the crossbow, climb the giant cedars of Lebanon, peep into the grotto where the Regent had entertained the Emperor of Russia and the King of Prussia after Waterloo, admire the small tombstones dotting a corner of the lawn that commemorated the Duchess of York's sixty-four pet dogs, and spend long happy days in the green glades of the park. With its rabbits and deer and innumerable birds the park was a paradise for children; they explored and dreamed and picnicked and were happy.

Charles only came for week-ends. Without riding or shooting, which he could not afford, the country bored him and he was too tall for the tiny cottage. But his wife had never been more contented; the place was pretty, yet there was room for improvement. At the back, a delightful garden sloped up to a still more delightful orchard; but the front was ruined by a monstrous hill of sand, as large as the house, which the landlord refused to remove. Mrs. Kemble fretted over this eyesore; the problem seemed beyond her, but at length, after much cogitation, she solved it. She had the sand-hill hollowed out, graded, turfed and lined inside with evergreen shrubs through which a path led to the front door. It was now the Mound, an oddly pretty, green, four-square erection, so suggestive of an old fort that John, the oldest boy, always climbed it in the morning to wake the household with a blast from his bugle. Everyone agreed that the Mound was an extreme proof of Mrs. Kemble's gift for bringing beauty from ugliness.

But landscape gardening was only one of Mrs. Kemble's many open-air activities. Like the children, she considered an hour spent indoors was an hour wasted; only nightfall drove her under cover, and not even stormy weather could keep her from the river. The fishing was poor, pike and not many of them, but for her fishing was not a sordid matter of catching fish. Rain or shine, windy days and sunny days, were alike to her; any day was a day for fishing. She would start out early in the morning; sometimes alone, sometimes accompanied by Aunt Dall and all the children carrying picnic baskets, tackle and bait. Sometimes only Fanny went along; she came the

nearest to sharing her mother's passion for fishing. But even
Fanny could not rival her mother's patience. Mrs. Kemble
could stand all day long without one real bite, leaving off only
when it was too dark to see her float. Fanny was more temperamental. Often she would let the whole day go by, lying
lazily in the sun on the grassy river bank, regarding her
mother's alert figure with sleepy eyes; imagining that at any
moment Sintram might come riding through the wood or a
kelpie with seaweed in his hair rise beckoning from a pool,
and scribbling verses reminiscent of Fouqué and Wieland.
But, in another mood, like her mother she could fish from
light till dark.

Why did she enjoy fishing? Fanny sometimes wondered.
She hated to see a fish gasping on the bank, hated that pro-
testing wriggle of a worm strung on the hook—though she
wouldn't let the boys bait the hook for her; if there was something horrid to be done one must do it oneself. Strange, that
in spite of wriggling worms and gasping fish, fishing should be
delightful! Her mother could have told her why they both
liked fishing. Hope made it exciting; the setting—flowing
musical water, sweet air, grassy banks—made it soothing; and
a stimulant combined with a sedative was good medicine for
impatient, highstrung, passionate creatures like Theresa Kemble and her daughter Fanny.

So the Weybridge days slipped pleasantly by. Fanny was
too contented to miss the girls at school or realize that she
needed companionship until, one spring, she went to stay
with her aunt-by-marriage, Mrs. John Philip Kemble, at her
country place in Hertfordshire. Heath Farm had been lent to
Mrs. Kemble by Lord Essex, after the death of her husband
"Glorious John," and overlooked the gardens and lawns of
the Essex estate, Cassiobury Park. Fanny's visit was scented
all through with the spicy breath of carnation and honeysuckle, and made memorable by a friendship (a friendship
that was to last for more than fifty years!) with another guest,
Harriet St. Leger, an Irish lady much older than Fanny. In

her own strange way Harriet was beautiful; though too tall
and thin she walked like a Diana, and in character she so
filled the ideal of the St. Leger motto, *Haut et Bon,* that
Fanny could forgive a certain eccentricity of dress, her short
scant skirts and Quakerish collars. But it was Harriet's mind
and conversation that Fanny found so satisfying. At home
conversation was usually confined to small events in the theatre and in society, and if a serious subject came up Fanny was
too young to be asked for an opinion. Harriet was not only
cleverer and more highly cultivated than anyone Fanny had
ever met before, she could be talked to on an equality. The
two talked and talked and talked. They discussed metaphysics
and politics, religion and literature, themselves and their families. Harriet would describe her Irish home, Ardgillan Castle,
not really a castle, but a country house on a grassy hill beside
the sea with the picturesque fishing village of Skerry lying in
one direction and in the other the Morne Mountains rising in
purple folds. Fanny envied Harriet her home; but still more
she envied Harriet her saddle-horse and gallops along the
beach in the early morning. Fanny had never owned a horse;
she determined that when her ship came in her first purchase
should be a saddle-horse.

Fanny's background seemed colorless in comparison, but
Harriet did not seem to think so; in fact, Harriet showed a
surprising interest in the stage for so serious-minded a person,
and would have liked to talk of what was going on in the
theatrical world. But, to Fanny, this was the dullest of dull
topics; she announced a detestation of the theatre and turned
to the discussion of literature in general and her own writing
in particular; her poems, a translation of Sismondi's history
of Italy she had undertaken for Dr. Malkin, her brother
John's headmaster, and a novel about Françoise de Foix, just
begun and very exciting . . . Harriet was an incomparable
listener. And so safe. Confiding in Harriet was like dropping
a pebble into the bottom of a well. Before long Fanny found
herself touching a subject still nearer home, the old old bur-

den of Covent Garden theatre: her father's troubles, her
mother's anxiety, the increasing difficulty of keeping the boys
at school. She ended with a vision of herself as the family rescuer, a female St. George slaying this dragon with one swoop
of her sword. With what kind of a sword? Oh, money of
course. But how to get it? Ah, that was another question. Literature perhaps. Or music. Fanny had a good voice, though
not so good as Adelaide's. Adelaide's voice was sweet and high
and clear as a bell, and her ear was so perfect that when she
practiced their mother never screamed and threw up her
hands in horror, as she sometimes did if Fanny were at the
piano. When Totty—Adelaide was too long a name—sang 'Oh,
there's a Mountain Palm,' their mother would sit with her
hands in her lap, smiling; everybody said Totty had a great
future. So perhaps it would be wiser for Fanny not to trust
to music as the best way of making money. There was always
her French; if the worst came to the worst a Parisian accent
ought to get one a position as a governess . . . A governess!
Harriet, listening, felt her heart sink. Impossible to picture
this eager, passionate, beautiful young creature, a genius if
ever there was one, wings clipped, teaching the A B C—like
seeing Pegasus chained to a desk in a counting house . . .

And then, all at once, with the suddenness so disconcerting
to less temperamental persons, Fanny's mood would change
Family cares went whistling down the wind, Covent Garden
forgotten, as she sprang to her feet and set off at a run across
the meadow to gather an armful of may, and busy herself
with a child's absorption twisting wreaths of pink and white,
a crown for Harriet as Ceres, and for herself—as Persephone?
Oh no, imagine not seeing the sun for six months! She would
be Hebe. Hebe must have lived in the sunshine or she would
not have been so healthy.

It was as well that Mrs. John Kemble could not see her
guests as they went wandering through the country lanes
crowned with flowers, Fanny singing at the top of her voice—
Fanny was never silent, when she was not talking she sang

—for Mrs. Kemble was the essence of propriety. They had one narrow escape; they had stopped at a little inn and were consuming a deliciously vulgar meal of bread and cheese and beer when Mrs. Kemble in her carriage drove past the window! She would have been still more shocked if she had caught Fanny one hot day gratifying, at last, an old desire experienced in the Parc Monçeaux of her school days. A bright flashing stream ran through Lord Clarendon's place; taking off her shoes and stockings she stepped into the cold foaming ripples, let the drifting weed caress her ankles and shivered at the inquisitive nibble of small silver fish . . . The river; the hawthorn trees like clouds of fragrant bloom; the first note of the nightingale's song between tea and bedtime remained as vivid memories of that springtime with Harriet.

When her friend returned to Ireland walks became restricted, for Mrs. Kemble's propriety forbade lonely wanderings for young females, and conversation was limited as Mrs. Kemble's response to a remark of Fanny's was sure to be "What a very odd girl you are, my dear!" But there were compensations. It was June now; there were strawberries and roses, and luckily Mrs. Kemble's taboos did not include reading. So another desire unfulfilled in her school days, as strong as her love for running water and somehow akin to it, could be gratified. Fanny read Byron from beginning to end.

Providing herself with a cabbage-leaf of strawberries and a bunch of roses, she would betake herself to a favorite oak tree, open her volume of Byron and let herself drift out on a sea of emotion. Emotion so intense and so varied—calm delight of finding in 'Parisina' the nightingale lines first glimpsed at school, waves of horror at the blasphemies of 'Manfred' and 'Cain'—that one morning she flung the book from her in sudden revulsion. She felt suffocated—it was like drowning—like being drugged with opium . . . But she could not give up Byron altogether! She would compromise—read Byron only every other day. And what should be sandwiched in between as an antidote? 'Coelebs in Search of a wife?' 'Letters of Ju-

nius?' And decided on 'Holy Living and Dying' as admirably
suited to her purpose.

So there Fanny sat under her tree in the sweet June weather,
sunshine flickering on her hair, making leafy patterns on her
bare shoulders and muslin frock, nibbling a strawberry or
sniffing refreshment from her nosegay; one day allowing Byron
to raise her temperature to fever heat and the next cooling
off with a chapter of Jeremy Taylor's spiritual consolations
. . . No wonder Mrs. John Kemble considered her a very odd
girl.

July took Fanny back to Weybridge but she returned willingly. The boys were at home now for the holidays; she played
cricket, practiced pistol shooting—she had a remarkably steady
hand—and roamed about the moors. With John and Henry,
even Byron could be forgotten. Then the happy summers at
Weybridge came to an end; the cottage was given up, and the
Kembles again divided their time between Bayswater and
London.

But those happy summers had been broken by one dreadful
interlude—the smallpox. Fanny happened to be in London
when Adelaide developed varioloid, a mild form of smallpox.
As Adelaide had been vaccinated, though not recently, Mrs.
Kemble, with her usual impetuosity, decided that vaccination
was useless, that old-fashioned inoculation was more efficacious, and sent for Fanny. Fanny, like Adelaide, would suffer
a few days' discomfort and be safe for life. Poor Mrs. Kemble!
Fanny obediently caught the smallpox but the disease that had
passed gently over Totty's face was cruel to Fanny. For days
she was not expected to live, and when at last she was well
again her mother could not look at her without a *serrement
de coeur*. It might have been much worse; her complexion
was not roughened, but its red and white was less vivid, and
her clear-cut features were a little blurred.

Wishing, perhaps, to make up to the poor child for this im-
pairment in her looks her parents now turned their attention
to her figure. She had an inclination to slouch and stoop and

poke, and to loll about in a most ungraceful and unfashion-
able manner. If Fanny were ever to go on the stage—not that
anybody dreamed of letting Fanny go on the stage—she could
not make a success with a figure like that. So she was encased
in a backboard, a steel harness strapped at the waist and
shoulders and sprouting a steel rod that held a collar encir-
cling the neck. But to the disappointment of her relations,
and to Fanny's relief, the machine produced none of the good
results that had been hoped for. It was abandoned, and a ser-
geant in the Royal Foot Guards, famous for teaching young
ladies how to carry themselves, was engaged to drill her. She
was an apt pupil and before long could be dismissed as "fit to
march before the Duke of York." Her parents were satisfied;
she had acquired the "flat back, well placed shoulders, erect
head, upright carriage and resolute step" they demanded, and
although her beauty had been dimmed by the smallpox, her
eyes were magnificent, her teeth perfect, and her hair as
thick and dark as ever. But she was extraordinarily variable;
at one moment, her face would light with warm animation
very near to beauty and the next, color and glow would fade
leaving her almost plain. Mrs. Fitzhugh was justified when she
exclaimed:

"Fanny Kemble, you are the ugliest and the handsomest
girl in London!"

CHAPTER VI

Fanny Takes to Literature

"If I may without breach of good manners, imagine that any pretty
young creature is void of genius, and would perform her part herein
very awkwardly, I must nevertheless insist upon her working, if it be
only to keep her out of harm's way."

—THE SPECTATOR.

BAYSWATER SEEMED tame after Weybridge, but the house was
the largest they had lived in at Craven Hill and Fanny, for
the first time in her life, could have a room of her own. With
family interruptions shut out her scribblings at once took a
serious turn. She decided to become a professional writer. A
poet?—she had written reams of verse. No; poetry didn't pay.
A novelist? She had a novel well under way, but so much fiction was written nowadays that a novel wouldn't bring much
glory. What would bring both cash and kudos? There was no
timidity in Fanny; she decided to write a drama. A successful
play always paid, and it would be amusing to see "by Miss
Frances Anne Kemble" at the head of a Covent Garden play-
bill. The only drawback was that, at seventeen, you hadn't
much experience of life. Never mind, imagination must take
the place of experience. And, anyhow, there was a better reason for writing a play than either making money or becoming
famous; Fanny wanted to write a play. She could not help
writing a play any more than she could have helped being
blown about by the wind as she walked across the common.
But she did not tell anyone, not even Aunt Dall. Time enough
when the play was done, and she could hand the manuscript
to her father and assure him that all his worries were over.

For there was one family topic that even a room of your
own could not shut out; Covent Garden theatre. Fanny was
old enough now to realize the weight of the burden her father

52

had so light-heartedly assumed. The theatre was in difficulties (Charles was never personally in debt); its affairs had been thrown into Chancery, and stayed there. Family economies had to be discussed, and Charles debated taking Henry away from Dr. Malkin's school; but it was agreed that, whatever happened, John must get his degree at Cambridge. John had the makings of a great lawyer; Charles fully expected to see John on the woolsack, and that would make up for a little skimping and scraping now . . . Mrs. Kemble broke down under the strain; a curious illness, for a time she could neither hear nor see and was haunted by visions . . . No wonder that Fanny decided to write a play and make money for the family.

And then with one of those sudden fluctuations of fortune characteristic of Covent Garden affairs took a turn for the better. Charles produced Weber's 'Der Freischütz.' London went wild over it; every air, duet and chorus was sung and whistled and hummed and played in London streets and London drawing-rooms until nervous persons declared they would lose their minds and one old gentleman, advertising for a valet, added the proviso, "incapable of whistling a note of 'Der Freischütz.' " Fanny and Adelaide soon knew the opera by heart from overture to finale; Fanny even imagined a romantic devotion for poor Weber himself, and sewed an engraving of his cadaverous face inside a silk case to wear on a string around her neck.

All financial difficulties forgotten now, Charles was in fine spirits; he bought new clothes and presents for the family, and asked Weber to write an opera especially for Covent Garden. Weber was delighted. He wrote 'Oberon' and came to London to superintend the rehearsals. 'Der Freischütz' was revived, and night after night Covent Garden overflowed, for everybody wanted a glimpse of the great musician conducting his own opera. The rehearsals went smoothly; Charles spent money like water. At length 'Oberon' was presented. But it had been over-advertised. Although the cognoscenti agreed that the music was better than 'Freischütz' the public complained that the airs were not catchy; no hand-organs played them, valets refused to whistle them, and London discovered that Weber was sadly unattractive, for, just then, Rossini, a gay talkative Italian, arrived in England.

So 'Oberon' on which so many hopes had hinged was only a partial success, worse in fact than an out and out failure; for as long as 'Oberon' kept on running, Charles had to keep on spending money. Weber took to his bed and died of tuberculosis, hastened by fatigue, disappointment and jealousy of Rossini, and Fanny received a lock of his hair as a memento—not that any of the Kembles were likely to forget Herr von Weber.

In the meantime, Fanny had been writing busily. When it was found that 'Oberon' had eaten up all the money that 'Freischütz' had earned, she felt it was time the family had something to look forward to and decided to tell them about her play. It was half done now and had a name, 'Francis I;' the plot was exciting, the heroine stabbed herself in the end; the costumes were lovely, and there was a last scene in the Certosa at Pavia, with troops of monks singing *de profundis* in pitch darkness, so drenched in gloom that Fanny wept as she wrote. She disclosed her secret; the effect was disappointing. Her mother was kind, but she showed some surprise when Fanny outlined the plot, had coughed almost as if she wanted to laugh—which was, of course, impossible for 'Francis I' was tragedy from beginning to end. Her father was more satisfactory; he said the plot was fine; the public always liked a betrayed maiden, and, God knew, Covent Garden could do with a good play; he promised to read 'Francis I' as soon as he could find the time. John—she had expected sympathy from John, for he was literary—smiled teasingly; he seemed to think Fanny did not know enough history to write a play founded on fact. Henry and Adelaide just said "What fun!" and hoped her play would be as nice as 'Freischütz.' And then they all went on discussing their own affairs exactly as if 'Francis I' had never been mentioned.

It was disheartening, but Fanny kept on writing. She could not have stopped now if she had wanted to; her Garcia and Françoise de Foix and Louise seemed more real to her than her own family; she thought in blank verse, and lived in the narrow crooked streets of ancient Paris and Pavia. Aunt Dall remarked that it was a pity for a young girl to spend her days writing in her own room, that if she never went out in society society would forget her, and Mrs. Kemble agreed. But Fanny scarcely heard these protestations; she had no time for frivolity, and became increasingly absorbed in her work. At length family indifference changed to interest. When another act of 'Francis I' was submitted for criticism her mother went through every scene with scrupulous care, suggesting better stage effects and more telling lines, and Charles, impatient for the play to be finished, told Fanny that Covent Garden was ready to give her two hundred pounds for 'Francis I,' the price they had paid for Miss Mitford's 'Foscari.' But the last act still hung fire. Then one afternoon she found that her father was to be at home the next evening—he was seldom free from the theatre—and she determined to finish that obstinate fifth act at one sitting or die in the attempt. She finished it. After five hours of continuous work, she wrote "curtain" at the bottom of the page with an exhausted satisfaction that showed in her face as, late that night, she went downstairs and met her father just returned from the theatre. He needed no answer to his delighted:

"Is it done, my love? I shall be the happiest man in the world if it succeeds!"

The next day dragged, but at length it was evening. The family gathered in the drawing-room and Fanny read her play.

It was a pretty scene, a true English "conversation piece;" handsome family group; warm, softly-bright room, with its Aubusson carpet and graceful furniture, coal fire on the hearth, wax candles in Empire candelabra on the high Adam mantelpiece, a candle under a hurricane shade on the mahogany stand beside Fanny's straight-backed chair, a bowl of mignonette scenting the autumn evening with a reminiscence of summer. Fanny, seventeen, slim and upright, in ruffled India muslin short-sleeved and low-necked, a scarlet ribbon tied high around her waist, coral beads, feet in neat crimson morocco shoes with ribbons crossed around the ankles, thick wavy hair parted and drawn up at the back into a Grecian knot; her hands trembling and her voice not quite under control as she opened her manuscript, and began: "Good morrow to my lord of Alençon!" but steadying as she forgot herself in the sorrows of Françoise de Foix and the haughty wickedness of Queen Louise.

Charles sat leaning back in a flowered brocade armchair, slim legs crossed, fingertips together, nonchalant but attentive, critical but proud—little Fan read damn well, she had profited by his lessons in diction. Her mother lying full length on the fauteuil in a Récamier pose, graceful head supported by a graceful hand, her dark eyes fixed on Fanny's face; Aunt Dall with her knitting, also intent; Adelaide and Henry in the window-seat, Henry fidgeting; John very serious, nodding or frowning with the critical solemnity expected from a man whose recent oration had been, according to his tutor, "the best that Cambridge had heard for many a year."

And as the inevitable end of the tragedy became clear Henry forgot to fidget, and there was a gasp from Adelaide as Françoise snatched her lover's dagger, plunged it in her own heart, and fell dead. But Fanny's voice went steadily on, quivering only as she reached the last line, "Crown the strange tale of this illustrious day," laid down the manuscript and looked up, eyes shining with expectation.

Charles sprang to his feet, and kissed her with an enthusiasm that lifted her up into his arms; Dall clapped applause; Henry and Adelaide joined in; John cried "Bravo!" and Fanny came near crying as her mother held her close, murmuring caressing congratulations, then turned to Charles, exclaiming that the play must be produced at once. Charles agreed enthusiastically; he himself would take the part of Francis, and Young would make a fine Bourbon; the king's costume must be made in Paris. What did Fanny think of amber-colored velours épinglé with a cloak of violet velvet trimmed with imitation sable? Fanny laughed delightedly. Then her face fell; Charles went on to remark that the last act needed cutting; those monks singing *de profundis* were too gloomy, had better be omitted altogether; he took the manuscript and scrawled long black lines here and there along the margin. Her mother had another idea; the play, she said, ought to be published before it was acted; there were lines such as

"Men still are men, the stream is still a stream,
 Through every change of changeful tide and time,"

that would be lost in the theatre. John agreed, Charles objected. They began arguing. Fanny stood back, chin in the air, soft mouth compressed. There was a touch on her arm—Aunt Dall, murmuring: "You have had two hours of perfect happiness, that is something to remember!"

Fanny smiled. She had had two perfect hours and she was not ungrateful, but she had also had a taste of theatrical criticism and the gilt was off her gingerbread. Describing the reading soon after to her friend Harriet St. Leger, she wrote: "Now that the effervescence of my poetical *furor* has subsided, and that repeated perusals have taken the charm of novelty from my play, my opinion of it is, that it is a clever performance for so *young a person*, nothing more." For already, at seventeen, she was too clear-sighted, she saw too many flaws; she could not whole-heartedly admire her own work.

'Francis I' finished, life seemed empty and society more unsatisfying than ever. She was always restless in a town, crowds and noise got on her nerves; she missed John, who had gone to Cambridge, found Henry uninteresting and was annoyed by Adelaide's incessant singing. To her mother's disappointment she declared that balls were dull, all young men danced badly, and most of them were bores. Even the joy had gone out of her writing; for her father decided that 'Francis' must be acted before it was published, and proceeded to hack and chop and interpolate until only a mangled remnant of her drama was left, and then postponed production to a more favorable time of year. All literature became vanity and vexation and in a fit of depression she flung everything else she had written that year, some eight hundred pages of manuscript, into the fire.

Only the theatre still kept its charm. Kean was acting; fired by his genius Fanny asked herself whether the stage might not, after all, prove her best chance of attaining that "independence of mind and body, which," she wrote to Harriet St. Leger, "is the greatest desideratum of life." But Covent Garden misfortunes loomed too large; she dismissed the idea. A new novel, Mrs. Jameson's 'Diary of an Ennuyée,' confirmed her suspicion that the world was a bubble and increased her dislike of London. She dreamed of Italy, of blue skies and blue seas. Then some Edinburgh relations, Mrs. Harry Siddons and her daughter Lizzie, came to stay and they were fresh from a trip to Switzerland. Fanny could have cried to think how absurdly the gifts of heaven were distributed, for Lizzie, who had seen the Jungfrau, *Manfred's* mountain, been caught on the lake at night in a thunderstorm and gathered edelweiss, only remarked languidly that "the Alps were very nice."

But Lizzie was a dear girl for all that, and when she was left with the Kembles for a long visit Fanny forgot her rôle of *ennuyée*. The girls' first fancy ball was great fun. In her most depressed mood Fanny could take an interest in dress, and her Anne Boleyn costume of white satin, point lace and pearls raised her spirits to rapture; she danced until daybreak and could have danced until noon. As this livelier mood showed that young companionship was what Fanny needed, when Lizzie's visit came to an end and Fanny in her turn was invited to Edinburgh, her parents were glad to let her go. She was enchanted; Scotland was not so blue as Italy or so icy as Switzerland, but it was notoriously romantic.

CHAPTER VII

Romance, Religion and Disaster

"Youth is the time to go flashing from one end of the world to the other both in mind and body; to try the manners of different nations; to hear the chimes at midnight; to see sunrise in town and country; to be converted at a revival."

—ROBERT LOUIS STEVENSON.

IN 1828 EDINBURGH was still the centre of Scottish society. Nobody dreamed of going up to London for the season; with the first cold weather country estates were deserted and all the nobility and gentry who could afford a winter of gaiety opened their houses in "Auld Reekie" and settled down to amuse themselves. The background was more picturesque than London's, more colored by the past; Highland lairds sported kilts; powdered hair, knee breeches and silk stockings were worn by ancient dignitaries such as Baron Hume; sedan chairs carried the elderly to routs and assemblies, and princes "over the water" were held in remembrance. Society was less insipid than in London; for men like Scott, Wilson, Brougham, Jeffrey, Hogg and Sydney Smith could not be ignored by even the ultra-fashionable. So the groups mingled, and as both were enthusiastic patrons of the drama, proud of their theatre and devoted to its proprietors, Mrs. Harry Siddons and her brother William Murray—Edinburgh liked to speak of Mrs. Harry as *our* Mrs. Siddons" to distinguish her from her mother-in-law, the "Tragic Muse"—an agreeable mixture of fashion and intellect was to be found at her house.

This environment suited Fanny. The family atmosphere was stimulating but there were no storms. Mrs. Harry ruled with effortless sweetness, and there was a serenity in the household that a woman of Mrs. Kemble's excitable temperament could not impart. Fanny felt at peace as she seldom felt

60

at home; her mind was fed and her spirit soothed. Immature in some ways—emotionally, a child of six—her mind was full grown, and though the conversation she heard seemed at first dazzlingly clever she soon adjusted herself. William Murray was a cultivated man, a witty talker, with a delightful voice for Moore's songs—his wife was a sister of Tom Moore; writers, scientists and philosophers gathered at his dinner table. Few girls of seventeen would have listened in absorbed silence to such grave conversation and fewer still could have followed their dissection of the political and economic problems of the day. She was more than an intelligent listener, she was inspiring. One night, sitting next to Robert Chambers at a dinner party, the flattering attention in those big dark innocent passionate eyes of hers led him on to describe the struggle with poverty that in their youth had nearly killed his brother and himself; and as he spoke of the two hungry boys standing outside a baker's shop sniffing the smell of new-baked bread but turning away because every farthing must be saved to buy books, Fanny shuddered. Every farthing? Her family thought they had their share of anxiety about money, but the Covent Garden debts that worried her father ran to many thousands of pounds! It was Fanny's first realization of a poverty that could count farthings.

The two Combes, George and Andrew, were among the family's most intimate friends. George just missed genius, sidetracked by a devotion to the new, so-called science of phrenology. He examined the skull of every person who would submit to his fingertips, so Fanny's of course soon came under observation. He told her that her bump of logic was very small, but it was only by accident that she discovered that he found her bump of alimentativeness unusually large. She was posing for Lawrence Macdonald, a young sculptor who had met the fate of every artist who saw Fanny. Having persuaded her to sit, and with a portrait bust well under way, he was beginning to suspect that he had undertaken the impossible. (All her life long it was the same story; painter or sculptor given one glimpse of Fanny's face felt an irresistible desire to interpret and perpetuate, discovered unsuspected difficulties, and, almost without exception, failed; her beauty was too evanescent to be captured.) Macdonald was getting discouraged and Fanny was getting tired—she had been perched on the throne for some time—when George Combe came into the studio. Macdonald welcomed him; conversation might bring back the glow and sparkle that was his model's chief charm. They talked, but Fanny was too tired to respond. She sat limp, a moment more and she would be very nearly plain, it was time to stop. The door opened and Mrs. Harry Siddons came in with a confectioner's paper bag in her hand. Fanny gave a start of joy. "Raspberry tarts!" she cried. Glow and sparkle came back as if by magic; she skipped down from her perch, snatched the bag and began nibbling a raspberry puff. Macdonald laughed, and George Combe remarked so triumphantly, "Didn't I tell you!" that Fanny, looking from one to the other, smiled between bites, for the shocking truth was plain—her bumps had told the "apostle of phrenology" that she was too fond of raspberry tarts!

Andrew Combe was a doctor, humorous and tender-hearted. Fanny, invited to accompany him on his rounds, would accept with enthusiasm. Perched on the high seat of his gig they explored remote neighborhoods so reminiscent of Scotland's romantic past and the Waverley novels that she was always hoping they might meet Sir Walter himself; but they never did. Before long Fanny's mother, who possessed a *naso fino* for romance, heard of these unchaperoned expeditions, and recalling a remark of her nephew Horace Twiss, now a proverb in the Kemble household: "A woman will go anywhere, at any time, with anybody, to see anything—especially in a gig!" was inclined to disapprove. How old, Mrs. Kemble inquired, was this Doctor Combe? Fanny laughed as she thought of the doctor's thin pale face and bony figure. "Old as the hills!" she wrote back, and Mrs. Kemble was satisfied—as she might not have been if she had seen Doctor Combe with her own eyes rather than a young girl's, for he was thirty-one. But there may have been a dash of sentiment on the doctor's side; when Fanny left Edinburgh he presented her with a document drawn up in the form of a deed, binding his ghost to appear to her at death; not, he laughingly assured her, accompanied by a flare of brimstone and corpse candles, nor wrapped in a depressing winding-sheet, but wearing the familiar brown greatcoat of their pleasant drives together. So perhaps the distance between thirty-one and seventeen was less vast than Fanny supposed.

As it happened, Mrs. Kemble had more reason to worry over another affair. It was as well she did not know that Fanny and her cousin Henry Siddons, a handsome young officer, were embarked on a sentimental intimacy; for Mrs. Kemble would not have been able to resist interfering and the flirtation might have crystallized into an engagement. Mrs. Siddons was wiser. She affected to be unconscious of what was going on, and the two cousins danced and walked and talked together, until he departed for the Orient, and though he took with him Fanny's name engraved on the blade of his sword the memento did not hold him long for he found a bride in India—and spent several fruitless hours with pumice-stone and sandpaper trying to eradicate that inconvenient dedication.

But Fanny was not inconsolable, she too had been merely amusing herself; moreover, her imagination was so stirred by the poetry and history of Scotland that she felt no need for more personal romance. In letters to Harriet St. Leger she exhausted her vocabulary of praise, moved most by the very ancient ballads "whose monotonous burdens," she wrote, "soothe and relieve the tragic tenor of the tale like the sighing of wind and the murmuring of water," and "the clarion-hearted Jacobite songs with their fragrance of heather and white roses, breathing a death-defying devotion." The melodies were as haunting as the words; as she wandered about the countryside she sang, and found solitude more adapted to her present mood than even a lover's companionship.

For she walked much alone, exulting in a freedom denied her in London. Often in the early morning before her cousins were out of bed she would climb the Calton Hill to refresh herself with a whiff of its chill air, or dash down to the sands at Portobello for a swim in the sea that would send her home ravenous for her breakfast porridge. But if she chose she was free to ramble to remoter shores, such as Newhaven and Cramond Beach. These lonely walks brought her in touch with the country people. She would stop at a cottage door to fondle a puppy or laugh at a laughing baby—children and animals, all helpless creatures, had for her an irresistible appeal; the guid wife would welcome her in, they would chat for a moment, and Fanny would go on her way, perhaps pitying the woman's poverty, more often envying her a little; poverty could be borne if one had children and lived in the country.

One stormy morning in spite of a wind that nearly blew her off her feet she succeeded in reaching Newhaven, a quaint fishing village. As she stood watching the waves, fascinated by their run and leap over the end of the pier, she felt a sudden need to become a part of the storm, to push out into the midst of its dancing tumult. A knock at the door of the nearest hut brought the fishwife, who summoned husband and son; wrapped in tarpaulins Fanny was rowed out on the Firth. Five minutes finished her; the men laughed and brought her back, paler and wiser than when she left the shore. That was the first of many visits to the Newhaven cottage. Fanny made friends with the fishwife, a beautiful woman whose calm gaze, foam-fresh complexion and easy strength suggested a Greek caryatid come to life. She liked to play with the children, a dozen of them, as strong and beautiful as their mother. She liked to watch her friend and the other fishwives gather on the shingle as the fishing smacks came in, plunge into the water, seize the boats, haul them in above high-water mark, sort the catch and trudge off to town with full baskets while their husbands rested; and all as easily as Fanny herself could pick a bunch of flowers. It was always a pleasure to meet the fishwife climbing Edinburgh streets barefooted, her massive beauty softened by the white handkerchief tied over her fair head, her high sweet voice calling "Caller haddie" as she went in the pensive cadence that is the most melodious of street cries.

But the blessings of freedom and solitude were to be found indoors as well as in the country, under Mrs. Harry Siddons's rule. Fanny was given a room of her own. If, late in the evening, she chose to venture into the dark garden to gather a sprig of myrtle for her aunt, it would be accepted with an unquestioning smile. If she chose to step out on the balcony to bid good-night to Inchkeith's revolving light, rising and setting like a sea star, and lingered there in the cold enthralled by a wonder new to her, the fire dance of the aurora above the northern horizon, no one called her in or fetched a shawl. She might wander and shiver in peace.

Peace was the best blessing of this Edinburgh winter. Fanny was so easily submerged in waves of emotional excitement—a line of poetry, the most trivial family disagreement could sweep her off her feet—and she so detested the inevitable backwash of repentance, that she had come to regard calm as the chief necessity of life. Forever experimenting, she had discovered several recipes calculated to preserve or restore self-control. Routine was one; punctuality, set hours for work and play, Byron and Jeremy Taylor on alternate days. Violent exercise in the open air was usually efficacious. So was fishing. Sleep, nature's specific, was the best and was apt to close down upon her uninvited after any access of joy or sorrow or anger. At such times she might sleep the clock around before she awoke, restored. At others she would appeal to some friend who possessed soothing powers. Harriet St. Leger could induce blessed drowsiness with a few strokes of her hand. In

Edinburgh, after an emotional crisis Fanny would hurry to find her aunt, and fling herself on the floor—always in such moods she experienced a need to get close to the ground; Mrs. Siddons's fingers would begin a gentle smoothing of the head pressed against her knee and almost with the first touch sleep would come.

But a susceptibility that could so feel the impact of a noble nature as to yield to it without a shadow of reserve had its drawbacks. Fanny's antipathies were as strong as her sympathies. They overtook her without warning. Meeting a stranger she would shiver with intense aversion, imagining that a chill wind blew from him to her. Introduced to an apparently harmless lady she would turn away abruptly as if an unseen hand had pushed her back—she might even walk out of the house before she came to herself wondering what inner quality had made the woman so repugnant.

Such antipathies were less apt to afflict her in Edinburgh than in London; the atmosphere did not encourage unreasoning likes or dislikes. Her over-taut nerves relaxed, already she had become far less excitable when she discovered another and more lasting cure for an uneven temper—religion. There was no especial emphasis on religion in Mrs. Harry Siddons's household; Fanny herself could not understand why it was that here for the first time religion should seem real. In her Paris school religion had been carefully taught. At home the family always went to church on Sunday; every morning her mother read a chapter of the Bible aloud to the children before breakfast; they studied Mrs. Trimmer's and Mrs. Barbauld's little books and were taught the catechism. During their childhood Charles liked to have his offspring kneel beside his chair at bedtime to receive his "God bless you, and make you good and happy and healthy and wise!" In the Edinburgh household this same routine of churchgoing and family prayers was expected as a matter of course. Outwardly, there was nothing more: but Fanny became aware of an inner and spiritual grace. Religion became real to her. She made up

her mind to be *good*. Whether or not she received those other
gifts of her father's good-night blessing—happiness, health
and wisdom—she could at least be good. She vowed that she
would never again quarrel with Adelaide and Henry, oppose
her mother, criticize her father, or disobey Aunt Dall; and
then, feeling that a vow should be consecrated by sacrifice,
she determined to offer up her most cherished pleasure or possession. After long consideration she decided to give up Byron. The old enchantment still held; she still shuddered and
thrilled, turned hot and cold, when she read 'Manfred' and
'Cain' and 'The Corsair.' She would shudder and shiver no
more. In future, Byron's poetry should be for her as sealed a
book as the angel's in 'Revelation.' In return she hoped, and
expected, that God would make her completely and perma-
nently good.

Whether or not this bargain was registered in heaven
Fanny found home life less trying when she returned to it.
The winter had given her superb health and high spirits, and
although her temper might not have acquired the calm that
perfect goodness demanded it was smoother and could bear
the ordinary small annoyances of every day. London too
seemed pleasanter. The Kembles were living now in James
Street, Buckingham Gate, and they had agreeable neighbors,
such as the Nortons at the other end of Birdcage Walk—Caroline and Fanny were the third generation of Sheridans and
Kembles who had been intimate. One met any number of
clever people crowded into Mrs. Norton's small drawing-
room; nobody, however, except her sisters, who could compare with her in looks. Fanny, always intensely aware of feminine beauty, envied Caroline Norton her rich coloring and
classic features framed in braids of blue-black hair even more
than she envied her wit and a talent for improvising that rivalled that of Theodore Hook, the most popular parlor en-
tertainer of the time. Either one could be given a subject, go
to the piano and sing a string of original nonsense verses so

pointed with humor and sarcasm that the audience would dissolve in helpless laughter. Fanny herself preferred Mrs. Norton's less spectacular impromptus for Hook happened to be an "aversion;" she detested his blazing red face, staring eyes and raucous voice and the cruel tongue that spared no one if he were in a bad humor. Even Mrs. Norton was not immune. Walking home from church one day with Fanny she let herself go; Hook was insufferably coarse and intolerably ill-natured; it was amazing that he should be tolerated in decent society. Fanny murmured that wit was no doubt a temptation. "Wit!" the angry lady cried, "it is easy enough to be witty if one fears neither God nor Devil!" and Fanny suppressed a smile, wondering under which head the magnificent Caroline placed herself.

The Montagues' house in Storey's Gate was another where clever people gathered spontaneously, and where the Kembles were intimate. Basil Montague's romantic background may have had something to do with his success—he was the son of the Earl of Sandwich and the beautiful Miss Wray who had been murdered in her box at the theatre by a German lover—but it was his genius for personal intercourse that made him notable in even that exacting age. His wife was as clever as he; she was beautiful, and dressed beautifully regardless of the prevailing fashion. Soft-falling, soft-colored satins and silks and floating lace scarves set off an old lady's looks, Fanny decided; when her hair turned gray she too would adopt some such becoming and fashionless style of costume. Mrs. Montague's daughter, Mrs. Procter, "Barry Cornwall's" wife, was another of Fanny's admirations—though a sharp tongue had earned the name of "Our Lady of Bitterness"—and she liked to play with fragile little Adelaide, imagining that she saw in that wistful face "the prophecy of a poet," though John insisted there was something weird about the little creature; she was an elf child. Of course John, as well as Fanny, was always glad to accept an invitation from

Mrs. Procter; an invitation was a compliment, for it was said of her drawing-room that "no bore ever got in twice."

Wit must have been at this time the best passport in London society. Hook's occasional lapses were forgiven, and a turn for impromptu verse and clever conversation were enough to get Horace Twiss into very smart houses and, eventually, into Parliament. Their friends watched this success with some surprise; the Charles Kembles, dining at Horace's, smiled and agreed when Tom Moore whispered that this was "a strange mixture of company," for their fellow guests were the Duke and Duchess of Devonshire, Lord and Lady Bathurst and Theodore Hook! Such mixtures were not uncommon in the easy, supremely agreeable society of the first thirty years of the nineteenth century. According to Trevelyan, "in the breed of men and in the noblest trophies of arts and letters" they were the greatest thirty years in England's history. There can be little doubt that they were also the pleasantest in English society and not only in literary circles such as the Procters'; even in the most aristocratic houses cleverness could get you in and dullness keep you out. That authority, Charles Greville, describing a Chatsworth house party in his diary, would note that "every one did what he liked best. In the evening they acted charades, or danced, there was plenty of écarté and, as Sydney Smith says, 'conversation raged';" and his worst condemnation of any party was a yawning "I was bored." Money and birth seem not to have been essential. Tom Moore, without a penny and the son of an Irish grocer, was made to feel almost at ease; Luttrell, whose father could only be guessed at, was welcome because of his clever epigrams; so was Washington Irving, although he was an American and had arrived in London with a letter to Mrs. Charles Kemble as his one introduction.

During the early years of this agreeable epoch the pace had been set by the Regent, a Stuart as intolerant of bores as Charles II and, in his rococo way, a patron of the arts; Marie

Thérèse De Camp was one of many who would remember
George IV with gratitude. But her "Prince Charming" was no
longer a figure in society; he had become ridiculous, so obese
that he could not bear to be laced into his stays till the day
was half over, so clouded in mind that one moment he would
declare that he had led the heavy dragoons at Salamanca
and the next that he had ridden Fleur-de-Lis for the cup at
Goodwood. One attractive quality seems to have remained;
"Prinny" still liked children and almost his last entertain-
ment was a children's ball given in honor of the little Queen
of Portugal and Princess Victoria, described by Charles Greville as "a short, plain-looking child, not near so good-looking
as the Portuguese"—no doubt Greville would have written
with a still sharper pen if he had foreseen the changes that
short plain child would bring about, a court where Mrs.
Procter's rule would be reversed, where bores could not only
get in but stay in!

That day was not yet. Fanny, brought up by a mother who
hated bores and a father who loved gaiety, was exacting
enough; but she found little to complain of in London society after her return from Edinburgh. She met Mrs. Jameson
at the Montagues' and although the "Ennuyée" was disappoint-
ingly red-haired and plumpish, she was clever and the two became intimate; and she met Rammohun Roy there, an Indian
Rajah and philosopher whose conversation was worthy of
Edinburgh. On the other hand Moore's melodies seemed
tame after Scotland's heart-stirring ballads, and though it was
an honor to be asked by Mrs. Norton to sing with Tom
Moore himself it was an ordeal; Fanny was obliged to swallow half her full rich contralto voice as she sang second to the
poet's pipe, and sometimes feared she might choke before she
got through one of his saccharine effusions.

At home too there was now no lack of good conversation.
John brought his Cambridge friends to the house and even in
"Auld Reekie" men such as Frederick Maurice, Richard
Trench, William Donne, Alfred Tennyson, Richard Monck-

ton Milnes, Edward Fitzgerald and William Thackeray would have been considered worth talking to. All of them were young, so she did not feel at a disadvantage; all of them were clever. Most of them, and John himself, belonged to the "Cambridge Apostles," a radical group, burningly aware of social problems, eager to right wrongs and ready to discuss any serious subject. The "Apostles" were extremely serious-minded. Frivolity was out of fashion at Cambridge and wisdom was admired more than wit. The easygoing first thirty years of the century were almost over. Reform was in the air. The aristocracy felt less secure. Property was becoming less sacrosanct; now and then the machinery of a factory would be threatened, or a farmer's ricks set on fire. There were disquieting rumors of a new disease, the cholera, said to be creeping into Europe from the Orient. Of all this—except cholera—the young and ultra-modern approved. What did a few ricks and spindles matter? The main thing was to raise the condition of the working classes. The only men worth listening to were Jeremy Bentham and John Stuart Mill—they were neighbors of the Kembles and John never passed their houses without raising his hat.

But though Fanny listened and talked and argued, and admired Trench and Maurice and the other "Apostles," there were moments when she was glad that not all John's friends were so earnest and turned with relief to Dicky Milnes who was distinctly frivolous, or to Tennyson who was poetical, or to Edward Fitzgerald and William Thackeray whom she had known all her life. These two were on the most intimate footing in the house, they had been John's school fellows at Doctor Malkin's school. In Thackeray's case this might not have been a reason for friendship; his nose had been broken at school, accidentally of course, by John and another boy named Venables while they were playing. But he was much too good-natured to bear malice and was the most amusing and best company of any of John's friends—he was not an "Apostle," he was too humorously inclined. Take them all round, however, there was not one bore in the lot and Fanny decided that if only they had danced half as well as they talked she would have been more than satisfied.

But there were others. London gave her ample opportunity for her favorite pursuit. Unfortunately an invitation to a ball could not often be accepted, for Charles's financial difficulties were increasing. Fanny's allowance of twenty pounds a year did not afford many new ball dresses but she hated to take even that small sum from her father; carriages were expensive, and return entertaining, in the lavish way that was the only way her parents enjoyed, was out of the question. So parties were limited to near-by, intimate houses, and Fanny darned stockings and mended broken fans, and cried when she found her ruffles torn by a clumsy partner, and wondered what she would have done without Aunt Dall who could work miracles with faded wreaths and limp ostrich feathers, and tried to be good and did not always succeed, because of one drawback inevitable in London, a lack of outdoor exercise.

Country cottages were out of the question now. It was all Charles could do to pay for the town house. Walking in the airless London streets she would long for the breezes of the Calton Hill, the blossoming hawthorns of Heath Farm and the ferny woods of Oatlands park. On a sunny day she would stand for long minutes in the back garden looking up at the patch of sky between the branches of the two poplars and the one sycamore that shook their leaves as if to make sure they had not been robbed of all their green by London smoke and smut, wishing she were rich. If she were rich she would have a house in the country, and she would have a saddle-horse. She envied the girls riding in Hyde Park, and quoted Wordsworth, "The horse and rider are a happy pair," and when her family, laughing at her, remarked that riding seemed to be her idea of heaven, she declared that she did not want to be an angel unless she could be an angel on horseback. She envied the children playing in the square who were allowed to run and shout; she hated the trailing, full-gathered skirts she wore that forbade easy motion and the tightly laced bodice that discouraged a deep breath; knowing what she needed, she wrote to Harriet: "Violent bodily exercise, riding or climbing up steep and ragged pathways, are my best remedies for the blue devils."

And then, suddenly, dreams and annoyances alike became unimportant and even poverty was forgotten in a new anxiety. The family began worrying about John, the brilliant "Apostle," whose future had seemed so secure. John came home one day and told his father that he was leaving Cambridge without taking a degree, that he had decided to give up studying law and was going into the church. Charles was disgusted. It was not that he felt any contempt for holy orders —with a martyr in the family no Kemble could object to the church as a profession—but the *volte-face* was too abrupt to seem sincere or safe. However, Frederick Maurice and Richard Trench approved, and Tennyson wrote a sonnet in honor of John's dedication to the church—the sonnet to J.M.K. beginning:

"My hope and heart is with thee—thou wilt be
   A latter Luther and a soldier priest"—

so the family anxiety subsided and their ambitions took a new form. Fanny dreamed now of keeping house for dear John in a country rectory embowered in roses, and his parents discussed bishoprics. But before long mitres and aprons went the way of wigs and woolsacks. John changed his mind again! Not that the church had ceased to beckon, he still wanted to be a clergyman; but he doubted whether he had a vocation. Anyway, Anglo-Saxon literature was more interesting than theology, and Heidelberg a better place to work in than Cambridge, and off John went to Germany.

The family imagination could not follow John into this unknown region; their ambitions had nothing to feed upon now. It was as if John were dead. They all missed him, Fanny most of all. Henry was a nice boy, cheerful and remarkably good-looking—Thackeray described him later as "the most beautiful boy I ever saw"—but with no brains to speak of; Adelaide was only fifteen and so absorbed in her music that she thought and talked of nothing else. Fanny not only missed John terribly, she was worried and puzzled; worried about his future, puzzled by his lack of decision. It seemed so strange not to know what you wanted! She always knew what she wanted—and made for it with a rush that sometimes ended in a tumble. But tumbles didn't matter—you picked yourself up and hurried on. John wasn't like that. John was timid, saw obstacles where none existed, and could not forget his mistakes. Fanny sighed, failing to understand her favorite brother; for, at heart, she was still the child who "never lamented, resented or repented."

Then all at once the family stopped worrying about John and Fanny forgot to miss him. Covent Garden affairs took a sudden turn for the worse. They had been running down-hill for the past year, but Charles had not expected any immediate crisis. He was away from home, touring Ireland, when the crash came one never-to-be-forgotten day in the autumn of 1829. Mrs. Kemble had gone out for a walk. Fanny was practicing; she heard her mother come in, and turned abruptly from the piano for there was a wildness in those hurrying footsteps on the stairs. Mrs. Kemble dashed into the room, dropped half fainting on the sofa, and burst into tears. It was some time before she could speak; at length the dreadful news was sobbed out. She had passed Covent Garden theatre—the walls were plastered with bills—the property was to be sold at auction—the theatre would be closed and all the employees turned adrift—seven hundred of them, and many more at Christmas and Easter—all left to starve. As for themselves— they would all starve too. Charles—so proud and hardworking —Charles would die of the disgrace. There would be no money to finish John's education; not a penny for the commission in the navy Henry had set his heart on; Adelaide—Adelaide with her golden voice—must give up studying music . . . At length poor Mrs. Kemble, sick with grief, went to lie down—windows wide open and Aunt Dall hovering over her with Cologne water and murmurs of encouragement—and Fanny shut herself up in her own room to think and plan. Literature, from which she had hoped so much, she could no longer consider as a means of making money. 'Francis I' still lingered in obscurity, neither published nor produced . . . In the end a governess job seemed the only possibility, and to make the decision seem real she wrote to her father asking his permission.

But Mrs. Kemble had also been thinking things over. When Fanny told her of the governess plan her mother nodded, but without enthusiasm, and then asked a startling question: did Fanny think she had any talent for acting? Fanny hesitated, recalling her school success as Hermione; but that was a long time ago. She shook her head. No; she did not believe that she had any dramatic talent. Mrs. Kemble persisted; she told Fanny to study some part, anything she happened to fancy. Fanny chose Portia, her ideal of womanly perfection; she learned the part word for word with her usual ease, and recited it to her mother. Mrs. Kemble listened, made no criticism, remarked that Portia gave too little scope for passion—she must have guessed where her daughter's genius lay—and told her to study Juliet. Again Fanny studied, recited; again her mother made no comment . . .

Charles came home, the governess letter was not mentioned; Fanny did not dare to speak of it. Her father looked dreadfully ill. He was taking the Covent Garden catastrophe hard. His pride was deeply hurt; he would not admit that his years of hard work were "years that the locusts had eaten," and that Covent Garden's law suits had become a joke. The jingle that everybody was repeating:

"The case of Kemble, Willet and Forbes
Much of the Chancellor's time absorbs;
If I were the Chancellor I should tremble
At the mention of Willet, Forbes and Kemble,"

did not seem in the least funny to Charles and his colleagues. But he acknowledged that he was at his wit's end. Perhaps it would be better to throw up the sponge now without waiting for further developments, follow his brother John's example and spend the rest of his days in exile. Theresa had better take the children abroad and settle down in some cheap place where he could join them if his creditors became too importunate . . . One morning Mrs. Kemble told Fanny that her father wished to hear her recite Juliet when he returned from the theatre that night.

Fanny recited Juliet's lines with the determination of an intelligent child. No fire flashed down from heaven to give life to Juliet as it had flashed for Hermione. Charles's: "Very nice, my love, very nice indeed," was not convincing. Fanny escaped as soon as she could and ran away, stopping for a moment to sit on the stairs and cry because she had been a failure, and then went to bed to forget all the family anxieties as soon as her head touched the pillow . . . Several days went by; no allusion was made to Juliet. Fanny took for granted that her failure had been as apparent to her parents as to herself . . . Then one morning at breakfast Charles remarked that he would like to try Fanny's voice; she was to go with him to the theatre, he wanted to find out whether her voice was strong enough to fill the building.

CHAPTER VIII

Success

"... The children of the crown were graced
With nearer seats, and lords by ladies placed.
Scarce were they seated, when with clamours loud
In rushed at once a loud tumultuous crowd,
The guards, and then each other overbear,
And in a moment fill the spacious theatre."

—DRYDEN.

THE STAGE of Covent Garden was enormous. Fanny stepped out into that vast emptiness and paused to look about her. Overhead, a confusion of criss-crossings cutting darkness; behind her, a confusion of meaningless shapes peering out awkwardly from another darkness; at the sides, racks of pasteboard and canvas—streets, forests, dungeons and banqueting halls—drawn away, leaving her the centre of an empty cavern. It was cold. The air smelt dusty. Her feet made no more sound than a mouse's as she crossed the smooth green baize floor. In front, a still vaster emptiness opened out; the curtain was up, the amphitheatre rose tier on tier, boxes empty, seats swathed in gray holland. No movement broke the stillness; the only light came from far above, a single ray that pricked down from some opening in the roof, alighted on the floor at her feet and spread to a round bright spot.

Fanny felt very small and young as she stood there, a newborn star told to twinkle in an empty sky with no companions to encourage her. Her father had moved out of sight; his voice seemed to reach her from miles away. But she was not frightened. The still loneliness was, somehow, inspiring, like the stillness of a mountain top. Her father bade her begin. She spoke. Her voice rang clear as a bell, soared up and out. She thrilled at the sound, rejoiced in its power, exulted in the

77

beauty of Juliet's lines. She forgot her father, forgot herself . . .

It was over, her father kissed her. A figure emerged from nowhere, came walking in—Major Dawkins, an old friend, who had, it appeared, been listening, hidden in the back of a box. He was a critic whose opinion Charles valued. Major Dawkins said: "Bring her out at once; she will be a success." If Charles had doubted he doubted no longer; nor did Fanny's mother. There was no time to lose; if Covent Garden could by any possibility be saved—and even Charles did not believe it could be—the attempt must be made without delay. They told Fanny that she was to come out in three weeks.

Three weeks! No child of a great theatrical family really begins at the beginning; from babyhood Fanny had heard stage matters discussed and analyzed, already she knew more than any outsider could know. But this was in itself daunting for she realized what lay before her. The other members of the company were strangers, she must make their acquaintance; she must learn all the intricate stage business; learn how to carry herself towards an audience; learn how to concert her own actions with those of her fellow actors, bring out every possible effect in her own part and yet not injure theirs. When she thought of all this three weeks shrank to three hours. But it had to be done. She set herself to work like a child given a hard lesson.

To her parents, with so much to teach, the time must have seemed even shorter; but they were not dismayed. Charles, like all the Kembles, was spurred on by difficulties, and the need for haste was in itself exhilarating to her mother. Morning rehearsals began at once; and the evening brought consultations at home to decide the question of Juliet's dress. Mrs. Kemble was an authority on costume, but so was Fanny's friend Mrs. Jameson, and they did not agree. Mrs. Jameson begged for a gorgeous brocade stiff with embroidery and jewels, such as a Capulet would have worn in ancient Verona. Mrs. Kemble took a different point of view; she had no wish

to return to the old way of acting historical plays in modern
dress; Garrick's Macbeth in knee-breeches and a powdered
wig had been ridiculous enough, and Mrs. Siddons should
not have worn a hoop as the Grecian Daughter. But she perceived technical difficulties that Mrs. Jameson did not allow
for. Asked to criticize a sketch Mrs. Kemble's first thought
would be: How will this dress look when it walks, runs,
rushes, kneels, sits down, falls and turns its back? So now she
insisted that appearance must be subordinated to action; a
ruff would prevent free movement of the head and neck, and
heavy sleeves ruin gesture. Moreover, the consciousness of being "dressed up" was fatal to passion, and any peculiarity of
costume might easily divert the attention of the audience from
Juliet herself. Charles agreed. Mrs. Jameson's drawings were
put aside and Fanny was told that her Juliet would make no
departure from the conventional. She was to wear a white
satin ball-dress with tight bodice and full skirt, low neck and
short sleeves; her thick wavy hair parted in the middle and
caught into a loose knot at the back with a comb as she usually wore it. Except for a diamond girdle and a train three
yards long—Mrs. Kemble realized the value of a sweeping
train—she would look as Juliet was expected to look, and feel
as if she were appearing at a party given by the Montagues of
London rather than by the Capulets of Verona.

This decided, a still more important question remained:
Romeo. Charles was Covent Garden's Romeo and extremely
popular, but now the part was forbidden him, the public
would not like seeing a man make love to his daughter. Various candidates were rejected. At length Charles suggested
that Henry might do. Henry was too young and too cheerful
and he detested acting, but a more beautiful Romeo could
not well be imagined and it was hoped that his expression
might soon become less cheerful as he had recently fallen in
love. So Henry, to his horror, was told to study the balcony
scene. The family assembled to hear him recite; their ordeal
was brief. His matter-of-fact gabble, interrupted by giggles,

was so absurd and the mortification that clouded his boyish face so unlike love's anguish, that a few minutes was enough. Charles smiled and flung his book on the floor. Henry, seeing which way the wind blew, clapped his arms to his sides and let out a cock-a-doodle-doo of mingled relief and triumph that sent his audience into shrieks of laughter. They laughed and laughed. And Henry was assured that he might consider himself forever immune from a dramatic career.

In the end it was decided that Mr. Abbot would have to do. The public rather liked Mr. Abbot; he was fairly good-looking though too old for the part, and knew his business. Fanny, of course, made no objection to the choice; she was too inexperienced to wish for a more passionate Romeo; in fact it did not occur to her that Romeo was important one way or the other. But at rehearsal she discovered that Mr. Abbot was given to ranting and roaring and rushing about the stage with a violence that was disconcerting and often terrifying; for the poor man was unsteady on his feet and she feared that at any moment he might slip and fall and carry her down with him. However, she soon learned to avoid his onslaughts and the rehearsals went on without mishap.

Mr. Abbot was the weakest spot in the cast; Mr. Keely made an excellent Peter and Mrs. Davenport a perfect Nurse. Fanny's mother was to take Lady Capulet, although it was years since her retirement, for she knew that her presence would give Fanny courage, and Charles was to act Mercutio. (It became his greatest part; then and later critics agreed that "Charles Kemble's Mercutio was incomparably the best that ever trod the English stage.")

Fanny herself remained an unknown quantity. At rehearsal her performance was so uneven that no one could feel sure of her. Now and then a gesture or tone would recall her aunt, Mrs. Siddons; but such flashes of genius were rare and they came and went like fireflies. Fanny's parents realized, of course, that artistry such as Mrs. Siddons had achieved after years and years of study could not be expected and agreed

that her only assets were youth, imagination and willingness
to work. But when Mrs. Kemble went on to lament the child's
lack of self-control as a disadvantage, Charles demurred—sup-
pressing a smile, for self-control was not Theresa's long suit;
to him, Fanny's lack of ambition seemed a more serious drawback, and he shook his head with a puzzled sigh. A Kemble
who could act and did not want to was something new in the
family history!

Apart from this anxiety the outlook was bright. Covent
Garden's misfortunes had worried the public almost as much
as they had worried Charles; theatre-goers were shocked when
they saw the walls of the old play-house plastered with bills of
sale, and the news that another Kemble was to appear on the
stage was received with rejoicing. Enthusiasm took a practical
form; several wealthy patrons of the drama started a fund to
insure a handsome production of 'Romeo and Juliet;' the
King's theatre gave a benefit, and the principals in the Covent
Garden company made a present of their services for the first
few weeks. The advertising also was in a sense free, for the
story advertised itself. It was so romantic, this story of a
daughter coming to the rescue of her father like another Iphi-
genia! And the girl was very young, only nineteen. And very
clever, a second Mrs. Siddons. As beautiful as the "Tragic
Muse?" Far more beautiful! As great a genius? Far greater!
Miss Fanny Kemble was a *natural* genius, entirely untrained.
Entirely untrained? So much the better!—for, as usual, the
public liked to believe that genius is miraculous and springs
like a rabbit out of a top-hat at the bidding of some celestial
conjuror. So there was much talk of Fanny's lack of dramatic
training as well as of her youth and beauty; and as few people
could boast of having seen her an element of mystery was
added to the tale of filial devotion and all London thrilled
with sentimental admiration. Everybody was urged to help
the dear child, everybody wanted to. Everybody agreed with
Sir Walter Scott when he wrote: "I love and honor Miss Kemble for giving her active support to her father in his need, and

preventing Covent Garden from coming down about their ears."

Seats for 'Romeo and Juliet' sold like hot cakes and there was a clamorous demand for boxes, and managers of other houses began to hope that theatre-going might again become popular with the upper classes. It had not been fashionable of late, for several reasons. Most of the new plays were so poor that only a great actor like Kean could draw an intelligent audience; politics had become so absorbing that the young and ultra-modern had no time for amusement, and the wave of evangelicalism, having purified the lower orders, was washing so high that some of the very smartest people had come to perceive that the stage was wicked, that even Shakespeare smelt of brimstone and that it was a good deal safer to hear his plays read than to see them acted.

These prejudices and predilections were now forgotten. The most straitlaced could not deny that filial piety should be encouraged; the intelligentzia allowed themselves an interval of frivolity, and rank and fashion fought for the privilege of seeing Miss Kemble act. The Kembles' friends did not of course need any sentimental stimulus to rally them. Mrs. Siddons consented to honor her niece by appearing in the small stage box that had been fitted up especially for her; Mrs. Fitzgerald ordered a new purple velvet gown and notified her son Edward that he might come up from Cambridge, and the "Apostles" to a man lamented John's absence and prepared to do their best for his little sister.

But Fanny, the centre of all this emotion and commotion, remained curiously indifferent, curiously *young*. Nineteen, nearly twenty, and intellectually a woman, she faced what lay ahead of her like a docile child. She did what she was told; she spoke, curtsied, moved this way and that, smiled or wept, put on a frock or took it off, like a child anxious to please; always a little aloof, as if she were wondering what all the fuss were about. A letter to Harriet at this time is suggestive. Not until several pages had been devoted to a recent illness in the

St. Leger family, the health of her own parents, and regrets
that Mrs. Harry Siddons was leaving London after a long
visit, did she remember to tell Harriet that the future so often
discussed at Heath Farm had been decided for her; she was to
go on the stage, the play was to be 'Romeo and Juliet,' she
wished it were all over, and ended this brief mention with an
apology; her own affairs would not have been alluded to at a
time of such anxiety for Harriet but she did not want her
friend to receive the first notice of her début from the newspapers.

At length the great day arrived, the twenty-sixth of October, 1829. There was no rehearsal that morning. Fanny, told
to rest and keep calm, resorted to routine. Her usual hour of
practicing on the piano was followed by her usual walk in St.
James's Park; then she took up a book she happened to be
reading, Blunt's 'Scripture Characters,' and became so absorbed that she looked up with a start when Aunt Dall came
to tell her it was time to go to the theatre.

Daylight was still brightening the streets as Fanny and her
mother and Dall drove to Covent Garden. A ray of sunlight
shone into the carriage and touched Fanny's hair and Mrs.
Kemble murmured: "Heaven blesses you, my child!" But her
voice was not steady, and when they arrived she hurried off
to her dressing-room afraid that her agitation might be contagious and left Fanny, still fairly calm, to be dressed by Aunt
Dall.

Dall and Fanny's maid and the theatre-dresser buzzed about
her, enjoying their task. Fanny stood like a lay figure while
the folds of her costume were twitched and smoothed, a stitch
taken here and there, a loop of hair adjusted and rouge applied. At length she was set down on a chair, with her train
draped over the back, to wait. And now calm deserted her and
she could no longer distract her mind with thoughts of Scripture characters; she was experiencing a new sensation, fear,
and might have been waiting for the guillotine as she sat
there, bolt upright, hands clasped palm to palm, heart beat-

ing in her throat. Now and then a tear would hang trembling on the long thick dark eyelashes that were her greatest beauty, and roll slowly down her cheeks. Each time Aunt Dall with a smile of pity would repair the damage to her make-up. Now and then her father would come to the door and Fanny would hear him ask: "How is she?" and each time Dall would send him away reassured . . .

But there was satisfaction as well as anxiety in the air; it filtered back-stage and reached Fanny's dressing-room. The house, they said, was jammed to suffocation; Mrs. Siddons herself had never met a better audience. The Leveson-Gowers had just come in, and the Duchess of St. Albans; Lady Dacre was already in her box; the Earl of Essex was expected. There were plenty of lesser lights such as young Mr. Wortley and the Reverend Mr. Harness and the Grevilles. Everybody was chattering and laughing. Miss Kemble was assured that she had nothing to fear . . . But Fanny did not hear these kind words, she was too far gone. She just sat and waited, numb and cold, waited for the axe to fall . . .

At last a brisk tap at the door, a voice: "Miss Kemble called for the stage, ma'am." She stood up, Aunt Dall lifted her train, she was led to the side scene directly opposite the one where her mother stood waiting to go on. Lady Capulet advanced. A roar of applause came from the audience, Fanny sank half-fainting into her aunt's arms. The company gathered about—Charles was nowhere to be seen, he could not bear to watch Fanny's entrance. "Poor thing! Poor thing!" they murmured. Mrs. Davenport gave her a warm: "Courage, courage, my dear!" Kind Mr. Keely said in that funny voice of his: "Never mind 'em, Miss Kemble. Don't think of 'em any more than if they were a row of cabbages!" . . .

Then a voice from the stage, Lady Capulet's voice:
"Nurse!"
Mrs. Davenport waddled on. Turned, called:
"Juliet!"

Aunt Dall stood Fanny on her feet, gave her a push and sent her running straight across the stage. Stunned by the deafening applause that rose to meet her, the green baize floor seeming to heave under her feet, a mist before her eyes, she reached her mother, caught at her, and stood staring at that sea of faces. Her mother whispered—the lines came to her— she spoke. But the voice that had rung so full at rehearsal was gone. Scarcely a syllable of Juliet's lines in the first act could be heard; the audience looked pityingly at each other and clapped half-heartedly . . . The ballroom scene went better. Little by little Fanny forgot herself; the part took possession of her; at last, as she leaned from the balcony to her lover the heavenly fire flashed down and she was all Juliet. Exalted by the beauty of Juliet's words, blushing with Juliet's passion, paling with Juliet's fears, her voice rang clear as a bell,

"O, Romeo, Romeo! wherefore art thou Romeo?"

and from the top gallery to Mrs. Siddons in her box the whole house knew that little Fanny Kemble was a great actress.

The applause was deafening. Young gentlemen stood on the seats and waved their hats; John's friends forgot they were "Apostles" and shouted like school-boys; young ladies clapped their gloves to shreds and flung bouquets at Fanny's feet. Here and there an elderly person might whisper that the girl could not be compared to Mrs. Siddons in talent or looks and that she was too small for tragic parts, but nobody listened to them. Most people declared that Miss Kemble was the image of her aunt—though Mr. Harness added: "Seen through the wrong end of an opera glass"—while others commented on her remarkable likeness to Malibran both in face and figure. Wave after wave of applause rose and fell, and rose again; the audience seemed as if it would never tire of demonstrating affection for the Kemble family and admiration for Fanny's genius and youth and courage . . . At last it was over. Half an hour in the greenroom of congratulations, embraces and tears of unutterable relief, and then Charles and Theresa Kemble took their child home.

Fanny was too dazed to feel any elation; the familiar streets seemed strange to her, their own house had an unnatural look, and her parents' kisses and expressions of thankfulness did not touch her; everything, she herself, seemed unreal. It was not until they sat down to supper and her father laid a little jewelled watch beside her plate that Fanny came to. A watch! She had never owned a watch—a watch was something tangible—the diligent child had been awarded a prize. Fanny laughed and cried with delight, and could not understand why Mr. Washington Irving, and the other friends who had dropped in to wish her joy, seemed amused by her enthusiasm as she kissed the little watch and declared she would christen it Romeo . . . When at length she was free to go to bed, after praying to be preserved from the many temptations of the stage she fell asleep at once; for her watch was under her pillow and she had been repaid for her weeks of hard work and even that horrible hour of stage fright seemed worth while . . . In spite of the great minds of Edinburgh, and the improving conversation of John's friends, Fanny was still very, very young!

CHAPTER IX

Life of a Star

"We were all in love with you and had your portrait by Lawrence in our rooms."

—THACKERAY (TO F.K.).

A TURN of the kaleidoscope had altered the pattern of Fanny's life. Every hour of the day was different now and all other occupations must give way to her career. As Juliet needed no more rehearsing her mornings were her own but they must be spent in quiet exercise. She dined in the middle of the day and as frugally as a Harrow boy, usually on a mutton chop, the Kemble idea of a proper diet for the profession—Mrs. Siddons's butcher had found her "a wonderful one for chops." 'Romeo and Juliet' was acted three times a week. On these days Aunt Dall took Fanny to the theatre and deposited her in her dressing-room, where she would wait, soothing herself with a bit of needlework and thinking over the next scene and the various effects it demanded, until the call came; then Dall would gather up that expensive satin train, spread it out for Fanny's entrance, remain on guard at the side-scene until she came off, gather up the train again, wrap a shawl about her shoulders, and escort her back to her dressing-room. She saw very little of the other members of the company and seldom spoke to them except while she was acting, for the green-room was forbidden ground. It was feared that there her thoughts might be distracted from the business in hand, or that she might, as her parents expressed it, "form undesirable acquaintances." Only once was she permitted to visit the treasury of the theatre; the first Saturday she was told she might receive her salary in person; she took her thirty sovereigns with satisfaction, jingled them in her hands and carried them

87

in triumph to her mother, the first money she had ever earned.

But the most careful chaperonage could not prevent her becoming aware of the adulation that surrounded her. One group of young men soon succeeded in making themselves conspicuous; they never missed a performance and always contrived to secure seats in the front row of the pit although these seats could not be reserved, and having fought their way in would greet the new star with an exuberance that the audience found extremely annoying. But Fanny was not annoyed; she delighted in that faithful row and grew so dependent on their cheers and encores that she would have felt lost without them. All these young men were of course hoping for an introduction to Miss Kemble, but that was even more difficult to achieve than a front seat in the pit. As no stranger was permitted to speak to her at the theatre and no one could get an introduction except through a friend, you met her in society or not at all. So most admirers were obliged to content themselves with buying her picture. The shop windows were crowded now with engravings; cups and saucers appeared adorned with Fanny's head; fashionable young men flourished buff handkerchiefs patterned with violets that proved on close inspection to be not flowers but Fanny. Hayter made some pretty drawings of her as Juliet; they were published with a eulogy from Mrs. Jameson, and Lane the publisher made over three hundred pounds from the first impression. In a short time Miss Kemble's face became as well known as the King's and much better known than that of the little Princess Victoria, though she too was painted that same year by Hayter, "in simple white muslin and ringlets, seated on an ottoman." Fanny's looks were a matter of hot discussion; some insisted that she was always supremely beautiful; others that she was handsome only when she was acting; Washington Irving wrote: "She is much more beautiful in private than on the stage, and the nearer one gets to her face and to her mind, the more beautiful they both are." A few saw little to admire; Lady Caroline Lamb was lukewarm; Charles Greville's diary noted disappointment. Fine eyes, hair and teeth did not compensate for too large hands and feet, and while allowing her some grace and some cleverness and much energy and spirit, he ended: "She does not move me."

Henry Greville on the other hand could find no flaw in Fanny either as a beauty or as an actress, and all fashionable young men were of his opinion. For it was soon discovered that Miss Kemble was the best dancer in London, and she could talk as well as dance and she could sing as well as talk! If her parents had been less careful of her health every evening not spent in acting would have been spent in dancing. Invitations poured in. Fanny, from being merely one young girl among dozens of others more important and better dressed, became in one night a "little lioness," the talk of the town. Other dancers would stop to watch her dance; they crowded about the piano when she sang, and listened with respect when she spoke. There was money enough now for all the frocks, gloves, shoes and bonnets the most extravagant girl could desire, and Aunt Dall might devote herself to the care of a new wardrobe rather than the repairing of an old one.

Fanny, the belle of every ball, found her rôle enchanting—to be a success at a party meant far more to her than being a success on the stage, and probably no belle ever attained that position with intenser delight or gave greater pleasure to her partners. For apart from her exquisite dancing, she possessed those still more essential gifts—vitality and an inexhaustible capacity for enjoyment. One moment she would be sitting beside Rammohun Roy, her soul in her eyes, listening as if her life depended on the perception of every beauty of 'Sakuntalà,' and the next she would be waltzing away from him, whirling about the room with some agreeable light-weight such as Henry Greville, laughing—that gay laugh of hers was another gift of the gods—chattering about nothing, every serious emotion forgotten in the bliss of rhythm and music and

swift motion, to return, glowing and refreshed, to her rajah
with renewed enthusiasm for Indian literature.

It was this vividness of Fanny's even more than her good
looks and accomplishments that made her remarkable, in the
same way that Mrs. Norton was remarkable, for herself not
for her talents. Some people found her *too* vivid. Charles
Greville would raise supercilious eyebrows as he watched her
dance, and warn his young brother Henry that it was a mistake to become intimate with theatrical persons, even a superior brand such as the Kembles. While that connoisseur, Sir
Thomas Lawrence, found a strong resemblance to Mrs. Siddons, and wrote to a friend that she had "ease and grace, a
fine brow, a voice both sweet and powerful, and a manner
characterized by modest gravity." For already, at nineteen,
both in public and private life, Fanny Kemble was either
heartily admired or cordially disliked, either loved or hated;
she could never by any possibility be ignored.

She was not herself aware of these differences of opinion.
With the lack of self-consciousness that is apt to characterize
vivid natures the impression she was making was the last
thing Fanny cared about, and she was too absorbed in amusing herself to consider anything else. If she could dance she
was happy and her greatest grief was to be forced to decline
an invitation, though it was almost as sad to accept and find
the ballroom too crowded; for the horror of crowds and noise
that was, perhaps, prenatal would return to ruin the evening.
The stare of so many eyes—she was stared at now wherever
she went—the heat and the clamor of voices, would become so
unbearable that sometimes she would rush away and out into
the fresh cool night air. But she was acquiring self-control, at
least in appearance; after a ball given by the poet Campbell,
she wrote to Harriet that although one "could not stand without being squeezed or sit without being stifled," and a lady
had spilled a cup of coffee all over the front breadth of her
new white merino frock, she had managed to keep on smiling
and had been rewarded; the poet had asked for her bouquet

in order that "he might immortalize it in verse," and she had had an hour's dancing after twelve o'clock when the rooms thinned out: "You know," she ended, "when I am dancing, I am 'o'er all the ills of life victorious.' "

And that winter added another pleasure. Acting often left her too excited to sleep, so it was decided that riding on horseback would be beneficial and her mother took her to Captain Fozzard's riding school, the most popular in London where Mrs. Kemble herself had been taught. Fanny was welcomed with enthusiasm by "Old Fozzie," as his pupils called him, for he remembered Miss De Camp's superb horsemanship, and as she had inherited her mother's fearlessness and grace she soon became a perfect rider—except for one defect, her hand remained a little too heavy for the mouth of a sensitive horse. She could slip her foot out of the stirrup, fold her arms behind her back or sit left-sided, and go through a plunging, rearing and kicking lesson, and take her horse over the bar, without the slightest fear of going off. This proficiency led to a little incident that she liked to remember.

She had gone to the school one day for exercise and was taking a solitary canter in the tan when a little door under the gallery opened and Captain Fozzard appeared, ushering in a lady and a little girl. He left them, stopped Fanny and put her through various evolutions obviously for the benefit of the spectators. She was proud of her riding and had no objection to displaying her ability; she went through several difficult feats; then, at a sign from the lady, Captain Fozzard opened the little door again and ushered the two out. Returning in a moment to dismount Fanny he told her that the ladies were the Duchess of Kent and her daughter, and that they had been so impressed by Miss Kemble's riding that the little princess was to be placed under his tuition at once. It was Fanny's first sight of Victoria.

Before long she could afford to buy herself a good horse and one for her father—she already had her own carriage—and now she was no longer a spectator in Hyde Park but one of the happy band she had envied only a few weeks before; she was, as she had longed to be, "an angel on horseback." And she looked it! Charles and Fanny were a handsome couple as they rode in the Mall on a bright morning, and heads would turn to follow them, and she would be pointed out to strangers, and the strangers would exclaim: "Miss Kemble? Why I thought you said Miss Kemble was not a beauty!" For no one who saw Fanny on horseback, then or later, ever doubted that she was always—as Mrs. Fitzhugh had said she sometimes was—"the handsomest girl in London."

As the winter wore away her circle of acquaintances among the habitués of the theatre inevitably widened. One of these, Lord Wilton, she soon met as he was a friend of her father's. Another admirer was less fortunate; the Reverend Lord Augustus Fitzclarence—one of the many illegitimate sons of Prince William, afterwards William IV—was kept waiting a long time for an introduction, although from the first he had never missed a performance and finally succeeded in getting behind the scenes. There he stood, night after night, patting his kid-gloved hands together in applause, until at length his patience was rewarded; Charles introduced him. But that was all; Augustus was forced to content himself with a bow as she passed him going on or coming off. Then one night they met at a ball. He rushed at her as she entered the room, and his lively: "Do dance with me, there's a dear good girl!" was so engaging that she laughed and took his arm. He danced, she discovered, surprisingly well for a clergyman and his conversation proved still more unclerical.

"Who are you nodding at?" he asked, as she threw a smile across the room. "Your father? You're very fond of him, ain't you? Now as for mine—" and he launched out into such a frank description of his royal parent that Fanny, thinking he was a little drunk, told him he must change the subject or she would sit down. He apologized, but insisted on telling her the sad story of his life. He hated being a parson, his heart was in the navy and he had been trained for a sailor; but unluckily a brother died and there was this living in the family, so they took him straight off the ship, bundled him into a black coat and made him vicar of Mapledurham! Didn't she think it was a hard case? Fanny did, but she urged him to make the best of it. He sighed: "Some people have a natural turn for religion—you have, I see. But I have not. And my sermons are no good. I wish you would write one for me. Mrs. Norton has." Fanny laughed, remembering the many sermons she had written for her Paris schoolfellows; the quadrille ended, and she walked away with another partner. But she felt sad and a little shocked. Thank Heaven, if John became a clergyman, he would not be that sort!

But of all her new acquaintances only one, Sir Thomas Lawrence, became a friend. In former years very intimate with the Kemble family, long estranged because of his unhappy love affair with Mrs. Siddons's two beautiful daughters —as everybody knows, Lawrence became engaged to one of them, found he loved the other better, but married neither for both died—and happening to meet Charles in the street just before Fanny's début, he stopped, spoke sympathetically of her approaching ordeal, and asked if he might come to call. Charles was delighted and when the call was followed by a request to be allowed to paint Fanny as Juliet her parents agreed, although most of the many artists who wished to paint her had to be refused for her days were crowded.

He began a pencil sketch at once, preparatory to a full length in oil. Fanny found that she liked sitting to Sir Thomas; he was still extraordinarily handsome, his manner with women was perfect—he had had vast experience—and she enjoyed his conversation. While he was working he was apt to be silent, except for an occasional remark—Fanny had a double row of eyelashes which was most unusual, the sheen of her white satin dress pleased him, he had once tried to paint a blush and had produced merely a red face; but while she rested, or when he came to call, he would talk of the past and recall great beauties he had known such as Lady Jerning-

ham, George IV's mistress. He had once seen Lady Jerning-
ham standing in front of a mirror staring at her reflection, and had heard her mutter: "I swear it would be better
to die and go to hell at once, than to live to grow old and
ugly!" That sort of anecdote shocked and saddened Fanny as
Lord Augustus's irreverence had shocked her, and she preferred Sir Thomas's discourses on dreams. In a dream, he
said, the dreamer preserves his real age and even when revisiting the scenes of one's childhood one never becomes a child
again.

Their usual topic was her acting. Lawrence, an excellent
critic, had been charmed by her Juliet, and predicted success
even in a part such as Lady Macbeth; for he insisted that an
audience would soon forget her lack of height and realize
that "creatures of the most daring energy were to be found
among men and women of small stature." But as he also perceived her ignorance and lack of technical skill, he warned
her not to "go fagging on in all the nakedness of talent," as he
himself had done, "without the material of knowledge or sys-
tematic information," and set himself to teach her all he
knew. No inflection, no gesture, was too trifling to escape him,
and the day after a performance he would either drop in to
talk it over, or he would write her a note suggesting an altera-
tion, sometimes drastic, but so delicately expressed that she
was never hurt, and she came to value his criticisms more than
anyone else's. Her father's elation at her success prevented
severe criticism, and her mother was too temperamental.
After watching Fanny's performance from her box—she had
acted Lady Capulet for only a short time—Mrs. Kemble always arrived behind the scenes in a too exalted mood; she
might fold Fanny to her bosom and exclaim: "Beautiful, my
love, really beautiful!" Or, and more often, would greet her
with a sad: "My dear, you were not fit to be seen. I really
think you had better give the whole thing up!" that would
send poor Fanny's heart into her shoes. But Sir Thomas contrived to hit the happy medium; and Fanny looked forward

to his visits and treasured every remark; she would take his last letter with her to the theatre and read it over just before going on for fear of forgetting his instructions; she even began to wonder whether, in spite of his age, the feeling she had for him could be love.

In the meantime, 'Romeo and Juliet' was running serenely on. Charles Greville noted: "Miss Kemble fills the theatre every night," and this happy condition seemed as if it might last forever. But the managers realized that the most successful run must have an end, and when the season was half over they began to discuss another play for their new star. Finally it was decided to revive a very old play, Otway's 'Venice Preserved,' chiefly because the part of Belvidera had been one of Mrs. Siddons's conspicuous successes and the public must not be allowed to forget the connection between aunt and niece. Fanny was appalled. Otway so entirely lacked Shakespeare's fire that she could not hope for the inspiration she had come to depend upon—she wrote to Harriet: "I must be excited myself or I cannot excite others"—and Belvidera was fantastically untrue to life, not a suffering woman but a lay figure being knocked about. She could not understand the part and she was afraid of it; she dreaded the comparison with her aunt, knowing that she could not rise to Mrs. Siddons's mental stature any more than to her physical. Even as Juliet she had been wearied by the inevitable comparison; it was a bore to be told that Mrs. Siddons always did this and Mrs. Siddons always did that; she wanted to make her own reputation, and stop feeling like a little girl dressed up in the cloak that her aunt had relinquished. But grumbling was useless, she must do what she was told and she set herself to learn the part, hating Belvidera's preposterous lines, but untroubled by another drawback that would have discouraged most actresses; the part was one of the longest known to the stage, but she had kept the faculty of rapid memorizing acquired at school and learned the part in three hours!

Again there was much discussion of costumes. What dress

should Belvidera wear in the first act? After her husband's
bankruptcy only plain black was permissible, but Fanny
pleaded for one pretty frock, and it was finally agreed that before poverty overtook her the heroine might be allowed an
embroidered robe, jewels and a hat. Fanny was enchanted, for
the hat, designed by Sir Thomas Lawrence, was ornamented
with a beautiful long curling white feather and with that
splendid erection perched upon her head she felt older, taller,
more important and a little less afraid of failure.

She need not have been afraid, Belvidera was successful
beyond the wildest hopes of her family or the management;
prices were high, orchestra seats sold at a guinea for the first
time since "Glorious John's" farewell, but the curtain went
up to a crowded house. Most critics had insisted that a girlish
part such as Juliet would prove the limit of Miss Kemble's
capacity, and only a few believed her capable of rising to
greater heights. No one was prepared for her Belvidera. One
of her admirers, young James Stuart Wortley, wrote to his
mother of that memorable first night: "She surpassed all that
I had been able to imagine or anticipate. Several times she
was interrupted by thunders and regular rounds of cheers,
and at the end the applause was perfectly terrific; one general
shout and cheer which continued until Charles Kemble appeared to announce the play for repetition when the whole
pit became one moving mass of raised hats. Amidst the stun-
ning thunders of applause it seemed as if it reeled from the
number of hats and handkerchiefs which were floating back-
ward and forward in every part. I both cheered and waved my
hat most lustily. There is an end to all the cavillers and false
critics. She is now established, and you must see *her* to know
the pleasure of once more seeing a first-rate, great, magnificent actress. Poor Charles Kemble says it was the happiest day
of his life. Think of *Alexander Baring* confessing that he
cried his eyes out. I saw him *in a state.*"

Sir Thomas Lawrence's prophecy had come true, the audience forgot that Miss Kemble was too young and too small for

tragedy; but the splendid hat he had designed for her did not prove an unmixed blessing. For when she had to give it up for a trailing black veil the contrast was too depressing; the gloom of the enveloping folds so increased the gloom of the play that Belvidera's agony became real, and in the last scene Fanny lost control of the part. Luckily it happened at the very end when Belvidera, having gone mad, digs in the earth for the dead body of her husband, discovers it, and lets out a prolonged blood-curdling shriek. This shriek Fanny had found impossible to rehearse and had trusted to the inspiration of the moment. But when the moment came too much inspiration came with it. The first blood-curdling shriek was followed by another and another, each higher and more blood-curdling than the last, and then she rushed off the stage and ran, still shrieking, downstairs and through passage ways and had reached the street before Charles caught her and brought her back, sobbing wildly, to her dressing room. At the time this hysterical outburst passed unnoticed by the audience; when the story leaked out some people laughed, and others considered it a proof of dramatic ability.

Fanny herself was deeply mortified. But in any case she was to remember 'Venice Preserved' with sadness rather than triumph; for shortly after her first appearance as Belvidera Sir Thomas Lawrence died. She had seen him only a few days before, they had laughed together about her hat; when the news was brought to her she was reading over a letter from him and noting his criticisms. And now he was dead . . . Lawrence's last hours, they told her, had been spent "looking wistfully at a portfolio of engravings of Miss Kemble." His sketch of her Juliet was his last drawing.

It was her initial encounter with death. She missed Lawrence's friendship, she missed his advice. When another play, Murphy's 'Grecian Daughter,' was put in rehearsal there was no kind friend to help her breathe life into a wooden part. She disliked the dreary heroine, Euphrasia, the play was dull and had been chosen for a reason that seemed to her revolting; the public would enjoy a drama of filial piety acted by a father and daughter known to be devoted to each other in real life. This appeal to sentiment proved unnecessary; Fanny's first entrance as Euphrasia brought down the house. The Grecian princess was lovely to look at in her white robe and scarlet sandals as she came stepping out heralded by a tremendous flourish of trumpets, and she was alive. Later, however, there came one bad moment, for poor Mr. Abbot's unsteady legs brought about the catastrophe Fanny had dreaded; as Phocion hurried to meet Euphrasia he lost his balance, fell and dragged her down with him. But she sprang to her feet and gave him his cue and got the scene going again with such grace and presence of mind that the audience's laughter changed instantly to applause. After that all went well, even the last scene, although, here, Fanny had ventured to depart from the Siddons tradition. After stabbing the tyrant Mrs. Siddons always fell on her knees asking pardon of Heaven; now it seemed to Fanny that a deed considered noble by the Greeks would not require pardon, and that any young girl would shrink from the sight of blood. So she let the dagger fall, and with her other hand lifted a fold of the robe and covered her face. Later on she improved the gesture; she still hid her face, but she raised the dagger high as if calling the gods to witness and approve. Both poses were classic; they may have been suggested by a memory of David's stately figures studied long ago in her Paris school-days.

Her handling of Mr. Abbot's misfortune had given her a sense of security, but if she imagined that she had attained complete self-control she was soon disillusioned. The next play, 'The Gamester,' ended with one of the dead husband scenes that had shattered her nerves in 'Venice Preserved' and again the agony became too real to be borne. The heroine, Mrs. Beverley, wearing gray silk and a charming bonnet, was expected to fall upon her husband's breast and stay there weeping in a ladylike manner until the curtain went down; but Fanny screamed as Belvidera had screamed, and could not stop herself; her father had to pick her up and carry her off in his arms.

After this second mortifying ordeal she set herself to overcome her tendency to hysteria, and as Isabella in 'The Fatal Marriage' succeeded in losing her mind and expiring without a single scream and to the entire satisfaction of her audience. But it was a relief when a comedy, 'The Provoked Husband,' was put on, and she enjoyed her part, being too inexperienced to realize (as she did later) that she had made Lady Townley a *modern* lady of fashion, listless and affected, totally unlike the coarse, high-spirited, humorous dame of an earlier time that Vanbrugh had created. But no part of that winter really pleased her except Juliet; Juliet had set her standard too high. It was with deep thanksgiving that she prepared to return to Shakespeare when 'The Merchant of Venice' was chosen for her benefit. Portia was her ideal woman, she told Harriet St. Leger, "so generous, affectionate and wise, so arch and full of fun and such a true lady," and the costumes her mother had designed were perfection. One was of levantine shot-silk, white and rose-color, with diamonds in her hair and in the bows of her shoes, another of white satin, trimmed with old point lace and pearls was topped by a crimson velvet hat ornamented with one of her favorite sweeping plumes; even the sombre dress of the trial scene had its good points, for the lawyer's cap, copied from an old picture, gave a touch of frivolity. She looked forward to her benefit with pleasure and without fear, secure in the belief that she must by now be immune from hysteria and stage fright.

The night came; she faced a crowded house, the applause was enthusiastic. But her letter to Harriet next day showed little elation. In spite of a noble part and magnificent dresses she had been "frightened flat," and it was discouraging to be told by her parents that stage fright could not be outgrown, that the greater an actor became the more easily he was betrayed by his imagination. Portia's comedy, she went on, had been received with such marked approval that she felt it must have been pretty good, but on the whole she was dissatisfied; only in the casket scene had she succeeded in producing the precise effect she intended.

Her parents could have told her that this dissatisfaction was in itself a sign of growth. She took seven star parts that winter, and from each she learned something. Towards the end of the season she wrote to Harriet that good acting required, in addition to a poetic imagination and the power of assumption, "a sort of vigilant presence of mind. This watchful faculty never deserts me. Even when I am uttering the exquisite poetry in Juliet's balcony scene, while I feel as if my whole soul was on my lips, and my color comes and goes with the intensity of the sentiments I am expressing, it prevents me from setting fire to myself from the lamps placed close to me, or from leaning on my canvas balcony when I appear to be throwing myself over it. It is altogether a curious and complicated process." Her mind was at work, she had become deeply interested in the technique of her art; but enjoyment still eluded her. The letter ended with a reflection that is pathetic in its childlike simplicity; she was in no danger of being spoiled by admiration for she still liked better to "curl up in an armchair and *read* Shakespeare's glorious imaginings than to act them— white satin, gaslights, applause and all."

Strange conclusion. Her success had been phenomenal. No other girl of nineteen, before or since, ever met with such instantaneous recognition. She had given Covent Garden a new lease of life, the box office receipts were enormous whenever she acted, and in that one season she cleared her father a debt of eleven thousand pounds; but she could write to Harriet: "I go out a great deal and that I like whenever there is dancing, but not else; my own home spoils me for society."

And with full spring even dancing lost its charm; she felt an increasing nostalgia for the country. One May day desire crystallized into poetry and in the midst of her work and all the demands upon her she found time to dash off a sonnet dedicated to Harriet St. Leger and their first meeting,

" 'Twixt the last violet and the earliest rose," when Heath
Farm had been sweet,

"With all the fragrant freshness of the spring,
With odorous lime and silver hawthorn twined."

June came. She was restless now and glad to start off on her
summer tour. For though it would take her from one town
to another—Bath, Edinburgh, Glasgow, Dublin, Liverpool,
Manchester, Birmingham—there would be glimpses of the
country in between and breaths of clean reviving country air.

CHAPTER X

Fanny Rides the "Iron Horse"

"The locomotive Monster, carrying eighty tons of goods, and navigated by a tail of smoke and sulphur, coming thro' every man's grounds between Manchester and Liverpool."

—CREEVY.

LITTLE PRINCESS VICTORIA herself could not have been more carefully chaperoned than was Miss Fanny Kemble during her summer tour. Her father and Aunt Dall always accompanied her, and her cousin John Mason, who had been chosen to replace Mr. Abbot, and usually Mrs. Kemble and Adelaide. Henry had gone to Paris for a holiday and though John was in England, having in the end returned to Cambridge and taken his degree, he had secluded himself in a quiet village to prepare for ordination. But the family party was large enough without John and Henry. Fortunately Fanny liked the society of her family—the Kembles might quarrel but they seldom bored each other—and she took supervision as a matter of course, never having known freedom except for a taste of it in Edinburgh.

Bath came first, with 'Romeo and Juliet.' Bath had changed very little since her childhood, Fanny decided. It was the same gay, pretty, pleasure-loving town; the gigs and ornate coaches of 1814 had given way to tilburies and barouches; the young ladies tripping through Cheap Street and Union Passage in 1830 needed more room for their spreading silk skirts than the clinging India muslins of their predecessors had required; but the faces were as pretty and the chatter as empty, and the pump-room and the riverside walks looked much the same. To find Bath unchanged by the years that had changed her so much gave Fanny a sense of sadness; but the tickets sold well for everybody wanted to see the new actress that London had been raving about all winter, and the rehearsal went well. Fanny's indignation that Shakespeare's lines must be cut in deference to provincial prudery that objected to such words as *shirt* and *smock* was counteracted by her satisfaction in a new Romeo. John Mason was young, good-looking, fairly competent and, unlike poor Mr. Abbot, was steady on his feet and so strong that when he had to carry Juliet's corpse down the stage, though she came near laughing as he muttered: "Jove, Fanny, you *are* a lift!"—her slimness and smallness were deceptive—she was not in the least afraid of being dropped. Minor parts were well taken, for Bath, like all large towns then and long after, kept a good stock company ready to support stars from London and the Continent who might stop there on tour. The audiences were excellent; they made lots of money, and then off they all went to Edinburgh.

An Edinburgh audience never gave strangers a very warm welcome; no exception was made in Fanny's case, and the critics seemed more impressed by her small size than by her acting. But she enjoyed every minute of that two weeks' engagement. She was in Edinburgh, she was staying with Mrs. Harry Siddons; Mrs. Harry was as lovely as ever, Edinburgh had lost nothing of its romance, and it was most amusing, Fanny discovered, to find oneself shining as a star where only a year before one had been treated as an insignificant schoolgirl. The meeting with Sir Walter Scott came about quite naturally now. She and her father were riding on horseback down Princes Street when Sir Walter came towards them on foot; he stopped Charles, and asked to be introduced to Miss Fanny. She liked his kind plain face and his border burr; she was enchanted when he praised her horsemanship, and distressed that an invitation to Abbotsford had to be refused because of her engagements. But they went to breakfast with Scott at his town house, and she sat beside him though Miss Ferrier and other celebrities were there; he told her thrilling tales of the Debatable Land and the Forty-five, and altogether it was a memorable occasion. After this of course she wished more than ever to see the country of Ellen and Marmion, but she might have been obliged to leave Scotland a second time without this experience if the King had not happened to die on the twenty-sixth of June. The death of the man who had been so important to Fanny's mother, the "Prince Charming" of the "little French fairy," meant nothing to Fanny. The younger generation had no tears for George IV; his name stood for nothing but obesity and extravagance, and in her heart she was delighted when the poor man died and the theatres were closed for she had three days' holiday and could go to the Trossachs. She brought away a heavenly remembrance of water and sky and wood; a white rose from Dumbarton in memory of Mary Stuart, an oak branch from Loch Lomond, and a tuft of heather plucked on the rocky shores of Loch Long.

Another day she found time to drive out to Newhaven to visit her friend, the gray-eyed fishwife. The good creature stood staring for a moment at the lady smiling on the threshold in her lilac silk and French bonnet, so unlike the linsey-woolsey girl of a year ago. Then she cried: "Ech, sirs! It's yer ain sel', come back at last!" drew Fanny in with a triumphant: "I's gotten anither ain!" and led her through a laughing crowd of children to where a new baby, an eleventh infant Hercules, lay asleep in his cradle.

Glasgow's welcome was warmer than Edinburgh's, but it was not until she reached Ireland that Fanny met with the enthusiasm to which London had accustomed her. Dublin was great fun! Night after night a crowd would be waiting for her at the stage door to salute each member of the family with: "Three cheers for Misther Charles! Three cheers for Misthress Charles!"—this for Aunt Dall, whom they took for Fanny's mother—and then, "Three cheers for Miss Fanny!" One admirer would exclaim, "Bedad, she looks well by gaslight," and another, reprovingly: "Och, and bedad, she looks well by daylight too!" Often as many as two hundred hurrahing gentlemen would form a bodyguard to escort her back to her hotel, open the carriage door, let down the steps and form in line, clapping and cheering, as she hurried across the pavement; some of them dropping on their knees to peer under her bonnet as she ran, head bent, laughing, a little frightened, into the hotel.

Dublin society was lively too; Lady Morgan, author of 'The Wild Irish Girl,' gave Fanny a huge party, and would have danced an Irish jig for her, but after running through room after room, calling at the top of her voice for a certain member of the vice-regal staff for a partner, she discovered he had gone home and Fanny never saw Lady Morgan's Irish jig. But it was almost as entertaining to see her "fairly tipsy" with joy when the news of the July revolution came from France; she could not contain her delight at the overthrow of the tyrant Charles X and declared she would be off to Paris as soon as her new novel was out.

But Ireland gave Fanny a far keener pleasure than parties or success; she was allowed to visit Harriet St. Leger at Ardgillan Castle. She saw its green hill, blue sea and distant mountains; she galloped a horse along the firm white sand of the beach, bathed in the sea, and sat for long hours talking her heart out to Harriet in a flowery dell, or lay on the rocks in the sun listening in silence to the wind as it came across the water. Best of all she enjoyed a run along the shore on a stormy day when the tide was coming in, the wind blew through her hair, and she could taste the salt spray on her lips. She told Harriet that the power of wind and water must be *catching;* she felt strengthened in mind and body and three inches taller when she was running by the sea. The Morne Mountains were too far away to seem real, but even that glimpse gave her a strange sense of excitement; her heart leaped as she imagined herself some day climbing a mountain and standing on the topmost peak.

After her country holiday Dublin's noise was harder to bear, and work at the theatre wearied her more than ever; dislike of cities was an old story, but that acting still gave her so little pleasure needed explaining. Having considered the question for some time, she wrote to Harriet that she had discovered one reason for her persistent lack of enthusiasm. Acting could not free the imagination, as writing and painting could free it, for acting was too dependent on the body, and to practice an art so tied to the body was "like dancing a hornpipe in fetters"; she added that no success on the stage had ever given her a sense of inrushing power such as the forces of nature could give.

But there were compensations; she was making money for Covent Garden and her father. Money kept on rolling in all through the tour. Liverpool was especially enthusiastic, but her visit there was memorable for another reason: Fanny made a discovery; the imagination could be freed by science as well as by art, and the forces of nature she reverenced could be coerced by machinery.

The summer of 1830 set a new high-water mark in the rising tide of industrialism. A railway had just been finished between Liverpool and Manchester and Stephenson's new engines were being tried out, in spite of the opposition of the aristocracy who feared for their parks, and the farmers who prophesied that steam-carriages would "blacken the wool of sheep, cause horses to bolt, cows to cease giving milk, and ladies to miscarry."

Even in Liverpool Stephenson's engines were considered dangerous, but invitations to trial trips were in demand, and when Charles Kemble and his daughter were asked to join a party he accepted. Fanny, to her delight, as the guest of honor was seated beside the great man himself on the bench of the engine; she made the most of her opportunity. He was a plain, rugged man, so shy that he might as well have been dumb, but Fanny found this taciturnity stimulating; she exerted herself, her gay simplicity was irresistible and perhaps for the only time in his life George Stephenson talked. Next morning a long letter went to Harriet.

"A small sheet of paper," she wrote, "is enough for love,

but a foolscap extra can alone contain a railroad and my ec-
stacies . . . We were ushered into a courtyard where several
carriages of peculiar construction stood, ours was a sort of un-
covered char-à-banc, with six seats placed across it back to
back. The wheels were placed upon the iron bands which
formed the road, and then it was set in motion by a mere
push, which rolled us down an inclined plane into a long
tunnel. At the end we emerged from darkness, and, the
ground being level, we stopped. Here we were introduced to
the little engine which was to drag us along the rails. She—for
they make these curious little firehorses all mares—consisted
of a boiler, a stove, a small platform, a bench, and behind the
bench a barrel containing enough water to prevent her being
thirsty for fifteen miles . . . There is a chimney to the stove,
but as they burn coke there is none of the dreadful black
smoke which accompanies the progress of a steam vessel. This
snorting little animal, which I felt rather inclined to pat, was
harnessed to our carriage, and we started at about ten miles
an hour. The steam-horse being ill adapted for going up and
down hill, the road was kept at a certain level, and appeared
sometimes to sink below the surface of the earth, and sometimes to rise above it. You can't imagine how strange it
seemed to be journeying on thus, without any visible cause
of progress other than the magical machine, with its flying
white breath and rhythmical, unvarying pace, often between
rocky walls already clothed with moss and ferns and grasses;
and when I reflected that these great masses of stone had been
cut asunder to allow our passage below the surface of the
earth, I felt as if no fairy tale were half so wonderful. Bridges
were thrown from side to side across the top of these cliffs,
and the people looking down upon us from them seemed like
pigmies standing against the sky. After this rocky defile, we
found ourselves raised upon embankments ten or twelve feet
high; we then came to Chatmoss, a swamp of considerable extent, on which no human foot could tread without sinking,
and yet it bore the road which bore us. Mr. Stephenson told

me this had been the great stumbling-block in the minds of the committee of the House of Commons, but he had succeeded in overcoming it. A foundation of hurdles, or basketwork, was thrown over the morass and the interstices filled with moss and other elastic matter. Upon this, the clay and soil was laid down, and the road *does* float, for we passed over it at the rate of twenty-five miles an hour and saw the stagnant water trembling on the surface of the soil on either side of us.

"We had now come fifteen miles, and stopped in a wide deep valley; Stephenson made me alight and led me down to the bottom of this ravine over which he has thrown a magnificent viaduct of nine arches, the middle one seventy feet high, through which we saw the whole of the beautiful valley. It was lovely and wonderful beyond words. He told me many curious things about the ravine; how he believed the Mersey had once rolled through it; how the soil was so unfavorable that his bridge had been built upon piles driven in to an enormous depth; how, while digging for the foundation, he had come to a tree bedded in the earth fourteen feet below the surface; how tides are caused, and how another flood might be caused. He explained the whole construction of a steam engine, and said he could soon make a famous engineer of me, which, considering the wonderful things he has achieved, I dare not say is impossible. His way of explaining himself is peculiar but very striking, and I understood all that he said to me. We then rejoined the rest of our party, and the engine having received its supply of water, the carriage was placed behind it, for it cannot turn, and was set off at its utmost speed, thirty-five miles an hour, swifter than a bird flies—they tried the experiment with a snipe. You cannot conceive what that sensation of cutting the air was; I stood up and with my bonnet off 'drank the air before me.' The strong wind seemed to weigh my eyelids down. When I closed my eyes the sensation of flying was delightful and strange beyond description, yet I had a perfect sense of security and not the slightest fear . . . The master of all these marvels is a man of about fifty; his face is fine though careworn, dark, and deeply marked; his mode of explaining his ideas is peculiar but very original, and although his accent indicates his north country birth, his language has not the slightest touch of coarseness or vulgarity. He has certainly turned my head . . . The railroad will be opened next month; the Duke of Wellington is coming down, and there will be thousands of spectators. The directors have offered us three places, which is a great favor, for people are bidding almost anything for a place. I hope my father will not be obliged to go abroad at that time.

"We open in Manchester on Monday. My father has received a pressing invitation from Lord and Lady Wilton to stay with them at Heaton, five miles from Manchester. There seems to be every prospect of our having a prosperous season this winter, London will be particularly gay, and the king and queen are said to be fond of dramatic entertainments."

In the midst of these pleasurable excitements, present and to come, the Kemble family's peace of mind was unexpectedly shattered. Fanny received a letter from John, written in Spain! John was supposed to be studying for Holy Orders, what had taken him to Spain? She opened the letter with trembling fingers, and the news was even worse than she had feared: John was about to give his life for the cause of Spanish freedom! But why? Fanny and her father asked each other —luckily Mrs. Kemble happened to be in London. Why? John had never shown the smallest interest in Spanish affairs, and war was strange preparation for a clergyman. The letter was mysteriously worded; they gathered that the more radical of the "Cambridge Apostles," becoming excited by the news from France and disgusted that a revolution should have come off without their help, and looking about for other likely affairs of the same sort, had discovered General Torrijos and the band of Spanish exiles he had rallied about him in London to plot the overthrow of the tyrant Ferdinand VII. Here was the opportunity John and his friends had hoped

for; they had embraced the cause, encouraged the general
to strike at once, evaded the English police and had finally,
by various routes, succeeded in reaching the scene of action.
So there they all were in Spain; Trench, Tennyson and
Hallam, Barton and Robert Boyd, and John himself; all
champing the bit, crazy to invade Spain, if the English authorities at Gibraltar would let them.

Fanny and Aunt Dall and Adelaide cried. Charles did not
know whether to laugh or curse, but he told Fanny not to
worry—though the news must be kept from her mother—the
revolution would soon fizzle out. Perhaps, after all, the army
would suit John better than the law or the church. John
would make a fine general.

So Fanny tried not to think about John any more than she
could help but she set off for Manchester with a heavy heart,
though with one small consolation; she could attend the
opening of the new railway in September, for her father was
not going abroad. Charles had intended to meet Henry in
Paris and take him to Heidelberg for a course of study, but
now that Germany had proved so unsettling to John the plan
was given up, and Henry was told he might come home and
go shooting instead. As Henry, asked at a tender age what he
wanted to be when he grew up, had lisped: "A *gentleman* and
wear leather breeches," and this was a first experience, his
family hoped that killing pheasants and hares might prove as
effectual as German university life in taking his thoughts
away from the sea.

Fanny too was enjoying a new experience. Heaton was the
first large country place where she had stayed and she discovered, rather to her surprise, that luxury was extremely
pleasant. She told Harriet that she liked a "silver fork existence;" it was delightful to have a magnificent barouche ready
to take her to the theatre in Manchester when she was acting,
and a thoroughbred—Lady Wilton's favorite mount—to ride
in her leisure hours. No one could be kinder than Lady
Wilton; she was Lord Derby's daughter but her mother had

been an actress, the celebrated Miss Farren, so she was interested in theatrical affairs; she lent Fanny a habit as well as a horse, and even allowed her to dress for the theatre before dinner. It was great fun to come down decked out in Portia's Venetian brocade and velvet, or the golden head-dress of a Greek maiden, and be greeted with applause by the other guests!

There were interesting people in the Heaton house party: the Barings, clever and agreeable; Anne and Isabella Forrester, beauties of renown, one blonde, the other brunette, but both scorning the prevailing fashion of tight bodice and full-gathered skirt and always wearing very décolleté clinging gowns that showed so much that Fanny, with her admiration of feminine beauty, longed to see a shoulder-strap slip and reveal even more of that snowy whiteness. Then there were the Batthyanyis, an Austrian count and countess, and Lord Francis Leveson-Gower, charming in face and manner and very clever, and Henry Greville who had all the social graces. Henry could dance and sing and play and act, and had, in Fanny's eyes, the great merit of being crazy about her and her genius, considering her far superior to Mademoiselle Mars.

The visit began with two days' leisure; Fanny rode and walked and danced and played battledore and shuttlecock and was taken sightseeing. She was shown the carved wainscoting of Hopewood Hall and the looms and spinning jennies of the Manchester factories. Lord Wilton was an excellent cicerone; Fanny liked him. He turned out to be less artificial than he had appeared to be when they met behind the scenes at Covent Garden; he played the organ; he read family prayers on Sunday evening in a most exemplary manner, and encouraged his peasantry to preserve their ancient customs—one afternoon during Fanny's visit a rush-bearing procession came winding across the lawn led by morris dancers waving bright handkerchiefs and stepping to the music of the village band. But this liking for old world pageantry no doubt added to his inherited dislike of innovation, and when it became clear that any railway between Manchester and Liverpool must inevitably cross his estates the earl fought Stephenson for all he was worth, even turning out his farmers and gamekeepers with pitchforks and guns to drive away the surveyors when they first appeared on his property.

But of course in the end he had been obliged to give in, and now that the railway was an accomplished fact the Wiltons were as anxious as anybody to attend the opening ceremonies. They were given seats in the Duke of Wellington's carriage; Fanny and her mother sat farther back, about midway of the long train that carried eight hundred people through the suburbs of Liverpool and out into the country, applauded by thousands of cheering spectators. As the speed increased Fanny's spirits rose, but her mother was frightened; Fanny was trying to reassure her when the train slowed down and stopped. Everyone began asking questions. Then came exclamations of horror—an accident—someone had been hurt —Stephenson? No; the name was Huskisson. Not the *great* Mr. Huskisson? Yes: it was the great Mr. Huskisson, the statesman who had saved the Bank of England in the panic of 1826! No one seemed to know whether he were dead or merely injured; but it was agreed that these steam railways were frightfully dangerous. Then the Kembles were joined by Lady Wilton and she told them what had happened. Mr. Huskisson had alighted when the train stopped for water, and a parading engine had run him down while he was shaking hands with the Duke of Wellington who was leaning out from the carriage; his leg had been crushed. Lord Wilton had succeeded in tying the femoral artery, and then the railway's first victim had been hurried off at a speed of thirty-five miles an hour to Eccles. The Duke wanted to give up the celebration, but it was finally decided that Manchester must not be disappointed. So at length the train moved on again and reached Manchester in a downpour of rain to be greeted, not with cheers, but with hisses and groans; for both the "Iron Duke" and the "iron horse" were unpopular in the factories, and a mob had gathered to demonstrate their hatred of this last triumph of machinery that would enrich the rich and starve the poor.

It was all most annoying and discouraging. The Wilton house-party sat down to dinner that evening in a depressed frame of mind. The gloom deepened when Lord Wilton returned from Eccles with the news that Mr. Huskisson was dead. Then a whisper went round; it was perilous to cross the path of the Duke of Wellington. Canning had been taken, and now another able adversary had been removed in the nick of time by an all-wise Providence and one of Mr. Stephenson's horrid little locomotives! Everybody agreed that England was in a bad way. There was much talk of the "spirit of unrest" manifest both in town and country, and of the ingratitude of the lower classes, the church catechism was quoted, and anecdotes exchanged proving the modern lack of respect. It was agreed that when you saw how village girls dressed nowadays one could not be surprised at *anything* . . . Fanny, outside the charmed circle, listened with some amusement for her imagination told her that what they had seen in Manchester that day was more than a matter of ribbons and curtsies, and her mother listened with impatient sadness; Mrs. Kemble could remember what it was like to be really cold and really hungry, and these good people knew no more what they were talking about than if they had been born and bred in the moon!

CHAPTER XI

Spring in London

"The footman, in the pride of his nonchalance, stands swinging from East to West upon his springy toes. The horses rush along amidst their glancing harness. Spotted dogs leap about them, barking with a superfluity of noise. The hammercloth trembles through its fringes. The paint flashes in the sun."

—LEIGH HUNT.

LONDON HAD been looking forward to the winter but it was not after all very gay. When the excitement over the Duke of Clarence's sudden elevation to the throne had evaporated it was discovered that a crown did not fit a dull man for society—the duke had never been in society. Charles Greville's diary noted: "No one had ever invited him into their house or treated him with any mark of respect." William IV was the same old William, almost as dull as his brother of Gloucester, and ridiculous for his "grotesque, meddling curiosity." Of the two new sovereigns society decided that the Queen was to be preferred, for Adelaide's manners were good, though her complexion was bad and she was prudish about low-neck dresses. However, a dull court could have been put up with if the "spirit of unrest" infecting the lower classes had not created such a depressing atmosphere. The lower classes kept on being discontented. That November of 1830 every post brought news of riots, risings, conflagrations, destruction of machinery, associations of laborers and demands for higher wages. The Duke of Richmond went down to Sussex and quelled a mob with fifty of his tenants and a good-natured speech; but the end was not always so happy. The starving peasantry were hanged, imprisoned and transported by the hundreds, and still they persisted in being discontented and ungrateful. As if this were not enough, it was rumored that cholera had appeared in Russia.

But the season opened well at Covent Garden. The King and Queen were often seen in the royal box signifying their approval of Miss Fanny Kemble's acting; the old plays kept on filling the house, and the new ones were successful, with one exception: 'The Jew of Aragon' was hissed. For the first and last time in her life Fanny was greeted with that ominous sound and although the hisses were not for her acting but for the play, which was dreary stuff, she was, she told Harriet, "as frightened and furious as if they had been the whistling of bullets." But the theatre was crammed from floor to ceiling for Milman's 'Fazio'; her portraits and fancy articles ornamented with her face were still popular, and she was kept so hard at work that she was thankful the new house her father had rented in Great Russell Street, next door to the British Museum, was so large that she could have a large room of her own with an open fire.

Here she found the solitude she needed for reading and writing—she had begun a new play called 'The Star of Seville'—or, tired out, crouch beside the hearth mesmerized by the leap and fall of the flames, searching in vain for words in praise of fire, remembering that even Shelley, like herself a fire-gazer, had found "the motions and colors of fire unspeakable." Riding was a more exhilarating relaxation. She was allowed a man's horse now at the riding school, an Arab, and could sit him through his wildest gyrations. In the Park she had Adelaide for a companion, and in their brown habits with red velvet waistcoats the sisters looked and felt as gay as robin redbreasts. Henry's companionship also added to her pleasure —though he enjoyed teasing her, professing to find a resemblance between his agile passionate sister and the tigress at the Zoo—for he danced almost as well as she did herself; but his lack of occupation worried her. Mrs. Kemble still opposed Henry's going into the navy, and as the army was considered less dangerous Charles talked of buying him a commission.

But nothing was done, Charles could not find the money; for no matter how much Fanny made Covent Garden debts swallowed it all.

Now once again Fanny's thoughts turned to literature; if Mr. Murray still wanted to publish 'Francis I' she might be able to buy Henry a commission. So she corrected some faults of metre that Mr. Milman had pointed out, and sent the manuscript to Mr. Murray; he renewed his offer, and there seemed every prospect of getting a sum sufficient for Henry's needs when a disagreeable incident occurred that threatened to divert it for a less satisfactory purpose.

The editor of 'The Age,' a scurrilous newspaper, had been hurt by a chance remark of Charles Kemble's and for some time past had been revenging himself by publishing a weekly paragraph abusing the Kembles and Covent Garden. But Charles had kept his temper until Fanny was alluded to in an offensive manner and then, happening to meet Mr. Westmacott in the street, Charles gave him a thrashing. Fanny was horrified; not for herself—no one they knew ever read 'The Age' and her reputation was too secure to be injured—but the man might sue for damages. She wished that her father, with so many law-suits already on his hands, could have found some less expensive way of defending her honor, but for a time it seemed as if Mr. Murray's money might have to be used to pay for her father's outburst.

But in the end the affair blew over, and the new year of 1831 began well; Fanny and Henry spent the evening at Mrs. Harry Siddons's, dancing without stopping from eight until twelve. A few days later she was refreshed by a trip to Brighton. "After rehearsing," she wrote to Harriet, "we all went for a walk. When we reached the downs I was completely happy. I gave my muff to my father and my fur tippet to Dall, for the sun shone powerfully, and I ran along the edges of the cliffs enjoying the solemn sound, and even the fear that came to me as I peered over, until my father called me away and to console me for not being allowed to dash myself to pieces, ran races with me and beat me hollow. We had walked about four miles, when a sailor came toiling up the cliff and I discovered his winding stair cut in the chalk wall. I felt as if I were hanging between heaven and earth, but I got down safe and ran to the water's edge, danced a galop on one smooth little sand island, waited till the incoming tide just touched my toes, gave it a kick of defiance, and then scrambled up the cliff again, enchanted with my expedition. A fight with smugglers up that steep staircase at night, with a heavy sea rolling and roaring close under it, would be glorious! . . . Our house at the theatre that night was very fine. Next morning I had time to run down to the beach, and had a few moments alone there. The fishing boats were, one by one, putting out into the calmest sleepy sea; I longed to be taken on board one of them, but I was summoned away to the coach."

That spring she could write to Harriet: "Why are you not here to kiss and congratulate me? Mr. Murray has given me four hundred pounds for 'Francis I'! Only think of it—was there ever such publishing munificence! My father says it is not enough, but looks so proud and pleased that his face shows it is too much by a great deal; my mother is enchanted, and I am so thankful, so surprised and charmed that what gave me nothing but pleasure in the doing has brought me such an after harvest of profit; it is too good to be true, and yet it is true."

So now there was money enough for Henry's commission and a little over. Fanny bought a present for Adelaide, a guitar adorned with a long blue silk scarf that must have been very becoming for, years later, Thackeray recorded a remembrance: "Miss Totty playing on her guitar, the most enchanting figure imaginable." Fanny treated herself to an expensive blue velvet gown from Dévy and daily bunches of violets, and set to work on 'The Star of Seville' with renewed enthusiasm, having discovered, she told Harriet, that "it was pleasanter to earn than to save"—and not, apparently, considering the immense sums her acting brought in as *earned* for that money belonged to her father.

In every way life was so full that she usually kept to her old rule of accepting only dancing parties. But some dinner invitations could not be refused. The Kembles dined with Lord Melbourne, and Fanny wrote afterwards to Harriet that she had a little fallen *out* of love with her host for he had been too absorbed in Mrs. Norton, and had consoled herself by falling *into* love with Lord Ossulston, "the most beautiful creature of the male sex" she had ever seen. And they dined at Devonshire House now and then to meet Fanny Arkwright—the Kemble cousin who had married well at the time Aunt Dall's love affair ended so disastrously—for she and her husband always stayed with the Duke when they came up to London as they were intimate neighbors in Derbyshire. Dining with the Dacres or the Leveson-Gowers was never dull, and Lady Cork's was another house Fanny found amusing. Lady Cork was very very old and very very eccentric, but she still enjoyed life and had no wish to exchange London for a heaven which she feared "would be just sitting on a damp cloud and singing God Save the King," until Lady Francis Leveson-Gower suggested a livelier prospect; *she* imagined heaven as "all splendid fêtes and dinner-parties; like the London season, only far pleasanter for there would be no bores."

There was much easy coming and going at the new house in Great Russell Street. William Thackeray and Edward Fitzgerald and Dicky Milnes, and other friends of John's who had not become involved in the Spanish expedition, often dropped in and Fanny saw a good deal of Chantrey, the sculptor; he was shy and silent, but she liked him and was grateful to him for not asking her to sit. Painters and sculptors gave her little peace that winter. Usually she managed to escape; but Pickersgill was allowed to try his hand, for he had been commissioned by Charles's old friend Major Dawkins, although his portrait of Charles had been so poor that when

Mrs. Kemble saw it, she cried: "That fat, red, _pudsy_ thing! God bless my soul! the eyes are no more like Charles's than mine are. And as for the jaw, how could the man miss it? Why, thé Kemble jawbone is as notorious as Samson's!" So it was a relief when Mrs. Jameson criticized Mr. Pickersgill's work with such frankness that she hurt his feelings and Fanny's portrait was given up.

But of all the Kembles' guests that year Sheridan Knowles, the playwright, turned out to be the most important as far as Fanny was concerned. One memorable afternoon in April she came in from riding to find her father and mother and Mr. Bartley, the stage manager of Covent Garden, in the library with Mr. Knowles and the manuscript of a new play. It was 'The Hunchback,' written for Drury Lane and Kean, but rejected; partly because the managers, like other managers before and since, failed to recognize a good play when they met one; partly because Kean had seen that his part, Mr. Walter, was overshadowed by the heroine, Julia. Covent Garden was now Knowles's best hope; he spoke to Charles, and was asked to come to the house and read his play.

Knowles read well; they all listened with interest. At the end Mr. and Mrs. Kemble expressed moderate approval; Mr. Bartley shook his head; only Fanny was enthusiastic. As she was too inexperienced to be worried by technical faults she could consider the play as a whole and from the point of view of the audience; she insisted that it was both original and exciting, that the situations were dramatic and the dialogue lively, and she saw, what Kean had seen, Julia was a magnificent part, a part that would "play itself." When 'The Hunchback' was finally accepted by Covent Garden, though the greenroom shared Mr. Bartley's doubts, Fanny could for the first time look forward to a play that was not Shakespeare's with real satisfaction.

The spring brought another excitement. News came from John. Most of his friends had already returned from Spain, among them Alfred Tennyson and Arthur Hallam, who had been satisfied with a very few political meetings, wandered about in the Pyrenees for a while, and finally wandered home again. But still John did not appear and his family became increasingly anxious. Then one day Richard Trench turned up. He said that the Torrijos expedition was a fiasco and that John would soon be back. Even John had been convinced that Spain had no desire for freedom after they had waited all night tossing about in a small boat for the beacon that was to signal the outbreak of revolution at Algeciras. No beacon had been lighted. The English authorities had quietly collected their young radicals on board a man-of-war and quietly returned them to Gibraltar. Only John and Robert Boyd still stayed on there; even now they could not bear to desert Torrijos. That was so like John, Richard Trench said; John was a noble soul; and he called John a "soldier priest," and prophesied a great future for him if he decided to go into the Church. But John was also considering politics and that, Mr. Trench feared, would be a mistake; John was too extreme for politics. John's family agreed; Charles said that radical ideas had done enough harm as it was, the radical and reforming element was responsible for England's present miserable condition, and Mr. Trench nodded sadly when Charles added that if the Reform Bill went through the country would inevitably go to the dogs. They quoted Colonel Napier who believed civil war was imminent, and Mr. Southey who said England was no place for a poet and he was considering transporting himself and family to America. Charles added that if these damn statesmen went on fighting among themselves every theatre in England would have to shut up shop. Mr. Trench took a more exalted point of view; he said there was only one side possible for a gentleman and a Christian; an aristocracy was necessary for the well-being of a nation; he "would welcome the bloodiest civil war rather than submit to a government of clubs and unions," and the future Archbishop of Ireland bade the Kembles goodbye, leaving Fanny with an impression of dignity and high-mindedness, and taking with him a similar impression of her. He wrote to Donne: "Kemble's sister seems to estimate things at their right value; she has apparently no sympathy with the shows and vanities wherein she is mixed."

Charles Kemble's fears were justified; the second reading of the Reform Bill came off on the same night as Fanny's benefit; the House of Commons was crowded and Covent Garden was not. The agitation continued and increased, no theatre could hope to compete with the illuminations, fireworks, torchlight processions and window smashings of the political drama going on in the streets, or lure society from its disastrous absorption in serious questions. However, the London season ended better than it began; Lord Francis Leveson-Gower got up an amateur performance of 'Hernani' at Bridgewater House and for a while the dreadful Bill could be forgotten.

As the Leveson-Gowers were old acquaintances Fanny was of course asked to take the part of the heroine, Donna Sol. She knew that the rehearsals would interfere with her work and tire her to death, but the affair promised to be so amusing that she could not resist and was at once caught up into a whirl of arguments and quarrels and discussions as to scenery and costume that made the production of a real play seem a mere nothing and her everyday life at the theatre restful by comparison. But it was all intensely amusing. The rehearsals were funnier than any farce. Except for herself and Mrs. Bradshaw, the former Maria Tree, the cast was made up of amateurs, and the poor things were so terribly in earnest and so solemn and so slow that she nearly died of suppressed laughter, and never ceased to be amazed at their difficulty in memorizing a single line and the vast number of swords, slippers, jewels, moustaches and wine glasses they managed to strew about behind the scenes. Her company at Covent Garden would have been amazed if they had seen their leading lady, the unapproachable Miss Kemble, laughing and clapping, gay as a lark, scolding one stupid boy and encouraging

another, and romping like a child let out of school. No Aunt
Dall to wrap a shawl about her shoulders, no watchful parents
to wave away intruders; for such young men as Lady Francis's
brother, Henry Greville, Mr. Craven, Mr. St. Aubin, Captain
Shelley and Mr. Mitford could scarcely be considered "undesirable acquaintances" even by the Kembles. At first they
seemed equally incompetent; but as the rehearsals went on
Augustus Craven, who took the part of Hernani, showed real
dramatic talent. He was the only one; the others remained
amateurish, even Henry Greville. However, they were all delightful young men; all of them dancing attendance on her—
she was the only girl in the cast—all of them flattered by a
word from her, all of them a little in love with her. Fanny
had never been so amused in her life. Then came a startling
discovery; acting with Mr. Craven was very different from
acting with poor dull Mr. Abbot, or a commonplace cousin,
or one's father. Mr. Craven had no difficulty whatever in
keeping his feet; he never groaned, "Fanny, you are a lift!"
As for her father— Well, acting with Augustus Craven was
not in the very least like acting with one's father! To be made
love to by a handsome spirited young Lochinvar was a most
agreeable change, and flirting began to rival dancing as a
favorite pastime.

The theatricals encouraged both amusements; after a rehearsal the cast of 'Hernani' usually hurried off to a ball. Of
one dance Fanny wrote in her diary: "I was enchanted with
everything. Such shoals of partners! such nice people! such
perfect music! such a delightful floor! Danced until the day
had one eye open. The carriage had been ordered for two
o'clock, but my father said he would not *spoil sport,* so he
angelically waited till past four. He is the best of fathers, the
most benevolent of men. It is pleasanter to be chaperoned by
one's father than one's mother. The latter, poor dear, never
flirts, gets sleepy and wants to go home before she comes; the
former flirts with every pretty woman he meets and does not

care till what hour in the morning. After all, I had to come away in the middle of a delightful mazurka."

Everyday life took on a peculiar brightness. Exercising in Russell Square was not a mere round among dusty privet bushes; she wrote in her diary: "A cold, damp, piercing day, delicious with lilac, syringa and new-mown grass—and Shakespeare to think about. How grateful I am for so much enjoyment. When I got home, I corrected the proofs of 'Francis I' and thought it looked quite pretty in print." Watching a procession from the windows of Bridgewater House was extraordinarily entertaining. "The King," she wrote, "was going to the House of Parliament and Palace Yard was thronged with people. At about one the royal carriages set out—such lovely cream-colored horses, with blue and silver trappings; such splendid, shining coal-black ones, with blue and silver trappings—it was like a fairy story." Even work at Covent Garden became tinged with romance; of 'Romeo and Juliet,' her journal noted: "John Mason had a cold, but he got on uncommonly well. My mother said I played *beautifully*, which is much for her. I was delighted, for the Francis Levesons were there, and Mr. Craven."

If London could be so glorified by 'Hernani,' the country would be paradise. When the Leveson-Gowers invited some of the cast to Oatlands, where rehearsals could go on with fewer interruptions, Fanny was overjoyed.

CHAPTER XII

Oatlands

"Le temps a laissie son manteau
De vent, de froidure et de pluye,
Et s'est vestu de brouderie,
De soleil luyant, cler et beau."

—CHARLES D'ORLÉANS.

OATLANDS HAD seen various occupants come and go in the years since Fanny's childhood at Weybridge but its eccentricities of landscape gardening remained unchanged and guests of the Leveson-Gowers could be amused with the same pleasures enjoyed in the Duke of York's time when, according to Charles Greville, a week-end was spent "eating fruit in the garden, shooting at a mark with pistols, playing with the monkeys and bathing in the cold bath in the grotto, clear as crystal and cold as ice." The Duchess of York's menagerie had gone, but there were plenty of horses in the stables now which had not been the case during her régime, and Lady Francis could promise Fanny a good saddle-horse and thus add a final touch to the pleasure she felt at seeing Weybridge again.

Even the weather condescended to bless that visit to Oatlands; a pale May sun was shining overhead as Fanny and her mother left London in an open carriage for their twenty-mile drive. The earth had not yet lost its spring freshness, along every hedge the hawthorn lay fragrant and white like snow the winter had forgotten to melt, and as they went on the road became delightfully familiar—Walton Bridge—the Thames— same old chestnuts along the banks, same smooth smiling fields, same white swans riding in happy majesty on the blue water ... They reached Oatlands an hour before dinner. Mr. Craven had not yet arrived, but Lord John Russell was there and several other pleasant people. They had time for a stroll. Fanny showed Lord John the dogs' graveyard, and the sharp-visaged little gentleman made himself so agreeable that it was surprising, later on, to find him more than able to hold his own even in that anti-reform atmosphere; at dinner "Pie-and-thimble" parried awkward questions about the Bill with the smile of a man who is entirely sure of himself.

Next morning before anyone else was astir she slipped downstairs and out into the spring-scented air and made her way along well-remembered paths to their old cottage. But "desolate was the dwelling of Morna," the grape-vine torn down, the shrubs trailing their blossoms, and the Mound in ruins. Fanny climbed to the top, and stood there for a moment thinking of John perched on the Mound and waking the echoes with his bugle. Where was John now? Alive—still blowing a bugle in some forlorn hope? Or lying dead on the Spanish seashore? . . .

Augustus Craven came that afternoon. The rehearsals went well; Donna Sol and Hernani loved and wept and parted and died in each other's arms; and, in the intervals, Fanny and Mr. Craven walked and drove and rode on horseback, except on Sunday when the horses were never taken out and then they went for a row instead, moving lazily up and down the river singing and quoting poetry. And there was much talk of the past, and of their first meeting in Paris at the ball at the boys' boarding school in the rue de Clichy; she had worn a white muslin frock and a magnificent *ponçeau* sash. Did Mr. Craven remember her sash? Of course; Mr. Craven remembered every moment of that never-to-be-forgotten evening. And they recalled a French wedding they had attended with its quaint ceremony of the distribution of *la jarretière de la mariée,* and laughed over Mr. Craven's conundrum: *"Quelle est la sainte qui n'a besoin de jarretières? Ste. Sebastienne—ses bas se tiennent."* Another topic that interested Mr. Craven was the stage, for the family background was slightly professional; his grandmother, the Margravine of Anspach, had written a successful opera and one of his aunts had been a Covent Garden actress before becoming Lady Craven. But Fanny refused to talk shop. She was on a holiday, and Covent Garden was allowed to fade into the distance as they wandered about the countryside, on foot and on horseback, revisiting the places she had loved in childhood. She missed a favorite oak beside the river—Lord King had been cutting timber, and she could have cried at the ruin his axes had left —but Oatlands park had suffered no desecration, and the circle of giant trees she had long ago christened her Cedar Hall she found inviolate.

But the Cedar Hall was a place for solitude. Fanny went there alone. Before the dew was off the lawns she would hurry out of doors, run along the terrace, pelted with syringa blossoms as she ran, and step in under the flat dark roof of interwoven branches, stop for a moment to look up at the bit of sky that shone down through a round opening like the window in a temple dome, and sniff the resinous odor, and then hurry back to the house to appear at the breakfast table as if she had just come downstairs. Sometimes after dinner she would contrive to slip away from the drawing-room while the ladies waited for the gentlemen to finish their port, and tiptoe out into the night. Through the branchy roof of the cedars she could see the stars now, and from the velvety darkness all around came small sounds—whisperings, rustlings, chirpings —that were mysterious but not unfriendly. Fanny was not afraid. Was she an Undine? she wondered. An *elemental?* A creature too closely tied to the material universe? Too sensitive to its lights and shadows, scents and sounds? Why was it that wind and fire and water gave her a feeling of companionship? . . . But a strange excitement always seized her as she ran back to the house; she would pause on the terrace to let her heart quiet down, and standing there looking into the brightly lighted drawing-room would think again of Undine bidding a last goodbye to the home where she had been happy before returning to her fountain. Were all lovers faithless? . . . She went in. The room seemed too warm and crowded, the talk trivial. They were discussing Lord and Lady Blank and their ménage. What should, would, could, a woman do under such circumstances? Endure and endure until her heart broke? Could any man be so cruel as to break a woman's heart? Then in a moment they were all laughing at another of those funny French conundrums of Mr. Craven's: "*Que font les vaches à Paris? Des vaudevilles—des veaux de villes.*" Augustus Craven was so amusing . . .

Back in London again; Mr. Craven dropping in to bring Fanny a sketch of the costumes for 'Hernani,' to discuss a line or a bit of stage business. More rehearsing at Bridgewater House; a dress rehearsal. Then at length the first performance. Fanny went through her usual moment of stage fright, Mr. Craven forgot his opening speech, a mountaineer was struck dumb; otherwise everything was perfect. Everybody admired the pretty costumes, declared that Lord Francis's version of the play was an improvement on Victor Hugo, and applauded Miss Fanny Kemble's acting. The second performance went more smoothly still, and then that too was over and the cast could sit down to supper with intense relief and in the wildest high spirits. Next day London buzzed with congratulations; a splendid basket of flowers arrived for Fanny from Cassiobury Park; the Leveson-Gowers' friends clamored for a third performance, royalty expressed a wish to see 'Hernani;' Fanny had another invitation to Oatlands . . . In the midst of the gaiety and turmoil John came home.

John was changed. He seemed older and he was strangely silent. He admitted that Torrijos was doomed, and that he was anxious about Robert Boyd, who had insisted on staying on in Spain. But that was all. He would not talk of his adventures even with Fanny. Yes; John was changed. But he was alive, and she could resume discussion of a possible third performance of 'Hernani' with a light heart.

But for a time it seemed as if the visit to Oatlands would have to be given up because of her professional engagements.

Then fate intervened. Mrs. Siddons died. Though she had been fading for months her death came as a shock to the public, and five thousand people attended her funeral in Paddington churchyard. Charles was of course saddened by this second break in the Kemble chain, but to the younger generation Mrs. Siddons had long seemed a mere emblem of past glory and Fanny felt no sense of personal loss. When Covent Garden, as a mark of respect for "the greatest actress the world had ever seen," excused the Kembles from playing for a week, and the invitation to Oatlands could be accepted—with the proviso that because of their mourning there would be no other guests—Fanny was not too depressed to be grateful.

As before they made the trip in an open carriage, reaching Oatlands in time for dinner. Lady Francis had not kept her promise of "positively nobody;" there was one guest, Augustus Craven. But he was such an old friend now that he did not count, nor could any objection be made to Lady Francis's father and mother, the Grevilles, when they too arrived. So altogether it was a pleasant party. They rode and walked and made hay on the lawn, and one evening Fanny and Augustus Craven acted several scenes from 'Andromaque,' the success of her Paris schooldays, and for the second time Fanny's Hermione brought a murmur of awed amazement from a parlor audience.

That sort of evening was apt to be followed by a restless night and a gloomy awakening. But she knew a sure remedy: at the first moment that it was possible to elude her friends she would hurry out of doors and climb trees until her "blue devils" had been safely exorcised. An hour seesawing up and down perched on a flat cedar branch, another hour mounting from limb to limb in a bower of resinous shade, higher and higher until she could survey the landscape from the topmost bough; a perilous descent, and she would return to the house in high spirits, ready for lunch and conversation.

A holiday so varied by companionship and solitude passed far too swiftly; Fanny hated to leave Oatlands when her seven days came to an end. But the drive home was delightful; Mr. Craven accepted a seat in their carriage, and he and she had plenty to talk about for a third performance of 'Hernani' had been arranged.

But when it came off in the latter part of June it proved rather less amusing than the other two. The audience was too grand. All the royalties except the King were there; Queen Adelaide, the Duke and Duchess of Gloucester, the Duke and Duchess of Cumberland, Princess Elizabeth, Prince Leopold and the Duke of Brunswick, and the grandeur did not make up for the dullness of these great people, nor for the lack of applause—applause not being considered etiquette in the presence of royalty. So although Fanny was pleased at being presented to the Queen after the last curtain, it was a relief to have the whole thing over and adjourn to Lady Gower's for supper. Supper was great fun. Lady Francis and her mother, Fanny and her mother, Charles Greville and several members of the cast, were all squeezed into a little boudoir opening off the great saloon and commanding a view of the royal table, where they could enjoy Sydney Smith's idea of heaven, "eating *fois gras* to the sound of trumpets," and laugh at poor Lord Francis, condemned to dullness and politeness at the royal table. After supper they all went downstairs to watch the royalties depart, and then Fanny said goodbye to the friends with whom she had become intimate, knowing that it might be a long time before she saw them again, and she and her mother drove home. They set Augustus Craven down at his door just as the sun was rising.

Fanny was so tired next day that she stayed in bed. But Mrs. Jameson came to call, and they talked pleasantly about 'Hernani' until, somehow or other, Fanny found herself discussing marriage and then, as she spoke of a wife's chances of happiness, such a strange look saddened her friend's face that Fanny, remembering the Jamesons did not get on, returned hurriedly to theatricals as a safer topic . . . That strange look was haunting. It was depressing, too, to remember that Aunt

Dall had a poor opinion of marriage, especially for an actress. Aunt Dall said that an actress lost much and her husband gained nothing, for of course no *gentleman*, however poor, could allow his wife to make money. But why bother about the world? Fanny asked herself rebelliously. There were greater things in life than fame and fortune. And then that strange warning look of Mrs. Jameson's came back to her; she picked up a volume of Dante and found his picture of devils boiled in pitch a refreshing change from her own thoughts.

Two weeks later Fanny and her father and Aunt Dall left London for their summer tour of the provinces—Bristol, Exeter, Plymouth, Weymouth, Portsmouth, Southampton. She was thankful to get away. The days had been crowded with preparations and packing; and they had not only been hurried, they had been miserable. (What happened is not clear; perhaps an engagement was broken, perhaps it was merely a flirtation ended too abruptly; in any case, the experience left its mark. Forty years later she wrote: "The theatricals at Bridgewater House were fruitful of serious consequences; they bestowed on me a lasting friendship and an ephemeral love; the one a source of much pleasure, the other of some pain.") She set out on her travels feeling that she knew the inner meaning of Donna Sol's lament:

> "All now is o'er, the torches out,
> The music done,"

and with no anticipation of pleasure from a change of scene.

Yet, in another mood, she would have enjoyed the trip; long drives by coach and carriage took them from town to town through a smiling country of orchard and pasture; she was often refreshed by a sight of the sea, and their audiences were good wherever they stopped. Weymouth was especially enthusiastic, for Fanny's mother had been popular there in the time of George III, and Fanny thought of her as she stepped into the quaint little theatre so small that the actors' heads almost touched the pasteboard sky, and recalled her stories of the royal family; the King and Queen Charlotte never missed seeing Miss De Camp act, the princesses liked to dress her up in their own finery for her various parts, and little Princess Amelia had given her a coral necklace for a keepsake . . . The past soon faded. Fanny's mind turned to the sea—too near in Weymouth to be long forgotten; the moon was rising now, a fresh tide flooding into the basin, salt breezes blew along the beach; how strange, she thought, that on a night like this so many people were willing to sit indoors, crowded into a hot gaslit theatre, and weep to see poor Juliet fling her life away! . . . The curtain fell. She would have run straight out into the moonlight and down to the shore if Dall had not caught her. Dall would have none of such folly; she was taken home and put to bed.

Early morning found her on the beach; steeped in sun and wind she would stand watching the waves until their call became too urgent to resist and she dashed into the water, and swam and swam and chased her "blue devils" out to sea and drowned them . . . But not for long. At night they had a way of reviving: "An actor's life," she wrote in her journal, "is the shadow of a cloud, the echo of a sound, the memory of a dream, nothing come of nothing. The finest actor does not create, he is but a translator of another man's work . . . I wish that I were a stone, a tree, some senseless, soulless, irresponsible thing; the restlessness of the sea is obedience to the law of its nature, not a striving against it, no miserable 'life within' urges it to ceaseless turmoil and agitation."

The summer went slowly. At length came Southampton—made pleasant by a visit to Bannisters, the Fitzhughs' country place near by—and then the tour was over. Fanny was glad; she wanted to get home, for her father seemed on the edge of a nervous breakdown. He talked incessantly of Covent Garden, of his determination to leave the old theatre to sink or swim, and, more than once, he had spoken of going to America for a tour of the States! It was a dreadful idea. Fanny hoped with all her heart that her mother and his friends in London would be able to dissuade him, or that the theatrical outlook would brighten when once the Reform Bill was passed.

Her hopes were not realized. The radicals, considering theatre patents an anachronism, were getting ready to deprive the two great old theatres, Drury Lane and Covent Garden, of their monopolies bestowed by Charles II, together with the exclusive right to the title "His Majesty's Servants" that had given them prestige. As for politics, no one, high or low, seemed able to think of anything else. Orators wrangled about the Reform Bill at every street corner, politicians became poets and sang its perils:

> "Earl Grey he proposed to have a reform
> To save old Britannia from a threatening storm.
> But let us not boast till the battle is won;
> For we see and we know that reform's not begun.
> For certain great snakes still lies in the grass,
> That use all their power for the Bill not to pass."

Trade suffered; fear of riots often closed the London shops; there were meetings every day and processions every night, the windows of Apsley House were smashed, and Wellington's Achilles was pelted with mud. It was worse in the country; night skies blazed with burning ricks and bands of miners out of work terrorized the countryside. That October the cholera landed for the first time on British soil.

Late autumn found the Kembles oppressed by a more personal anxiety; Charles was taken ill with inflammation of the lungs. Dall nursed him; Mrs. Kemble, too excitable for a sick-room, cooked invalid dishes, and calmed herself by moving the furniture—Fanny helped her mother move the furniture four times during that illness! It was a bad time for the whole household; in a way, Fanny suffered most. Her work at the theatre could not be given up, night after night she had to leave home afraid she would find her father dead when she returned, and to act in such anxiety was a frightful strain. But at length Charles was pronounced out of danger. She was allowed to sit with him, and give him the latest news of Covent Garden; 'The Beggars' Opera' promised to have a long run, rehearsals for the Christmas pantomime were going well, her Bianca costume of gold tissue was much admired and the critics called her a "golden pheasant." She amused him with political gossip: Lord Grey was haunted by the ghost of Castlereagh sent by the devil to tease him into committing suicide; Brougham had gone down on his marrow-bones begging the Lords to pass the Bill, but they would not listen to "Old Wickedshifts;" Horace Twiss would lose his seat if the Bill went through—Mr. Macaulay had said "the face of Twiss was as the face of the damned," after the second reading. She talked of the riding school; Fozzard wanted her to try out a hunter for Lady Chesterfield; Lady Grey's horse was restless and Fanny had changed mounts, given her Gazelle and ridden the troublesome horse quiet; the Duchess of Kent and Princess Victoria had come in, Victoria was "an unaffected bright-looking girl" and had spoken pleasantly when Fanny was presented. Usually her father liked to discuss the points of a horse she had lately bought for him, and the perfections of her own little mare, named Donna Sol; but sometimes he would break off with a groaning, "a dying man had no need of a horse," and she would hurriedly change the subject, speak of the American tour and agree that it might, after all, be the surest way of making a fortune that could be saved for the family, not wasted on Covent Garden. But this topic too would often end by Charles turning his face to the wall muttering that he was more likely to cross the Styx than the Atlantic, and Fanny would have to prepare for her evening performance in utter discouragement.

December wore itself out. Christmas brought no merriment; for as if illness in the house were not enough news came from Spain that confirmed John's worst fears. Torrijos had made a last attempt and had failed; he and all his followers, including Robert Boyd, had been captured and shot! So the Christmas of 1831 was remembered by the young Kembles as the first sad Christmas they had ever spent.

But a few days later things took a turn for the better. Charles came down to breakfast, announcing that he felt so strong he would be able to act in another week, and 'Catherine of Cleves,' a play that had been waiting at Covent Garden for his recovery, need no longer be postponed. That evening in a sudden reaction from the misery and constraint of the past month Fanny's spirits rose to "champagne height"; she challenged Henry to a game of hare and hounds—Totty was in Paris studying music—and even John joined in; round and round the drawing-room she ran, in and out of the library, with the boys after her, hurdling chairs and tables, hiding under sofas, until at last she shrieked for mercy and dropped on the hearth-rug, weak with laughter, her hair tumbling about her shoulders. So the Old Year did not end badly after all; they all sat up to see the New Year in, played quadrille, enjoyed an excellent supper, drank the absent Totty's health, and when the clock struck midnight everybody kissed everybody else, exchanged good wishes, and went to bed in the best of spirits—fortunately the Kembles could not foresee that this was the last New Year they would welcome as a united family, and that England was to label 1832 as the wretchedest year of the nineteenth century.

For a time England was able to ignore the cholera—most sensible persons agreed with Macaulay that it was not contagious and "reposed great confidence in the excellent food and the cleanliness of the English"—and Fanny was too busy to think of anything but her work. That winter was the most exciting of her theatrical career. It began with 'Catherine of Cleves,' a melodrama by Dumas translated by Lord Francis Leveson-Gower, liked by the Parisians but so violent in action that it ran some risk of offending British sensibilities. However, it was fairly well received. Lord Francis's blank verse was praised, and Fanny's acting; although she herself was far from satisfied; she knew she was not tall enough for a duchess and not powerful enough for the scene parodied in the 'Ingoldsby Legends':

"De Guise grasped her wrist
  With his great bony fist,
And pinch'd it, and gave it so painful a twist
That his hard, iron gauntlet the flesh went an inch in—
She did not mind death, but she couldn't stand pinching!"

But in spite of what came to be known as the "pinching scene"—perhaps because of it—'Catherine' ran for some time to good houses, and Lord Francis and Fanny could afford to laugh together over the truth of the 'Ingoldsby' finale:

"Catherine of Cleves
  Roar'd 'Murder!' and 'Thieves!'
From the window above
  While they murdered her love;
Till, finding the rogues had accomplish'd his slaughter,
She drank Prussic acid without any water,
And died like a Duke-and-a-Duchess's daughter!"

The next Covent Garden production was a very different matter; laughter could not help Fanny now, for it was her own play 'Francis I' and it had been so often postponed, so discussed, torn to pieces, criticized and altered, that when rehearsal began she was already heartily tired of the whole thing, and would have wished she had never written a line of it except that Murray was bringing it out at the same time and she looked forward with some pleasure to seeing her drama in print. Publication and production had been of course timed to coincide; the theatrical reviews would sell the book and London would flock to see a play written at seventeen by a girl who was now appearing in it herself. The cast

was good; Fanny was the Queen-Mother, Charles took de
Bourbon and Ellen Tree Françoise de Foix. It all worked
out as Mr. Murray and the Covent Garden management had
planned; Charles Greville's diary noted: "Fanny Kemble's
new play is a complete success, an odd play for a girl to
write." Leigh Hunt compared her favorably to various great
playwrights of the past and Lockhart's eighteen pages of fine
print in the 'Quarterly' told the world that Miss Kemble "was
full of golden promise and had sprung at once into the fore-
most rank, not only of living actors, but of modern drama-
tists." But Fanny was too clear-sighted to believe them. A
hundred Hunts and Lockharts could not have persuaded her
that 'Francis I' was great poetry, and personal experience
had shown her it was not a good acting play; moreover she
was so absorbed in 'The Hunchback,' now in rehearsal, that
she had no time to brood over her deficiencies as poet and
playwright. When 'Francis I' was withdrawn she let it go
without a sigh.

Since the afternoon when Sheridan Knowles had read his
play in the Kembles' drawing-room and Fanny alone of all his
hearers had given it unstinted praise, she had been looking
forward to its production, having never wavered in her belief
that 'The Hunchback' would be a success and that Julia was
a part that would "play itself." She was right. The first rehearsal made that plain. Except for the plot it was a modern
play; the situations were natural, the conversation that of real
people. Julia, a very young, high-spirited girl, brought up in
the country, impatient of restraint and eager for pleasure,
when exposed to the excitements of London society throws
over a good lover and becomes engaged to a bad one, realizes
her mistake, fears it is too late, confesses her fault, and is re-
united to the man she really loves—and all with the passionate
abandon of youth. Both Knowles's play and Fanny's acting
took London by storm. The critics who had insisted that, in
spite of her name, Miss Fanny Kemble belonged to the realis-
tic school, the school of Kean, were triumphant; those who

had believed she was a tragedienne *per se* and could never reach the more difficult heights of comedy were obliged to eat humble pie. Charles Greville's diary noted: "Great acting." Knowles freely acknowledged his indebtedness: "Her Julia," he wrote, "has outstripped my most sanguine hopes. The soul of Siddons breathes its inspiration upon us again." What was more important, Fanny herself was happy; she enjoyed playing Julia as she had never enjoyed any part except Juliet; more, in fact, for she was satisfied with her interpretation; she knew that it was true to life. No doubt the love affair of the previous spring helped her now; the vagaries and perplexities of a girl "crossed in love" had been studied at first hand—a psychologist would say that love "sublimated," was giving fire to art—and she was able to create a type new to the stage; sometimes cruel, sometimes kind and always enchanting, her Julia was the sort of girl that every girl would like to be and no young man can resist. It is scarcely surprising that Julia "charmed the town" and that 'The Hunchback' ran for the rest of the season to crowded houses in spite of reform, revolution and cholera.

Yet in the end the combination was too much for Covent Garden. Fanny had saved the theatre the year before; if the times had been propitious she and Julia would have saved it again. But the political horizon was black as ink. All winter England had been living in fear of a "French Revolution"; the Whigs insisted that reform would avert it and the Tories that any change in such a crisis was suicidal. Early spring found the Lords wavering; by May the pressure had become impossible to withstand and the Reform Bill was passed. But Whig rejoicings were cut short, for England was now face to face with a calamity more terrifying than revolution; cholera became epidemic. The death rate was not quite so high as on the Continent—ten thousand died that spring in Paris—but it was high enough. In London a money panic added to the universal gloom, and the country was infected by a superstition common in Europe; the doctors could not be trusted;

they had started the plague and were poisoning people to increase practice! Charles Greville's diary recorded "scenes of uproar, violence and brutal ignorance. The awful thing," he went on, "is the extent of the misery which prevails and the evidence of the rotten structure on which the whole fabric of this gorgeous society rests."

The cholera, in addition to all that had gone before, gave Covent Garden its *coup-de-grace!* Head over ears in debt and with a winter of depression ahead, the management decided to sell and the Kembles realized they would have to look elsewhere for a living. Charles was penniless; his forty years of hard work had left him with nothing but a reputation, and the money Fanny had earned—thousands of pounds, a fortune if she could have kept it—had been poured into the bottomless bucket of insolvency.

But no Kemble ever wasted time in lamentations. Charles was game; his vague idea of touring America at once became a plan. England, he told Fanny—she was of course to go too as leading lady—was no place for actors. America could not well be worse; presumably the States had had their fill of revolution and were in no immediate need of reform; cholera might not cross the Atlantic. Fanny saw the force of these arguments and reconciled herself as best she could. The family must have money and it was up to her and her father to make it. Henry had his commission and John would soon be independent for Mr. Murray thought well of his 'Beowulf'; but there were still her mother and Aunt Dall and Adelaide to be provided for, and Adelaide's musical education must of course be continued. Ten thousand pounds would be enough. Two years in America—her father said they must stay two years or it would not pay to go—and then, safe home again, whatever painful experiences lay ahead of her now would soon be forgotten.

But two years was a long break; the Kembles had never been separated except during John's Spanish excursion and this break was worse for it cut the family in half; Mrs. Kemble must stay with the boys and Adelaide, and Aunt Dall was going with Fanny to America. Dall hated leaving home; she was a poor sailor and had no desire for adventure, but Fanny could not travel about in a semi-barbarous country without some woman to look after her, dress her for the theatre, wait for her in the wings and guard her from "undesirable acquaintances." As usual, Dall ignored her own likes and dislikes and, to Fanny's intense relief, consented to expatriate herself. They were to sail about midsummer, but Charles planned to give a few farewell performances in Edinburgh, Manchester and Liverpool, so they would be leaving London in June.

The news of the Kembles' American tour was received with mixed feelings. The profession agreed that America was a Tom Tiddler's ground for actors. Junius Booth and Mrs. Whitelock, neither of them great, had succeeded there, and though Kean had gone through many vicissitudes in New York he had only himself to thank, and his son had done well. So had Charles Mathews, in spite of a yellow fever epidemic. Mathews had not of course liked America. Nobody liked America. Mathews was only one of many who had found the American peasantry "rude in speech and manner and lacking in humor, never joking among themselves or enjoying the jokes of others;" although he admitted that the better sort of persons were easy and polite and the melons and the Madeira remarkedly fine. But the Kembles must be prepared for frightful discomfort except in a few large towns. Such ramshackle stage-coaches, broken-winded horses, dirty inns, boorish servants and uneatable food! Even the large towns were dull. Philadelphia was the best of them, clean and rather pleasing but laid out like a draft board and almost as lifeless. As for the climate, the American climate was the most dangerous in the world; torrid heat one day, arctic cold the next, scorching sun, torrential rains, dust, mud, snow and wind. The Yankees themselves were all sickly. Mrs. Mathews begged Fanny to wear flannel next the skin and warned Dall to air the sheets herself, to keep a flask of brandy by her, insist on a hot brick in the bed at night and never to go out without an umbrella. However, Mr. Mathews admitted that he was thinking of going again very soon, and Tyrone Power was planning a trip; on the whole the profession saw the advantages of the tour and approved.

But the Kembles' other friends could only offer their deepest sympathy. Tom Moore recalled memories of America that were almost without exception disagreeable. Mrs. Trollope's privations were recounted, and everybody quoted Sydney Smith's tirade that ended: "Who sleeps in American blankets? Under which of the old tyrannical governments of Europe is every sixth man a slave, whom his fellow creatures may buy, sell and torture?"

So it was with no expectation of pleasure, no desire "strange countries for to see," but in very low spirits and upheld only by a sense of duty and the hope of making money for the family, that Charles, Fanny and Dall prepared for their journey to a land that to them seemed "far as the solar walk or milky way."

Innumerable farewells of course added to the misery of leaving home. Harriet St. Leger came from Ireland and Emily Fitzhugh from Bannisters; Fanny bade goodbye to Mrs. Norton and Lady Dacre, the Leveson-Gowers, the Basil Montagues and the Procters, and would have gone to see Lady Cork but that lively octogenarian called in person, and startled the neighborhood by shouting from her carriage window that Fanny was "a supernatural creature." Mrs. Fitzgerald came, magnificent in green velvet, and Mrs. Jameson and Alfred Tennyson and Arthur Hallam and Henry Greville, and promises of frequent letters were exchanged. The horses took their share of goodbyes—the carriage horses as well as the saddle-horses were to be sold; Fanny had her last ride on Donna Sol. Carlo, Mr. Drinkwater Meadow's Newfoundland dog, who often visited her behind the scenes, was patted for the last time. And when all this was done there still remained the farewell performance at Covent Garden.

The evening was one of mingled pain and pleasure for the Kembles, with pain uppermost. Charles needed all his courage to get through it without breaking down. Covent Garden was just turning the century—it opened in 1732; his family had built the present house, he loved every stick and stone of it, and now the long history had ended in disaster and under his management. Fanny, too, though she did not share her father's sentimental feeling, found it a heart-breaking experience. The play was 'The Hunchback'. After the final curtain Mr. Bartley made a speech; he praised Sheridan Knowles, asked the public's good will for the new management and finished with an allusion to the approaching departure of Miss Fanny Kemble and her father. Knowles came out and was warmly greeted; then the audience began clapping for the Kembles, and when they appeared the whole house rose to receive them, waving hats and handkerchiefs, shouting farewells and good wishes, until Fanny could bear it no longer and snatching a little bunch of flowers from her sash flung it out into the pit with a handful of kisses and, as her father led her off, burst into tears. But she had no time to cry. There were dozens waiting to say goodbye; the company, friends, servants and stage hands; old Rye the property man, his boy Louis with two nosegays for her, her own pretty little maid left sobbing in her dressing-room . . . When Mr. Harness at supper that night remarked cheerfully that the world was on the whole a happy place, Fanny found it hard to agree with him.

Because of the trip to Scotland family farewells came piecemeal. The travellers were to go north by sea, and Mrs. Kemble decided to go with them to Edinburgh. So Adelaide and Henry were kissed for the last time in London, and John went as far as Greenwich, but he would not go on board the steamboat. He stood on the shore and Fanny on the deck leaning over the rail; gazing at each other; as the boat moved out into the stream, Mrs. Kemble began to cry, Fanny signalled him not to wait; he waved once in return, ran along the beach and was gone.

Edinburgh was less gay than usual; cholera was raging and Sir Walter Scott had just been brought home to die. But it was still beautiful and dear. Fanny saw all her old friends; one day she made time for a long ride with Mr. Murray and two other men, past the links to Habbies How and Woodhouse-leigh. As they left the Ghost Walk Mr. Murray pointed to a sprig of heather she wore and told her it should be the badge of a new order of knighthood; they three would be her knights; they would drink her health every fourteenth of June until her return and when that happy day arrived they would all meet together in the Pentlands Glen.

But Mrs. Kemble had no such consolations; the suspense soon became too much for her; she returned to London, and now it was Fanny's turn to watch a ship move slowly from the shore . . . When she and her father reached their hotel the vessel was still to be seen from the windows; the feather of steam dwindled, left the coast, moved on towards Inchkeith, and vanished. Charles broke down. Fanny tried to console him, but her heart was too frozen . . . Then came Liverpool. A few performances there, a few in Manchester; houses crammed, excited audiences shouting farewell; a last attempt of Charles's Covent Garden creditors to prevent his sailing, hurried adjustments . . .

Then, at last, Fanny, Charles and Dall on board the good ship 'Pacific,' all sail set—no steam to help them along—outward bound, with five dull weeks between them and New York.

CHAPTER XIII

The New World

"O say, simple maid, have you form'd any notion
Of all the rude dangers in crossing the ocean?
When winds whistle shrilly, ah! won't they remind you
To sigh with regret for the grot left behind you?"

—INKLE AND YARICO.

SUNDAY MORNING; a glorious September day, not a cloud in the sky, a brisk breeze sending the 'Pacific' curtsying over the whitecaps to the tune of nine knots an hour. If the wind held, they would soon be in. Fanny was below packing when a shout, "Land! Land!" sent her running to the deck. There along the horizon, between the blue of the sea and the blue of the sky, lay a low dark line. Through the glass she could see hills and trees. They said it was Long Island. The voyage was almost over.

It had been a short voyage, only five weeks. Of the eighteen passengers Fanny liked two, a young girl and her brother going to Boston; the others—a fat old woman and a fat young one, a colonel and a doctor, several commercial travellers—were well enough. The weather had been fairly good. In a dead calm, the gentlemen would fish for hake and dog-fish, go for a row, or let out a couple of geese from their coops—there were geese, chickens, ducks and a cow on board, whose voices provided an oddly rural accompaniment to sunrise—and put them down over the side for a swim. There had been one storm bad enough to snap the mainmast and send a wave through the skylight of the ladies' cabin frightening poor Dall almost to death, and terrifying the man at the wheel so that he had to be driven back to duty by the mate with a hatchet. Even Fanny was overcome for a time; but a raspberry tart and some grapes proved good medicine, and she

143

was able to get on deck to watch the last of the storm and stretched on the bowsprit feel herself part of the billows and spray.

In good weather the passengers danced *la Boulangère* and the *Monaco,* or played dumb crambo and blind-man's-buff. When it was cold they drank champagne and when it was warm they drank lemonade. Sometimes they would all gather in the round-house, and the Colonel would read 'Quentin Durward' aloud, Fanny would read 'Childe Harold,' or Charles declaim a speech of Daniel Webster's. On Sundays Charles always read the church service to the assembled company in the ladies' cabin. Fanny made friends with some of the ninety steerage passengers stowed away down below; her passion for exercise took her walking the deck for hours at a time, usually with the nice Boston girl who was almost too excited by Fanny's society and wept at being allowed to see a lock of Mrs. Siddons's hair that Fanny happened to have in her dressing case—everybody on board wanted to see that lock of hair and it was passed reverently from hand to hand. Often Fanny would escape from the crowd and read some book she had brought with her—Moore's 'Life of Byron,' 'Pelham,' 'The Adventures of a Younger Son,' study German, embroider a nightcap, or write letters to be sent home from New York. One day an eastward-bound ship passed so close that she gave her Boston acquaintance a letter to Harriet and he weighted it and tried to fling it across to the other boat, but it fell short and went to the bottom instead of to Ireland. If she felt too sad for letter-writing she wrote poetry; homesick verses and verses reminiscent of 'Hernani' and Oatlands such as the poem ending:

> "Why art thou weeping,
> Over the steadfast faithful dead,
> Who can never change,
> Nor grow cold and strange,
> Nor turn away,

In a single day,
From the love they bore,
And the faith they swore,
Who are true for ever,
Will slight thee never,
But love thee still,
Through good and ill,
With the constancy
Of Eternity:
Why art thou weeping,
Oh, fool, for the dead?

They are your only friends,
For where this foul life ends,
Alone beginneth truth, and love, and faith;
All which sweet blossoms are preserved by death."

In this mood she would turn for consolation to the sea and sky, and forget herself as she gazed down at the pearl-edged waves rippling past and up at the flocks of gulls and the stormy petrels that circled about the ship like black butter-flies. Once a sea-swallow fell exhausted on the deck; she made a cage for it and fed it with seed but the poor thing would not eat and very soon it died.

And now, the voyage nearly over, as she stood watching the Long Island shore draw close, another bird came to greet her. At sunset a wood pigeon flew out to the ship, fluttered around it and alighted for a moment on the masthead, and that, Fanny told herself, was a good omen, a welcome from the new world. The moon came up. They danced on deck until midnight, and went below expecting to get in next day. But they woke to a dead calm. The sails hung limp, the sea was oily smooth, the sky glass, the decks scorching hot; all the morning the passengers yawned and whistled for wind. But in the afternoon a small boat belonging to a brig that had been standing aft for hours arrived to ask for help; they were eleven weeks out from Bristol and needed food. Everybody lined the rail to watch the boat load up with provisions, and while it was making its return trip a breeze sprang up and the 'Pacific' went on her way. There were ships all about now. A schooner came alongside with a news collector; he was pelted with questions about business, the tariff, cholera. The cholera, he admitted, was pretty bad; it was in Boston now as well as in New York. At dusk they reached Sandy Hook; then a pilot came on board; not long after, they saw the lights of New York and the anchor went down. They sang a last song, drank a last health, and went to bed.

Next morning it was raining. A steamboat, a strange look-ing boat with three decks, came through the fog and took the passengers ashore. The Kembles packed themselves into a hackney-coach that bumped over cobblestones and in and out of mud-holes and finally set them down at the American Hotel on Broadway. It was a cheerless looking place, the rain came down in torrents. But there was a piano in the drawing-room; Fanny had not seen a piano for five weeks, she flew to it; someone brought her a glass of lemonade and a cake; rain and homesickness were forgotten.

The American was the best hotel in New York and the Kembles' drawing-room was large and pleasant but the bed-rooms were as shabby as in the old Shelbourne in Dublin; paper peeling off the walls, beds without curtains and, what was far worse, insect life abounded! Clouds of mosquitoes buzzed and bit; the wash-basins crawled with red ants; one clothes closet was infested with moths and another with bugs. Pier glasses adorned the walls and the furniture was ornate; but there was no bathroom, and as cisterns were few and water pipes non-existent—conservative persons still believed it unsafe to drink water that had run underground—drinking water had to be brought to the hotel in huge butts every day. However, a bath in one's room turned out to cost less than in an English inn, and Fanny soon discovered a bathing establishment behind the City Hall, the Arcade, neat and clean and as well equipped as similar places on the Continent. The food at the American was better than appearances would have led one to expect. At five o'clock dinner the first day— the Kembles dined in their own room, the ordinary was too noisy—there was an abundance of fruit and ice, and the wine was fair though rather expensive—champagne and claret eleven shillings and sherry, port and Madeira from nine to thirteen. But soup, fish and meat were all put on the table at once, then the puddings, tarts and cheese; there were no finger glasses, and the waiters reminded Fanny of the Highland lads of Glasgow, only these were wild Irish not wild Scotch. After dinner Fanny played and sang for some time, and when she went upstairs was amused to find the hall full of men, sitting on the floor and smoking, who had gathered to listen.

The next day was hot; walking was out of the question, but there was much to be seen from the windows. New York was foreign-looking, Fanny decided; many of the houses were of wood and brightly painted red or white, straw color or pale gray, most of them had bright green Venetian blinds. The streets were bordered with trees; the sidewalks were red brick; even the clothes of the people who emerged from their homes in the cool of the evening to promenade up and down Broadway were gayer than at home and French rather than English in fashion; an occasional black face, crowned with a gaudy turban or bonnet, added an exotic touch. There were few well dressed people, but Fanny was told that the upper classes, as in England, usually went to the country for August and had not yet returned. There seemed to be no poor; no beggars, nobody in rags, very few with bare feet; they all looked well fed and were talking and laughing cheerfully; the voices were shrill, loud and nasal. Many of the women were pretty though they looked delicate, and walked badly, like Frenchwomen and as though their shoes were too tight; the men seemed more polite than in London, often a man would step off the sidewalk to let a lady pass. There were many omnibuses with high-sounding names—Lady Washington, Lady Clinton, Lady Van Rensselaer—but no handsome carriages; no graceful barouches such as one saw in London; only funny old-fashioned coaches, hung high, without hammercloth or footboard, and the men servants not in livery. The hackney coaches, on the other hand, were cleaner and more comfortable than at home and not expensive; a mile cost twenty-five cents, and a long drive, such as the "Sandy Hill tour" round Mr. William Neilson's country place at Washington Square and back, only came to a dollar. Good horses, except trotters, were few; none of the saddle-horses appeared to be well- broken, and they were ridden entirely on the snaffle, held their heads badly, and they were not properly groomed. In fact, the whole town had an unkempt air; the grass in the little square enclosed in white palings they called the City Hall Park had not been cut, the street was rough with ruts and mudholes, the sidewalks broken, and pigs rooted in the gutters. Fanny went to bed that night with a confused impression of color, light, noise and dust that was very unlike home.

Next day did not alter her first impressions; a walk in almost any direction brought one to untidy suburbs; it was hot and dusty. Not until evening could Fanny see any beauty in New York. But at sunset, as she and her father strolled north on Broadway the end of every side street gave a bright glimpse of river and farther shore under a sky far more brilliant than any English sky. And as they went on the moon rose, a larger brighter moon than any English moon; it whitened the outlines of a temple-like church on Canal Street, the Church of the Ascension, and Fanny could imagine herself in a classic land, under a southern sky. The next evening they walked south, down Broadway to a marine promenade called the Battery that had been, they were told, formerly frequented by fashionable persons but was now given over to the rabble, though it lay along the water and was shaded by fine trees. Here Fanny stood in silent delight watching the sunset gild the bay and the thickly wooded slopes beyond the water, purple a red fort on Governors Island and draw a belt of orange across the sky such as she had never seen except in a picture of Claude Lorrain's, while vessels far more graceful than any English boats went slipping past, their sails dark against the light. Then night fell; and as the band began to play at Castle Garden, a sort of Vauxhall, and its colored lamps shone flickering through the tree branches with prettily Parisian effect, and moonlight turned the town to silver, Fanny admitted that New York, at sunset and at night, could be incomparably beautiful. Her spirits revived. The sea breeze came fluttering in, and as her father, turning to meet it, exclaimed that the American climate agreed with him, and she saw that he did indeed look young and well, she felt repaid for her sacrifice in leaving home and more hopeful as to the future.

She needed whatever refreshment beauty and hope could give her for the week that followed was hurried and confused. Twenty-one enormous boxes, passed unopened by a polite custom house, had to be unpacked and as the dresses and bonnets needed freshening after the long sea voyage—a lovely Dévy bonnet emerged almost crushed to death—Fanny and Dall were obliged to go shopping and Fanny hated shopping. There were only two good shops, Stewart's and Bonfanti's; both were more expensive than London and the shopkeepers too familiar in manner. Many of the shop windows were so small that the goods were shown heaped on the sidewalks or draped across the front, and lengths of calico and flannel flapping in the wind gave another touch of color to the streets. There was color too in the market; laundry baskets heaped with melons and wild grapes; downy pink and yellow peaches in tall, bright red baskets; pears, apples and vegetables; fish and game. The fruit and vegetables had been carelessly picked and nothing was well displayed, but as a piece of color the market was superb.

What with shopping and sewing Fanny and Dall were busy enough; they were also overrun with visitors. Fanny found

the lack of privacy unbearable—she could not even appear in
negligée at breakfast; their fellow passengers from the
'Pacific' felt at liberty to run in and out of the Kembles' drawing-room at any hour, and all New York seemed to think they
would be grateful for a call—even persons employed by the
newspapers actually attempted to see her! But this impertinence was soon put a stop to; Miss Kemble announced that
under no circumstances whatever would she see a news collector; she had never submitted to that sort of persecution in
England and most certainly would not allow it in America.
Actors of course received a different reception; Mr. Wallack
and Mr. Hackett and Charles Kean were among the first to
pay their respects. Mr. Wallack was handsome but theatrical
in manner; Fanny liked Charles Kean much better; his face
was plain but his voice reminded her of his great father,
Edmund Kean. Most of the visitors were notables in New
York society; at first more gentlemen than ladies came, for
families were staying on in the country because of the cholera.
As it abated, ladies began dropping in. Amiable ladies, but
provincial in their interests and so inclined to resent any criticism of America that Fanny was glad she could say she had
never read Mrs. Trollope's obnoxious book, and return calls
would have been rather boring except that she wanted to see
the inside of New York houses. Many of them were square
comfortable dwellings, red brick trimmed with white, of a
type usual in England; but the newer ones showed tall narrow
fronts of brown sandstone with a tall narrow door approached
by a flight of steep steps. All the drawing-rooms were alike in
giving an effect of coolness; they were pleasing to the eye in
their summer dress of white matting and gray linen with the
sunshine softened to a green twilight by drawn-down Venetian blinds, and so were the ladies in their ruffled muslins
made in the French fashion. Both ladies and gentlemen were
kind. Young men sent her flowers—the only florist was far
uptown at Twenty-third Street—and presented books of poetry,
the latest efforts of Bryant and Halleck; one wanted to give

her a Newfoundland dog, another promised to find her a
good saddle-horse as soon as the weather grew cool enough for
riding. But their conversation was not interesting to a
foreigner for politics was the absorbing topic—a New Yorker,
Martin Van Buren, had just been nominated for the vice-
presidency—and Fanny was so busy that for some time her
visitors remained an almost indistinguishable company of
strangers.

Then individuals emerged. One was Miss Catherine Sedgwick, a novelist from Boston; Fanny liked her extremely. Mr.
Gouverneur Kemble was another acquaintance who soon became a friend; he was so agreeable and so good-looking that it
was pleasant to believe him a cousin and though he and
Charles, comparing notes, could not trace any close family
connection, his theory that *Kemble* harked back to those
notorious freebooters of the Mediterranean, the *Campobellos,*
enchanted Fanny; pirate ancestry was delightfully romantic.

Mr. Philip Hone, a former mayor of New York, also succeeded in making an impression; Charles had brought a letter
of introduction to him from Mr. Vaughan the British Minister, and Mr. Hone called at once—he lived just around the
corner. Only Fanny was in. That evening Mr. Hone's diary
praised Miss Kemble's "good figure and easy manners";
Fanny's recorded the visit of "a good-looking elderly man who
sat himself down, pottered a little, and went away."

On the heels of the call came an invitation to dinner.
Fanny did not want to go. She was rehearsing 'Fazio;' Mr.
Keppel, the Park Theatre's leading young man, knew nothing
and seemed incapable of learning; her costume needed altera-
tion, and as it never crossed her mind that it was nice of the
Hones to invite theatrical people—many New Yorkers were
"evangelical" and abhorred the stage—she believed that she
was conferring rather than receiving a favor when she consented to accompany her father and Dall to Number 235
Broadway at five o'clock.

Some twenty people—English and American, diplomatic

and literary—had been asked to meet them. Most of the men
talked well and the American ladies were all pretty, and well-
dressed, though their hair was frizzed in the French fashion
and they were in demi-toilette—long sleeves and thread-net
capes over bare shoulders—while Fanny of course wore full
dress. The dinner was good and the wine excellent. Mr.
Hone's cellar was famous. But there were too few men servants and no finger bowls; coffee was served after dinner, but
not, to Fanny's annoyance, tea. The piano to which she was
led was a ridiculous little cabinet affair stuck against the wall
and pitched too high for her voice; she sang badly and was
glad to give way to Mr. Dominick Lynch, to whom the ladies
listened with the adoration that Henry Greville and Lord
Ossulston received in London, and Fanny, as no one told her
that Mr. Lynch had brought Italian opera to New York and
started Malibran on her career, with the tolerance of a professional for an amateur and an almost unbearable homesickness; she had last heard 'The Phantom Bark' sung by Tom
Moore with Mrs. Norton hanging over his shoulder. She was
blue, she was tired, she wanted to go home. That night her
diary devoted a page to the dinner party—a page that, later
on, she was to regret—and various little oddities of the
"aborigines" observed during the evening.

Mr. Hone's diary also recorded various little oddities—of
the English. "Miss Kemble," he wrote, "like all young persons
who have become celebrated, has many admirers. Her manners are somewhat singular. Allowance must be made for her,
just arrived among strangers, one of the lions of the day and,
as such, an object of curiosity. She talks well but will only
talk when, and to whom, she chooses, and she has an air of
nonchalance not calculated to make her a favorite with the
beaux . . . She has astonishing requisites for the stage. Her
features separately are not good but combined they make a
face of great and powerful expression. She is said to resemble
her aunt Mrs. Siddons. I am of the opinion that she does not
like her profession. It is not her favorite theme of conversa-

tion. Her father is a gentleman of fine manners and dignified deportment, somewhat stiff—he is a Kemble—but evidently accustomed to good society."

Next day, a Sunday, Mr. Hone's diary noted that he had given the Kembles seats in his pew at Trinity, and they were "evidently accustomed to attending divine service, a practice which is not so frequent among persons of their profession as could be wished;" Fanny's, that it was surprising to find no pew opener or clerk to make the responses, and several alterations in the liturgy, such as *prosperity* for *wealth*, seemed to her affected, but the service was read "with fewer vices of pronunciation or vulgarities of emphasis" than in England, the music both at Trinity and Grace was good, and although Grace Church was as bare as a dissenting chapel she enjoyed the vicar's sermon. A few days later she met the vicar of Grace at dinner and liked him so much—"Dr. Wainwright," she wrote, "is enchanting!"—that it came as a shock when he expressed pleasure at being able to meet her *in private*—it seemed that clergymen in America never went to the theatre! Later he gave her another surprise. They met at a ball; when he bade her goodbye she remarked that he was leaving early and he explained that he never stayed in the room after the dancing began! She was amazed. Strict parents at home sometimes considered waltzing objectionable and agreed with Sheridan Knowles that no gentleman would tolerate seeing his fiancée "in the coil of another," but she had never heard of anyone who minded looking on. All her friends danced round dances. Where was the harm? Next day she was enlightened. Dr. Wainwright came to call and he came as a missionary. He pointed out the impropriety of allowing "any coxcomb to come up to a lady and, without remorse or hesitation, imprison her waist, and absolutely whirl her around in his arms," and he spoke so feelingly of the dignity of womanhood that Fanny promised with tears in her eyes that she would give up waltzing, except with her brothers or another girl. "Farewell sweet German waltz!" she wrote in her journal.

"I shall never again keep time to your pleasant measure. No matter, anything is better than being lightly spoken of."

But dinner-parties, dancing and church-going were interludes. A week after the Kembles arrived in New York Charles appeared at the Park Theatre in 'Hamlet'. There were rival attractions; Wallack was acting at the American Theatre under Mr. Barrymore's management; Peale's Museum promised that "THE GREAT ANACONDA would be fed with a live rabbit," and a picture of Adam and Eve at the Rotunda "in a semi-nude condition," according to the critics was "much censured and therefore largely attended." Nevertheless 'Hamlet' drew a large audience, 'The Evening Post' gave the play three columns, and Mr. Hone told everybody that Charles bore a remarkable likeness to the elder brother, "Glorious John," whom Mr. Hone had seen in London.

But there was a note of expectancy in the air; it was Fanny the public wanted. Perhaps London had over-praised Miss Kemble? New York, critical and expectant, was waiting. New York was not disappointed. She was the first great actress that New York had ever seen and New York told her so. The newspapers forgave her for being rude to their reporters. Mr. Hone forgave her for being "nonchalant:" "Bianca," he wrote, "is a fine part, well calculated for the display of the strongest passions of the female heart—love, hate and jealousy . . . The curtain fell amidst the deafening plaudits of an astonished audience."

Juliet and Mrs. Haller drew crowded houses. When 'The Hunchback' was put on, enthusiasm rose to ecstasy. As in London, Fanny's appeal was especially to the young; every boy and girl in New York wanted a ticket; a few, after prayerful consideration, received permission from their parents and for these it was an unforgettable experience. The future of one very young spectator, Clara Ogden, was determined that night: "Never have I beheld any creature so perfectly bewitching," the little girl wrote of Julia, "the tones of her voice were richest music, her dark flashing eyes seemed to penetrate my soul, and I laughed and wept immoderately;" and Clara became an actress, Mrs. Mowatt, and a playwright, the author of 'Fashion.' Another youthful admirer, a boy of thirteen, saving every penny, contrived to come over from Brooklyn again and again to see the new star. Years later, Walt Whitman wrote: "Fanny Kemble! Name to conjure up great mimic scenes withal—perhaps the greatest! . . . She came to give America that young maturity and roseate power in all their noon, or rather forenoon, flush . . . Nothing finer did any stage ever exhibit—the veterans of all nations said so, and my boyish heart and head felt it in every minute cell," and he added that, in some mysterious way, Fanny's acting had helped in the making of 'Leaves of Grass.'

It was a pity Fanny could not know she was inspiring a great poet for that would have seemed to her supremely worth while. As it was, praise came as a matter of course and New York's was too lacking in discrimination to be taken very seriously; she was more amused than pleased by the critics' fulsome paragraphs. How funny the American newspapers were! she thought, laughing as she read. Even the advertisements were funny; "Portuguese leeches, citron and boneset lozenges;" *new* music—'Gaily the Troubadour touched his Guitar,' and 'Malibran's Bagelitto Waltz'—that everyone was tired of at home. Droll items recalled the anecdotes Aunt Eliza had told so long ago; a missionary had been found skinned, "whose head, it was supposed, had been taken as a curiosity as he wore his hair remarkably long." The foreign news seemed oddly chosen; who cared whether or not Count Tolstoy had fought a duel with Count Troubetskoy?

And, as it happened, no praise could have offset the misery of acting with Mr. Keppel. The poor creature was such a pitiable spectacle as he stood groping for a forgotten line, rolling his eyes, gasping and gagging like a man in a fit, that Fanny could not help feeling sorry for him, and although he ruined her best point lace veil in one of his clumsy embraces she continued to prompt and push and pull him about the

stage until everybody's patience was exhausted. Mr. Keppel
was dismissed and Charles took his parts, to Fanny's relief and
the satisfaction of the public who soon forgot that this handsome hero was in reality the heroine's father.

Without Mr. Keppel things went better; the company was
adequate, the Park Theatre large, handsome and well
equipped; Fanny would have enjoyed acting if she had not
been so fatigued by the noise and confusion in which she
lived at the hotel, and its lack of solitude. She was never alone,
and might have broken down under the strain if she had not
been refreshed by an occasional country excursion. With
cooler weather her New York acquaintances remembered
their promise, and with them she explored the neighborhood.
A country so beautiful and unspoiled by civilization lay
within easy reach of New York that every moment would
have been a delight if she could have found a really good
saddle-horse—American horses all seemed to have hard
mouths and an inclination to fall into a horrible gait called
a *rack*—and she longed for her own little mare, Donna Sol.
Some of the most charming excursions—to Weehawken,
Hoboken and Sandy Hook—began with a trip on the water. A
small steamboat ran back and forth across the Hudson carrying dozens of tradespeople's and laborers' families to the
Elysian Fields of Hoboken to spend the afternoon; prosperous people, so unlike the half-starved London population that
as Fanny watched them chatting and laughing she became reconciled to the absence of picture galleries, good music and
other amenities of civilization she missed in the New World.
At the landing the crowd would hurry off to the swings and
circular railway that Colonel Stevens, the proprietor of the
Elysian Fields, had installed below the bluffs where his house
stood surrounded by waving forests. But Fanny's friends did
not mingle with the *hoi polloi,* or stop for refreshments at the
Pavilion, where the Turtle Club was wont to partake of
"spoon exercise;" they turned in another direction, climbed
a steep path and emerged on a grassy flower-sprinkled knoll

where the picnic baskets of champagne, cake and cherry-bounce were unpacked by Negro servants under the shade of magnificent trees framing vistas so brilliant with autumn foliage and blue water and so gay with birds and butterflies, that Fanny could almost—but not quite—forgive Hoboken its mosquitoes.

Sometimes a trip up the Hudson would be arranged. "Nothing," Fanny wrote in her journal, "can exceed the comfort with which the steamboats are fitted up, or the skill with which they are managed . . . But to an English person the circumstance of being the whole day in a crowd is a nuisance. The Americans live all their days in a throng, sleep five or six in a room, eat in droves, and travel by swarms." But among the swarms pleasant acquaintances were often to be met; visitors on their way to Mr. Gouverneur Kemble's country place at Cold Spring, or the Hosacks' at Hyde Park. The return trip, irradiated by sunset light, was enchanting and pages of Fanny's journal would that evening be devoted to the scenery of the Hudson and the Highlands.

After such heavenly glimpses the hotel seemed drearier than ever, and the city dingier—New York was passing through the shabbiest decade of its history. When in October the Kembles' first engagement came to an end they were thankful to shake from their shoes the dust of streets unswept since the previous winter, and set off for their next stopping place, Philadelphia.

CHAPTER XIV

The City of Brotherly Love

"There is much beauty in Philadelphia as well as neatness—just as
you may often detect a pretty face under a demure bonnet."

—BASIL HALL.

THE JOURNEY from New York to Philadelphia in 1832 was not
lacking in variety. It began with a steamboat trip that landed
travellers at a wharf in New Jersey where a row of coaches
stood waiting in a waste of red mud to convey them to the
Camden and Amboy railway. The coaches, boatlike in shape,
seemed designed for discomfort, three passengers being
crowded on seats built for two and only partially protected
from the weather by flapping leather curtains. They were
drawn by four horses; the roads were deep with mud, crisscrossed by tree roots and obstructed by stumps, but the pace
was brisk—half gallop, half trot—and the passengers were
tossed up and down, back and forth, until Fanny screamed,
Charles swore and poor Dall sighed and groaned in acute
misery. But no one else appeared to mind this bone-racking
experience; the ladies laughed and talked; like all American
women they were so small and delicate looking that Fanny
was surprised at the loudness of their voices—it was like hearing mice roar! She noticed an occasional mispronunciation,
such as *vaggary* and *vitupperate*, but she was too absorbed in
keeping her equilibrium to join in the conversation or to
study the landscape. However, there was nothing to see. The
land was flat, the trees second growth; the fields bristled with
black stumps; the cottages, few and far between, were no better than the huts in France and Ireland, and ragged barefoot
peasants stood staring as the string of coaches rattled by.
There were wild flowers in the underbrush, but no gardens

158

brightened the monotonous expanse intersected by rail fences that went zigzagging across the country like the herring-bone on a flannel petticoat . . . At last the coaches drew up in a swampy field where the railroad began, but as the road had not yet been equipped with steam-engines, such as Fanny had been introduced to in Liverpool, the carriages, though running on iron ledges, were drawn by horses. Next came another steamboat; it was pleasant sitting on deck as the boat moved up the huge Delaware River stopping at pretty little villages along the way, and Fanny would have enjoyed herself if her chair had not been surrounded by tobacco-chewing men; the habit of spitting anywhere and everywhere struck her as peculiarly nauseating and, as she had never been in Italy, peculiarly American. At Philadelphia the Kembles were met by the proprietor of the Mansion House; his inn was much more comfortable than the American Hotel in New York, and Fanny's first walk gave her an agreeable impression of the place.

"The town," she wrote in her journal, "is perfect silence and solitude compared to New York; there is greater age about it too, which pleases me. The red houses are not so fiercely red, nor the white facings so glaringly white; in short it has not so new and flaunting a look. We passed a bank in Chestnut Street which is a beautiful little copy of the Parthenon, and other buildings of white marble in harmony with the extreme brilliance of the sky in this country. The shops here are better looking than those at New York, the windows are larger and there does not seem to be the same anomalous mixture of vendibles. The streets were full of men hurrying to their town houses to give their votes. The democrats, or radicals, are for the re-election of General Jackson, but the aristocratic party favor Henry Clay. There is the usual shouting and breaking windows and bonfires that we are accustomed to on these occasions. I saw a caricature of Jackson and Van Buren, entitled the 'King and His Minister'; Van Buren held a crown in his hand and the devil was approaching Jack-

son with a sceptre . . . Nothing can exceed the civility of the
people in this hotel; the enchanting Mr. Head has allowed
me a piano-forte, and the house is extremely well kept. I am
in high delight with this Quaker City."

As in New York, 'Fazio' was chosen to introduce Fanny to
the public. The house was jammed; the audience was attentive, but warmed slowly. Not until the end brought a tremendous burst of applause was she sure of her success and
even then the audience did not rise in her honor as they did
in London. But the box office reported "fighting and rushing
and tearing of coats" to secure seats for 'Romeo and Juliet'
and 'The Hunchback' when they came along, and it was said
that one daring individual had actually made forty dollars
by purchasing tickets and selling again at an advanced price.
According to Henry Wickoff, a young man about town who
later recorded his impressions of the time: "That single performance of 'Fazio' stamped Fanny Kemble in my mind as
the greatest of living actresses," and of 'The Hunchback:'
"The town went Kemble mad; the affecting phrases of the
idolized Julia were repeated at every corner . . . I did nothing
but frequent the theatre and abandon myself to the fascination of this bewitching actress." So the Philadelphians could
be forgiven for reserving applause until the close of a performance.

They turned out to be slow in another respect, slow in coming to call. New York's stream of visitors had been so overwhelming that it had been a relief to escape; but now, as the
days went by and no ladies and no persons of importance left
cards, Fanny became indignant; there wasn't, she exclaimed,
a town in Europe where her father's arrival would not have
been recognized at once by all the prominent citizens! Then
young gentlemen began coming, and they brought her
bouquets of hot house flowers, music boxes, and the latest
Annuals and Books of Beauty. She made friends with some
children staying in the hotel and with a Newfoundland puppy
she met in the street, and discovered a fairly good riding-

school, where her horsemanship created a sensation. It was amusing to hear that the cap she wore was styled the "Kemble cap," and that all the girls had begun taking riding lessons and had ordered habits like hers, which would, she felt, be an improvement on the calico skirts and flowered bonnets usual in the riding-school. Better horses were found for her than the school animals her journal described, "like old trunks covered with shaggy angry-looking hair, a donkey's head and cart-horse legs," and every young gentleman in Philadelphia seemed anxious to show her the sights of the neighborhood.

At first they seemed merely an agreeable group of attentive young men; then one, Mr. Pierce Butler, emerged as more agreeable and more attentive than the others; he was good-looking, musical and literary, and rode well. Through him, she met his cousin Thomas Sully, the painter; this had one drawback, Mr. Sully wanted to paint Miss Kemble's portrait; but she liked him and in the end both she and her father consented to sit. He painted her as Juliet and gave her a pretty, innocent little face recalling Mrs. Siddons in her youth. It was the first of many attempts but he was never satisfied; always the essential Fanny Kemble seemed to escape him. He tried again and again—one portrait went to Harriet St. Leger in Ireland; whenever she was willing to sit he was more than ready to paint. Strange to say, the most life-like, to Fanny's mind, was a Beatrice—not a pretty little girl, a beautiful passionate woman—which was painted from memory. Sully had seen 'Much Ado', caught a single brilliant glance, hurried home and recorded it as he might have recorded the flash of a bird's wing or a breaking wave.

By this time Philadelphia had waked up. Important elderly gentlemen followed in the wake of young Butler and young Sully, and soon Fanny's drawing room was as crowded as in New York. Politically it was a critical time; she heard much discussion of states rights and slavery, and entries in her journal indicate she was already taking sides: "Carolina," she wrote, "is in a state of convulsion. The Nullifiers and the

Unionists have had a fight in Charleston, and the Carolinians have threatened to secede from the Union . . . I am horrified at what I am told of the state of negroes in the South. To teach a slave to read or write is to incur a penalty of fine or imprisonment. So great is the dread of insurrection on the part of the white inhabitants that the blacks are kept in the most brutal ignorance, and too often treated with barbarity. Oh! what a breaking asunder of old manacles there will be some of these fine days; what a fearful rising of the black flood; what a sweeping away of oppressions and tyrannies; what a fierce and horrible revenge for wrong so long endured! . . . They say 'Old Hickory' means to lick the refractory southerns; why, they are coming to a civil war! However, the grumblers haven't the means of fighting, without emancipating and arming their slaves."

But politics and other masculine topics were not allowed to usurp conversation in Fanny's drawing room for very long. Heads of households having brought good reports of the Kembles the ladies decided they might be called upon in spite of their connection with the stage. Invitations followed. Fanny's first ball was at the Willings. "I wore," she wrote, "the same dress I wore at Devonshire House at my last ball in England and looked at myself in amazement to think of all the strangeness that has befallen me since." But the rooms were too crowded, huge fires blazed on the hearths; she did not like stewed oysters and terrapin, "the refreshments invariably handed round at evening parties in America," and "all the world and his wife" stared and asked strange questions. So the evening ended, as it so often ended at home, with thankfulness: she was glad to get away and hurry out into the cold moonlight. "The sky here," she wrote, "is an earnest color that is solemn to look at; the stars are more vivid than in our heavens, and there is a variety of hues in their light—some reddish, some violet and others of the palest silver."

But her spirits were reviving. Of another ball she wrote:

"The floors were duly chalked, the music very good, the women very lovely; and I fell in again with my dear kinsman, Mr. Gouverneur Kemble, whom I love most devotedly, and whom I jumped half across a quadrille to greet, which must have edified the assembly." A few days later she was asked to join a riding party to Laurel Hill and by this time she was in the highest spirits, gay as a lark. A radiant Fanny scribbled that night in her journal: "It was winter, but winter in its most dazzling array of sunshine and crystal; dry, crisp, hard roads, with delicate rime tipping the ruts with sparkling jewelry, and the waters curling under the breath of the arrow-like wind. We dismounted, and ran, slid, slipped and scrambled down to the shore; far below a natural rocky arch overhung the river all glittering with pure long diamond icicles; he convoyed me there, and broke off one of the wintry gems for me. I called up to Dall, and the echo answered me. I ran up a scale, as loud and high as I could, and from the sunny fields a voice repeated the threaded notes; I stood in enchantment, provoking the hidden voice in the air that answered me as though a mocking spirit fled along the hill tops . . . At the house we partook of cakes, wine, 'cordial' and preserves, the invariable refreshments presented to visitors at Laurel Hill. Our host waited himself most attentively upon us and refused all remuneration save thanks. We were very late getting back to the hotel. He stayed to dinner. To my surprise, he seems to dislike the Doctor—or at least he is troubled by the Doctor's admiration of my singing."

Who was the *he* who rode with her that day and stayed to dinner? and who was the doctor? Their names can only be guessed at. She was pursued and plagued and flattered by dozens of fashionable young men, all jealous of each other, all trying to push a little nearer to the throne; an attempt to distinguish any one would be futile. But Pierce Butler was the most persistent and his attentions were becoming marked. Henry Wickoff observed that Butler seemed likely to "carry off the splendid prize, and was envied and almost detested by a swarm of rivals." The dowagers were less complacent; they did not want to lose one of the most eligible bachelors in Philadelphia. Pierce Butler was young and handsome and descended from the Irish Earls of Ormonde and the Middletons of Carolina, a combination that even Philadelphia considered genteel; he was rich, for he and his brother had inherited the Middleton property from their grandfather Butler, on condition that they changed their name from Mease to Butler, and that was a very nice property indeed; fine rice and cotton plantations in Georgia and hundreds of slaves. So when it was rumored that this desirable young man was so taken with Miss Kemble that he proposed to follow her on tour and play the flute in the orchestra in order to be near her, society was shocked to the core; it looked as if what was known as "Mr. Butler's infatuation" might end in marriage! Unluckily, no less respectable outcome could be hoped for; Miss Kemble, unlike most actresses, was known to be very particular. She was far more carefully chaperoned than an American girl; wherever she went either her father or her aunt went with her; no visitor ever saw her alone, the aunt always sat on the sofa. So Philadelphia feared the worst; what was the world coming to if an actress could walk off with a *parti* that a Willing or a Cadwalader or a Wharton would have accepted with joy!

Meanwhile, the centre of the storm, Fanny herself, remained calm. She was too accustomed to "infatuation" for Mr. Butler's to seem very exciting; she had known plenty of young men in London richer and better born and quite as good-looking and agreeable; but it must have been pleasant to have a passionate adorer always on hand. It must have been reassuring. She had left England with a heartache, and the "ephemeral love" of 'Hernani' and Oatlands seems to have overshadowed her first weeks in New York. Now, in Philadelphia, the cloud lifted. She recovered her zest for life, her delight in dancing and outdoor exercise. Now, if assailed by "blue devils," she no longer wrote mournful verses but rushed out and bought a rocking horse for the children in the hotel.

"The dear babies," she wrote of them, "are delightful to me; their laughing voices have power to make me happy, and when they come dancing to meet me, my heart warms fondly towards them;" and of Americans in general: "The people are more civil and considerate than can be imagined. I sent yesterday evening for some water-ice; the confectioner had none; when lo! to-night he brings me some, made on purpose for me. I admired a fan in a lady's hand; at the end of the play it was sent to my dressing-room; these sort of things are done by me ten times a day. Nothing can exceed the kindness and attention which has encountered us everywhere since we have been in this country. The Americans have shown us un-mingled good will, and cordial, real kindness."

But along with this increasing light-heartedness an increas-ing dislike of her profession is noticeable in Fanny's record of the time. "I acted like a wretch," she wrote one night. "Oh, Juliet! vision of the south, rose of the garden of the earth! How I do loathe the stage, these wretched, tawdry, glittering rags flung over the forms of ideal loveliness, pitiful substitutes for the glories of poetry. Pasteboard and paint for the thick breathing orange groves of the south; green silk and oiled parchment for the solemn splendor of her moon at night; an actress, a mimicker, a sham creature—*me*, in fact—for that most wonderful conception, in which all that is true in nature, and all that is exquisite in fancy, are moulded into a living form. To *act* this! to *act* 'Romeo and Juliet.' Horror, horror, how I do loathe my most impotent and unpoetical craft!" This outburst is exaggerated even for Fanny. No doubt Pierce Butler was responsible; after the adoration of a real suitor, stage passion would have been peculiarly distasteful.

Christmas, a dull day in Philadelphia, came and went, and the first gray dawn of 1833 found the Kembles on their way to Baltimore. The journey was uneventful, the town so quiet that but for the number of rakish clipper-ships crowding the wharves one would never have believed it a haunt of pirates. Barnham's Hotel lacked comfort, but the proprietor procured

a piano for Fanny, her audiences in the Holliday Street theatre were enthusiastic and she was serenaded every night
after she went home; the country could not, to her disappointment, be explored because no side-saddle was to be had
in any livery stable or saddler's shop in the town. The inhabitants, however, were delightful. Fanny liked the Balti-
moreans, and they liked her. They were gifted with a softer
intonation and a gentler manner than the Northerners she
had met, and there was an old-fashioned flavor in households
such as the Catons' that reminded her of home. Mrs. Caton—a
sweet woman, in mourning for her father, Charles Carroll, the
last of the signers of the Declaration of Independence—had
known and admired Fanny's aunt, Mrs. Whitelock; the
daughters of the house were married to well-known English-
men and it was pleasant to see Lawrence portraits adorning
the walls. Pleasant too to hear Mr. Caton speak of his slaves
as "the best and most faithful servants in the world," and to
realize there might be a kinder side to plantation life than
she had supposed. Her stay in Baltimore was further brightened by a meeting with an old friend, Mr. Washington Irving;
"always," she wrote, "simple, unconstrained, kindly and
good." He spoke of her mother who had befriended him
when he first arrived in London, young and unhappy; of her
début and the little gold watch her father had given her at
supper that night, and it was delightful to find they would
soon meet again for he too was on the way to Washington.

Gadsby's, the best hotel in Washington, was a scramble of
crooked wooden galleries, rambling passages and innumerable staircases and doors; a village in itself. But the theatre
was minute, no larger than the baby's playhouse at Versailles,
and the company as forlorn as a band of strolling players
pictured by Hogarth. But Washington society was accustomed
to these drawbacks, everyone came to see Fanny act and applauded her to the echo. Dolly Madison and John Quincy
Adams, Judge Story and Daniel Webster, laughed and wept;
even Chief Justice Marshall was reduced to tears by the sor-

rows of Mrs. Haller. Everyone left cards on the Kembles: Edward Everett, an impressive figure, was one of their first visitors; he had just come from the White House and reported the President in a belligerent mood, little inclined to give in to Carolina. Mr. Everett was of the same opinion; it would, he thought, be better to fight than to admit the right of every individual state to dictate to the whole government. The President was another personage who came up to Fanny's expectations. After being presented at the White House—in private; the public levees were too crowded, ladies perched on the mantelpiece and men knocked each other about trying to reach the presidential hand—she wrote: "His excellency Andrew Jackson is a good specimen of a fine old well-battered soldier; very tall and thin, but erect and dignified in his carriage; his manners are simple and quiet and therefore good, and his niece, the lady of the house, is a very pretty person." But the White House was disappointing; handsome but comfortless inside, and forlornly set in a withered grass plot with palings in front and at the back a stretch of waste land sloping untidily to the river.

These contrasts seemed to be characteristic of Washington. When Daniel Webster spoke in the Senate his majestic oration was interrupted again and again, Fanny wrote disgustedly, by "a regiment of ladies sitting among the senators, whispering, talking and fidgeting." The dome of the Capitol emerged from a confusion of hovels, in the very heart of the town spaces of half-cleared ground dotted with small cheap houses alternated with tracts of untouched moorland and swamp, and every avenue soon faded out in open country.

But this easy access to the country and the mild climate— already, in January, the air tasted of spring—gave Washington one advantage; it was delightful for riding. Every young gentleman in town wanted to show Miss Kemble the neighborhood, and she could have borrowed a good horse whenever she chose if she had been willing to take the responsibility. As a rule she refused; but in Washington she did yield to over-persuasion—and regretted it! One fine afternoon a party of friends appeared at her door accompanied by a stranger, a Mr. Fulton, on a tall gray horse which, it appeared he expected her to ride. Fanny thanked and declined; Mr. Fulton insisted and went on insisting. At length she had to give in and mounted the gray, with a laughing remark—"she supposed if she gave Mr. Fulton two dollars the horse would become a hired horse and then it would be all right;" Mr. Fulton laughed; they all rode away together and Fanny never gave the matter another thought. But a few days later Charles was informed that his daughter had insulted America in the person of Mr. Fulton; she had told Mr. Fulton that she did not choose to ride the horse of an American gentleman and had actually offered him two dollars for its hire! Washington's feelings were hurt; if an apology were not forthcoming at once the results might be unpleasant; there was talk of hissing Miss Kemble off the stage at her next appearance! Fanny, bewildered and angry, explained; Charles explained; the explanations were accepted. When Fanny, shaking in her shoes, stepped on the stage that night she was greeted with cheers and the affair appeared to be over.

But it was not. The newspapers had made the most of the incident and when, soon after, the Kembles returned to Philadelphia they found that the story of Mr. Fulton's horse had preceded them. As the second act of 'Fazio' ended handbills came fluttering down into the pit giving a garbled version of Fanny's innocent remark and calling upon the American public to avenge the insult. This time Charles went before the curtain with his explanation. His speech was clapped; Fanny came out and was greeted with an outburst of applause that made it clear Philadelphia was on her side; and when the engagement came to an end and she left the theatre after the last performance, a huge crowd gathered at the stage door to bid her goodbye; as she drove away they broke into hurrahs and that night she wrote in her journal: "I love the whole city of Philadelphia from this time forth forever more."

But New York was pleasanter now. The Hones and the Hosacks and Mr. Gouverneur Kemble seemed like old friends; there was plenty of dancing and riding, and Mr. Pierce Butler came on so often that Fanny did not miss Philadelphia and was rather sorry when in April they left New York for Boston. But, luckily, Mr. Pierce Butler was able to accompany them, and the journey was remarkably comfortable. After a luxurious night in the Sound boat, an "exclusive extra"—a coach with no other passengers—took them rapidly over smooth hard roads and at the end of six hours landed the party at the Tremont House in fine spirits. The hotel was excellent; the theatre, just across the street, well equipped, and the company the best the Kembles had acted with since leaving London. Boston audiences, as in Edinburgh and Philadelphia, warmed slowly; but before long everybody was cheering and shouting, and there was such a demand for tickets that the scenes at the box office often drew Fanny to the hotel window. The crowd would gather early; here and there one would see an isolated figure, a speculator who had smeared his jacket with molasses hoping to keep rivals at a distance. But when the bolts were withdrawn stickiness was forgotten; there would be a mad rush forward that would send men tumbling over each other, fighting and swearing, to emerge with bruises and torn coats as well as with tickets they could sell again at an enormous profit.

Boston was agreeably reminiscent of England in appearance—the houses reminded Fanny of London houses, the Common of Constitution Hill and Beacon Street of Park Lane—and its citizens struck her as the most highly cultivated she had met with in the States. New York, she had been told, was supposed to boast of money, Philadelphia of birth and Boston of brains. But New York had not seemed to her very luxurious or Philadelphia very aristocratic—Mr. Butler said she would have to go to Carolina to find an aristocracy—so it was a surprise to discover that Boston's share of the adage was justified; Channing and Emerson, Daniel Webster and John

Quincy Adams would have been welcome even in Edinburgh. And yet society, in the lively Edinburgh sense, was almost non-existent. Very little entertaining went on in those large comfortable houses where, Fanny wrote: "I saw more pictures and sculpture, and more books, than I have seen anywhere else." The Boston ladies lacked vitality; they were languid hostesses, remained in the background and left conversation to the gentlemen. However, the town exerted itself for the Kembles. Fanny dined and danced, and was taken sightseeing, and walked in the blossomy Boston streets where each spring day seemed to bring another charm and another fragrance. Overhead horse-chestnuts shook out their white stars, lilacs overflowed the dooryards, every grass plot became patterned with tulips and every fence veiled itself in flowering vines. The country beckoned; at length the roads were dry and she could ride.

The New England landscape, with a few more swift brooks, would have been as beautiful as Scotland. Jamaica Pond, the Blue Hills and Mount Auburn were wild and lovely, and the farmland exquisite now; meadows sheeted with green and gold, orchards billowing pink and white. Birds new to English eyes chirped in the hedges, new wild flowers showed among the drifts of last year's leaves. There was a new enchantment in the air, as Fanny and Pierce Butler rode side by side through brown forest paths or galloped their horses along the hard white sand of Chelsea Beach. Even the sea spoke with sweeter music, there was a sweeter tang in the air, as she and Pierce, leaving the horses, wandered on and on gathering shells and colored pebbles; on and on until their friends were out of sight and they were alone. They reached a hut, built by sportsmen who came there to shoot plover, and Pierce took her hand and pulled her up to the flat roof smelling of warm salt shingles, and they sat talking idly, half asleep; the sun shone, gulls wheeled, sandpipers tiptoed at the water's edge. Fanny sang a little, scribbled a little poem, and was happy.

CHAPTER XV

Fanny Makes Up Her Mind

"High on the sea-cliff ledges
   The white gulls are trooping and crying;
Here among rooks and roses,
   Why is the sea-gull flying?"

—STEVENSON.

SPRING WENT fast that year. Its first freshness was on the wane when the Kembles left Boston and in New York they found full summer. But heat and dust could be endured, for the end of June would see them northward bound. The trip promised well. Canada was notoriously romantic; a land of huge rivers, enormous waterfalls, vast stretches of primeval forest; and two agreeable men had joined the party. Pierce Butler was, of course, to accompany them, and Charles had also invited an Englishman to whom he had recently been introduced in New York, a Mr. Edward Trelawny, an explorer who wrote books and had known Byron and Shelley.

The first lap of the journey only got them as far as Cold Spring to spend a week-end with Mr. Gouverneur Kemble; a mild beginning but not without adventure. Fanny met her first waterfall and it came near being her last. The streak of foam looked harmless enough as it came dashing down over the rocks and, as always, swift-moving water awoke in her a strange excitement; she insisted that she had to climb it and she did. No one could stop her. The wet rocks were slippery as glass; she pulled herself up from ledge to ledge, soaked through, her muslin frock clinging to her ankles; up and up, until, blinded by the spray and deafened by the roar, she missed her footing, thought she was gone, caught at a branch, climbed on and stood at last on the summit, triumphant, but dizzy—if that branch had broken! . . . For the time being she

171

was satisfied with safer pleasures; picking wild flowers, playing with a pet lamb on the lawn, eating strawberries, drinking lemonade and watching the testing of a string of cannon from Mr. Kemble's foundry destined for West Point—a magnificent spectacle; coppery smoke went billowing up the mountain side and every gorge resounded with the bombardment. When the warm still night closed down they went rowing on the river. But rowing was less peaceful than it might have been, for the oars could not agree. Fanny, steering, found it impossible to keep a straight course; Mr. Trelawny and Mr. Butler were inclined to pull against each other; the boat went zigzag. She laughed, the crew grumbled . . . Then the moon rose. Fanny began singing. The boat drifted, slipping in and out of the mountain shadow . . . It was midnight when they left the shining river and climbed the hill to the house.

Next day the travellers were on their way again up the Hudson in the Albany boat. The morning was hot and bright, and the passengers noisy. Pierce discovered a corner on the upper deck where Fanny could sit under the shade of an awning, sewing, or scribbling poetry—a song about the wild flowers she had gathered at Cold Spring; one line pleased her:

> ". . . the leaves of the wild vine, that shine
> Like glass without, and underneath are white
> And soft as a swan's breast";

that was accurate, that was good. Pleasanter still to do nothing; watch the river escape from the Highlands, widen to a bay, flow on between low banks of orchard and pasture, exchanging an occasional remark with the two men who sat at her feet ready to retrieve a thimble or wandering reel of thread that might slip from her lap.

But she soon forgot the landscape. Trelawny began talking; about himself, his adventures, and his friends, Byron and Shelley. Pierce got up and walked away; but she did not no-

tice his departure for Trelawny was describing Byron's death
at Misselonghi and the funeral obsequies on the shore of the
Gulf of Spezzia. He showed her a letter from Claire, Byron's
Claire, mother of Allegra; he spoke of Mary Shelley, the poet's widow, who had corrected the spelling and punctuation
in his book, 'The Adventures of a Younger Son'—"he was no
good at that sort of thing"—and Fanny realized with surprise
that the story she had read on board the 'Pacific' was true;
the buccaneering exploits, the sojourn in the mountains of
Greece, even the marriage with the chief's sister, were fact not
fiction! . . . They were both so absorbed, he in telling, she in
listening and questioning, that they failed to see a thunder-
cloud darkening the sky until the storm was upon them and a
gust of rain had soaked her dress. But it did not matter. Mr.
Trelawny knew the way to the engine room, and in the red
glow of the furnace fire they went on with their conversation.
That night Fanny wrote in her journal:

"He's a curious being, a savage in some respects, a giant for
strength and ability, taller, straighter and broader than most
men; yet with the most listless indolent carelessness of gait,
and an uncertain wandering way of dropping his feet to the
ground, as if he didn't know where he was going, and didn't
much wish to go anywhere. His face is as dark as a Moor's,
with a wild strange look about the eyes and forehead, and a
mark like a scar upon his cheek; his whole appearance giving
one an idea of toil, hardship, peril and wild adventure. The
expression of his mouth is remarkably sweet, and his voice is
low and gentle. His hands are as brown as a laborer's; he
never profanes them with gloves, but wears two strange magi-
cal-looking rings; one of them, which he showed me, is made
of elephant's hair."

Trelawny was an ideal companion for a romantic journey;
he shared Fanny's adoration for wild nature, he even shared
her mystical passion for waterfalls; he understood her when
she exclaimed, beside the Falls of the Cohoes, that "the foam
looked so nice and soft and thick and cold, she longed to be

in the middle of it!" When he assured her that of all the
world's wonders he had travelled far to see Niagara was the
only marvel he cared to visit a second time, she thrilled with
impatience.

Meanwhile there were small pleasures to enjoy; a case of
musical glasses at one little inn, a bouquet of flowers at another; an old meek-eyed, yellow-white cart horse she found in
a field, with a man's saddle on his back, gave her a refreshing
gallop. The drives in stage coach and carriage often took
them through deep woods, and the days on the canal boat
winding along the valley of the Mohawk went by in lazy
peace. They would sit on deck, sewing and talking; Charles
and Trelawny would discuss Kean's acting; Trelawny would
read aloud a chapter of 'Don Quixote' in that strange mild
slow voice of his, or perhaps fling down the book and break
into a poem of Byron's, declaiming with fierce abandon until
a low bridge sent his audience flat on their faces for fear of being scraped off the deck. Trelawny was extraordinarily stimulating; but Pierce too had his uses. Pierce was so helpful with
the luggage, so attentive to Dall, so respectful to Charles, so
thoughtful—knowing the discomforts of frontier travel he had
even brought some silver forks from home—and before long
he developed an admiration for the beauties of nature almost
as ardent as Trelawny's. It was Pierce, not Trelawny, who introduced Fanny to her first "wonder," Trenton Falls. It was
Pierce who took her hand and led her inch by inch along the
narrow slippery path above the boiling pool flecked with
foam. He found a ledge where they could crouch, their feet
dangling over the abyss; he held her when she bent too far
tossing flowers and leaves into the rapids to watch them rush
away; twist for a second, cling, rush on again; feel the drag of
the whirlpool, and vanish—the whirlpool never let anything
go, the guide said; a man had once struggled and twisted in
the rapids, helpless as a leaf; in the end the whirlpool got
him! . . . Trelawny came wandering by, glanced at them, wandered on again. Fanny scarcely saw him. The terror of the

scene in some strange way gave reality to Pierce's passion and there beside the swift water she discovered that she loved him.

Trelawny may have realized that Pierce's star was in the ascendant that day; perhaps he was merely waiting for a grander "wonder," Niagara. At Queenstown, where a conveyance had been engaged to drive the party to the Falls, Trelawny brought Fanny a bunch of roses he had stolen from a garden, while Pierce's gift was only a glass of milk. When they neared the village, after driving miles and miles in a rickety cart over a rough road straining ears for the first murmur of the cataract, Trelawny told the driver to stop. And now, at last, a far-off roar broke the stillness of the woods and from above the river treetops a cloud of silver mist rose like incense! It was an intense moment, Fanny wrote in her journal that night:

"A frenzy of impatience seized upon me. I could have set off and run the whole way, and when at length the carriage stopped at the Niagara House, waiting neither for my father, Dall nor Pierce, I rushed down the foot-path cut in the rocks. Trelawny followed me. Down, down I sprang, and saw through boughs the white glimmer of a sea of foam—Trelawny shouted, 'Go on! Go on!' In another minute I stood upon Table Rock. Trelawny seized me by the arm and, without a word, dragged me to the brink. I saw Niagara— Oh God! who can describe that sight!!!" A characteristic letter went to Harriet; her three days at Niagara, Fanny wrote, were spent "under the water, on the water, and more than half in the water. Wherever foot could stand I stood, and wherever foot could go I went. I crept, clung, hung and waded. I stood alone under the arch, water thundering overhead and the noon day sun looking like a pale wafer, drenched through, almost blown off my feet—bare for safety—and my delight was so intense that I could not bear to come away."

After Niagara even the Falls of Montmorency seemed tame, and although their audiences in Montreal were good and Quebec, she decided, was "fiercely picturesque," Fanny was tired of sight-seeing and not sorry when the tour came to an end and the party turned southward. Every one agreed that it had been a magnificent trip, and that to have travelled so far with only one accident was an achievement. For there had been one accident. Near Rochester their driver had made too short a turn and upset the coach. As it went over, Charles was flung on top of Fanny; they extricated themselves unhurt, and found poor Dall sitting in the road her face streaming with blood and Trelawny lying unconscious beside her. But Trelawny soon revived, Pierce had escaped without a bruise; the cut on Dall's forehead was bound up, and they all sat down to supper at the little inn at Murray in good spirits, feeling they had been lucky to get off so well.

Autumn found the Kembles acting again in New York, Trelawny gone to Virginia and Pierce Butler still dancing attendance on Fanny. There was much comment. Were they, or were they not, engaged? His friends insisted that Pierce was amusing himself; no scion of Butler and Middleton would condescend to marry an actress. Fanny's admirers retorted that the condescension was all the other way; she would sacrifice a brilliant career for a narrow life with a narrow-minded man! Catherine Sedgwick wrote to a friend expressing "a thousand fears:" she considered Fanny "a most captivating creature, steeped to the lips with genius. A complex being, made up of glorious faculties, delightful accomplishments, immeasurable sensibilities—and half a hundred faults;" while Pierce Butler was "a gentlemanly man, with good sense and an amiable disposition, but so infinitely inferior to her that the experiment of marriage might be dangerous."

But Fanny's friends were agreed on one point; her acting that autumn touched heights she had never reached before. One spectator—a passionate, unawakened New England girl— was transported into a new world by Fanny's acting in 'The Stranger.' Margaret Fuller wrote: "I could scarcely keep from rushing on the stage. All my soul was satisfied. Miss Kemble sank to the earth, her head bowed upon her knee, her white drapery falling in large graceful folds about this broken piece of beautiful humanity, crushed; it was the triumph of the poet actress. I burst into tears." Mr. Hone wrote in his diary: "Fanny Kemble played Mrs. Haller with the most affecting pathos. Probably her last engagement, if the report be true that she is married, or about to be married, to Mr. Pierce Butler of Philadelphia."

By this time rumors had crossed the Atlantic and London was buzzing with conjecture. Only Harriet St. Leger and a few others knew the truth; Fanny was neither married nor engaged, but Pierce Butler was persistent and she might at any time give way. Her family were alarmed, and worried letters flew back and forth across the Atlantic. Charles waited helplessly; too kind to remind Fanny that the family finances would suffer if she married, and too tactful to suggest that she might better wait for a compatriot, or recall various friends who had achieved strawberry leaves. After all, Pierce Butler seemed to be a nice young man and a girl must decide for herself. This was all that Dall could say; but Dall was wise and must have been anxious. Could a girl so undisciplined, so ignorant of life, so dependent on stimulating society and so accustomed to admiration make herself happy in a humdrum American town? Fanny was in love—no doubt of that after Trenton Falls—but would it last? Dall knew that only a great passion would satisfy Fanny; she must have seen that Pierce was weak and might be fickle, and suspected that obstinacy and not constancy accounted for his long pursuit and, like Charles, wished with all her heart that the American contracts could be broken and they could take Fanny home at once. As that was impossible they could only mark time and hope that Fanny would get tired of Pierce, or he of her, before it was too late.

Autumn went by, winter came, Fanny was still in love and so happy that no one seemed to exist except Pierce and herself. Then Dall was taken desperately ill; an injury suffered when the coach upset, unsuspected at the time, became apparent and the doctors said that if she lived she would be an in-

valid. Fanny forgot herself and her happiness and began planning for Dall. Dall hadn't a penny of her own and must be
provided for. As usual Fanny's thoughts turned to literature
rather than acting as the surest way of earning money—
Charles's finances were still too tangled to be depended upon
—and she finally decided to sell her journal to a Philadelphia
publisher who had been trying to convince her that this carelessly written, too frank, private record might with propriety
be given to the public. Mr. Carey's offer was good, and he had
assured her again and again that if the names were left blank
no one's feelings could be hurt, but she could not bring herself to consent until now. Now she needed the money for
Dall; she told Mr. Carey he might have the journal and the
sooner it came out the better.

But, wise or not, her decision came too late. Dall's illness
took a sudden turn for the worse. They were all in Boston;
Fanny was acting, and night after night she had to leave her
aunt—as she had left her father during his long illness—afraid
that Dall might die while she was at the theatre; and the anxiety was greater, for then the family had shared it and now she
was practically alone; Charles was so overcome that he was
useless.

In April Dall died. It was Fanny who arranged the funeral
and chose the grave and prepared for their departure from
Boston—they were to return to New York immediately after
the funeral; Charles could not even pack his own boxes. And
as Fanny, tears running down her cheeks, forced herself to
pack their theatrical wardrobes in the room where Dall lay
dead in her coffin—the wreaths, scarfs, jewels, slippers and
plumed hats that Dall had cared for, the doublets that Dall
had trimmed and the cloaks that Dall had darned and brushed
—her distaste for her profession became revulsion. She hated
her trade and her employers, the cruel public that could make
a girl work on while her heart was breaking, and bitterly regretted hours wasted in amusing strangers that might have
been spent with Dall. Surely, of all the occupations open to a

woman, acting gave the least of "that freedom of mind and body" which, she had long since decided, was "the greatest desideratum of life." Home ties pulled strongly now, and a few days after the funeral she wrote to Harriet:

"Dear Dall has left us. She died in my arms. I have almost cried my eyes out for the last three months. I am working again, and go about my work stunned and bewildered. Dall is buried in a lonely lovely place in Mount Auburn cemetery where Pierce and I used to go and sit together last spring in the early days of our intimacy. I wished her to lie there, for life and love and youth and death have their trysting place at the grave . . . We shall probably be in England on the 10th of July."

But before that letter reached Ireland Fanny had changed her mind. For more than a year she had resisted Pierce's pursuit. Now, weakened by sorrow and loneliness, her resistance broke and she turned to Pierce. Pierce loved her; he offered her a refuge in a stormy world; he offered her more than a refuge. Fanny's hopes were high; she expected as much as Margaret Fuller who believed that in marriage "regions of her being that else had lain sealed in cold obstruction would burst into leaf and bloom and song." She told Pierce she would marry him.

What were Pierce's sensations when Fanny suddenly accepted him? The chase had been so long and his quarry so elusive that he must have been amazed as well as triumphant. Did he experience any misgivings? Did he realize that asking a passionate young genius to become a wife was like asking a leopardess to change her spots and dwindle to "a harmless necessary cat," or wonder whether he were big enough for the job he had undertaken? Probably not. He was too complacent. Philadelphia husbands never had any trouble with their wives. Fanny would soon conform. She would learn which side her bread was buttered—if she didn't, there wouldn't be any butter! It was all quite simple. Pierce did not anticipate any difficulties.

To Charles, Fanny's news must have been distressing. With the date fixed for their departure he had flattered himself that the danger of losing her was over, and although the American tour had been profitable much of the proceeds had been deposited in the United States Bank, Mr. Nicholas Biddle's bank in Philadelphia, which was in difficulties. Fanny knew this, and she had worked so long and so hard for her family that she could not bear to leave them to shift for themselves. Fortunately, her share of the profits was safe in a New Orleans bank, and she decided to make this sum over to her father for his life. That this would leave her with no fortune of her own did not seem to her to matter much. Pierce was rich; when she had spent what she had on hand Pierce would give her some more. Ever since her début she had had money of her own to spend or misspend as she chose. She was not extravagant, but she came of an extravagant family and she had lived in the most luxurious society the modern world had known. Pierce Butler considered himself well off; neither he nor Fanny realized that when London thought in thousands of pounds Philadelphia thought in hundreds of dollars, and he rather liked the idea of having his wife dependent on him for every penny. In short, the rôle of King Cophetua was admirably suited to Pierce, while Fanny, in spite of her varied theatrical experience, had never before been cast for any part resembling that of the Beggar Maid.

Fanny Kemble and Pierce Butler were married by Bishop White in Christ Church, Philadelphia, on the seventh of June, 1834. Next day she returned to New York with her husband to finish her theatrical engagement at the Park Theatre. When, ten days later, she bade farewell to the stage, she was at the height of her powers. Ireland, the annalist of the American stage, calls her "the most intellectual, passionate and original English actress of the age. To the state and dignity of the Kemble school she added the fire and impetuosity of her own original genius; from her mother she inherited a grace and fascination in her comic delineations that no other of the blood of Kemble ever knew. In girlhood she had a dainty lightness of figure; her glorious dark eyes, soft in repose, could with a single glance express the intensest shade of every varying passion. Her triumph in America was complete; she was the acknowledged Queen of Tragedy from Boston to New Orleans, without a rival near her throne. To her, whom all eyes admired, and all tongues praised, wooers of course thronged in—hearts and fortunes were laid at her feet."

CHAPTER XVI

Marriage

"What do they know of love who do not know
He builds his nest upon a windy ledge
Above a precipice?"

—W. B. YEATS.

THE SUMMER was not yet over when Mr. and Mrs. Pierce Butler after an agreeable honeymoon returned to Philadelphia. Philadelphia is not at its best in hot weather, and it was annoying to find that their house at Branchtown—or rather the house that had been lent to Pierce by an aunt—was not ready for them. Fanny had been delighted when Pierce told her that her home was to be in the country and that Butler Place was old as such things went in America. But an old house meant repairs, and several weeks had to be spent in town choosing wall papers and carpets, engaging servants and driving out to the farm, as she preferred to call the place after she had seen it, to hurry the workmen and direct operations. They were staying with Pierce's brother, and Fanny did not like staying with relations; but she was too busy, and too sure of herself, to give much thought to her in-laws or to consider their prejudices. She took admiration for granted and did not suspect that they found her as disconcerting as a flock of domestic fowls would have found a wild, bright-plumaged bird from the tropics. The Butlers were not a Quaker family, they were Unitarians and went to Dr. Furness's church; but they lived in an atmosphere tinged with Quaker thought; a dim atmosphere devoid of high-lights, where all extremes—bright colors, passionate music, strong perfumes, sensuous poetry— were considered vulgar if not wicked. And Fanny was nothing if not extreme. Her in-laws were shocked by her moods, her quick laughter and sudden tears; they deprecated her choice

182

of deep rich colors and expensive fabrics for her new house, and were puzzled by her insistence on a flower garden. The poor girl seemed to think roses more important than potatoes, a piano than a dinner table and a saddle-horse than a cow. As for servants, what did she want of a lady's maid? Scarcely anybody in Philadelphia had a lady's maid; that seamstress she had engaged would not stay, the woman would feel the ignominy of a menial position. As for manners and training, Mrs. Pierce need not expect any free-born American to say *ma'am,* or a cook to cook and a waitress to wait without being taught. Certainly Mrs. Pierce's own manners were often most peculiar; you never knew how she would behave with visitors. The family would be sitting comfortably in the parlor after supper in a peaceful silence except for the buzzing of the mosquitoes around the lamp, for it was too hot for conversation and it was not healthy to talk after a hearty meal; the ladies busy with their fancy work, the gentlemen with their newspapers; Fanny silent, except for an occasional yawn. The bell would ring; she would start and look eagerly at the parlor door until the visitor came in, and then there was no counting on her. It might be one of the very best people in Philadelphia, a judge or a bank president, she would sink back, looking plain and dull, and sit there like a stone, refusing to respond if anyone tried to make her talk about London society, and if she were asked to sing she would say she was tired. But if Mr. Sully, the young man who painted pictures, happened in, or that strange wild, savage sunburned person, Mr. Trelawny, she would spring to her feet and scream with joy. Now, if they wanted her to sing she would dash to the piano and break out into a wild ballad about love or war, so passionate as to be not quite nice, and her cheeks would get red and her eyes would flash and her voice would rise and swell, until you shuddered, wondering what the passers-by in the street would think of such embarrassing sounds. Indeed, it was difficult to believe that Mrs. Pierce had moved in good society in London, as Pierce said she had, for she had no dis-

crimination. She said quite openly that she did not care who
people were so long as they were not bores, and spoke of a
fishwife in Edinburgh as a *friend*. She had no sense of fitness.
She did not realize Philadelphia could tolerate persons like
Sully and Trelawny because Sully's mother was a Middleton,
and Trelawny, in spite of his outlandish ways, was also of
good family. When a Mr. and Mrs. Charles Mathews, a couple
of English actors, arrived in Philadelphia, she actually suggested that they should be invited to dine. This was too much.
Pierce, infatuated though he still was, put his foot down. But
he was kind; he told Fanny he would see that Mr. Mathews
received an invitation to a banquet that he and Penn Smith
were giving in honor of Sheridan Knowles. Fanny said this
wasn't enough, and she went on about this Mr. Mathews's
mother being an old friend of her mother's and of their having gone to France together when they were children, until
Pierce was obliged to remind her that marriage had raised
her to a higher sphere where some of her former associates
could not hope to be admitted. With that she flew into a passion. She told Pierce to his face that he didn't know what he
was talking about, and went on raving about the Kembles
and George IV and the Duke of Devonshire, and that she,
Fanny, had been presented to Queen Adelaide—which nobody believed for a moment—and asking whether kings and
queens and dukes would be received in America—which was
simply silly—and when Pierce tried to explain about Philadelphia society she just flung up her hands, rushed out of the
room and upstairs, and wouldn't come down to dinner. It was
all very very sad. Poor dear Pierce. But what else could a man
expect when he married beneath him?

There was also that annoying matter of the 'Journal,' the
book Fanny had written about America and sold to Carey,
Lee and Blanchard before she decided to get married. Pierce
had hoped it could be withdrawn; but neither Fanny nor the
publishers seemed to realize that what was suitable enough
for Miss Fanny Kemble, the actress, was not at all suitable for

Mrs. Pierce Butler. Fanny just said the book was sold, and the publishers declined to give in. So Pierce had to content himself with correcting the manuscript; he cut out many objectionable passages, such as allusions to slavery and jokes about America, and he also improved the style which was colloquial and often undignified. But far from being grateful for her husband's assistance Fanny seemed to resent it. She could not see that nobody cared how dull the book became provided it did not in any way reflect on the Butlers or Philadelphia society—luckily, the most indiscreet remarks were about New York. In fact, the more he helped her the angrier Fanny got. But Pierce behaved admirably. He kept his temper; he went on quietly correcting and improving, scoring out sentences and supplying dignity, until—without the slightest warning—Fanny flew into a rage. There was another scene. It was all most unpleasant. Poor Pierce! The more the family saw of Fanny, the sorrier they were for Pierce.

Meanwhile, Fanny also was feeling sorry, not for Pierce but for herself. She was bored to death. She wrote to her friend Mrs. Jameson: "You can form no idea—none—none—of the intellectual dearth and drought in which I am existing at present." But she would not acknowledge that her marriage had been a mistake; if marriage had turned out less romantic and her husband less sympathetic than she had expected, it was her own fault, she had expected too much: "No two human beings were ever fashioned absolutely alike . . . My life and all its occupations are of a sober neutral tint, but I do not despair of attracting towards me some of my own kind." But these attempts at philosophy were not very successful and as the visit was prolonged Fanny became increasingly restless and probably increasingly annoying to her in-laws, and everybody in the household from Mr. John Butler to the knife boy must have shared her impatience. But at last the house was ready, and Fanny with her dozens of boxes, her canary, her black squirrel, her maid, six servants and her husband moved out to Branchtown.

By this time she was of course familiar with Butler Place and had recovered from her first disappointment at finding it so unlike what she had expected. Pierce had, quite naturally, described it as a country estate for the house stood in three hundred acres of its own, six miles out of Philadelphia in the heart of the country. But that overvivid imagination of hers had pictured an English country seat. Not a grand place like Oatlands or Heaton, she was not so foolish as to expect a deer park or Italian gardens; she imagined a place like Bannisters, the Fitzhughs' place near Southampton. A house with an air of distinction, well-kept grounds, velvety turf, peacocks, swans floating on a stretch of ornamental water, a lodge where a neat woman would run out curtsying to greet the family carriage as it passed. When Pierce spoke of barns and a dairy she revised this first idea, and willingly, for she thought now of flower-scented Heath Farm where she had stayed as a girl; a farm would provide occupation; she would skim cream, mold pats of butter and gather new-laid eggs.

But Butler Place was not like either Bannisters or Heath Farm. The house was fairly large, and old enough to be spoken of with respect by the neighbors; but it was too like a farmhouse for Fanny to give it the admiration that her in-laws expected. To English eyes it was not even a picturesque farmhouse. Approached by a short avenue of maples, it stood close to the highroad—dusty in summer, muddy in winter and rough at all seasons—with a cornfield on one side and an apple orchard on the other, and farm buildings in the background. There was no lawn, the rough grass around the house was mowed only twice a year; no gravel paths; no garden worth the name, just a part of the kitchen garden squared off by a row of mangy box bushes where flowers grew reluctantly because, according to the gardener, they were "frivolous creatures."

But after all Butler Place was in the country. Farmhouses stood far apart; fields were interspersed with patches of forest and watered by brooks; there would be birds and wild flowers in the spring. She settled down contentedly to enjoy a winter of domesticity and rural pleasures and carry out various improvements she had in mind. For Fanny was determined to be an ideal lady of the manor. The aged poor should bless her as they blessed Lady Wilton; the sick should be nourished with soup; the naked clothed with red flannel petticoats, and the ignorant instructed. Perhaps old world customs might be revived, such as rush-bearings, morris dances and maypoles; the children might be encouraged to dance on the village green, and sing carols at Christmas time—there was so little color in American life! At home too there was much to be done; flowers of course to be planted, bushels and bushels of flowers, fresh butter churned every day, the lawn must be cut twice a week in summer and the paths raked, some of the more objectionable outbuildings ought to be removed . . .

Pierce listened kindly, but he was not encouraging. He pointed out, what Fanny had forgotten, that the place was not really theirs but only lent, and that the farm was "run on shares." This, she discovered, meant that neither its produce nor its laborers were at her command. When she betook herself to the dairy and smilingly begged to be supplied with fresh butter every morning, the dairymaid turned away with a brief: "Don't thee fill theeself up with the notion I'm going to churn butter for thee more than twice a week." Not so much as a hen coop could be removed for fear of hurting old Miss Butler's feelings. She soon found out how absurd the Lady Bountiful dream had been. There were no poor; the sick and aged were cared for by their families; the children were taught in the public school. Visiting, except on an equality, would have been an insult, and her nearest approach to a charitable deed was lending a dress to the farmer's wife who wanted to copy the pattern.

So, more and more, she was driven in on herself for occupation and amusement. She spent hours correcting the proofs of her 'Journal'; tiresome hours, for the book gave her no pleasure now. She tried to forget Pierce's criticisms, but their quarrel over the manuscript had left a sting. Dear Dall, to whom the proceeds had been dedicated, was gone. Reading it over for the last time, the 'Journal' seemed immature, and she wished with all her heart that it could have been withdrawn. When the proofs were done, determined to be a model housewife she took up the study of bookkeeping; but her attention wandered; she found herself weaving romances based on the losses from shipwreck, bankruptcies and fire catastrophes. She mapped out a course of serious reading, though she read alone now, Pierce having lost the taste for literature evinced during his courtship when they had pored for hours together over a volume of very modern poetry—Alfred Tennyson's first—that her brother John had sent her. She rode on horseback; at first one of the horses from the farm and then a saddle-horse of her own, a bright bay with black points, tall and strong, built like a hunter. Fanny wrote to Harriet: "I have christened him Forester after the hero of my play; he grins with delight when I talk to him and pat him, he has high courage and a good temper; I do not like to think what would become of me if anything were to happen to him." Whatever the weather—through snow and rain, mud and dust —Fanny rode; but she rode alone. Pierce seemed to have lost his fondness for riding. Occasionally they would drive in to Philadelphia for a dance, and she still loved dancing, or a dinner party where, now and then, she had a talk with some interesting man, such as Dr. Furness. But there were very few oases in her intellectual desert. When Miss Harriet Martineau, the English writer and reformer, arrived in Philadelphia with her ear-trumpet "formed of a tube of gum-elastic," and a female companion, Fanny went to see her again and again; that Pierce did not approve of Miss Martineau probably lent excitement to the friendship.

There could scarcely have been a stranger contrast. Fanny —young, handsome, a bride, beautifully dressed in the latest fashion, talking too fast, laughing too often—was too vivid to suit the restrained spinster taste of the other with her shrewd

emaciated face, grotesque features, scanty hair strained back
from a high pale dome-like forehead, and angular frame clad
in garments as plain as her face. Fanny's disposition was warm
and generous; Miss Martineau's cold. Fanny's senses were too
easily excited; Miss Martineau was stone deaf, she had no
sense of taste, no sense of smell. Characteristically, she had
gone to America not for pleasure but for self-discipline; fearing to become tainted with luxury, she had left home to mor-
tify the flesh by the inevitable discomforts of travel in a semi-
barbarous land.

However, Harriet Martineau could be a most agreeable
companion. Fanny liked Miss Martineau, but Miss Martineau
did not like Fanny; Miss Martineau despised temperamental
natures; she considered passion vulgar and any display of
emotion ill-bred. So Fanny chatted on, excited at meeting
someone from home and stimulated by her new friend's intellect, and never suspected that Miss Martineau was summing
her up as self-willed, capricious and histrionic, and even
shared Philadelphia's pity for Fanny's husband, for Miss Martineau contrived to combine hatred for man in the abstract
with a coy admiration for men as individuals. But Miss Martineau kept her disapproval to herself, and criticized the
'Journal' proof sheets with so much tact that she contrived
to cut out thirty pages without hurting Fanny's feelings or
showing that she considered it frivolous except for a few remarks on slavery. Slavery was indeed the only serious topic
the two had in common; for although Fanny was deeply religious, the intricacies of dogma seemed to her unimportant,
and with all her longing for personal freedom she remained
uninterested in the cause of women's rights. But Miss Martineau found no lack of response when she spoke of abolition.
Fanny shuddered at tales of cruelty, wished that she might
accompany Miss Martineau to the South and see plantation
life for herself, and felt more keenly than ever her own deg-
radation in being supported by the proceeds of slave labor.
Before her marriage she had been so ignorant of conditions

in the South that she had not realized that owning plantations implied owning slaves, and the discovery that Pierce was a slave-owner had come as a shock. But she repeated to Miss Martineau what Pierce had told her; the slaves on the Butler plantations were happy and carefree and far better clothed and lodged than the peasants of Europe, they loved and reverenced their masters; they did not *want* to be free. Pierce said that if Fanny could see the darkies dancing and singing like children she would realize that the abolitionist tales were lies, or, at best, exaggerations. That story, for instance, of Madame Lalaurie of New Orleans; it was true that the bodies of seven slaves had been found in her cellar tortured to death, but everyone knew that the woman was insane. No sane person kept slaves for the purpose of torturing them. Pierce said that if only the abolitionists would mind their own business everything would be all right. But here Miss Martineau was obliged to differ from Mr. Butler; and Fanny, remembering that her New England friends also differed, could only reiterate that the Butlers were such kind people—uninteresting, inartistic people, but extremely kind—that she must wait to judge them until she had seen their plantations for herself, and promise to do so at the very first opportunity.

But Miss Martineau's talks left Fanny with an uneasy conscience. Her vision of playing Lady Bountiful to the villagers was replaced by another. She saw herself now as a missionary consecrated to the conversion of the blacks; she would teach them to read, instill in their childish minds a desire for freedom, and, in the end, persuade Pierce to set all his slaves free. Pierce was so high-minded; he would see his duty when it was pointed out to him. She did not, of course, keep these sentiments to herself—Fanny never kept anything to herself—and the Butler family must have been heartily tired of Miss Martineau and Miss Martineau's opinions before the lady departed for the South accompanied by her ear-trumpet and her female companion, and taking with her a humming-bird's nest from Fanny's garden as a souvenir of Butler Place.

Fanny missed her; there was no bracing conversation to reward her now for a long dull drive in to town. Time went slowly that winter. Her book came out; when the two thin volumes bound in shiny dark red muslin arrived she experienced a momentary glow of elation; but reaction soon came. Though the effect of the 'Journal' had undoubtedly been anticipated by the publishers it was most surprising to the author. Fanny had sold her diary in order to make money for Dall, never supposing that her girlish comments on American manners and morals would excite more than brief amusement. To her astonishment the book was taken seriously on both sides of the Atlantic. America was angry, England was impressed. American newspapers devoted many pages to the new book, tinged with bitterness for Miss Kemble's scorn of "news-collectors" still rankled; they said she spoke of reporters as if they were insects, and a farce called 'The Bugs' became popular in New York. Edgar Poe contributed a long article to the 'Southern Literary Messenger,' a dull article but respectful in tone; he praised her descriptions of scenery, and averred that to imagine she had *insulted* America was absurd: "There is much sound sense," he wrote, "and unwelcome truth, in her remarks on the situation of married females in our fashionable circles, though more applicable to northern females." He admired her style, except for the use of words and phrases too vulgar for a lady's pen; it was not nice for a lady to write that her "feet were perishing with cold," or that "yesterday began like May, with flowers and sunshine, and ended like December, with the sulks and a fit of crying," and such expressions as *dawdling, gulping* and *pottering* were words that a lady should never use, much less print. Mr. Poe was forced to conclude that the gifted authoress was lacking in delicacy. Many critics likened Miss Kemble to Basil Hall and Mrs. Trollope—hateful names in America! Parodies came out, and books of caricatures illustrating every trivial incident in the 'Journal'; the overturn of the coach with Fanny and her father, Dall and Trelawny strewed about on the ground and Pierce perched on the roof of the vehicle; the Kemble family eating oysters as big as trunks—she had commented on the size of the American oyster; Fanny fondling a Newfoundland puppy larger than a cow. Her visit to Washington was parodied in 'Miss Fanny Thimble's Journal,' and a skit in the form of a play satirized her account of a bazaar in Boston: "Enter Miss Fanny Capulet," it ran, "attended by gentlemen from Philadelphia. She exclaims 'This oppressive crowd!' Twenty-five gentlemen offer her their arms. She disappears. She reappears: 'Be so good as to inquire the price of that India shawl. Quick! Abridge my sufferings!' She lets her purse fall, the assembled crowd falls on its knees to pick it up." And so on, for a dozen pages that probably seemed very funny to Boston at the time.

But society, as a whole, was too incensed to enjoy the 'Journal.' Everybody read it, everybody found it entertaining; but most people were shocked, many thought it vulgar, a few were hurt. For the omission of proper names that Fanny had imagined would rob her remarks of their sting only increased the excitement, and the 'Journal' became the cross-word puzzle-book of its day. Who was "the bright youth who rode very like an ass on horseback?" Who gave the dinner party where they had no finger-bowls? Could "the wild-eyed, flowing-haired, white-waistcoated" admirer be meant for Arthur Middleton? And when the conundrums were answered the fat was in the fire; Fanny, at last, realized what she had done. She had hurt people who had been kind to her; people such as the Hones, whom she really liked.

Unfortunately, few people were as tolerant as Mr. Hone. After reading the 'Journal,' he wrote in his diary: "Here is all the light gossip, the childish prejudice, the hasty conclusions from first impressions, in which the diary of an imaginative young traveller in a new country would naturally abound, but her remarks on the private habits of persons who received her with hospitality are in bad taste. Its publication now that she has become the wife of an American gentleman is injudi-

cious in the extreme." His allusions to the memorable dinner
party were good-humored, and he had the best of Fanny when
it came to finger-bowls: "We have them in the house," he said
calmly, "but we do not use them, for we do not like the foreign habit of rinsing the mouth and squirting the polluted
water back into the vessel, which was formerly the habit in
this country and still prevails abroad."

In England the 'Journal,' like all criticisms of America,
sold well, and was duly noted in the diaries of the time.
Charles Greville wrote: "Went to Charles Kemble's in the
evening. Kemble told me he had never read his daughter's
book until it appeared in print, that it was full of sublime
things and of vulgarities. Her mother said she 'was divided
between admiration and disgust, threw it down six times and
as often picked it up.'" Henry Greville wrote: "Called on
Mrs. Charles Kemble, a most entertaining woman, shrewd
and droll; she told me all the circumstances of Fanny's marriage. I am reading the Journal, it is very amusing, full of
eloquent passages descriptive of scenery and interspersed with
some charming poetry." Little Princess Victoria was "not
amused;" she and Poe seem to have thought alike, for she
wrote in her diary: "The Journal is certainly very pertly and
oddly written. One would imagine by the style that the author
must be very pert and not well-bred; for there are so many
vulgar expressions in it. It is a great pity that a person endowed with so much talent as Mrs. Butler really is, should
publish a book which is so full of trash and nonsense, which
can only do her harm. I stayed up till 20 minutes past 9."

By now Fanny was aware that the 'Journal' had "done her
harm;" she was tired of explaining and apologizing, and of
trying to keep her temper when Pierce said, "I told you so!"
Even Philadelphia, though given less cause for complaint
than New York, was annoyed to find terrapin lightly spoken
of, and Miss Willing did not enjoy being reproved for asking
her guests to dance on carpet. However, after a while most of
the tantalizing blanks had been filled in and Mrs. Butler and

her 'Journal' ceased to be the chief topic of conversation at American tea tables from Boston to New Orleans. But life at Butler Place probably seemed flatter than ever when the commotion died down.

It was mid-winter and the roads almost impassable. The carriage horses were seldom taken out; day after day went by, each the counterpart of the last and each as flat as a pricked balloon. When Pierce came home in the afternoon—he had business in town—and found his wife standing in the window of her drawing-room looking out at the bare landscape, watching gray rain slant across brown cornfields, or snow whiten the highroad, did he guess that the song she was humming under her breath—Fanny had a tiresome way of humming and singing all the time—was an old song of Poitier's heard long ago in Paris? As she sang:

"Ji! Ji! mariez-vous,
Mettez-vous dans la misère.
Ji! Ji! mariez-vous,
Mettez-vous la corde au cou,"

did he ask himself if she were happy? Probably not. His wife had everything that a wife needed; food, clothes and shelter.

So it annoyed him when Fanny, in her extremity, began teasing to be taken to England for a visit. They had often spoken of going abroad, but Pierce did not want to go now. He was not sure that he wanted to go at all. If Fanny's London friends were as grand as she said they were he might feel at a disadvantage, an uncomfortable sensation for a Butler and a Philadelphian, and if they were not—well, Pierce flattered himself that no one could call him a snob, but he did admit a preference for good society! He tried to put her off; he said he couldn't afford it and he was too busy. But she was persistent and he still loved her—off and on; finally he promised to take her to England in the summer, if nothing turned up to prevent. Something did. Fanny found she was going to

have a baby; a long voyage was out of the question. The Butler connection heaved a sigh of relief; now, at last, Pierce's
restless wife would settle down!

The baby, a girl, arrived in the spring. Fanny had wished
for a boy; "The lot of women," she wrote to Harriet, "is seldom happy, owing I think to mistakes in female education. I
cannot believe that the just Creator intended one part of his
creatures to lead the sort of lives that many women do, or that
the agony attendant upon the entrance of a new creature into
life was ordained, but is rather the consequence of our abuse
of our constitutions and infringement of God's laws. One
item alone—the tight stays, tight shoes, tight garters, tight
gloves, tight waistbands, tight armholes and tight bodices, of
which we are accustomed to think so little—must in many ways
affect health. American women soon lose their looks and
health; they never go out without veils, they pinch their
pretty little feet cruelly and, of course, cannot walk . . . I am
sorry to find that my physical courage has been shaken by my
confinement. Our horses ran away the other day. I had the
child with me, and after getting her safely out of the carriage,
I shook from head to foot, for the first time in my life, from
fear."

But the baby was a delight; a nice pink and white baby
with bright yellow hair; they christened her Sarah and called
her Sally. Life at Butler Place was no longer flat; idling away
one's time with a baby was very different from idling alone;
it was spring, there were wild flowers in the woods and daffo-
dils in the garden. When summer came and Philadelphia siz-
zled in the heat, Pierce consented to take his family to the
Berkshires to spend a month with the Sedgwicks. The visit
passed off pleasantly, for everybody, knowing that Mr. Butler
was a slave-holder, contrived to avoid the ticklish subject of
abolition, often with difficulty for feeling ran high. The previous summer had seen riots in New York and Mr. Hone's
diary had noted: "The diabolical spirit which prompted this
outrage is not quenched, and I apprehend we shall see more

of it." Now, in the summer of 1835, he wrote: "The abolitionists are certainly engaged in a most mischievous undertaking, which may bring destruction on their own heads and
civil war into the bosom of our hitherto happy country, the
remedy is worse than the disease. I do not choose to surrender
the power of executing justice into the hands of the slave-
owners of South Carolina." New England was less uncertain.
There was abolition in the air, and though Fanny refrained
from argument she was uncomfortable; an inner voice whispered that slavery was wicked and that it was wrong to live
from the proceeds of slave labor.

However, it was a happy month; she was devoted to the
Sedgwicks, and the climate agreed with Sally. When Pierce
took the family home in the autumn his wife was looking
splendidly well and seemed contented. So it was disappointing that before the winter was half over—a severe winter,
snow mountains high, Fanny and the baby shut indoors for
weeks at a time—she should begin pining for England. Pierce
still loved her—at least, when other men admired his wife he
was conscious of the pride of possession; he promised that he
would take her abroad in the spring, if nothing turned up to
prevent. Again something did. It almost seemed as if Providence were watching over Pierce's affairs for, in the spring,
old Miss Butler died. As Pierce and his brother John were her
heirs there was much business to attend to and even Fanny
realized that it was impossible to leave America.

Unfortunately for the peace of the household Pierce had
not only inherited Butler Place but, with his brother, was
now directly responsible for the management of the Georgia
plantations, and the problem at once became too personal to
be ignored by any wife with "northern" sentiments, especially
a woman of Fanny's romantic nature. When a member of the
family remarked that if cotton raising in Georgia became un-
profitable they might move to Alabama where a vast fortune
could be made with slave labor, and went on to ask Fanny
how she would like living in the wilds, her answer brought a

shiver from the family group. She cried that she would go anywhere, suffer any privations; she would gladly freeze, fry, starve, provided she were given the opportunity of "at once placing our slaves on a more humane and Christian footing." There was a moment's appalled silence. Then everybody began talking about something else. Poor Pierce! He had married beneath him; gossip said that Fanny had a terrible temper and that she denied a wife's first duty was obedience; she had no tact and had written a horrid book. Sad, very sad; but nothing—nothing—compared to this last shameless avowal. Fanny Butler was an abolitionist!

Pierce went about his preparations for a necessary visit to the South with his brother John in a worried frame of mind, for Fanny wanted to go too. Her teasing to be taken to England had been tiresome enough; this last demand was too absurd for discussion, but it took a long time to convince her. Finally she was forced to agree that little Sally could not be left behind and that it would be unsafe to take a baby to such a comfortless country. Pierce on his side realized that it was cruel to ask her to spend the winter entirely alone in the country, and he was by this time so weary of discussion that when she asked to be allowed to spend the winter in England with her father he consented and promised to come and fetch her back in the spring. So Pierce and John Butler went to Georgia, and Fanny sailed for Liverpool with little Sally and her nurse Margery, so overjoyed at the prospect of seeing England again and all her friends that she could for a while forget the vexed question of slavery and her own duty as the wife of a planter.

CHAPTER XVII

Presentiment

"Presentiment is that long shadow on the lawn
Indicative that suns go down;
The notice to the startled grass
That darkness is about to pass."

—EMILY DICKINSON.

LONDON SEEMED unbelievably gay after America. It was so long since Fanny had seen crowds of well dressed people bent on amusing themselves; elegant carriages painted blue, pink and scarlet, with coats-of-arms, gold-embroidered hammer-cloths and servants in smart liveries; handsome shops, and street corners bright with the heaped baskets of flower girls. It was such fun to have a baby, the first grandchild, to show her family; they were enchanted with Sally; everybody was enchanted with Sally. It was fun to talk nonsense—nobody in America ever talked nonsense—and to say the first thing that came into one's head without remembering American prejudice; enchanting to meet all one's old friends and find them unchanged except that the Leveson-Gowers had become Egertons, Earl and Countess of Ellesmere, and to be told that she herself had not changed a particle. Sydney Smith insisted that the American husband was a myth! She was suffering from an hallucination and he offered to "exorcise" her; and Fanny held up her hand with its wedding ring and cried "But, oh! the *baby!*" and his expression sent the dinner table into shrieks of laughter. Life went with a rush now; invitations came in dozens and all were accepted with girlish enthusiasm —except one: "Who do you think," she wrote to Harriet, "Adelaide and I dined with last Friday? You will never guess, so I might as well tell you—the Cravens! The meetings in this world are strange things. She sought me with apparent cordiality and I had no reason whatever for avoiding her. She is handsome and amiable, with the simple good breeding of a French great lady [Mrs. Augustus Craven was Pauline de la Ferronays, author of 'Le Récit d'une Soeur'] and the serious earnestness of a devout Roman Catholic. They are going to Lisbon, where he is attaché at the Embassy."

That Adelaide was often invited to her parties, as on this occasion at the Cravens, added immeasurably to Fanny's enjoyment of the winter's gaiety. For the sisters, now that the difference in their ages no longer counted, were in perfect sympathy and discovered that they would rather be together than with any one else in the world. Adelaide was tall and handsome, a Kemble in face and figure, and her voice gave promise of such a brilliant future that the family were planning and hoping for her as they had once planned and hoped for Fanny. But Fanny was not envious; one small Sally, she told herself, was worth more than a thousand careers, and she could discuss Adelaide's prospects with as much pride as her parents. Another family topic of that year was Charles's retirement from the stage. Of his farewell, Fanny wrote to Harriet: "The house was immensely full, the feeling of regret and good will universal and our own excitement, as you may suppose, very great. My father bore it all far better than I had anticipated, and I hope that his occupation as licencer of plays may prevent his feeling the loss of professional excitement, the dram he has taken nightly for more than forty years."

The most important public events were the death of King William and the accession of Victoria. Fanny went with Lord Lansdowne to see the new queen meet her houses of parliament—Lady Lansdowne, as Mistress of the Robes, was one of the group around the throne—and shared the universal emotion, a wave of sympathy and pity, that swept through the crowd as their sovereign came stepping in. For the little Queen was so *very* little. She looked like a child as she stood there, with her small pink face, candid eyes and serious expression; a graceful child with a slender figure and beautiful hands and arms, and an exquisite speaking voice. Fanny wrote to Harriet: "I have never heard any words more musical in their gentle distinctness than the 'My Lords and Gentlemen' which broke the breathless stillness of the illustrious assembly; it would be impossible to hear a more excellent utterance than that of the queen's English, by the English Queen."

Yet with all that was going on in private and in public Fanny, to her surprise, found time to write. She had felt no desire to write during the past year, there was too much leisure at Butler Place. Now, stimulated by the swift movement of events all about her, imagination revived and in odd half hours she wrote 'An English Tragedy,' which she considered "the only good thing I ever wrote," a play founded on an incident in the life of Lord de Ros, a notorious roué who had recently finished himself by cheating at cards. There were many bitter jokes at his expense. One wit composed an epitaph: "Here lies Henry, twenty-second Baron de Ros, in joyful expectation of the last trump," and Lord Alvanley remarked that if he ever called on the fellow he would "mark the card so that de Ros would know it was an honor." Charles had heard the incident in question mentioned at a dinner party at Lady Blessington's and spoke of it to Fanny when he came home; she sketched the outline of her play and wrote the principal scene the same night before she went to bed.

So Fanny was busy as well as happy and her contentment would have been perfect except for one flaw; uncertainty. She had left America with the understanding that Pierce would soon join her in London; but what with his tendency to procrastination and important affairs—he was a delegate to the Convention which was revising the constitution of Pennsylvania—the weeks went by, and summer came and was half over before he was ready to sail, and then he wrote that the Convention had been adjourned and he would have only a month in England. It was terribly disappointing; she had been planning amusements for him, she wanted him to meet

all her friends and have them meet him; but she hurried off
with Sally to Liverpool—Pierce would never forgive her if
they were not there when he arrived—and waited fourteen
interminable days. Calm weather delayed the ship and Pierce's
month was cut down to a fortnight.

But they crowded all that was possible into those two weeks.
A few days were spent at Bannisters, a few with the Dacres at
the Hoo. But an invitation from the Lansdownes to Bowood
had to be declined—Pierce would have liked to be able to tell
people at home that he had stayed at Bowood—and there was
no time for a visit to Sydney Smith at Combe Florey. The last
hours were a frantic medley of shopping, packing and farewells; then they were back in Liverpool again, waiting to
sail.

Pierce had enjoyed himself; he had moved in the best society and everybody had treated him with consideration. But
something had rubbed him the wrong way; perhaps he was
tired of playing second fiddle to his wife, or he may have been
shocked to find that while English girls were strictly chaperoned, married women were given more freedom than in
America; anyhow, he decided that it was high time he asserted
himself. When they reached the quay they found the ship
lying off shore and the captain standing disconsolately on the
wharf. There was no wind; it was Sunday, the captain said he
doubted whether he could get a steamboat to tow his ship out,
and walked away. Fanny begged to be allowed to return to
the 'Star and Garter'; but Pierce was firm. He bundled his
family into a small boat; they boarded the ship, stowed themselves away in their cabins—and waited. The wind did not
come up, the captain did not return. They waited all day.
Then the captain came back and the wind came up, but it was
the wrong kind of wind. The ship dragged her anchor and all
night they tossed and pitched. Everybody was seasick. In the
morning Pierce bundled all his family ashore again. When
they finally sailed everybody was cross. It was not a good beginning for a rough voyage of thirty-seven days; long before

they reached New York Fanny and the baby were worn to shadows.

That winter Sally had scarlet fever; one of her tonsils became enlarged and the doctor said she would suffocate unless it were removed. As the operation was not usual in Great Britain, Fanny described it to Harriet: "With children," she wrote, "they use a double-barreled silver tube through which two wires are passed, making a loop which is tightened around the tonsil so as to destroy its vitality, and left for twenty-four hours projecting from the patient's mouth, causing some pain and extreme inconvenience. Then the tube is removed and the tonsil left to rot off. Our physician said the functions of the tonsils were not understood, but that removal did not affect the breathing, speaking or swallowing, and as the baby could not be allowed to choke, we submitted to the inevitable. The medical mode of treatment here seems to me frightfully severe, and must often be fatal to people so delicate as the Americans. All the household have had violent sore throats. I had a hundred leeches applied to mine; they did little good, and enraged me beyond expression."

But Sally got well, and spring came at last and found Butler Place ready to burst into bloom. Fanny had planted hundreds of trees and shrubs, the garden had been cut into a more interesting shape and stuffed with plants, a double row of lemon trees in pots ornamented the entrance. One sunny day, in that May of 1838, she wrote to Harriet: "I am sitting on the veranda, or piazza as they call it here, watching Sally in a buff coat zigzagging about the lawn. It is a late spring; hardly a fruit tree is in blossom, but looking abroad over the landscape I can detect here and there faint symptoms of that exquisite green haze that hangs like a halo over the distant woods at this season." A few days later, on Sally's birthday and at the same hour when Sally had been born, Fanny's second child came into the world, a girl; she was christened Frances Kemble.

Spring-time peace did not extend beyond the garden. There

were riots in Philadelphia; a mob broke up an abolition meeting and burned down the hall. Mr. Hone's diary had noted not long before: "The terrible abolition question is fated, I fear, to destroy the union of the states"; now he wrote: "This dreadful subject gains importance every day." Many families, North and South, were in mourning, for the steamer 'Pulaski' had been lost with nearly everyone on board. Butler Place had its lesser tribulations; little Sally caught the measles, and summer brought the hottest weather Philadelphia had ever known.

In August Pierce took his family to cool off at Rockaway, a new and very fashionable summer resort on Long Island. They revived; but Fanny was not happy. The huge wooden hotel that stood staring across rough sand hills to the sea was full to overflowing, the food was wretched, and far too many bathers were crowded into the omnibus that crawled back and forth through deep sand to the beach; there were only two small bath houses and she had to dress and undress in the company of many strange women. But the sea air was good for the children and she met a few old friends. One meeting was noted in Mr. Hone's diary: "I had an interesting conversation," he wrote, "with Mrs. Butler, who has seldom visited New York since the publication of her Journal. I was never very seriously offended at what she said, though I thought it a pity that so brilliant a woman should have given to the world her inconsiderate girlish remarks, and as soon as she entered the room, I seated myself by her side, told her I was happy to renew an acquaintance which had given me much pleasure, and danced with her. In the course of conversation, she said to me, with great earnestness: 'Mr. Hone, I cannot express to you how happy you have made me by the notice you have taken of me on this occasion. Believe me, I am extremely grateful.' The tear which stood in her flashing eye convinced me that this highly gifted woman possesses that warmth of heart for which I have never failed to give her credit."

It is doubtful if the "interesting conversation" that evening at Rockaway touched on abolition for Mr. Hone would not have considered it a topic to be discussed with the wife of a slave holder. But the question could not often be side-stepped now at the North—the South never mentioned the "institution" in polite society—and Fanny was not allowed to forget it. Her conscience gave her little peace. She had been taught that the path of duty was always made clear for the Christian soul, but now it seemed to fork. Her conscience, and Dr. Channing, said that slavery was wrong, Pierce said it was right. She was too intelligent to agree with her cousin Fanny Arkwright, that "a wife owed her husband unquestioning obedience because a man would have to answer for his wife's soul at the Day of Judgment," or with Mrs. Norton, who declared: "I believe in the natural superiority of man as I do in the existence of a God. The natural position of a woman is inferiority to man. Amen. That is a thing of God's appointing, not of man's choosing . . . I never pretended to the wild and ridiculous theory of equality." But Fanny did honestly believe that the husband was the head of the house in all temporal matters, such as the source of the family income. On the other hand, in spiritual matters a husband had no jurisdiction, and slavery was sinful; therefore the question became spiritual. In this dilemma even the Bible failed as a guide for both North and South quoted the Bible. One cleric insisted that if slaves had been necessary to society, slaves would have been created to tend and dress the Garden of Eden, whereas Adam had been expressly told to do the gardening himself. Another announced that the lashing of slaves was justifiable because Christ had driven the money-changers out of the temple with a whip of small cords. Many preachers spoke of compromise and of consequences. But Fanny loathed compromise; there were no halftones in her landscape, night was night and day was day, and Joan of Arc could not have been more contemptuous of consequences. Fanny would have lived on bread and water to free the slaves. She would

have died for her husband and children. Unfortunately, nobody wanted her either to live or die; all her family asked of
her was to sit still and hold her tongue! They might as well
have asked the sea to stop roaring!

A month spent in Lenox that autumn did little to quiet her
uneasiness. It began pleasantly, riding, driving and picnicking
with Mary and Fanny Appleton, who were also staying at the
Red Inn, and ended in sorrow; Fanny heard that her mother
was dead. Mrs. Charles Kemble had died rather suddenly
while she was staying in a cottage in Surrey she had inherited
from Mrs. Whitelock. Fanny was heart-broken, overwhelmed
with grief and homesick longing for her own country and her
own people, and thankful that she was with the Sedgwicks,
her most intimate friends in America, especially Elizabeth, in
her way as sympathetic as Adelaide.

But even deep grief could not deaden her anxiety as to the
rights and wrongs of slavery. Whenever she and Elizabeth
Sedgwick met they talked about the Georgia plantations and
Fanny's responsibility and, as they talked, one thing became
clear; Fanny must go to Georgia. Reports were contradictory;
she must see before she could judge. Having judged she could
act: spread her wings and flutter about the plantation playing
"ministering angel," a part in which she had long wished to
see herself. She would instruct the blacks, she would exhort
and convert the whites . . . Fanny returned to Philadelphia
on fire with zeal; if Pierce went to Georgia that winter, he
should not go alone!

To her surprise her plan met with less opposition than she
had anticipated—there had been no question of her going to
Georgia the previous winter because of the new baby. Now,
when she expressed a wish to see the South, the family hesitated. Either John or Pierce must go, and John did not want
to; when he said that the warm climate would be good for
Pierce's rheumatism the family agreed, and if Pierce went
perhaps Fanny ought to go along to make him comfortable.
There was still some talk of possible risk for the children's

health and the fatigue of the long journey. She was warned of many discomforts—the overseer's small house to live in; no fresh meat or white flour; salt pork and corn meal; dirty, shiftless, colored servants; no society, not one white person to speak to on the rice island except the overseer . . . Fanny declared her willingness to undergo fatigue, discomfort and solitude, and the family told each other that plantation life would be good for her; when she saw the darkies laughing and singing at their work she would realize that they *liked* being slaves and that slavery was a beneficent institution ordained of God. So, at length, it was decided. Pierce told Fanny to pack up; she and the two children and Margery might go with him to Georgia.

CHAPTER XVIII

Butler's Island

"Through torrid tracts with fainting steps they go,
Where wild Altama murmurs to their woe;
Where at each step the stranger fears to wake
The rattling terrors of the vengeful snake."

—GOLDSMITH.

IT WAS late December before the Butlers started on the thousand-mile journey to Georgia for Pierce's habit of procrastination had delayed them, and bitter cold was added to the usual discomfort of travelling in America; the Susquehanna was frozen over and the steamboat had to cut her way through thick ice. In Virginia they found warmer weather and here Fanny got her first glimpse of slavery. The slaves looked as she had expected them to look; dirty, lazy and reckless. At every station they gathered as the train came in; with loud laughing cries they would point to little Sally, praise her yellow hair and rosy cheeks, lift a pickaninny up to the car window and offer her, giggling, to "little Missis" for a waiting maid. And Sally would nod and smile and show her dimples; she was only three but old enough to enjoy admiration.

Ice and snow left behind, the travellers suffered from heat and lack of air. The earlier type of railway carriage had been replaced by a long narrow car with seats running cross-ways and an aisle down the middle where a cast-iron stove breathed out heat and coal gas. Restless children ran about, tobacco chewers spat at their ease, noisy vendors of cake and fruit pushed in and out; there was no ventilation whatever, Fanny, half suffocated, could only pray that Sally and the baby would survive, and marvel at her fellow travellers' tolerance of dreadful smells and apparent enjoyment of the din and jostling that played such havoc with her nerves.

But this was an old story, not until they were in North Carolina did Fanny begin to suspect that she had never tasted the full horror of American travel. All day the train had been crawling like a discouraged caterpillar through a fire-scarred country, robbed of natural beauty by the railroad and not yet civilized; there was not a single town; the few farms looked starved. Sometimes the road skirted cypress swamps where the trees thrust hideous purplish knees up through stagnant water as if trying to meet their overshadowing branches. Sometimes it ran through arid pine barrens, less serpent-haunted but as dreary as the swamps. At length they crossed the Roanoke and crawled on. It was dark now; at midnight the train stopped. The railroad was not yet finished; the passengers must disembark and go on by stage coach. In darkness streaked with the red flare from pine-knot torches held high by grinning negroes, they crept down out of the train and reached a cleared space in the forest where three coaches waited beside a huge bonfire ringed about by more grinning negroes squatting on their hams or lying about on the ground, their eyeballs and teeth gleaming white in the firelight. It was cold, the coaches were crowded, no one slept except the children; even the children stirred now and then, frightened, as the coach went splashing through deep water or rocked perilously on the corduroy road. All night the coach splashed and rocked; at last as daybreak whitened the sky they reached Stansborough, a single lone house in deep woods; breakfasted on eggs swimming in black grease and sour milk; and went on. At the River Neuse the coaches stopped. The bridge was unsafe, the passengers must cross it on foot. They all got out; the women, with the children in their arms and Pierce steadying them, shivered out on the rotten structure that swayed high above the river, stepping lightly and rapidly, trying not to see the swirling water that gleamed through the crevices. At last they were across; the coaches had followed them; they got in and went on, through deep sand now, and reached the railway at sunset. The train had not arrived; the passengers sat in the

coaches and waited . . . There was not a house in sight but as
they waited country people, "poor whites," came wandering
in from the woods; forlorn, fierce creatures, coarsely and fantastically dressed, drawn by curiosity, hoping to see with their
own eyes the queer "hot water carriages" that had already
passed twice, puffing fire and smoke, along the iron rails and,
it was reported, might come again. In the meantime here was
another spectacle almost as exciting, these coach loads of
strangers, rich white folks from the North dressed in fine
clothes, with boxes and bundles strapped on at the back of
the coach. Like suspicious cattle the "poor whites," attended
by a fringe of negroes, padded round and round the clearing
staring dumbly, all the men chewing and spitting, all the
women "dipping snuff" . . . Twilight fell, a cutting wind
sprang up; the men passengers lighted a fire and stood around
it discussing the situation, for the night could not be spent in
the open. Someone recalled a farm about a mile away; the
owner had been a colonel in the Revolution, he would give
them shelter. Fortunately, his house stood close to the railroad tracks; the women and children were lifted on to a truck
that stood on the rails, the luggage was piled around them,
negroes were commandeered to push; off they went, the men
passengers bringing up the rear on foot. For half an hour they
trundled on through the darkness. It seemed to Fanny that
she had reached the edge of creation as she sat there, watching
the landscape darken to night, cowering among the trunks
with Sally in her arms, Margery hugging the baby, while the
wind howled in the tree tops and the sweating negroes grunted
and groaned, shouting encouragement as they pushed across a
ravine spanned by a skeleton bridge, yelling with triumph
when the danger was past . . . Lights at last, twinkling ahead;
a house. The truck had outrun the walkers; Fanny clambered
down, and led her detachment up to an open door. A white-
haired, red-faced old gentleman sat dozing by the fire that
roared up an enormous chimney. The room was spacious, its
ceiling crisscrossed with rafters, furnished with a bed, an old

case-clock and a few rush-bottomed chairs; guns and powder-horns hung on pegs; the shelves were cluttered with medicine bottles, bunches of dried herbs, tools and turkey-feather fans. The Colonel welcomed the ladies politely; the other passengers arrived; all were invited to draw up to the fire. Negro boys and girls ran aimlessly about, bringing milk and home-made wine. The Colonel promised his guests a good supper. The blazing pine knots snapped and crackled; Fanny's spirits rose; she laughed and talked with her host, encouraging him to recount his war-time exploits. It seemed that this gallant old patriarch had fought side by side with General Washington! Fanny was impressed; less impressed when she discovered that he was patriarchal in more ways than one; a mulatto girl told her with pride that several of the slaves were his children. The long heralded supper appeared; moldy cheese, stale biscuits, bad butter, watery tea—and the Colonel smilingly demanded fifty cents apiece!

Still hungry they boarded the train; another sleepless night and they were in Wilmington—the first town since Suffolk, Virginia. It was before dawn and piercingly cold; there was no conveyance to take them to the inn a mile away. Carrying the children, lighted only by the winter stars, they made their way along the banks of the Cape Fear River. Mount Misery lay on the opposite shore—appropriate names Fanny thought, as they reached their destination. Uneatable food, no baths, only two beds for several women. But nothing mattered now except sleep; she gave Margery and the children one bed, flung herself thankfully on a mattress on the floor, and slept like a log.

The worst was over now; a comfortable steamboat took them to Charleston, and Fanny's letter to Harriet ended cheerfully: "We bumped on the Charleston bar on the morning of Christmas Day . . . The city is highly picturesque and although pervaded with an air of decay, 'tis a genteel infirmity, as might be that of a distressed elderly gentlewoman. It has none of the smug mercantile primness of the northern

cities, but a look of state, as of quondam wealth and importance, a little gone down in the world, yet remembering its
former dignity . . . Every house seems built to the owner's
particular taste; and in one street you seem to be in an old
English town, and in another some continental city of France
or Italy." The inhabitants as well as the houses pleased her;
they seemed to have more individuality than other Americans
she had met; there was a flavor of aristocracy in Charleston
society—Margery remarked that "they were the haughtiest
looking people she had ever seen;" the ladies who came to
call were charming, and everybody seemed to feel an easy confidence in themselves and their surroundings that one seldom
found in the North. But one saw more black faces than white
in the streets; at nine o'clock a curfew—drums beating, bells
tolling—called the negroes back to their quarters, and a new
guard house, very large for so small a town, hinted that with
all their self confidence the whites were taking no risks and
realized the danger of a vast slave population.

Then came Savannah, the Pulaski House, and delicious hot
baths. One more night in a tiny steamboat—the ninth night
since leaving home—and at sunrise they reached the coast of
Georgia, a sparkling sea, low reedy shores; a river, the Altamaha; a cluster of buildings, Doboy, and two ships lying at
anchor, one flying the Irish harp and the other the Union
Jack, a homesick elation in Fanny's heart. More reedy shores,
miles and miles of low reedy shores; forests of withered canes
rattling in the breeze, sedges whispering; twisting and looping
with the sinuous curves of inlet and creek, the boat wandered
on; reached another cluster of houses, Darien.

As the steamboat bumped against the wharf and Pierce and
his family emerged from the cabin and stepped on deck, a
shout came from the water where two pretty rowboats waited
manned by Negroes. Their master had come; his slaves greeted
him with ecstatic yells and whistles, bursts of jolly laughter,
and cries of "Oh Massa! How you do, Massa? Oh Missis! Oh
lily Missis! me too glad to see you!" Black faces glistened,

white teeth gleamed, eyeballs rolled, black hands seized the children, lifted them down; Fanny and Margery were helped into one boat, the luggage was piled in the other. Pierce nodded and smiled, gave orders. Black shoulders heaved, black arms pulled at the oars, the boats moved out into the stream, an improvised song of welcome rang out across the sunshiny water keeping time to the oars.

More low reedy shores, a vast sheet of water, but no glimpse of the blue sea; the sea shut out now by a strange, low-lying, yellow land of mud flats, swamps and innumerable islands. Islands that lay steaming under the hot sun, half submerged in the river, like amphibious monsters made of mud and sand and water, uncertain of their destiny, forever changing, sliding down, dissolving, becoming one with the Altamaha; itself so heavy with mud that it too was forever changing, giving here, robbing there, eating up a swamp, building a new island, as it made its way, turbid and relentless to the sea, streaked the blue with tawny yellow and was lost.

A strange sad wild landscape, Fanny said to herself, as she sat there in the boat, gazing out over the water of the vast river; so strange that it seemed unreal. She herself felt unreal; as if she might lose her hold on life, slide out from civilization and dissolve in barbarism. All the world one monotonous savage pattern now, black figures against a yellow background. Black. Only black was in harmony with the setting. What were white people doing here at the world's end? Pierce, herself, Sally so pink and white, dear good Margery with the tiny white baby? . . . She drew a breath of relief, they were across the river and had pushed into a creek overhung with glistening green, but it was only a brief respite from the savage pattern and sun dazzle; the creek became a canal, the "General's Cut," the canal dug, they said, in one night by General Oglethorpe's men escaping from the Spaniards—Oglethorpe, first British governor of Georgia, disciple of Wesley, who had forbidden slavery in Georgia. An ugly canal walled with dykes of mud. Out again into the river, another branch of the many-

armed Altamaha. The slaves gave a shout, Pierce pointed—
Butler's Island! Fanny stared at the island that was to be her
home; the same monotony of outline and color, a low shore
of sand and mud and sedge; a building, the steam rice-mill;
a wharf.

The steersman raised a conch shell to his lips and blew a
mighty blast—Fanny thought of Scottish clans in by-gone days,
summoned to the fray—and at once the wharf became black
with moving figures, others came hurrying, they gathered like
flies on a cake. It was Sunday, and every man, woman and
child on the plantation could join in welcoming the master;
as the boat drew near they milled round and round like
dancing dervishes, jumped up and down, sang, laughed, and
clapped their hands in a wild ecstasy of joy; cheering their
king and queen, shouting hosannas to the god-like beings who
had condescended to visit their worshippers. The boat touched
the wharf; a hundred black hands seized the prow, the slaves
fought for the privilege of assisting the master to alight. The
family stepped on shore and was surrounded; the centre of a
jostling yelling mob Fanny and Margery stood swaying, frightened by the confusion, trying to lift the children out of reach
of those over-affectionate black hands, hands that yearned to
touch and fondle. It was impossible; a timid finger would
poke the baby and feel of her dress; bolder souls would kiss
her feet. They kissed Fanny's hands, kissed Margery's hands,
stroked Fanny's velvet pelisse with grunts of awe, and gave
out yelps of admiration at Sally's pink and white beauty.
Pierce shouted to the overseer; he came running, the slaves
were driven back, but they closed in behind as the family
made its way up the path to the house. A gaunt negress broke
through the lines, snatched at Fanny and embraced her,
snatched at Margery; then she too was driven back. The house
seemed very far away, at last it was reached, they were in, the
door was slammed shut. Fanny dropped into a chair, half
laughing, half crying; of all the crowds she had ever encountered this was the worst! Chuckling laughter, the delighted

cackle of many voices, sounded from outside and at every window a dozen black grinning faces peered in . . . When a little later Fanny ventured out for a stroll they were waiting for her, with their strokings and fondlings. She tried in vain to shake them off and hurried home. Not until nightfall did the crowd disperse, satiated with sight-seeing.

That day was a foretaste of what was to come; Fanny was to find that the most trying feature of her lonely island life was its lack of solitude and quiet. All day long the steam rice-mill throbbed and the darkies chattered. Whenever she went out of doors a few pickaninnies were sure to spy her out and follow her wherever she walked. The house was too small for privacy. There were two rooms in the front downstairs, a sitting-room and a bedroom for Fanny and Pierce; and three very small rooms at the back, the overseer's bedroom, his office and a combined dressing-room and audience-chamber for Pierce where the slaves came to proffer petitions. Upstairs under the sloping roof there was a garret room for Margery and the children. As in all southern houses the kitchen was in a separate building, and the servants went home at night to their own huts. The furniture was scanty, all made on the plantation; the Butlers bathed in cedar tubs, ate off of a pine table, and sat on hard wooden chairs and benches; their clothes were hung on pegs. Plumbing was nonexistent; they drank the river water; for drainage, a deep ditch had been dug at the back and one side of the house, and a merciful tide washed in and out twice a day. Fanny had brought some chintz with her; she made cushions and curtains. She tried to train the servants—a man cook, a dairy woman, a laundry woman, a housemaid and two boys to wait on table; but except for the man who had his race's gift for cooking, a maid and one of the boys, they were too stupid and too lazy. They all went scrambling and shambling about their work getting in each other's way, giggling, scolding, breaking china and scorching linen. In the kitchen other Negroes strayed in and out like hungry hounds, squatting on the earthen floor, nibbling at any scraps of food that fell from the rich man's table and adding to the confusion. The house servants were less ragged than the farm hands but they usually went barefoot; all were filthy; all smelt to heaven. Fanny, told that this last was inherent in the negro nature but recalling a similar stench encountered in the cabins of Irish "bog trotters," bribed her servants to wash themselves, and the atmosphere of the establishment improved. The food was better than she had hoped for; there was game in the swamps and forests; wild ducks and wild turkeys, snipe, partridges and venison, and fish in the river; chickens, ducks and eggs could be bought from the slaves who were allowed to raise poultry though forbidden to keep pigs. A few sheep were pastured on the dykes, but as the plantation had no butcher the mutton was cut up into unappetizing square chunks by the carpenter. When Fanny complained he begged to be shown what she meant by *joints*. So a carcass was brought in and laid on the kitchen table; the smell of raw meat sickened her, but she stood resolutely over the corpse, carving knife in hand, considering; then marked it off by guess work into hind quarters, fore quarters and chops. Cabbages were the only vegetables grown on the island; there was no attempt at ornamental cultivation of any sort, no flowers or shrubs, though the alluvial soil was riotously rich and weeds grew to giant size, and not a tree shaded the house from the fierce southern sun or softened the glare from the water; the barrenness was unrelieved except for a few orange trees leafing out after a recent killing frost that had ruined a magnificent grove and left rows and rows of dead stumps as mementoes of scented acres of bloom and fruit.

The near-by landscape was featureless, for the whole island lay below high water mark. The river was walled out by dykes and let in through ditches and canals when the rice fields needed flooding. The cleared ground was interspersed with patches of steaming green swamp and luxuriant forests of magnolia, live oak, cypress and palmetto garlanded with creepers and gay with birds, but so wet and so infested with reptile life that walking was limited to a stroll along the raised margins of the canals that everywhere scored off the land into rectangles of hideous monotony. Across the rolling waters of the Altamaha the mainland and the white warehouses of Darien could be seen; in the other direction lay the sand hills of smaller islands and the shore of St. Simon's, a large fertile island where in the past the Butlers had made a fortune from their cotton plantations; but even long-staple, "sea island," cotton was taking second place to rice, only the poorer grade of slaves worked the cotton now and the strong healthy ones were kept for the rice.

There were three mills for threshing rice, run by steam and tide-water, on Butler's Island, and four slave villages, called "camps" by the Negroes; each a double row of ten to twenty cabins, roughly built wooden shacks held down by brick chimneys whose huge fireplaces gave out more smoke than heat. There was little furniture except a plank bedstead heaped with moss; sometimes not even that. Each cabin possessed a bit of garden, usually uncultivated, for a hoe was the last thing a slave cared to handle when his master's work was done for the day; at the back of the row ran a ditch for the tide-water that carried off the worst filth and garbage. A large infirmary was provided for the sick; each camp had its driver's hut, each had its cook shop and row of cauldrons presided over by an old crone who boiled the rice and corn grits doled out weekly by the head driver, who had the key of the stores. She gave their portions to the gangs when they left home at sunrise; part was heated in the field over a fire of sticks at about noon, the rest was eaten at night. The mechanics—the engineers, carpenters, coopers, blacksmiths and bricklayers—lived a little better, and the hedgers and ditchers occasionally got a bit of salt pork, but the common field-hands seldom tasted meat except at Christmas time when they were feasted on beef and whiskey. The slaves on the Butler plantation were not overfed, a child of ten was allowed only three quarts of grits a week; but they were never allowed to starve. Twice a year they were given a ration of clothing, a certain number of yards of flannel and "plains," a heavy blue or gray cloth like drugget, and two pairs of shoes.

Children under twelve were not expected to work; they "minded" the babies, carried them to their mothers in the field to be nursed, and brought them home again. Pregnant women were given somewhat easier work than the others; no woman was sent back to the field until her baby was three weeks old, and sometimes an obviously worn out woman was allowed to give up field work and give her whole attention to breeding. Each slave had a set task; that done, the remainder of the day was his own, he could idle or work for himself. The strong ones often finished in time to go fishing or set traps for game—firearms were of course forbidden; the more energetic gathered moss from the trees, made tubs and piggins, even built boats and sold them at Darien. They could get permission to go to Darien for this purpose, and once a month were allowed to attend church there, but not elsewhere as mixing with slaves from other estates was considered dangerous, nor could they be baptized—most of them were Baptists—without the express permission of the overseer, which was not always given. A negro preacher was allowed to read the Bible to them; he was almost the only slave on the island who knew how to read as the law that forbade teaching a slave to read was strictly enforced, and they might attend his prayer meetings. The regulations with regard to punishments were the same as in the time of Major Butler, Pierce's grandfather. No driver was allowed to administer more than a dozen lashes; sometimes he delegated the job—it gave point to a lesson if a woman were flogged by her own husband or father. The head driver might inflict only three dozen lashes; though he could order a man, or a woman, to be "tied up"—flogged with the wrists tied to a beam overhead so that only the toes touched the ground—or banish a troublesome hand to Five Pound, a remote settlement in a swamp infested with rattlesnakes. Even the overseer was limited to fifty lashes, and was not expected to maim or kill a slave. As for the owner, in remote places such as Butler's Island the owner was lord of life and death; the law, though it forbade flogging a slave to death, could not touch the owner, for the testimony of a negro could not be accepted in a court of law against a white person and the owner and his overseer were the only whites on the plantation. But the Butlers, being model proprietors, had never wished to flog any of their animals—negroes, dogs or horses—to death. Their old slaves were given food and shelter, though not very much food and shelter in the most tumble-down cabins. The Butlers seldom sold a slave, or hired one out, unless it were some fellow who had developed a mania for running away just as a dog gets a taste for killing sheep; an infrequent malady, the people had all been born and reared on one or other of the three plantations, so the unknown world beyond did not often lure them to forget their duty, and most of them were blessed with the contented spirit that goes with a black skin; there were very few mulattoes among them.

It was a simple code. Island life was simple. Pierce answered Fanny's questions frankly enough; he and his overseer were naïvely proud of their administration. Whatever might be the drawbacks of slavery in the abstract nobody could say that it did not work well on the Butler plantations; properly administered, slavery was a beneficent institution. But Fanny still doubted, she promised herself a tour of inspection as soon as her trunks were unpacked. Pierce had spoken of an infirmary; she would begin by visiting the sick; there might be some simple delicacy she could provide from her own kitchen, a glass of eggnog or a mold of jelly.

But before her house was in order she had two visitors whose appearance increased her desire to see the infirmary for herself. The first was a fat dirty old negress ushered into the sitting-room by Pierce himself, who introduced her with a laughing: "Rose, the mid-wife, wants to make your acquaintance." The woman threw up her hands in an ecstasy of admiration. "Oh Massa!" she cried, "where you get this lily alabaster baby?" and Fanny looked around for Sally before she realized that the compliment was intended for herself. The mid-wife's flattery was almost as disgusting as her appearance, but at last she went away. Fanny went on unpacking, and was again interrupted; a woman was waiting on the piazza to see her. It was the tall gaunt Negress who had embraced Fanny and Margery with such embarrassing fervor at the time of their arrival; a dreadful looking creature, all skin and bone, obviously very ill. Her name was Teresa and her tale of woe was piteous indeed; with her, field work and child-bearing had proved a disastrous combination. She ended by pulling up her ragged petticoat with a savage gesture—the Missis should see for herself! Fanny saw, and sickened at the sight. She did what she could; she gave the woman a bandage, showed her how to put it on, and gave her some advice. As soon as the woman had gone, Fanny left the trunks as they were, put on a hat and started off for the infirmary.

The path along the top of the dyke led her past settlement number one; she stopped at a cabin and looked in. It was dark and cold and filthy, a confusion of children and poultry, tangles of gray moss and bits of kindling wood. Ducks and chickens, wandering in and out at will, scratched in the ashes of the broad fireplace and picked their way among the children that crouched on the bare floor close to the hearth although the fire had gone out. The older ones were half naked, but every baby wore a thick cap on its wretched little head and was swaddled like an Italian baby in a strip of dirty red flannel—the same strip, Fanny discovered later, that it had been wrapped in at birth. The little creatures stared—eyeballs rolling, teeth shining—at the apparition in the doorway; not one of them had ever seen a white woman before, it was an awesome sight. They began to whimper. Fanny spoke encouragingly. She asked why they had let the fire go out, why they did not sweep up the ashes and drive out the poultry. Nobody answered. Some giggled, some cried; nobody understood. She tried pantomime; kindled a fire, swept up the hearth with a twig, shooed out the chickens, piled the wood in a corner. They watched, stupefied. Then burst into loud laughter. They understood now. It was a game, they mimicked her; swept furiously, piled more wood on the fire. She pointed to the babies, indicating disapprobation, and told one of the older girls that the babies were dirty; the babies must be washed. This was too much—babies were never washed! Babies died if they were washed! She persisted; taking a penny out of her pocket she held it up. She would give a penny to every "minder" whose baby had a clean face when she came next time. Did they understand? She could not tell, and went on to the next house. The same scramble of children and chickens . . . All the cabins in the row were alike in their dirt and discomfort. She went on to the infirmary.

A letter to Elizabeth Sedgwick recorded her experiences:* "The infirmary," she wrote, "is a large two-story wooden building containing four large rooms. The first I entered was half dark; some of the windows were glazed but encrusted with dirt and the shuttered openings were closed to keep out the cold. In the enormous chimney a few feeble embers glimmered and here many of the sick women were cowering on wooden settles, the poor wretches too ill to rise lay strewed about on the earthen floor without bed, pillow or mattress. Here, in their hour of sickness and suffering, lay those whose health and strength are spent in unrequited labor for us, those whose husbands, fathers, brothers and sons were, at that hour, sweating over the earth whose produce was to buy for us all the luxuries which health can revel in, all the comforts which can alleviate sickness. I stood in the midst of them, perfectly unable to speak, the tears pouring from my eyes, myself and my emotion alike incomprehensible to them. Here lay women expecting the agonies of childbirth, others who had just brought their offspring into the world, others groaning

---

* Here and elsewhere, quotations from F.K.'s writings are condensed, but the meaning is never in any way altered.

over the pain and disappointment of miscarriages—here lay some burning with fever, or chilled with cold and aching with rheumatism upon the cold hard ground, in draughts and dampness, dirt, noise and stench—here they lay like brute beasts, all absorbed in physical suffering . . . I told old Rose, the midwife, to open some of the shutters and myself went to the fireplace to build up the fire, but as I lifted a log, there was a universal cry of horror, and old Rose tried to snatch it from me, exclaiming: 'Let alone, Missis—let be! what for you lift wood? you have nigger enough, Missis, to do it!' I made Rose tidy up the miserable apartment. It was all I could do. The other rooms, one of them for sick men, were in the same deplorable condition of filth, disorder and misery; the floor was the only bed and scanty begrimed rags of blankets the only covering. And this is the hospital of an estate where the owners are supposed to be humane, the overseer efficient and kind, and the negroes well cared for! I left this refuge for Mr. Butler's sick dependents with my clothes covered with dust and full of vermin, and with a heart heavy enough, as you may well believe. When I reached home, I gave vent to my indignation to my husband and his overseer. The latter told me that when he first came a year ago he had thought the hospital in need of reform, but receiving no encouragement from either the former overseer, Mr. King, or from Mr. John Butler, he had left it as he had found it, in the same condition it had been for upward of nineteen years. This overseer came to us from Mr. Couper's plantation on St. Simon's Island where, I understand, the hospital is well managed. Mr. King was considered to be an excellent overseer, as the estate returned a full income under his management; but such men treat sick slaves as tools, to be mended if they can again be made available, or thrown away, with as little expense as possible . . . I went again today to the infirmary and was happy to perceive there had been some faint attempt at cleaning, in compliance with my desires. I remonstrated with one of the mothers, a woman named Harriet, who was ill herself, upon the horribly dirty condition of her baby and she assured me it was impossible for the mothers to keep their children clean, that they went out to work at daybreak and did not get their tasks done till evening and then they were too worn out to do anything but throw themselves down and sleep. Some of the babies are very pretty; I stopped to kiss a little sleeping creature that lay on its mother's knee and the caress excited the delight of all the women. Poor creatures, the contempt to which they are accustomed makes the commonest expression of human sympathy a gracious condescension . . . In another room a woman was lying on the floor in a fit of epilepsy, barking most violently; she excited no particular attention, the women said she was subject to these fits; she lay barking like an enraged animal. I stood in profound ignorance, sickened by the sight of suffering which I knew not how to alleviate. How I wished that, instead of music and dancing and such stuff, I had been taught something of sickness and health, that I might have known how to assist these poor creatures and direct their ignorant nurses. The swarms of fleas are incredible; I never come away from the infirmary without longing to throw myself into the water and my clothes into the fire.

"As I walked home along the street the people who had been working in the rice mill were taking their first meal of the day, sitting on their doorsteps or on the ground, eating out of little cedar tubs or an iron pot, some with broken spoons, others with bits of wood, the children with their fingers—a complete example of savage feeding. Some of the boys and girls were shouting like wild things; girls of eighteen will roll about in the dust, tumbling, kicking and wallowing regardless of decency, or loll on a bank in the sun dozing away their short leisure hour like so many cats and dogs. It is evidently considered meritorious to have large families; the older slaves often point to their children exclaiming, 'Look Missis, little niggers for you and master! Plenty little niggers for you and little Missis!' When I reached home I spoke to the overseer about Harriet, the woman who had complained to me that the mothers did not have time to keep their children clean; he seemed annoyed and assured me that it was not true.

"Next day at the infirmary I found poor Harriet crying bitterly and she and Rose informed me that the overseer had flogged Harriet that morning for having told me the women did not have time to keep their children clean. His visit had preceded mine by only a short time, or I might have been edified by seeing a man horsewhip a woman. None of the other women denied or contradicted her. I left her, because I could hardly restrain my feelings, and to have expressed them would have produced no single good result, and went home, full of the most painful thoughts. I told my husband of poor Harriet's flogging and said that if the people were to be chastised for anything they said to me, I must leave the place, as I could not but hear their complaints, and endeavor, by all my miserable limited means, to better their conditions while I am here. He said he would speak to the overseer, assuring me that it was impossible to believe a single word any of the people said. At dinner accordingly the inquiry was made and the overseer said she had not been flogged for what she had told me, but for impertinence. He had ordered her into the field, and she had said she was ill; he retorted that he knew better, and bade her get up and go to work. She replied: 'Very well, I'll go, but I shall just come back again;' meaning that she would be obliged to return to the hospital. 'For this reply,' he said, 'I gave her a good lashing. I gave it to Chloe too for some such impudence.' The conversation was prolonged to great length; he complaining of the sham sickness of the slaves and detailing the struggle which is always going on, on the one hand to inflict and on the other to evade, oppression and injustice. With this sauce I ate my dinner, and truly it tasted bitter.

"Taking a walk today I came for the first time upon one of the gangs in full field work. Upon my approach there was a momentary suspension of labor and the usual chorus of screams and ejaculations of welcome, affection and infinite de-

sires for infinite small indulgences. I was afraid to stop their
work, not feeling at all sure that the plea of a conversation
with me would be accepted as an excuse or avert the infliction
of an award of stripes. So I hurried off and left them to their
hoeing. On my way home I met London, our negro preacher,
who asked me for a prayer book and Bible. I promised him
his holy books and asked him how he had learned to read;
but I could not get him to tell me. He is a remarkable man.
After parting with him, I was assailed by a gang of children
clamoring for meat, as if I had had a butcher's cart in my
pocket; I began to laugh and then to run, and away they came
like a pack of little black wolves at my heels shrieking: 'Missis,
you gib me piece meat!—Missis, you gib me meat!' till I got
home. After I had been in the house a little while, I was summoned out to receive certain poor women in the family way
—'lusty women' as they are called here, who begged me to
have their work lightened. I said I could not interfere, that
they must speak to their master. They said they had already
begged Massa and he had refused; they thought if Missis
begged Massa for them he would lighten their tasks. Poor
Missis, poor Massa. Poor woman that I am, to have such prayers addressed to me! I had to tell them that I would try, and
choking with crying I turned away from them and re-entered
the house to a chorus of, 'Oh thank you, Missis! God bless
you, Missis!' The overseer tells me the work is not a bit too
much for these women, and that they are in the habit of *sham-
ming* themselves in the family way in order to obtain a dimi-
nution of labor. Poor creatures, I suppose some of them do.

"A day or two later I was accosted by Teresa, the gaunt old
negress who had come to see me when I first arrived to complain of her back being broken in two by hard work and
child-bearing, and had given me ocular demonstration of her
condition. She was in a dreadful state of excitement, but she
managed to tell me that the overseer had ordered her to be
flogged for having complained to me. I seem to have come
down here to be tortured. It is almost more than I can endure

to hear these horrid stories of lashings inflicted because I have been invoked, and though my husband, thanks to my passionate appeals to him, gives me little credit for prudence or self-command, I have some, and I exercise it too, when I listen to such tales as these with my teeth set fast and my lips closed. Whatever I may do to the master, I hold my tongue to the slaves, and I wonder how I do it. Later I had a painful conversation with Mr. Butler about the flogging which had been inflicted on the wretched Teresa. He maintained there had been neither hardship nor injustice in her case. She had been flogged, not for complaining to me, but because her field work had not been done at the appointed time. At the end of the day the driver of her gang—not knowing of course how she had employed her time instead of hoeing—had reported to the overseer and she had been ordered the usual number of stripes; the whole transaction had been perfectly satisfactory. I resorted, in my distress and indignation, to the abstract question, as I never can refrain from doing; the injustice of unpaid labor, the brutal inhumanity of allowing a man to strike and lash a woman, the mother of ten children, to exact from her toil which was to maintain in luxury two idle young men, the owners of the plantation. I said I thought female labor of the sort exacted from these slaves, and corporal chastisement such as they endure, must be abhorrent to any manly or humane man. Mr. Butler said he thought it was *disagreeable,* and left me to my reflections. These discussions throw me into a perfect agony of distress for the slaves: for myself, whose intervention sometimes seems to me worse than useless; for my husband, whose share in this horrible system fills me by turns with indignation and pity. But, after all, what can he do? How can he help it? Born and bred in America, how should he care or wish to help it? And, of course, he does not; and I am in despair that he does not; it is a happy and hopeful plight for both of us! . . . I have never been so busy in my life as I am here. No time, no place affords me a respite; asleep or awake, reading, eating or walking—in the kitchen, my bedroom, or the parlor, my innumerable petitioners flock in with their pitiful stories, and my conscience forbids my ever postponing their business for any other matter; for their nakedness clothes me and their heavy toil supports me in luxurious idleness."

But though Fanny's visitors seldom came without a petition of some sort the interviews were occasionally enlivened by a touch of the picturesque. Maurice brought an heirloom to show her, a silver cup that had been given to his father by the old Major as a token of appreciation for fidelity during the British invasion of Georgia. Of one strange visitor she wrote to Elizabeth: "Sinda is a hideous old negress who passed at one time for a prophetess among her fellow slaves; when, like Miller, she announced that the end of the world was coming at a certain date, they refused to work and the rice and cotton fields were threatened with ruin. Mr. King realized the uselessness of arguing and even flogging, for the authority of the overseer was nothing in the expectation of the universal judge of all. So, like the shrewd man that he was, he acquiesced; but expressed his belief that Sinda was mistaken, and warned her that if, when the day came, her prophecy proved untrue, she would be severely punished. Poor Sinda was wrong; the spirit of false prophecy was scourged out of her, and the faith of her people reverted to the omnipotent lash. But think what a dream it must have been while it lasted—freedom, without entering it by the grim gate of death!"

Old House Molly from St. Simon's Island was a less picturesque visitor but more agreeable, for she had been one of Major Butler's servants in the old days and retained the dignified courteous demeanor of a negro who had been brought up in the master's household. She brought her granddaughter Louisa with her; a nice looking girl, who made a shy curtsy and then stood silent while her grandmother talked about her. Louisa, it appeared, had recently run away! Why? Because she had been flogged for not getting her work done on time, and next day she had been too sick to work, and Driver

Bran told he was going to "tie her up;" so Louisa ran away. She hid in the swamp till she was starved out, and when she did come home she had to go to the infirmary, and she was sick so long that Driver Bran forgot to "tie her up." Molly ended: "Lor, Missis, 'tain't no use! What use nigger run away? De swamp all round; dey get in dar, and dey starve to def, or de snakes eat um up—Massa's slaves don't nebber run away."

Louisa's was only one of many similar stories; some Fanny believed, others she knew must be at least exaggerated. But each seemed to add a little to the barrier that was growing between Pierce and herself. She could not understand his tolerance of what seemed to her intolerable. "This evening," she wrote to Elizabeth, "Mr. Butler was called out to listen to a complaint of a gang of pregnant women . . . I turned away in bitter disgust . . . The details of slaveholding are so unmanly, letting alone every other consideration, that I know not how any one with the spirit of a man can condescend to them."

But now and then the cloud of discouragement would lift. "Today," she told Elizabeth a month after her arrival, "I have the pleasure of announcing that a second story is to be added to the infirmary and, to my unspeakable satisfaction, the apartments are to be furnished with bedsteads, mattresses, pillows and blankets; I feel a little comforted for the many heartaches my life here inflicts upon me." And Pierce could be astonishingly kind at times; when Shadrach, a boy to whom he was attached, was taken ill with pneumonia Pierce not only sent for the doctor but took turns with the overseer sitting up at night—a thing no English squire would have offered to do—and when the boy died, Fanny, rather to her surprise, found that she was expected to provide cloth for a winding sheet and to accompany her husband to the funeral.

CHAPTER XIX

Psyche

"A robin redbreast in a cage
Puts all heaven in a rage."
—BLAKE.

TWILIGHT WAS falling as Fanny and Pierce walked along the
dykes to Cooper London's cabin. "The coffin," she wrote to
Elizabeth, "was laid on trestles in front of the cottage; many
of the men carried pine-wood torches, and in the fitful glare
every pair of large white-rimmed eyes was turned upon Pierce
and myself, we two poor creatures, even on this solemn occasion, being objects of admiration and wonderment. The first
high wailing notes of a hymn—sung in unison, in the midst
of these unwonted surroundings—sent a thrill through my
nerves. Then all the people knelt down on the sand, and London began a prayer. His closing invocation of God's blessing
upon the Master, the Mistress and our children fairly overcame my composure and I cried, for, to me, we seemed as
legitimate a cause for tears as for prayers. When the prayer
was concluded we all proceeded to the people's burying
ground where London read parts of the funeral service from
the prayer-book. I was excited by awe and pity and a sensation
of wonder at finding myself on this slave soil, surrounded by
my slaves, as I knelt while the words proclaiming to the living and the dead the everlasting covenant of freedom mingled
with the heavy flowing of the vast river sweeping through the
darkness. The service concluded with an address on Lazarus
and the resurrection; the words were rustic, but there was
nothing grotesque in either the matter or the manner. When
the coffin was lowered, the grave was found to be half full of

228

water—the island is a swamp and the Altamaha only kept out by dykes; this seemed to shock the people and, for the first time, there were sounds of grief. But their chief expression of sorrow was when Pierce and I bade them good-night, on account of my crying; many of them mingling with their 'Farewell, good-night, Massa and Missis!' affectionate exclamations of 'God bless you, Missis!' 'Lor', Missis, don't you cry so!' My husband declined the assistance of the torch-bearers and bade them all go quietly to their quarters and we found the shining of the stars in the deep blue lovely night sky quite sufficient to light our way along the dykes. I could not speak, but continued to cry as we walked silently home, and whatever Pierce's cogitations were, they did not take the usual form with him of wordy demonstration, and so we returned from one of the most striking religious ceremonies at which I ever assisted . . . Think, Elizabeth, of that man London—a slave, the helpless creature of his master's despotic will, without a right or hope in this dreary world!"

There were others besides the preacher who stood out among the ignorant mass of blacks. Two carpenters had recently built a boat in their spare time and sold it on the mainland for sixty dollars. Engineer Ned, who managed the steam power of the mill, was extremely intelligent and had kept his youth better than most of the slaves as he had never worked in the fields; but his wife, he told Fanny, what with field work and too many children, "was most broke in two," and Fanny sighed, thinking of the life of an engineer's wife in the North. Headman Frank would have been notable in any community; during the absence of the overseer he ruled the island; he appointed the tasks, pronounced punishment, gave permission to visit the mainland, and kept the keys of the stores and doled out the weekly provisions for the slaves and for the family. His wife, Betty, was one of the nicest women on the plantation; Fanny was surprised when she came one day requesting permission to be baptized, and asked why the ceremony had been deferred. Betty explained that she had never been able to get permission from Mr. King, the former overseer, and was hoping that Missis might persuade Master to consent. Frank was a quiet, sad-faced man; Fanny would see him in the noon leisure hour sitting on the dyke looking out over the river, and wonder what his thoughts were. Was he asking himself whether his utmost exertions would ever conquer one inch of that far-off shore for himself and as a heritage for his children? It had been done; she was told of a Darien slave two generations ago who had been allowed to purchase his freedom with money earned in his spare time, although he was a carpenter—a carpenter sold for over two thousand dollars in the market—and in fourteen years of freedom had hoped to make enough to buy his wife from Major Butler; that was beyond him, but he had left seven hundred dollars to her and her children.

There were very few mulattoes on the island. Frank and Betty, jet black themselves, had a mulatto son. Another was Psyche, wife of Joe, who had been taken into the house to help Margery, and was envied by the whole plantation because Margery was white—a white person who was also a servant was such a novelty that for some time Margery had been supposed to be the Master's second wife! Psyche was a pretty, graceful little thing, but she seldom spoke and went about her work with the sad, timid air that seemed to characterize the more intelligent slaves.

Only the lower sort were quite as jolly and carefree as tradition demanded, but they were merry enough and Fanny laughed almost as often as she cried over the slaves, their doings and sayings. Any darky festivity was sure to be amusing. Soon after the arrival of the family the plantation was allowed to give a ball in their honor; a room in the infirmary was cleared out, with little regard for the sick crowded in elsewhere; Fanny was besieged by bands of pickaninnies clamoring for bits of finery, and a boat-load of slaves from the Butler cotton plantations were invited.

"I have seen Jim Crow, the veritable James!" Fanny wrote

of the ball. "All the contortions and capers that you have
been led to accept are but pale northern imitations. Words
cannot describe the things these people do with their bodies
and with their faces, the whites of the eyes and the whites of
their teeth, the strange outlines which, either by the grace of
heaven or by prolonged artistic practice, they are able to
bring into prominent and most ludicrous display. The efforts
of one enthusiastic banjo player who seemed to thump his
banjo with every part of his body at once, at last overcame my
gravity and I was obliged to retreat; considering the atmosphere, it was a wonder we were not made ill by the combined
effort not to laugh and not to breathe."

The naïve conversation of Jack, her special servant, never
ceased to divert her. Jack had a mild thoughtful face and as
they walked and rowed he would ask questions such as a small
child might ask about the world outside the island. Once
Fanny asked him suddenly if he would like to be free. His
face shone. But, instantly, the light died and he stammered:
"Free, Missis? Oh no, Missis, me no wish to be free—if Massa
only let me keep pig!" Jack took care of the family boats and
canoes, an important occupation for when the rice fields were
flooded island life was as watery as Venice's and everyone
went about in boats. Fanny enjoyed her expeditions with
Jack, sometimes fishing; sometimes slipping slowly along the
reedy banks teeming with alligators to the farthest rice mill
whose enormous wheel was turned by the tide. "No human
pen," she told Elizabeth, "ever wrote light or mine should
spread before you the full glory of these southern heavens;
sunset is a spectacle to make one fall over the side of the boat
with one's head broken off from looking adoringly upward.
Italy and Claude Lorraine may go hang!"

For the island, itself so unbeautiful, was set in beauty. The
marshes that bordered the horizon were the marshes of Glynn
and as Fanny gazed at that flat, sad-colored tranquil expanse
melting into the sea she felt the sense of release that Sidney
Lanier expressed when he wrote, dying:

"Oh, what is abroad in the marsh and the terminal sea?
    So mellow my soul seems suddenly free
From the weighing of fate and the sad discussion of sin,
  By the length and the breadth and the sweep of the marshes
    of Glynn."

At twilight if they had gone as far as Darien they would hear
a melancholy boat-horn sounding from up the river and pres-
ently one of the flat-bottomed barges known as Oconee boxes
would come floating down with the tide, piled high with cot-
ton-bags from the up-country. Now and then a school of por-
poises might brighten the water, a company of blue herons
stalking solemnly across a rice field would spread their heavy
wings as the canoe approached and throw themselves upon
the air, skinny shanks dragging after them, or a flight of birds
rise whirring from a swamp casting a shadow like a cloud,
and Fanny would recall the legends told by her aunt Mrs.
Whitelock, never until now believed.

For long expeditions she would order out the big boat and
eight oars would move swiftly over the water keeping time to
a barbaric chant. It might be "Caesar's song":

"The trumpets blow, the bugles sound—
    Oh, stand your ground!"

or a complaint:

"God made man,
    And man makes money."

Perhaps a single line would be repeated over and over:

"Oh, my massa tol' me there's no grass in Georgia,"

supposed to be the lament of a slave from Virginia where the
labor of hoeing the grass out of the crop was less severe. The

negro melodies were extraordinarily interesting. She wrote to Elizabeth:

"I can trace a popular melody in most of the boatmen's songs, such as 'Coming through the Rye,' the words changed to,

> " 'Jenny shake her toe at me,
> Jenny gone away,
> Hurrah, Miss Susy, oh!
> Jenny gone away!'

but some are wild and unaccountable. The way in which the chorus strikes in with the burden, between each phrase of the melody chanted by a single voice, is very effective, especially with the rhythm of the rowlocks for accompaniment. I often wish that some great musical composer could hear these semi-savage performances. With a little skilful adaptation and instrumentation, barbaric chants and choruses might be evoked from them that would make the fortune of an opera."

If Margery and the children were in the boat the songs were usually improvisations praising herself, "Massa's darling," for her "wire waist," and extolling Sally's brilliant coloring. One ending:

> "Oh Miss Sally,
> That's a *ruling* lady!"

brought a grin to every black face and the singers would glance affectionately at the child whose large gray eyes regarded her dependents with satisfaction. Indeed Fanny feared Sally was only too well suited to this rôle of princess; she had heard Sally say to the chambermaid: "Mary, some persons are free and some are not. *I* am a free person!"—Sally was three. As Mary did not answer, she persisted: "Some persons are free and some are not. Did you know that, Mary?" Finally Mary said: "Yes, Missis, *here*. I know it is so here, in *this* world," and Fanny concluded that the slaves must expect to be free in heaven. But a princess was what the island wanted, and wherever Sally went she was followed by admirers bringing presents: baby alligators, wild rabbits and bits of sugar-cane. Headman Frank gave her a chicken; a green ribbon was tied around its leg and it became sacred as "little Missis Chicken." Neither Sally nor the baby felt any fear of the negroes. Sally was not afraid of anything, and Fanny, thinking of the snakes and centipedes that spring would bring out and the child's plump bare legs, could have wished her less fearless.

Fanny's own fearlessness and energy never ceased to astonish the slaves, and at first her disregard of black-and-white etiquette was considered rather shocking. They would cry out when she seized a spade to show how a hole should be dug—she had begun improving the grounds and kept Jack busy planting trees and shrubs—or ran about in the sun giving directions. But bewilderment soon gave way to admiration, and the Missis was accorded the whole-hearted devotion of her slaves. One day a storm came up when she was out in the eight-oared boat far from shore; the men were not singing—it was all they could do to get the boat home—but she saw one of them make a remark which was answered by a general exclamation of agreement, and asked the steersman what they were talking about. He told her they were saying there wasn't another planter's lady in the whole of Georgia who would not have been afraid to go out with them in a boat *alone*—meaning, without a white man to protect her. Her smiling assurance that she was not afraid, for if the boat capsized she would have nine chances of being saved, was answered by a delighted chorus: "So you would, true for dat, Missis!" and they reached their destination in high good humor.

Such fearlessness would have been condemned by her white neighbors, the planters and their wives who occasionally braved the fatigue of the row from Darien or St. Simon's; and though the ladies might affect to admire Mrs. Butler's energy, in their hearts they considered her lacking in refinement. The South expected the fair sex to be languid in manner and delicate in appearance; no southern lady ever set foot to the ground if it could be avoided, and most of them "enjoyed poor health." But Fanny liked them. To be sure conversation seldom strayed beyond domestic matters—complaints of colored servants, envy of Mrs. Butler's white nurse—but they were gentle and well bred and very religious. She realized that they were sincere; they believed that slavery was good for the blacks, that whatever suffering their "involuntary servants"—a favorite euphemism—might undergo in this world was more than offset by their being given a chance to embrace Christianity; that heaven, in short, was worth the price of admission. They were not bigoted; the dogma that slavery was a divine institution impious to discuss had not yet been received by the South as a whole.

Now and then Fanny in her turn would row in state to call on her new acquaintances; but the distances were too great for real intercourse. Weeks would go by without her exchanging a word with any white person except her own family and the overseer, and days without even Pierce's society; for there were the cotton plantations on St. Simon's to supervise as well as the rice, and he was often away from home. During these absences Fanny and the overseer were left tête-à-tête. He was a well-meaning man, with very little education. Mrs. Butler's unnecessary preoccupation with the slaves and their concerns worried him a little; her attempts at ornamental planting he regarded as an absurd waste of time, assuring her that she would not find a really good flower garden or kitchen garden, except Mr. Couper's on St. Simon's, in the whole of Georgia. Slavery as a moral question did not interest him; economically he considered it a failure, but he insisted that so long as a prime slave brought a thousand dollars on the auction block it was not likely to be given up. He objected to any form of education for the negroes—reading was bad and religion was worse.

But not all overseers were quite so narrow-minded. When his predecessor, Mr. King, arrived for a short visit, Fanny as

well as Pierce found him an agreeable addition to island society. Mr. King talked well, and was worth listening to because of his nineteen years' experience as sole ruler of the
Butler plantations and their seven hundred slaves. Fanny
liked him. He seemed to be attached to some of the old slaves
he had known, and spoke kindly of House Molly and Engineer Ned, and declared that Headman Frank had "the prin-
ciples of a white man." Though born and reared in the South
he considered slavery "a curse," chiefly because of its effect
on the whites who had come to feel all labor beneath them,
and believed that it would "keep the slave states fifty years behind the others in improvement and prosperity." But he saw
hope ahead: "As soon," he insisted, "as people become convinced that it is to their interests to get rid of it, they will do
so."

Altogether Mr. King made such an agreeable impression
that when his visit came to an end it was disappointing to find
that his nineteen years' régime had not been as satisfactory to
the blacks as to the whites. The slaves told Fanny that Mr.
King forbade churchgoing, and as he did not consider their
marriages binding had a summary way of settling marital in-
compatibilities; if a couple disagreed he would hand the wife
over to another husband and give the man another wife
whether any of the four liked it or not. It shocked her still
more to discover that Mr. King's features could be traced in
several of the young mulatto faces on the Butler estates. The
parentage of Minda's children, Ben and Daphne, was unmis-
takable, and Jem Valiant—so called because his white blood
had given him uncommon courage—would not have needed
much wisdom to know his own father. The puzzling pallor of
jet-black Frank and Betty's son Renty was now explained; according to old House Molly, Mr. King had "borrowed"
Betty for a while and acknowledged that Renty was his son;
and the boy evidently hoped something would come of the
relationship, for after Mr. King's departure he asked Pierce
if a gun had been left for him and seemed annoyed that this

fatherly action had been neglected. Many lurid stories concerning Mr. King and the women slaves, and the cruelty of his punishments, were brought to Fanny; Pierce told her they were ridiculous lies, but she could not be sure and never saw a dusky replica of Mr. King's respectable countenance without a shudder that Pierce would have considered supremely absurd.

Another result of Mr. King's visit gave Fanny a more personal pain and widened immeasurably the breach between Pierce and herself. Soon after his departure, Margery came to her with a surprising message; Psyche, the pretty sad-faced mulatto nursemaid, would be grateful if the Missis would find out to whom she, Psyche, belonged. Fanny sent for the girl; it appeared that Psyche and her husband Joe had been worrying about this for some time but Psyche had not dared to ask. She knew that she had at one time belonged to Mr. King, and if Mr. King had sold her to Mr. Butler everything was all right for Joe was a Butler slave. But if she and her children still belonged to Mr. King he might take her down south, take her away from Joe! The girl broke down; Fanny told her she would find out at once, and rushed off to find the overseer. His answer gave a new turn to the affair; it seemed that *he* was the owner of Psyche. As it would be troublesome to take the woman and her children all the way to Alabama, Mr. King had offered them to him, and he "having no objection to investing a little money that way" had bought them. Fanny hurried back to Psyche with the good news. Psyche expressed her thankfulness, but added that she would feel even safer if she and her family all belonged to Mr. Butler, and Fanny promised to speak to the Master at the first favorable moment. Next morning before breakfast she heard a disturbance in Pierce's dressing-room, voices raised, and then a loud cry. She opened the door:

"There stood Joe," she wrote to Elizabeth, "Psyche's husband, raving, his voice inarticulate with passion and broken with sobs, reiterating his determination never to leave this plantation, never to leave his old father and mother, his poor wife and children, and then dashing his hat, which he was wringing like a cloth in his hands, upon the ground, he declared he would kill himself if he were compelled to follow Mr. King to Alabama. Pierce, meanwhile, stood leaning against the table, his arms folded, occasionally uttering a word of counsel to his slave to be quiet and not fret, and not make a fuss about what there was no help for. I retreated, breathless with surprise and dismay, and waited for some time, my heart and my temples throbbing so that I could scarcely stand. As soon as I recovered, I went to the overseer to inquire the cause of Joe's distress. He told me that Mr. Butler was so pleased with Mr. King's administration of the estates, that he had made him a present of the man Joe, and Joe had just been told that he was to go to Alabama next day! I realized that either Mr. King had sold the wife and children after he had been given the husband, or that Pierce had given Joe away knowing that Psyche belonged to the overseer; you may imagine that I prefer to believe the former.

"When this most wretched story became known to me I appealed to Pierce for his own soul's sake not to commit so great a cruelty. My pity for the poor wretch, and my wretchedness at finding myself implicated in such a state of things, broke in torrents of words from my lips and tears from my eyes. God knows! seeing any one I belonged to commit such an act, was indeed a new and terrible experience to me, and it seemed to me that I was imploring Pierce to save himself more than to spare these wretched ones. He gave me no answer whatever—I have thought since that the intemperate vehemence of my entreaties deserved that he should leave me without one single word of reply; and miserable enough I remained. Toward evening as I was sitting alone, my children having gone to bed, the overseer came into the room. I had but one subject in mind; I had not been able to eat for it, I could hardly sit still for the nervous distress which the thought of these poor people filled me with. As he sat there looking over some accounts, I asked if he had seen Joe that afternoon. He said, 'Yes, ma'am, he is a great deal happier than he was this morning.' 'Why how is that?' I asked eagerly. 'Oh, he is not going to Alabama. Mr. King heard Joe was kicking up a fuss about going, and he said he didn't want to be bothered with any troublesome niggers down there, so Joe might stay behind.' 'And does Psyche know this?' 'Yes, ma'am, I suppose so.' I drew a long breath. Joe was for the present safe. But I sat sewing, pondering his deliverance and the conduct of everyone engaged in the transaction and, above all, Pierce's share in it. I felt the weight of guilt upon my conscience and yet, God knows, I need not. When I married Pierce, I knew nothing of these dreadful possessions of his, and even if I had, I should not have formed any idea of the state of things in which I find myself plunged with those whose well-doing is as vital to me as my own.

"Pierce said not one word to me upon the subject all the next day; I was impatient of this reserve, as I was dying to prefer my request that he would purchase Psyche and her children from the overseer. In the evening, I was again in the sitting room, revolving in my mind the means of rescuing Psyche from her suspense. As I sat, calculating the value of my bracelets, brooches, rings, necklaces and earrings, and doubting if, all put together, they would equal the price of the woman and her children, for the first time, the power I had foregone of earning money by my own labor occurred to me, and my profession assumed a new aspect. During the four years before my marriage, I coined money, and never, until this moment, did I reflect on the means of good to myself and others that I had so gladly agreed to give up for a maintenance by the unpaid labor of slaves—toiling not only unpaid but under the bitter conditions the contemplation of which was now wringing my heart. In the midst of these thoughts, I suddenly asked the overseer to promise me that he would never sell Psyche and her children without letting me know, so that I might have the opportunity of buying them.

His squint obliges him to take some time in directing his gaze; he laid down the book he was reading and directed his head and one of his eyes towards me and answered: 'Dear me, ma'am, I am very sorry—I have just sold them.' My work fell on the ground, my mouth opened wide, I could not utter a sound. He deliberately proceeded: 'I didn't know, ma'am, that you entertained any idea of making an investment of that nature. I'm sure, if I had, I would willingly have sold the woman to you; but I sold her and her children to Mr. Butler this morning.' So you see, Elizabeth, though Pierce had resented my unmeasured upbraidings and had punished me by not telling me of his humane purpose, he had bought the poor creatures and, I trust, secured them from any such misery in future. I jumped up and left the overseer without another word, to find Pierce and thank him for what he had done. But think, Elizabeth, how it fares on other plantations where there is no crazy Englishwoman to weep and entreat and upbraid, and no master willing to listen!"

Unfortunately the affair left Pierce less ready to listen and Fanny more ready to upbraid. Pierce was proud of his estates; he saw himself as a wise and benevolent ruler of contented subjects, and had brought his wife to the South in the expectation that a glimpse of plantation life as it really was would dissipate her tiresome "northern" prejudices. But Fanny persisted in looking on the dark side of everything. If he spoke of the two carpenters who had earned sixty dollars in their spare time, she would exclaim that men of such intelligence ought not to be kept in slavery; she was forever complaining about the sickness among the negroes and describing their symptoms with unladylike frankness, yet when he enlarged the infirmary she had seemed to consider his kindness a matter of course; in an abstract discussion of the "institution" she would stop him with some sarcastic question which he could not answer at the moment; and instead of being converted, her horror of slavery seemed to increase every day. She was absurdly credulous, and believed any fairy tale the negroes chose to invent. She was utterly unreasonable; would overwhelm him with reproaches, fly into a rage that would end in tears and, half the time, he had so little idea what the fuss was about that he began to doubt her sincerity. Perhaps she was play-acting! missed the excitement of the stage and was treating her husband to these scenes just to keep her hand in—after all, she was an actress! Anyhow, he was getting tired of hysterics; tired of those great dark passionate eyes, her grand gestures, the solemn inflections of her voice. Often, now, if conversation threatened to leave the surface, instead of laying down the law he would walk away, ignoring Fanny —the most annoying thing he could do—and no doubt often wished that he could exchange his "crazy Englishwoman" for a well-trained southern wife who knew that smiles were more efficacious than tears and flattery than argument.

Then the winter with all its disappointments came to an end; and spring brought so many delights that Fanny could often forget her unhappiness. An unsuspected bush of pyrus japonica would burst into flamelike buds, perfume in the air reveal a clump of narcissus piercing through the rough grass of the door yard, or a rose growing on the dyke. The mainland was fragrant with jasmine; there were mockingbirds in the trees and shad in the river. But spring also brought centipedes, the hot sun would soon wake the rattlesnakes, and the damp atmosphere of the rice island was enervating in warm weather. It was time to go; in March Pierce moved his establishment to Hampton, the cotton plantation on St. Simon's Island, fifteen miles away at the mouth of the Altamaha.

CHAPTER XX

St. Simon's

"The oak fringed island homes that seem
To sit, like swans, with matchless charm
On sea-born sound and stream."

—W. J. GRAYSON.

THE BARGE 'Lily' manned by eight men transported the family to St. Simon's; the servants and all their belongings—pots and pans, chairs and tables, live stock, boxes and bags—were heaped in the bow and here among the bedding Psyche and her children perched. Fanny and Margery, Sally and the baby, sat amidships, and Pierce in the stern, steering; and so they moved slowly down the river, "all in the blue unclouded weather," Fanny quoted—under her breath, Pierce no longer cared for Tennyson—the oars keeping time to a chant of farewell to Butler's Island. "We are parted in body but not in mind," they sang over and over; then turned to praises of the family, of Psyche and Mary the housemaid. They passed Five Pound, the Siberia of the plantation, and wound on through a labyrinth of branches as the river, nearing the sea, fringed out into a hundred arms. The conch sounded, they had arrived.

The house was old, bare and inconvenient, but what did that matter? Live-oaks shaded the leaky roof, a peach tree was coming into bloom; there were tufts of narcissus and jonquils, millions of violets, a myrtle bush; in all directions alluring paths garlanded with yellow jasmine strayed off into the forest; there were wild flowers in the cotton fields and black and gold butterflies as big as birds. St. Simon's was not only far more beautiful than the rice island, the ghosts of a romantic past haunted her green glades: Guale, the Indian chief, who left his name to the group of islands, the Golden Islands of

242

Guale, that lie at the mouth of the Altamaha—Jekyl, Sapelo, St. Catherine's and their sisters; the Spanish fathers planting the cross, long before California's conversion, and achieving martyrdom; the Wesleys, preaching and suffering discouragement worse than martyrdom; Oglethorpe, winning the battle of Bloody Marsh that held America for the English; Ebo, the African chief, too proud for slavery, leading his tribe, singing, into the sea to drown. St. Simon's forests had given ribs for "Old Ironsides" (and later would give timber for the Brooklyn Bridge), they were scarred by fire but in Fanny's time hundreds of magnificent giants still stood and "Oglethorpe's Oak" was still a landmark. Only two houses, however, were left of Frederica, the settlement he had founded, and the fort bombarded by the British during the Revolution was a picturesque ruin wreathed with honeysuckle and roses.

This victory of nature over civilization seemed to be characteristic of the neighborhood. Darien's rickety buildings were half sliding into the river mud; the river would soon swallow some of the old houses on St. Simon's and had already taken a fine orange grove. Most of the gentlemen's residences scattered about St. Simon's and the mainland gave evidence of a losing fight; many were falling to decay. Here and there a bit of carving or painting in a room of fine proportions, or traces of a flower garden, would suggest past prosperity, but there was little present attempt at neatness, no beauty except the trees, and in every dwelling a horde of dirty, incompetent colored servants shambled and shuffled.

The old Butler house at Hampton, where the Major had given refuge to Aaron Burr after the duel, was uninhabitable now. As old House Molly showed Fanny through the musty apartments and up and down the rotting stairways, boasting of the past "before the war"—the War of the Revolution—Fanny wondered what calamity had wrought the decadence. No one seemed to know. If slavery were responsible, if slavery were a failure, why did not the planters realize it? It was plain that many of them were poor and growing poorer; few of them could afford to keep up their estates, or entertain with the reckless liberality of the old days.

A notable exception was Mr. Couper's estate at Cannon's Point; his house was large and comfortable; his flower garden, his date palm, his olives and mulberries were admired novelties. Fanny would return from a visit with a bouquet or a basket of new peas, and refreshed by conversation with intelligent men. For old Mr. Couper was a shrewd Scotchman whose opinion was worth having, and though he corroborated the stories she had been told of the suffering of the Butler slaves under the former overseers—the Kings, father and son—he was encouraging; better times would come now that the owners were taking a personal interest in their plantations. Young Mr. Couper was equally agreeable; a cultivated man with a flavor of romance about him because of his heroism during the recent wreck of the 'Pulaski.' Old Mr. Couper told Fanny the story; she was thrilled, and realized there was this to be said for slavery: it might develop arrogance and callousness in the white man, but it did prepare him to face danger. The ruler of a vast rebellious population must face danger every day of his life—the planters' wives told Fanny they lived in terror of the slaves, even Mr. Couper's had once conspired against him—and without plenty of courage and presence of mind would go under.

She was soon to experience a revulsion of feeling; the bringing-up of southern gentlemen had *no* good points! A long dispute over a boundary line between the doctor and a neighboring planter culminated in a challenge; a duel was arranged, the victor to have the unusual privilege of cutting off his victim's head and sticking it on a pole to mark the disputed line. But before the duel came off the antagonists happened to meet in the hotel in Brunswick; there were words, and the doctor shot his neighbor dead on the spot. To Fanny the whole affair seemed unbelievably brutal; the dead man was young and the only son of a widow. But the community did not share her horror; such revenges were taken as a matter of course, and it was agreed that although the doctor might have to go through the form of a trial no jury would dream of convicting him. And so it turned out; the widow buried her son, the murderer was tried and acquitted.

However, with all their unchristian disregard of life Fanny liked many of her neighbors, and riding on horseback permitted a freedom of intercourse impossible on the rice island. Shady bridle paths wound in all directions through the woods, and she longed for Forester, but any horse was better than none. The nearest thing to a good horse on the cotton plantation was a stallion, a powerful, high-spirited animal with a rough gait, that had never been ridden by a lady; the stable boys were horrified when they were told to bring out Montreal for the Missis. A crowd gathered, exclaiming and admiring, as the huge horse went plunging back and forth across the yard with Fanny on his back, rearing and flinging up his head; but he could not get her off, and with whip and spur and soothing pats on his handsome crest she soon brought him under control. Montreal never gave her any further trouble, and she much preferred him to the only other possible mount, a mare with a mouth like iron and so bad-tempered that when Fanny took Sally up on the saddle Miss Kate's snorts and bounces gave Fanny an anxious moment. But Sally was not afraid; she shouted with triumphant delight.

The bridle paths, at first seeming limitless, so often ended in fallen timber or a tangle of briar that Fanny told Jack she would pay any boys who would cut trails for her in their spare time, and as the cotton was in, Pierce made no objection. Paths grew; Margery with the baby in her little wicker carriage and Sally marching ahead, could wander further afield, and Fanny could explore new regions. Incidentally, riding gave her a respite from the petitioners that here, as on the rice island, besieged her with complaints and requests.

In some ways the conditions were worse; as the strong Negroes were needed for the rice, the derelicts were left on St. Simon's; the infirmary was no better, and the cabins more forlorn. For Fanny it meant many hours spent listening and consoling, making bandages and poultices, layettes and flannel petticoats. The response was touching, and often poetically worded. Bedridden Nancy, holding Fanny's hand, murmured: "I have worked every day, through dew and damp, through sand and heat; but, oh, Missis, me old and broken now!" Old Dorcas, come to beg a pinch of sugar, picked up Fanny's watch from the table and laid it down with a sighing: "Ah, I need not look at this, I have almost done with time." Often their gratitude was painful; an old crone boasted that when her strength had given out she had still been worth her keep, for she had "gone on making little niggers for master," and ended with an ecstatic, "While there's life there's hope, we done see Massa before we die!"

Wearying as Fanny found these ministrations to have them curtailed was misery, and soon after her arrival at St. Simon's Pierce told her she was ruining the slaves with her credulity and mistaken tenderness; she was making them discontented, and doing more harm than good. With the present price of cotton in the Liverpool market he had enough on his mind without this everlasting fuss about sick babies and religion and flannel petticoats! He forbade her to bring him any more tales; if she did, he would not listen.

She cried and implored. They both lost their tempers—the weather was hot now, the sand flies had come and white tempers were not at their best. Pierce became sullen and Fanny hysterical. At length he walked away, leaving her disintegrated with misery and mortification. What was she to do? The people would not stop begging her to "ask Master," or believe her when she told them it was useless! For a time Pierce had seemed open to suggestion; now he was as hard as a stone!

In a wretchedness so confused that she scarcely knew what she was doing, driven by a need for fresh air and a longing to escape from Pierce and his galling authority, she rushed out of doors and down to the wharf, jumped into a big boat,

called to the crew and bade them row her to the rice island.
She must get away, be alone, have time to think, decide
whether she should leave Pierce forever and return to England. A storm was coming up, the wind was high and the
water rough. Wind and water worked their spell. A night on
the lonely rice island soothed her, and when she awoke her
first thought was of the children; they might be needing her!
The storm had increased, but nothing could hold her now;
the boatmen wanted to wait, but she could not wait; half-way
they wanted to turn back, but she insisted on going on, and at
last they got the boat home.

Outwardly life went on as before. But Pierce's pride had
been touched—he could not forgive that night of desertion,
the incident was treasured in the back of his mind for future
reference—and a sense of failure added immeasurably to
Fanny's unhappiness. She took up her routine, her doles and
consolations; but the endless petitions to "ask Master" had to
be refused. She told the slaves it was useless for her to interfere; they did not believe her, and kept on coming. The "lusty
women" were especially pertinacious; they left her no peace,
and always the complaint was the same: "Missis, we hab um
pickaninny—three weeks in 'ospital, and den out upon de hoe
again—*can we strong* dat way, Missis? No!" Of one deputation
Fanny wrote to Elizabeth:

"They had all had large families, and ALL of them had
lost half their children. When they reminded me of my babies
and my carefully tended convalescence, and implored me to
use my influence so that they might be given some labor less
exhausting than hoeing during the month after confinement,
I held the table before me so hard in order not to cry that my
fingers ought to have left a mark upon it ... But they went away
exclaiming: 'God bless you, Missis! You sure will tell Massa
for we, he sure do as you say!' and I had my cry out for them,
for myself, for *us* ... I am helped to bear what is so painful to
me here by my enjoyment of the strange wild scenery. I rode
to-day across a salt marsh upon a raised causeway that was

alive with land crabs whose endeavors to avoid my horse's
hoofs were so ludicrous that I laughed alone and aloud. The
sides of the road were covered with an embroidery of moss
and lichens of vivid green and red, making my horse's path
look as if it were edged with coral, it was like a thing in a fairy
tale. I suppose one secret of my being able to suffer as acutely
as I do without being made ill, is the childish excitability of
my temperament and the ecstasy which any beautiful thing
brings me. No day passes without some enjoyment like this
coral-bordered road, and I almost despise myself for a rapidity
of emotion that sometimes makes me doubt whether anyone
who feels so many things can be really said to feel anything.
One thing I commend to you as a trainer of youth; cultivate
in young minds an equal love of the good, the beautiful and
the *absurd;* most people's lives are too lead-colored to lose the
smallest twinkle of light from a flash of nonsense. After my
crabs and coral, I came to thickets of evergreen and jasmine;
I sat there on my horse in a dream of enchantment, listening
to the mocking-birds and inhaling the heliotrope fragrance
of the jasmine . . . Coming home, I met Margery and the children, picked up Sally and took her for a good gallop."

Not only the scenery of St. Simon's was strange; indoors as
well as out, day and night, the impact of the alien life all
about was to be felt. "The Calibanish wonderment of my visitors is very droll," she wrote to Elizabeth. "To them, my rude
chintz-covered sofa and pine-wood table with its green baize
cloth seem the adornings of a palace. Often in the evening,
when my bairns are asleep and Margery keeping watch over
them, and I sit writing my journal, the door of the great barnlike room is opened stealthily and men and women come
trooping in, their naked feet falling all but inaudibly on the
boards, as they betake themselves to the hearth where they
squat on their hams in a circle, like a ring of ebony idols,
watching me writing at the other end of the room; you can
not imagine anything stranger than the effect of these glassy
whites of eyes and grinning white teeth turned toward me,

and shining in the flickering firelight. I often take no notice of them, and they seem absorbed in contemplation. My evening dress probably excites their wonder and admiration, no less than my rapid writing for which they have expressed compassion as if they thought it must be harder work than hoeing. When I speak to them each black figure springs up as if moved by machinery; they all answer, 'Me come say ha-do, Missis,' and then they all troop off as noiselessly as they entered, like a procession of sable dreams." But all existence was dreamlike now; and as she bent over her writing table again and began another letter it was with a sense of ghostlike unreality, for she was answering letters from England describing Adelaide's recent triumphant début in Venice. Adelaide seemed as unreal as a fairy queen, and Italy and England as remote as landscapes in the moon.

On Sundays the gatherings were less uncanny and gave her real satisfaction. As the slaves' church privileges were limited to once a month at Darien she had asked Pierce to let her read prayers to the house servants and their friends, and having chosen a propitious moment—he had been ill and was grateful for her care—he had consented. Some thirty negroes would come slipping quietly into the sitting room and listen with rapt attention, deeply moved by the sonorous sentences from Bible and Prayer-Book and the music of the Mistress's voice. Fanny herself was moved; there was something infinitely pathetic in that ring of dark faces, their blackness and humility accented by the pink and white dignity of small Sally enthroned in the midst, bland and superior as befitted a plantation princess. At the final amen they would rise, and with a gentle "We thank you, Missis," file out as solemnly as they had entered.

Spring was fast heightening to summer now; Pierce's illness had been a warning that Georgia would soon be too warm for white people, and he began, in his dilatory way, to prepare for departure; one day he would tell Fanny they were to go North at once, and the next postpone leaving for an indefinite time. But she was learning to accept her husband's vacillations; she packed her trunks and waited, oppressed by the blazing sunlight and the steaming fecundity of the earth, and bearing as stoically as was in her nature to bear the farewells that she encountered wherever she went on the plantation. The days dragged; she was half glad, half sorry, when Alec came to her with an unexpected request: would Missis teach him to read? It was against the law and Pierce would have to pay a heavy fine if it were found out; but Pierce's policy of silence had irritated her to the point of recklessness, and she consented. Alec was bright; encouraged by Sally's example—Sally, already embarked on 'Mother Goose,' was exhilarated by her competence—he mastered the alphabet, and Fanny could hope that some friend might help him to go on for she had discovered that more slaves knew how to read than were willing to acknowledge such a dangerous accomplishment. The last Sunday service came; her congregation were in tears when they bade her goodbye with many promises to remember what she had told them, to wash the babies and keep the cabins tidy. Of her last visit to the infirmary, she wrote to Elizabeth:

"I found an old negro named Friday lying on the floor of the damp, dark, filthy room; his glazed eyes and rattling breath told me that he was dying. A tattered shirt and trousers barely covered his poor body, he had nothing under him but a handful of straw that did not cover the earth on which he lay and under his head, by way of pillow, two or three rough sticks raised his skull from the ground. There he lay—the worn out slave whose life had been spent in unrequited labor for me and mine, without one physical alleviation, one Christian solace, one human sympathy—panting out his last breath like some forsaken beast of burden rotting where it falls. As I bent over him, blinded with tears of unavailing pity, there was a quivering of the eyelids and falling of the jaw—and he was free. How I rejoiced for him; and how, as I turned to the wretches who were calling to me from the inner room, I

wished they were all gone away with him, freed by death from
bitter, bitter bondage."

But there was beauty as well as sadness in those last days in
Georgia; last evening row on the Altamaha under a world of
stars; last moments on the shore at bedtime listening to the
surge of the ocean breaking on the beaches of Little St.
Simon's, and watching the revolving light on Sapelo that
warned ships away from the bar at the mouth of the river,
just as she had stood watching Inchkeith light from the balcony of her aunt's house in Edinburgh. Yet how unlike! This
languorous flower-scented air and melting sky were as unlike the crisp tingle and high sparkle of those northern lights
as she herself was unlike the gay irresponsible girl of ten
years ago.

Next day the Butlers were on their way. The plantation
visit was over. May found them once more settled at Butler
Place, and island life had faded to a fantastic dream. But those
months had left their mark. Fanny had been too inexperienced and too sensitive for an abrupt introduction to the
"wounds and bruises and putrefying sores" of human deg-
radation. She knew little of poverty; of disease made unendurable by poverty she knew nothing. The world had been
kind to her, and she had taken for granted that most people
were well-meaning; now she knew better. She was bitterly
disappointed in Pierce; Pierce was only superficially kind; he
was not high-minded, he was merely respectable. She was disappointed in herself; the "ministering angel" had come limp-
ing home, draggled and forlorn, and she could have laughed
aloud as she recalled her hopes and plans. She had expected
to find "much kindness on the part of the owners, much content on the part of the slaves;" to evolve some scheme for
"placing our slaves on a more Christian footing," and persuade Pierce to fall in with her ideas. And it had come to
nothing—Pierce said she had done more harm than good!

But there was one concrete result of her sojourn in Georgia,
the journal she had kept for Elizabeth Sedgwick and the let-

ters she had written to her. Abolitionist feeling was running high that year because of the "Amistad case," a trial following mutiny on a slave ship in which the captain and three of the crew had been murdered. Counsel for the negroes argued that they were not slaves but free Africans, and many agreed with him; but in the end President Van Buren ordered them to be sent to Havana and slavery. The Sedgwicks and Fanny's other abolitionist friends told her that this was the right moment to publish a book depicting slavery as it really was, and that she would do much to advance the cause of freedom. But she refused. Her husband would never forgive her; in a sense she had been a guest at the Butler plantations; she had seen what she would never have seen if she had not been Pierce's wife, and to give her criticisms to the world would be a breach of hospitality. The manuscript was put aside, but not destroyed; in the future, some crisis might arise that would induce her to change her mind.

CHAPTER XXI

Discord

"From below is heard the reverberation of a heavy door closing."

—IBSEN.

IN THE late autumn of 1840 the Pierce Butlers' long-discussed trip to England finally came off. It was five years since Fanny had seen her family, and Pierce rather wanted to go; again and again he had promised to take her, but as often he had changed his mind; for his habit of procrastination and inability to keep to a plan was becoming a complex.

The previous year had been poisoned by this lack of decision. After her unhappy winter in Georgia Fanny had not expected to be taken south again, but Pierce would not admit that he did not need her. In the autumn she had been told definitely that she was to go; they had all left Butler Place and moved into Philadelphia to stay with the John Butlers while Fanny made her preparations for the journey and a southern winter; the children were outfitted, supplies bought and trunks packed. Everything was in readiness, and still they waited. Autumn grew to winter; Fanny shuddered, remembering her first cold journey to the South. In January she was still expecting to go. February came; everyone said it would be folly to take the children south now, they would have to return so soon. But still Pierce backed and filled. At last John Butler came to the rescue; as part owner of the plantations he had a right to interfere, and he told Pierce that he did not approve of Fanny's going: "Her presence on the plantation was," he said, "a source of misery to herself, annoyance to others and danger to the property." Pierce agreed; it was settled; he and John would go south, Fanny and the children return to Butler Place. But, even then, Pierce did not tell his

253

wife; until the day before he started for the South, Fanny supposed that she and the children were to go with him.

Such lack of consideration was insulting. Mortified and indignant she moved out to the farm, unpacked the long packed trunks, and settled down to wait for the spring. Of her life at this time she wrote to Harriet: "I shall pass the rest of the winter teaching Sally to read and sliding through my days in a state of external quietude. I shall have nothing to talk to you about but Sally's sayings and Fan's looks, and I have a dread of beginning to talk about my children for fear I should never leave off. When bedtime comes and their little feet and voices are still, the spirit of the house seems to have fallen asleep, and my evenings are sad in their absolute solitude. I have taken vehemently to worsted-work, and am going to read Gibbon's 'Decline and Fall.' . . . You ask if I am writing anything; I occasionally make critical analyses of books that please or displease me, in the language in which they are written, but that can scarcely be called writing. No one here is interested in anything I write, and the isolation of my life from literary and intellectual society, which might strike fire from the sleepy stone, is not favorable to inspiration. I once thought the material lay within me, but it will moulder away now for want of use. It matters very little; my interest in life is the care of my children and my recreation is my garden. I am longing for the spring as I never longed before . . . The spring has come and even this uninteresting place is beautiful. There is a rosy bloom in the apple orchard, a tender green halo above, and a golden green atmosphere beneath the trees of the avenue, birds are singing. Tulips and hyacinths and lilacs and monthly roses shake about in the soft wind and scatter their petals like jewels among the young vivid verdure. Delicate shadows of delicate leaves lie drawn in quivering tracery on the smooth emerald grass . . . I do not believe I am a normal human being; at my death only half a soul will pass into a spiritual existence, the other half will go and mingle with the winds that blow and the trees that grow and the waters that flow."

In June a break came in the rural monotony; Fanny Elssler arrived in Philadelphia, and as Pierce and his wife still had one taste in common, the stage, they drove in to Philadelphia every night to see her. Fanny wrote to Harriet: "She is a wonderful artist, the only intellectual dancer I have ever seen; inferior to Taglioni and Grisi in grace and sentiment, she excells them both in dramatic expression." But hot weather brought discussion of summer plans, and vacillation; one day a twinge of rheumatism would fix Pierce's wavering mind on the Virginia hot springs, the next he would decide that it was safer to stay at home. Summer was half over, and the children wilted by the heat, before Fanny was finally permitted to take them to Lenox.

With autumn the arguments for and against a trip to England revived. Pierce promised to go, then decided it would be impossible for him to leave America; if Fanny went she must go alone. She hated going alone, but she began her preparations. Then a letter came; her father and Adelaide were spending the winter on the Continent, could Fanny join them there? Pierce at once withdrew his permission; it would not be suitable for his wife to travel on the Continent without a male escort. Fanny was in despair. Then a second letter came; her father had been taken ill, Dr. Liston and Dr. Bright said he could not live; if she wanted to see him again she must sail immediately. Pierce could not now refuse to let her go; while he was still hesitating, a kind Butler cousin intervened: "What would people say," she asked, "if a wife were allowed to arrive at her father's death-bed unaccompanied by her husband!" This argument was convincing; Pierce bestirred himself; the whole family, the children and their nurse Anne—Margery had left to get married—sailed for Liverpool.

When Fanny reached London her father was still at the

point of death. But to the doctor's amazement he soon rallied
—he told Fanny that her presence in England had "called him
back to existence"—and when the Butlers left the Clarendon,
where they had gone on arriving, and took a house in Clarges
Street, Piccadilly, Charles was able to be moved there, and
here Adelaide joined them on her return from Italy where
she had achieved a triumphant success in opera.

Again the kaleidoscope of Fanny's life had taken one of its
sudden changes and the pattern was as vivid as it had been
colorless. She wrote to Harriet: "We are lifted off our feet by
a torrent of engagements and our house is full from morning
till night. At my writing table at this moment sit Trelawny
and Charles Young; Charles Greville, Mary Anne Thackeray
and an Italian singer are beside my father and Adelaide, and
the door has just closed on an English youth with whom my
sister has been singing her soul out for the last two hours.
Friday my sister sings at the palace. I am a little bewildered
by the whirl in which we live after my solitary existence in
America . . . I was interrupted, and now it is another day.
Adelaide sits in the next room at the piano, singing sample-
singing for Charles Greville. The passionate words of love,
longing, grief and joy burst through the utterance of musical
sound, and light up her whole countenance with a blaze of
emotion. She is looking very handsome, and has acquired
something foreign in her tone and manner, and complains
of the darkness of our skies, and the dullness of our mode of
life . . . Again I was interrupted. We are off to St. John's
Wood to dine with the Procters; Pierce is not ready, my sister
is lying on the sofa reading an Italian letter aloud to me, and
the children are rioting around the room like a couple of
little maniacs. The first time Sally heard her aunt sing was
one night after she was in bed; when I went up, I found her
wide-awake, and she started up exclaiming: 'Well, how many
angels have you got down there, I should like to know?'
Richard Lane has been making medallion likenesses of us all;
Pierce and I in one eternity, and our chicks in another; their

two little profiles looking so pretty and funny, one behind the other. I enclose a silk chain for you from the Sedgwicks brought by Miss Fanny Appleton who has just arrived."

Adelaide had not yet sung in public in England; that June she made a semi-public appearance, with Liszt and Rachel, at Stafford House, lent by the Duchess of Sutherland for a concert for the benefit of the Poles. Fanny wrote to Harriet: "Adelaide sang beautifully and looked beautiful and was extremely admired and praised and petted. The great hall and staircase, with its scarlet floor cloths, marble balustrades and pillars of scagliola and roof of gold and white, and skylight supported by gigantic gilt caryatides, the sunlight shining down on the faces of the women and the soft sheen of their clothes, and every corner piled with pyramids of flowers, reminded me of Paul Veronese's most splendid pictures . . . I was a little overcome at this first appearance of my sister's, and Rachel, seeing how it was with me, was very kind and courteous . . . Her voice is like a fine deep-toned bell and expresses admirably the delineations of the passions—scorn, hatred, revenge, seething jealousy and the fierce love which sometimes springs from that bitter-sweet root. Pierce took me to call on her and I was much pleased with the excellent *bon ton* of her manner. She is completely the rage; the Queen throwing her roses out of her own bouquet, and viscountesses and marchionesses driving her about, *l'envie l'une d'autre*, to show her the lions of the town."

Soon after the Stafford House concert Adelaide accepted an engagement at Covent Garden for the following winter, and Pierce, to Fanny's delight, now intimated that he might stay in England for another six months or so, and made no objection when it was suggested that he and his family accompany Adelaide on her summer concert tour in Germany. And so it was finally decided; a house was taken in Harley Street, near Cavendish Square, that would be suitable for entertaining next season, and as the tour would not begin until August the Butlers started on a round of country-house visits.

One house, Cranford Hall, was new to Fanny for the Berkeleys were Pierce's friends; Pierce and Henry Berkeley had met in America. Lady Berkeley was a magnificent old lady. Fanny enjoyed hearing her anecdotes of the past. How "Old Charlotte," as she called the Queen, had tried to prevent her being presented at Court, for her marriage had been irregular as well as romantic; how, when her husband had been on the edge of ruin he had allowed her to take charge of the estates and been amazed when her reforms paid off an enormous gambling debt. "He called me an angel," she ended. "One is always an angel, my dear, if one holds the purse-strings, and the purse is full," and Fanny agreed, wishing she might make a similar experiment for Pierce's extravagance was giving his family much anxiety.

Cranford Hall had once been a part of Hounslow Heath; now highwaymen had given place to poachers, and Morton Berkeley often made the rounds of the estate at night with his keepers. One evening when the ladies of the house-party were going upstairs to bed, they saw his gamekeeper's outfit lying on a window seat, and Fanny was urged to "dress up." Laughing, she slipped into the pea jacket and buckled on the leather belt, and went marching up and down brandishing her cutlass, her ferocious upper half contrasting so amusingly with the rose-colored silk skirts flowing below that the girls insisted on showing her to the gentlemen. So down they went; Fanny's entrance was greeted with laughter, that rose to applause as she thrust her hand into a pocket and pulled out a pair of handcuffs. But before she could explore the other pocket Morton seized her wrist; she struggled to free herself; she drew the cutlass and threatened to chop off his fingers. But he was too strong for her and she had to let him take the coat. Later the mystery of the other pocket was explained by his sister; it had contained a miniature, the portrait of a girl, one of the house-party, with whom Morton was secretly in love, and Fanny forgave him.

Another house where she had never stayed before was the

Grotes' little country house near Burnham Beeches, the forest
that had given Mendelssohn the inspiration for his 'Midsummer Night's Dream,' written at the Grotes' except for the
overture composed long before and played in Mrs. Charles
Kemble's drawing-room. The Grotes were clever, the centre
of radical society, and Fanny enjoyed her visit; but when she
was asked a second time to meet Fanny Elssler—whose anony-
mous child Mrs. Grote had taken in, with a careless: "I don't
care who the father is, so long as it isn't that fool d'Orsay!"—
Sydney Smith's warning: "No, no; that's all very well for
Grota, my dear, but don't *you* mix yourself up with that sort
of thing," was so emphatic that the invitation was declined.

At the Hoo Fanny rode a fine horse that Lord Dacre had
named Forester in honor of her American horse, and a cricket
match was got up for Pierce's benefit as he had never seen
cricket. Then the Butler-Kemble ménage started for the Continent: Adelaide and Henry; the Butlers, with children and
nurse; to be joined by Liszt, Chorley the musical critic of 'The
Atheneum,' and other friends; one of those immense family
parties possible only at that time when railroads and steamboats had simplified travelling but tourists were not yet ex-
ploited, and a party of distinguished travellers arriving at an
inn would be welcomed by the landlord himself with bouquets and glasses of wine. The easy progress from one pic
turesque town to another along the Rhine was delightful,
although Fanny, remembering the Hudson, was inclined to
agree with nurse Anne who "didn't see why they made such a
fuss about the river." Professionally the tour was exciting;
Adelaide was admired, and Liszt in this year of 1841 at the
height of his power; young, and so handsome that even little
Sally was impressed and never forgot him. "Of all the pianists
I have heard," Fanny wrote later, "and I have heard all the
most celebrated of my time, Liszt was the first for fire, power
and brilliancy. None of his contemporaries ever produced his
volcanic effects—eruptions, earthquakes, tornadoes of sound
. . . But there was a sort of artistic charlatanry in all that

he did ... He could not go on being forever more astonishing than before, and in the end he paid the penalty."

Liszt's conversation was also to deteriorate to sarcastic repartee, but that summer he was a charming travelling companion and the centre around which the group of friends revolved. Adelaide too was in buoyant spirits, and Pierce, who was fond of music, seemed to be enjoying himself. But for Fanny there were drawbacks; travelling was not good for the children, and as artistic triumphs and fine scenery had become less important to her than the children's beds, dinners and amusements, she was not sorry when, in October, they all returned to London to prepare for Adelaide's début at Covent Garden.

Adelaide's Norma was the success of the season; no dramatic event since Fanny's début twelve years before had so stirred society and the public. To Fanny it seemed strange, and a little sad, to find history repeating itself; to see another Miss Kemble—not so pathetically childish as little Juliet, Adelaide was older and taller—stepping out on that vast dusty stage escorted by the same company of family ghosts, and arousing the same sympathy in her audience. For Adelaide had come, in her turn, to rescue Covent Garden from bankruptcy and to help her father—Charles had been unable to resist involving himself financially—and so the old futile attempt was repeated, and Adelaide, like Fanny, filled the Covent Garden bucket to the brim only to find that it was bottomless.

But Adelaide's personal success was without a flaw. Critics and public agreed that she was the coming prima donna in voice, face and figure, and some declared that she had an even greater future as an actress. 'Punch' in one number proclaimed her "a heroine of the lyric drama, one who can sing as if she had a soul;" and in another declared:

"Supercelestial is the art she practices,
     Transcending far all other actresses."

Fanny shared this uncertainty. Adelaide's dramatic talent was obvious; on the other hand, the career of an operatic star was the most brilliant open to a woman, the only career that placed a woman on an equality with a man; even Mrs. Siddons had been forced to give way to the Kemble men when it came to the management of Covent Garden. But that question could wait; the present triumph was enough. Charles's satisfaction was unalloyed, for he could not know—what Fanny may have suspected—that the letters Adelaide was receiving from Italy would settle the question between music and drama with an abrupt *neither*.

Her sister's success made the season exciting but Fanny was not happy; Pierce was deteriorating, too much pleasure had gone to his head. He was not very discriminating as to his associates, and he was inclined to dissipation; she suspected him of being unfaithful—that was nothing new, but he no longer loved her and she could not forgive him as freely as in the past. He was increasingly extravagant; Pierce considered himself a rich man, but London's standard was very different from Philadelphia's and she was sure they were spending more than they could afford. He kept her in complete ignorance of his business affairs, but she heard, in roundabout ways, that his family were worried by his absence and that she was being blamed. But although it had been difficult to bring Pierce to England it was still harder to get him away. He did not actually refuse to go, he merely put it off; he would fix a date a few weeks ahead and then postpone departure, and she began that living from day to day she found so intolerable; city life got on her nerves, and only an occasional country visit gave her strength to go on.

Pierce would not leave London very often but some invitations were too flattering to refuse. They went to stay with the Egertons, and he was even more elated at being asked to Bowood, the Lansdownes' place in Wiltshire. Fanny wrote to Harriet that, inside and out, Bowood was "a home of terrestrial delights," that Sally, taking a first run across the lawn to the lake and its swans, had cried: "Well, this is my idea of heaven!" and only American Anne had refused to be impressed, though she had admitted that "the staircase was well enough." Most of the guests were old friends of Fanny's, Charles Greville among them.

"The party here are all more or less distinguished," he wrote in his diary, "Moore, Rogers, Macaulay, Butler and Mrs. Butler, Lady H. Baring, Miss Fox. Mrs. Butler read the last three acts of 'Much Ado About Nothing.' Her reading is admirable, voice beautiful, great variety and equally happy in the humorous and pathetic parts . . . Charles Austin came yesterday, Dundas and John Russell today. Last night, Mrs. Butler read the first three acts of 'The Hunchback' which she was to have finished tonight, but she ran restive, pretended that some of the party did not like it, and no persuasion could induce her to go on. Another night Moore sang some of his melodies, and Macaulay has been always talking. I never passed a week with so much good talk, literary and miscellaneous, no scandal or gossip."

Why was Fanny "restive" that evening? Perhaps Pierce, annoyed that his wife received more attention than himself, had made some sneering remark. Anyhow, her unhappiness was apparent to one of her old friends; the poet Rogers, after mending a pen for her, by way of trying the nib wrote in his delicate hand:

"The path of sorrow, and that path alone,
    Leads to the land where sorrow is unknown,"

and walked away, leaving her to uneasy conjecture. Was it a quotation from his own poems? or an impromptu? Was it a seer's vision? or a friend's warning?

Whether or not Pierce was responsible for that particular fit of restiveness, his peculiarities of disposition usually took the edge off a pleasure before it arrived. When the Butlers were invited to a fête at Apsley House given by the Duke of

Wellington in honor of the King of Prussia there was so much discussion as to whether or not the invitation should be accepted that when, in the end, they went Fanny was too irritated to enjoy herself. There was one pleasurable moment when Lady Douro and Mademoiselle d'Este entered the ballroom together—both in white lace over white satin ornamented with huge cactus blooms sparkling with diamond dewdrops, pink for the blonde, crimson for the brunette—for beautiful women and beautiful clothes invariably delighted her. But that was all; the crowd was dense, and in her most light-hearted moods that old horror of crowds could still ruin an evening.

It was in fact increasing rather than diminishing and, aware that it was slightly abnormal, she had evolved a theory to explain it: "I am persuaded," she wrote to Lady Dacre, "that we are all surrounded by an atmosphere—a separate, sensitive, distinct envelope extending some distance from our visible persons—and whenever my invisible atmosphere is invaded, it affects my whole nervous system. The proximity of any *bodies* but those I love best is unendurable to my body." An encounter with a street crowd, during that same visit to London of the King of Prussia, was a horrible experience. She was taking the children and Anne to see the procession—the Queen going to open parliament attended by her German guest—from a window overlooking Whitehall; they left their carriage escorted by only one footman, were caught between the crowd on the sidewalk and the carriages in the road, pushed and jostled this way and that, Fanny expecting every moment to see the children dashed under the horses' hoofs; by the time the police came to the rescue she was shaking from head to foot and even the imperturbable Anne in tears. After all, the sight was not rewarding, there was so little enthusiasm; according to the Whigs, "the silence spoke of Paisley starvation and Windsor banquets."

Fanny must have been on fairly amicable terms with her husband that spring, for she wrote of a visit to the Duke of

Rutland: "I enjoyed my visit to Belvoir Castle very much. Our hosts were kind, the society free from constraint, and the mode of life both stately and comfortable . . . I received several rather mysterious invitations to the Duchess of Bedford's room and found her with a 'small and select' circle of female guests busily employed in brewing and drinking tea, with her grace's own tea-kettle." This visit at Belvoir not only introduced Fanny to "afternoon tea," but led to her being presented, willingly, to the Queen Dowager, and unwillingly, to Victoria.

The first affair was as informal as an ordinary call; Queen Adelaide was kind, they talked of French plays and whether or not they were improper, and Fanny came away from Marlborough House with an agreeable impression of the old lady. The Birthday Drawing-room was very different. Fanny had not wanted to go. When the Duke of Rutland sent word that the Queen had asked why Mrs. Butler had not been presented, she realized that the question was equivalent to a command, but she had no diamonds, a court dress would cost more than she could afford, and she had spent her allowance. She consulted Pierce, and he would not hear of her refusing. So a costume of white satin and point lace, with bows of scarlet velvet for the hair, was ordered from the same Madame Dévy who had made Fanny's best dresses when she first came out; a set of diamonds was hired from Abud and Collingwood; she was coached by Lady Francis Egerton who was to present her, and she made her curtsy to the Queen. "I kissed a soft white hand," she wrote to Harriet, "which I believe was hers; I saw a pair of handsome legs in fine stockings, which I am convinced were not hers but Prince Albert's, and this is all I saw of the royal family. I made a sweeping curtsy and came away with no impression but that of a crowded mass of fulldressed confusion, and neither know how I got in nor out of it."

Fanny's going to court had two results. One was harmless; Pierce now wanted to be presented, and so he was—by Mr.

Everett and to everybody's satisfaction except that of Anne
the nurse who was horrified that any free-born American
should degrade himself by kissing a queen's hand. The other,
Madame Dévy's bill, added considerably to Fanny's anxieties.
For Pierce was annoyed; when he began making objections to
paying it, Fanny declared she would pay it herself. She had
been writing off and on—poetry, criticisms, translations that
some editor might take; she might even write another play;
anyhow, Pierce need say no more about the bill—she would
pay it herself. Pierce's retort, that a married woman's earnings
belonged not to herself but to her husband, rankled. She
wrote to Harriet: "I cannot persuade myself that that which I
invent—create, in fact—can belong to anyone but myself! . . .
I wish that women could be dealt with, not mercifully, nor
compassionately, nor affectionately, but *justly;* it would be so
much better—for the men."

This old debate, matrimony versus a career, was taking on
a new interest at this time. For in May, 1842, Adelaide announced her engagement. Edward Sartoris lived in Italy, and
Adelaide adored Italy; he was an agreeable, highly cultivated
man, well off, in every way a desirable *parti.* A few years before Fanny would have rejoiced wholeheartedly in Adelaide's
happiness; now her congratulations were mingled with bitter
reflections. How long would Adelaide's happiness last? Had
art no claims? Adelaide was a great artist. Was it right to
bury such talent in a napkin, no matter how fine the damask
or how softly it was folded? And what if, later on, the napkin
turned out to be not damask but sackcloth? How would
Adelaide like it, when Edward criticized her milliner's bills?
. . . But there was hope for Adelaide; clever and sweet, she
could manage a husband if anybody could. And Fanny sighed,
wishing herself cleverer and sweeter; for she had no illusions
as to her own share in her matrimonial disappointment,
would indeed have borne it better if she had been less clear
sighted.

However, the bill that had caused the recent unpleasantness

was by now in a fair way of being paid. She had set to work writing and disposing of her productions with such success that, within a month, she had sold a ballet, 'Pocahontas,' and a translation of Dumas' 'Mademoiselle de Belle Isle' to Covent Garden, sent an article on Victor Hugo to her brother John, now editor of the British 'Quarterly Review,' and a chapter of her southern experiences—only the account of the journey to the plantation—to Bentley, and had outlined a play in five acts, a sequel to Kotzebue's 'Stranger.' The 'Stranger' had two endings; Germany allowed the husband to forgive his erring wife, England preferred a sterner finale, and Fanny had never been sure which was right. Now, one evening as she sat before the looking-glass brushing her hair she seemed to see the wife standing beside her, a mournful figure clearly defined, and seizing Sally's copybook she wrote out like lightning, act by act, scene by scene, almost speech by speech, a story of *consequences*. A husband might forgive but he could not remit punishment; and a wife's worst punishment would be the effect of her sin on her children.

Apart from the satisfaction of making her brains pay her bills there was consolation in finding that she would have been obliged, in any case, to buy a handsome dress; for the Egertons, still interested in private theatricals, decided to produce 'The Hunchback' at Bridgewater House. Fanny was of course to be Julia, and Adelaide, Helen. Henry Greville took the part of Clifford, Pierce was Modus, and various young guardsmen filled in the minor rôles. It went off well. There had been little hard work for Fanny who needed no rehearsing; but neither was there much pleasure—except for a moment of elation when a deep, "*Ah, bien, bien, très bien!*" came from Rachel in the front row as Julia read her lover's letter. The romance that had given the presentation of 'Hernani' so intense a flavor was of course absent, and Pierce, with his usual trick of spoiling a pleasure, had contrived to set her temper on edge just before the first performance. She had naturally expected to have some tickets for her friends, but had asked for only three for the opening night and given two of them away when Pierce interfered. He was shocked at the liberty she had taken—she had been on intimate terms with the Egertons for years; he said she had "committed an indiscretion," the ticket she still had must be returned and she was forbidden to ask for any more. This meant that several old friends would be disappointed, but she had to give in. When Pierce took the bit between his teeth she was helpless; she could subdue a stallion with a judicious mingling of pats and pricks but not her husband—though it is only fair to remember that, even with a horse, Fanny's hand was not sufficiently light. The last performance of 'The Hunchback' was tiresome for another reason; there was measles about; Fan had a cough and Fanny was so eager to get back to her "little white mouse" that she scarcely heard the applause and had no appetite whatever for champagne and lobster. Take it all around, an amateur play at Bridgewater House was a good deal more amusing for young girls than for wives and mothers!

Little Fan did not get the measles; a week of June weather at Oatlands was refreshing, and then they were all back again in London. Fanny wrote to Harriet: "Our life is now one of insane incessant dissipation. Thank God, I have not lost the power of sleeping." Pierce's restlessness was increasing as well as his extravagance; they would dash to Cranford, having a dinner engagement in town for the same night; miss the return train—Pierce was always late—and post back with four horses, although it was Ascot day and the cost ruinous. Reports from America were alarming; Fanny begged to be taken home. At length Pierce set a date in August; she told her family; they smiled, no one was surprised when he postponed departure to October.

And then something happened. There was a scene. Fanny left London and went to Edinburgh—alone. The break may have been caused by a trifle, Pierce's procrastination or some new petty restriction; but it seems more likely that suspicions of her husband's unfaithfulness now became certainty, for she wrote to Harriet in Germany: "I wish I was with you, seeing the Danube, that river into which poor Undine carried her immortal soul, and her broken woman's heart, when she faded over the boat's side, saying, 'Be true, be true, oh, misery!' " Whatever the cause, and whether or not she intended to return to her husband, she did return, and soon; she could not stay away from the children. But Pierce never forgave her, and they both added a black mark to the score they were keeping against each other.

In the meantime, probably to punish his wife for her escapade, Pierce let her think they were going home. He let her begin her goodbyes, her packing, all the complicated preparations for a voyage with young children; and as the lease of the Harley Street house had run out she fully expected to get off until she heard, in a roundabout way, that Pierce had told a friend he was not going. She would not ask. Ten days before the date fixed for their sailing, he told her they were staying on in England for an indefinite length of time. They all moved to the Clarendon Hotel; Anne the nurse was sent back to America, and a governess engaged in her place. Then another house was taken, 26 Upper Grosvenor Street near Hyde Park, for the following season; for Pierce spoke of entertaining on a larger scale than heretofore. Fanny wrung her hands; where was the money coming from!

In this December of 1842 Charles Greville summed up his impressions of the Butlers. He had never been one of Fanny's passionate admirers; she was too impulsive to please his sophisticated taste, and he preferred a more studied style of acting; his young brother Henry's enthusiasm for the Kemble family must have worried him—no doubt he heaved a sigh of relief when Adelaide's engagement reduced Henry to the lesser rôle, which was to be life-long, of her factotum. However that may have been, the elder Greville was not prejudiced in Fanny's favor when he wrote: "I have been seeing a great deal of Mrs. Butler, whose history is melancholy, a domestic tragedy without any tragical events. She went to America ten years ago in the high tide of her popularity and when she was making a fortune. Then Pierce Butler fell in love with her and she fell in love with him. She gave up her earnings to her father, left the stage, married and settled in America. And now after wasting the best years of her life in something very like solitude near Philadelphia, with two children, whom she is passionately fond of, what is her situation? She has discovered that she has married a weak, dawdling, ignorant, violent-tempered man, who is utterly unsuited to her, and she to him, and she is aware that she has outlived his liking, as he has outlived her esteem and respect. With all her prodigious talents, fine feelings, and lively imagination, she has no tact, no judgment, no discretion. She has acted like a fool, and he is now become a brute; the consequence is she is supremely and hopelessly wretched. She sees her husband brutal and unkind to her, ruining himself and his children by his lazy, stupid management of his affairs, and she lives in perpetual terror lest their alienation should at last mount to such a height that their living together may become impossible, and that then she shall be separated from her children for whom alone she desires to exist. Among the most prominent causes of their disunion is her violent and undisguised detestation of slavery, while he is a great slave proprietor. She has evinced the feeling (laudable enough in itself) without a particle of discretion, and it has given deep offense."

If Fanny ever read that merciless synopsis—suppressed in early editions of the diary—she would have agreed with tears that it was true. She knew she had been a fool, especially in her denunciations of slavery. She had refrained from any action that would place her openly on the side of abolition, and had refused to publish her Georgia journal. But she could not control her tongue; an allusion to slavery was a call to arms. Her eyes would flash and her voice thrill with passion, varying from pathos to satire and bringing tears or laughter

as she chose. Someone would speak of Channing's recent
death, and she would quote from his last sermon in the little
Stockbridge church describing emancipation in the West
Indies; as she told how the slaves had gathered in the
churches at midnight to wait on their knees for the stroke
of the cathedral clock that was the signal of freedom; how, as
the last stroke of twelve rang out lightning flashed and thunder pealed across the dark sky and there was a moment's awed
silence, and then every black man was on his feet shouting
alleluias, many of her hearers were deeply moved; but not,
one may be sure, her husband. When Fanny praised the
"sweet expression and noble countenance" of that violent
abolitionist Gerrit Smith, whom she had once met at Lucretia
Mott's and hailed him as "a confessor of the martyr age of
America," Pierce must have foamed at the mouth. If she told
an amusing anecdote, such as Catherine Sedgwick's story of
the old negress who had remarked, when her wicked master
died: "Massa pray God to forgive him! Oh, how he prayed!
And I'm afraid God heard him, for they say He is so good,"
everyone would laugh—except Pierce.

But no doubt Pierce was able to affect a certain complai-
sance knowing that he could have his revenge as soon as he
got his wife home; he could make her eat humble pie now as
often as he chose, he had found a weapon—or rather, he was
polishing and sharpening a weapon already found—the "terror" alluded to by Charles Greville, separation from her
children. For the nineteenth century was not yet old enough
to have discovered that children had more than one parent,
and a man was still the sole and undisputed owner of his
children.

So the New Year of 1843 turned a dubious face to Fanny,
and that winter was strangely striped with black and white;
but she got through it; there were alleviations. She renewed
her acquaintance with Lady Byron, whom she admired—
though she may have begun to doubt that lady's aphorism:
"To treat men as better than they are is the surest way to

make them better"—and summed up as "a woman capable of profound and fervid enthusiasm, with a mind of rather a romantic and visionary order." Other friendships were renewed; she met Dickens again, and Robert Browning; Mendelssohn was in London and gave the Butlers evenings of superlatively good music. Her high spirits and powers of enjoyment still stood by her. She could dance all night and never get tired; she contrived a ravishing Spanish costume for a fancy ball with a mantilla, a comb and a fan—the money her writing had brought in was gone—and delighted the children with a Christmas tree dressed in the pretty German fashion that Madame Lieven had introduced to England. But Covent Garden was in a bad way; Adelaide had not been able to save the theatre for as long as Fanny had saved it, it was full only on the nights she sang. So the property was sold to Mr. Bunn and as the Kembles no longer possessed a box, and Fanny could not afford to buy one, she missed some of her sister's last performances. Not that they gave her unalloyed enjoyment; of Adelaide's farewell in 'Norma,' Fanny wrote to "dear Granny," as she called Lady Dacre: "When I saw that grace and beauty and rare union of gifts, when I heard the applause break out simultaneously from all those human beings whose emotions she was swaying at will, my heart sank; this beautiful piece of art (for such it is now, and very near perfection) would be seen no more! If she does not find happiness what will atone to her for all this that she has left? It is a fearful risk. God help us all!"

Then Adelaide's career was over, and the winter was over, and London was on the edge of another season when some financial crisis—a break in the stock market, warnings from his family in Philadelphia, or pressure from creditors—brought Pierce to his senses, and he decided, reluctantly, that it would be well to go while the going was good. But they must leave a good impression; they must give a few parties.

So April rushed by in a turmoil of packing and entertaining. The Butlers' first large party of the season was pleasant enough, Pierce was satisfied; some two hundred people came, the music was good, Gunter had been told to do his best, six policemen were needed at the door. Then the children were dispatched to Liverpool with the governess—even after the lapse of years it will be more discreet to omit her name—who had been asked to accompany the Butlers to America, although Fanny did not like her as much as Pierce did; somehow her appearance at the party, very dressy in black satin with her hair curled in profusion all over her head, was vaguely disquieting. Another party came off, also a success; there was a last dinner party at Sydney Smith's, a last breakfast with Rogers; Fanny went to bid goodbye to Charles Greville laid up with the gout. May came; Fanny wrote to Harriet: "You ask how it goes with me. Why, pretty much as it did with the poor gentleman who went up in the flying machine t'other day which, when its tackle gave way, began 'to turn round in the air with the most frightful velocity,' and I shall finish as he did by 'falling in a state of senselessness into a steam packet.' Any one would suppose I was in great spirits for I fly about, singing at the top of my voice, and only stop now and then to pump up a sigh as big as a house, or I remember my leave-taking of my father and sister and turn deadly sick. Your present will be very dear. I was wearing my watch on an old silver chain. I love to feel yours round my neck."

The last goodbyes were said. They were in Liverpool with a long voyage ahead and only anxiety and discomfort to look forward to at the end of it. For, characteristically, Pierce was now preaching economy and his economies were as reckless as his extravagances. Butler Place was to be let, for he said they could not afford to live there; Sally burst into tears when she heard that dreadful piece of news, and Fanny was dismayed; she would lose her greatest pleasure, the garden, and when Pierce told her that he had engaged rooms at a boarding house in Philadelphia it was almost more than she could bear. She knew those American boarding houses!

CHAPTER XXII

The Turning of the Screw

"If the world were all Philadelphia, although the poultry and dairy market would be admirable, I fear suicide would be exceedingly prevalent. I look eagerly for the stars at night, for fear they would disappear in the dull air."

—EMERSON.

BOARDING HOUSE life was all that Fanny had imagined it. The noise, confusion and lack of privacy would have irritated any sensitive nerves, and the discomfort and ugliness of the badly furnished rooms offended any fastidious taste. The servants were incompetent, and so dishonest that the Butlers had to keep their doors locked, but in spite of this precaution within a few days of their arrival the gold chain that had been Harriet's farewell present was stolen, and as Fanny had no money she could not offer a reward or advertise her loss. She wrote to Harriet: "Whenever I think of that chain I feel so sad that I hate to speak or move . . . Of the discomfort and disorder of our mode of life I cannot easily give you a notion for you know nothing of the sort and, until now, neither did I; it is peculiarly trying to me, who have a morbid love of system and regularity and a delight in the elegancies of civilized life."

The picture was not exaggerated; Harriet would have found some such description in any book of travels in America during the first half of the nineteenth century; the American boarding house struck foreigners as an amazing novelty. Why was it, they asked, that all but the very rich found these places satisfactory, not merely as lodgings but as permanent homes? Why did so many young couples prefer to begin life in a boarding house? There were various answers, but the women were usually held responsible; their health was poor and most young wives could not stand housekeeping; their education

273

had left them ignorant of practical matters and husbands did not dare to risk home cooking. Boarding house food, according to Mrs. Trollope, was abundant but coarse and served in odd combinations; eggs and oysters came on together, beefsteak and stewed peaches, salt fish with onions. The bread was good but, Mrs. Trollope wrote: "The Americans prefer horrible, half-baked, hot rolls, and are 'extravagantly fond,' to use their own phrase, of puddings and pies. The evening parties are supremely dull."

This last criticism might have been given a wider application for dullness pervaded all American life of this time. Immigrants missed their street fairs and *fiestas*, their Christmas trees and Maypoles and processions, all the gay pattern that in recollection made up for the poverty of their old world life. Travellers invariably noticed the lack of amusement in city and country. Basil Hall hoped to find it at a New England cattleshow: "It was a sunny day," he wrote, "in a pretty valley, yet there were no signs of merriment; only groups of idle men smoking segars, and gaping about, looking listlessly at the cattle." At hotel dinner-tables he found "everybody very stiff and unwilling to talk; it might be supposed we had assembled for the purpose of inhuming the body of some departed friend." Dickens wrote of New York at night in 1842: "How quiet the streets are! Are there no itinerant bands; no wind or stringed instruments? No, not one. By day, are there no Punches, Fantoccini, Dancing-dogs, Jugglers, Conjurors, Orchestrinas, or even Barrel-organs? No, not one. Yes, I remember one. One barrel-organ and a dancing-monkey—sportive by nature, but fast fading into a dull, lumpish monkey, of the utilitarian school. Beyond that, nothing lively; no, not so much as a white mouse in a twirling cage;" and of the travelling public: "There is no conversation, no cheerfulness, no sociability except in spitting; and that is done in silent fellowship around the stove. The people are all alike, too; they travel about on the same errands, say and do exactly the same things in exactly the same manner, and follow in the same dull cheerless round."

Dull. Dull. Dull. Any number of travellers could be quoted to prove that in no other civilized country in the world—or in any barbaric land for that matter—would Fanny's life have moved to so dull a rhythm as in that Philadelphia boarding house of 1843. Moreover, few travellers, certainly neither Mrs. Trollope nor Dickens, were as sensitive as she to the sharp contrast between the American and the European scene for they were not a part of the luxurious, pleasure-loving, witty, stimulating society she had so lately left; nor, presumably, were they obliged to add, as she did, unhappiness to dullness, a miserable combination trying enough without another affliction—*heat*.

In July a hot spell descended on the town, the sky was brass and the pavements hot as the bricks of Nebuchadnezzar's furnace seven times heated. Sally and Fan grew pale and languid, the heat increased; the governess was prostrated, the nurse left, the children became ill, Fanny was afraid she might break down and be unable to take care of them. She begged Pierce to let them go to the sea-shore; the doctor said Fan needed sea air. Pierce shook his head; he could not afford country excursions. But the thermometer kept on going up; when the mercury stood at a hundred and nineteen in the shade Pierce gave in; the children might go to the country, but sea-shore resorts were too expensive; he would have to find a cheap place. He found one.

The Yellow Springs, thirty miles from Philadelphia, was a type of watering place common at this time in America that, like the boarding houses, roused all foreigners to invective. They did not realize—Americans themselves did not realize—that such places marked a transition. An earlier generation of rich city people usually owned country places in the suburbs and entertained their friends during the summer; the poor stayed at home. But the suburbs, though shady and sweet-

smelling, were not any too cool, and adventurous spirits began
experimenting. Huge comfortless hotels sprang up along the
coast. Sportsmen, recalling pretty spots in the wilderness discovered during a fishing or shooting trip, built cabins and
took their wives and children there to rusticate during the
month of August. A central dining hall would be built, and
then a ballroom, a manager would be engaged, the place
would become a sort of club where well-to-do people could
enjoy the beauties of nature, but in a surprising confusion of
dirt and discomfort. It was the fashion to joke about such
things; new comers were assured that corncobs could be
found in the mattresses, more ducks' heads and feet than
feathers in the pillows, and all sorts of suspicious and unappetizing oddities in the food. Of the most fashionable of
these resorts, the White Sulphur Springs, an English geologist,
Featherstonehaugh, wrote: "Language cannot do justice to
the scenes we have witnessed here yet the place is frequented
year after year by numbers of polite persons who have comfortable homes of their own. Situated in a romantic plentiful
country, it could be converted into a refined and rural paradise, uniting the use of the waters with fine mountain air and
the pleasures of society; but what might be a charming retreat from the heats of summer is disgraced by all the filth of
a common jail. The dinner scene—what with the clinking
of knives and forks, the confused running about of troops of
slaves, the exclamations of the new comers at the dirtiness of
the tablecloths, the nasty appearance of the incomprehensible
dishes, the badness of the water brought from the creek
where the clothes are washed—was perfectly astounding! Fortunately we could get something to eat at a nearby shanty
run up in the woods by a very odd fellow who had kept an
oyster cellar in Baltimore. He served various kinds of con-
fections, with Champagne, Madeira, claret, gin, lemons, sugar,
ice and all the appliances of a jolly existence, and here, at
rough tables set up under leafy bowers, we could admire his
skill in venison steaks and mutton chops, as well as inimitable

iced punch. His log hut was fast becoming a rival of the
hotel barroom, where cocktails, gin slings, gum ticklers, mint
juleps, phlegm cutters, and other American sherbets were
brewed from morn to night for the crowds of spitting and
swearing, cursing and coughing, smoking and stinking *reel*
gentlemen who passed their time there."

Yellow Springs was neither so large nor so popular as
White Sulphur, but the general plan—a hotel and *dépend-
ances*—was the same; the rooms were half furnished, the beds
lumpy, the food coarse, there was noise and confusion. The
country was not remarkable for picturesqueness, but it was
country, and to Fanny and her small pale children it seemed
paradise. She took long walks with Sally and Fan, and bathed
them in the clear cold swimming pool; they revived, Fan began to look as if she might live through the summer. There
were a few pleasant people staying at the hotel, people Fanny
liked and who liked her. Fenimore Cooper wrote to his wife
at this time: "Mrs. Charles Ingersoll met Mrs. Butler at Yellow Springs, and was delighted with her. It seems Mrs. Butler
is a good fisherman, and she made a great deal of *cancan* by
wearing pantaloons, with boots and straps, a man's hat, with
blouse over all. It was the dress of a page on the stage. She
rode miles on horseback alone, in petticoats, and fished in
pantaloons, which Charles said was unreasonable, if not in
bad taste. Still, Mrs. Charles says she is charming."

It is possible that Pierce overheard some criticism of his
wife's costume, perhaps he was taken by another fit of economy; anyhow, in August he ordered his family back to town.
Fanny was told at three o'clock that they were to leave at
five; that night they were all sweltering in the Philadelphia
boarding house. Of course the children wilted at once, Fan's
face took on that plaintive *doomed* look her mother dreaded.
After two suffocating weeks Pierce decided they would have
to get out of town. Yellow Springs was too expensive; they
were to go to a farm this time, three miles from the village
of West Chester.

Fanny wrote to Theodore Sedgwick: "Here there is indeed pure air for the children, and a blessed reprieve from the confinement of the city. But we eat at the hours and the table of these worthy people; we, who are sophisticates, with two-pronged iron forks; the more sensible Arcadians exclusively with their knives. The farming men and boys come in to the table from their work without their coats and with their sleeves rolled up, and we all sit down promiscuously to feed."

Nevertheless, country life brought peace, and autumn found her with courage restored, ready to face the winter's inevitable unhappiness and dullness. But not its lack of exercise. Her saddle horse, Forester, had been sold to a livery stable keeper; she determined to buy him back. The 'Knickerbocker' magazine accepted an article on Tennyson, Harper published a volume of fugitive poems, and Forester was hers again. She could escape now from the city streets, and that abiding "terror"—separation from her children—be momentarily forgotten as Forester took her briskly through the country lanes, or she felt light snow flakes kiss her cheek and the wind whistle in her hair as she gave him his head, and off they went at a gallop across the crisp gray turf of a wide meadow.

Unfortunately, the whole affair gave deep offense to Pierce. How could a man keep his wife in her place if she persisted in earning money? As for this mad passion for outdoor exercise, why could not his wife stay at home and lie on the sofa as most wives preferred to do? Heaven must have intended married women to be sickly or there would not be so many invalid wives. The whole thing smelt of insubordination; he was not surprised that it led, in the end, to open disobedience. According to Pierce (five years later he described the incident in question with a minuteness of detail that shows it had been venomously resented), he had happened to meet his wife starting off for a ride; he had asked her where she was going; to his amazement, she had answered that she was going to the wharfs. He told her the waterfront was not a suitable place for a lady to ride, she might be seen there by her friends, what would they think? expecting, of course, immediate acquiescence. But did she acquiesce? did she bow to her husband's better judgment as any right-minded female should? No; she merely tossed her head, muttered something about "this everlasting thinking about appearances," touched up her horse and vanished—headed for the waterfront!

But though Forester's redemption enabled Pierce to add another item to his list of grievances Fanny would have been worse off without her horse, for she needed all the health and courage that riding could give her; the spring of 1844 brought a new ordeal. She left no record of the affair; there is no hint of it in her published reminiscences; the months between the autumn at the West Chester farm and the following May are left significantly blank. But another person was less reticent. A Philadelphia gentleman—it will be kinder to call him Mr. X—was so excited by certain events in March that he felt impelled to take the public into his confidence, and in the process of laundering his family wash contrived to display a basketful belonging to the Butler ménage that Fanny, proud and loyal, would have died rather than see hung out on the line to amuse and horrify the neighbors.

It began with a trip to New York. The party consisted of Mr. X and Mrs. X—her maiden name, that of a well known Philadelphia family, it will also be kinder to suppress—Mrs. X's sister and Mr. Pierce Butler. They engaged rooms at the Astor House; Palmo's opera company was giving 'Figaro' at the Park Theatre, crowds were flocking to the American Museum to see the giant and giantess "descendants of Anak and Goliath," and smaller crowds to hear Dr. Hollick lecture on 'Lungs and Tight Lacing.' At the Metropolitan Library visitors could get tea or coffee, as well as literature, for ten cents, "served in either the Chess, Cigar or Conversation rooms;" and persons interested in architecture find inspiration on Chatham Street where a new hotel was going up, seven stories high and designed in the "Norman and Gothic styles intermixed." The shops were most alluring; a new style in silk mitts was being shown, and there were other novelties such as Paris-made, horse-skin gloves, Magic razor strops, and gentlemen's vests of figured satin and quilting; Dickens' 'Christmas Carol' was on sale at Wiley and Putnam's for sixty-three cents. In short, New York was living up to its reputation for brilliance and wild gaiety, and Mr. X's party never had an idle minute. All went well for the first few days; all might have continued to go well if Mr. X had not been taken by a slight indisposition—late hours and too much chicken salad at Delmonico's?—and was obliged to go to bed rather early; even then all might have gone well if Mr. X had stayed in bed. Unfortunately, in the small hours of the morning he was impelled to get up and go downstairs to the sitting-room where, to his surprise, he found his wife and Mr. Butler wide awake and in what he considered a compromising situation. He was perturbed; but, at the moment, it seemed best to pretend he had seen nothing; he controlled his anger, and went on controlling it for several days. But he could not forget his wrongs; he brooded; friends asked unkind questions. At length he worked himself up to action; he beat his wife and sent a challenge to Pierce Butler. It was of course accepted; Pierce's gallant southern blood rejoiced in affairs of honor. As the challenged he had the choice of weapons and could arrange details. He chose pistols, and stipulated that the opponents were to stand with their backs turned; at the word *fire!* they were to wheel, and begin shooting. Mr. X's seconds were horrified; they reminded Mr. Butler that Mr. X had a game leg; by the time Mr. X got around, he would be dead; perhaps Mr. Butler could be persuaded to leave out the wheeling? But Mr. Butler was firm; he had set his heart on wheeling; he said it was too bad that Mr. X had a game leg, but other men's legs were no concern of his; Mr. X would either wheel or apologize. There was no way out; poor Mr. X had to agree; off they all went to Bladensburg, the "historic dueling ground," and the duel was fought. The principals were placed with their backs turned; they wheeled; they fired; nobody was hurt. Dr. George McClellan had nothing to do. They shook hands; the seconds, Mr. Harrison Gray Otis, Mr. Hartman Kuhn, Mr. Alston and the others, shook hands; everybody said how nicely it had all gone off; it was over. No; not quite over; there was an aftermath. Mrs. X had found the whole thing most annoying, especially the beating; she accused Mr. X of cruelty, sued him for divorce, and got it. Mr. X, remembering the night in the Astor House, was both amazed and indignant. He had no legal redress, but he could write. He wrote a pamphletful of explanations; he described the sitting-room scene, and gave his reasons for not getting angry at the time and for getting too angry three days later. He was so pleased with his effusion that he had it printed and thus gave the "inside story" of the Butler-X duel wider publicity at the moment and also preserved it for future generations.

In the meantime, what was Fanny thinking of it all? How did she regard the duel and its mortifying sequel, the X divorce case? While the case was being tried—and no one knew whether Mrs. X, and incidentally Mr. Pierce Butler, would emerge whitewashed or black as ink—did she contemplate following Mrs. X's example? Did her friends urge her to sue Pierce, with Mrs. X as co-respondent, and assure her that, if she won, she would get the custody of the children? And did the outcome of the X case put an end to such hopes? When Mrs. X and Pierce were exonerated, did Fanny force herself to settle down again to the old routine of marking time, hoping against hope, but knowing that every day she spent with her children might be the last? Futile questions, left unanswered by Fanny, unanswerable by anyone now after the lapse of more than eighty years. All one knows is that this is what Fanny did: she settled down again to wait and hope, to live at first from day to day and then, literally, from hour to hour. For that summer Pierce, tired of the situation, began a system of petty persecution designed to end it.

Public opinion did not permit a man to dispose of his wife unless she were unfaithful, if a respectable woman left her children it must be of her own accord; so Pierce decided to squeeze Fanny out. He began by arranging a schedule of hours. He told her that as he did not approve of her influence over his children she was to see them only at stated times; she might spend an hour with them in the morning before breakfast and another hour between half-past six and half-past seven in the evening; during those hours she was permitted to walk and talk with Sally and Fan but forbidden to give any directions whatever to the governess. The governess was to be responsible for the children's health, morals, manners, dress, food and instruction; she was free to punish or withhold punishment; under no circumstances was Fanny to interfere. If Fanny chose to accept these conditions, she might stay; she might even be allowed to accompany the family to Butler Place when they went back there to live. If she refused, she would have to go.

If Pierce, trusting to his wife's passionate nature, expected instant rebellion he was disappointed. Fanny, incredible as it may appear, submitted! No mother who loved her children would willingly give them over body and soul to another person; in this case there was an added torture for gossip was coupling Pierce's name with the governess's, suspected of being his mistress. Evidently Fanny was not sure enough of this to risk open warfare. She submitted. She agreed to everything, the two short hours a day, the delegation of authority; she would promise whatever Pierce demanded provided he did not take the children away from her. This abject surrender left Pierce rather in a hole, for he had hoped to get rid of her before he returned to Butler Place. All he could do was to add another mortifying stipulation; if Fanny returned to Butler Place she must not behave as if she were the lady of the house. She would have her own suite of rooms so that she might live, as far as possible, apart from the family, and that she might have no excuse for bothering her husband she would receive an allowance of eight hundred dollars—Pierce had made inquiries, and found that no lady in Philadelphia was allowed more than that—and she was not to come to him for any more. Again Fanny submitted. Pierce was annoyed; but he thought of another straw that might perhaps break the camel's back; he told her that he was fed up with the Sedgwicks—or words to that effect; they were "vulgar and obtrusive people" (how astonished that blameless tribe must have been!), if she wished to return to Butler Place she must break off her friendship with the Sedgwicks, and he presented her with a paper to sign. "I promise," it ran, "to give up all intercourse whatever, whether by word or letter, with every member of the Sedgwick family, and hereafter I will treat them in every respect as if I had never known them." Catherine Sedgwick had been among the first to welcome her when she arrived in a new world; to Elizabeth she had confided the journal of her experiences in Georgia; and she depended on Theodore for advice in business matters. Giving up her annual visits to their Berkshire country houses meant giving up all that was pleasant in her life in America. But she signed the paper; she could not let Sally and Fan return to Butler Place without her.

It was useless. The dice were loaded, but she would not give in and the uneven struggle continued. It continued for eighteen months. No doubt many letters were dispatched to intimate friends during that wretched time, and were afterwards destroyed. The few that remain mention two accidents; in the spring of 1844 Fan tumbled downstairs and broke her arm, and the horse, Forester, slipped on a muddy road and injured his hip. Fan was soon well again, but Forester was less fortunate; he never recovered and in the end he had to be shot. Fanny wrote: "He was beautiful and powerful, high-spirited and good-tempered, almost a perfect creature and I loved him very much." Of inner anxieties she said nothing.

But that same spring Philadelphia was visited with a misfortune so remarkable in the city's quiet routine that it could not be ignored:

"We have had fearful riots here," she wrote in May. "The city has been lighted from river to river with the glare of burning Roman Catholic churches and private dwellings; whole streets of this city of brotherly love look like pandemonium avenues of brass and copper in the lurid reflected light. While one church was burning, the Orange band of music played 'Boyne Water,' and when the cross fell from the steeple these Christian folk gave three cheers. For three days, the civil and military authorities did not interfere, but as the city is obliged to pay for this sort of damage, the Militia at length turned out, decent citizens organized themselves into a patrol, cannon were planted around the remaining Catholic churches, the streets were lined with soldiers, and order was finally restored." In July she wrote: "The outrages have recommenced with more fury than ever. The old Orange spirit of bloody persecution has joined itself to the American hatred of popery; Philadelphia flares with burning churches and the Catholics are shot down in the streets and their houses pillaged in broad daylight. The spirit of lawlessness has been growing here for some time. People have been allowed to set fire to the property of negroes and to murder them without anyone caring what happened to the person or property of 'damn niggers'; the same turbulent spirit breaking out in other directions is less agreeable to the *respectable* portion of the community."

After this July of 1844 until October 1845 her letters to Harriet evidently became too intimate for publication. No doubt they described the miseries and mortifications of the life Pierce had mapped out. Small irritations; seeing Sally and Fan wearing frocks she had not chosen, reading books she did not approve, eating food that seemed to her indigestible. Sorrows that cut deep; watching them at play without being able to join them, knowing they were being alienated from her and fearing that their characters would suffer from association with the governess.

A life of such abnegation would have strained the patience of a Griselda; for Fanny, it was impossible. Patience and resignation were not indigenous in her nature; not hardy perennials like her generosity, her courage and her loyalty, but small weak seedlings planted unwillingly and watered with tears. She was doomed to failure. The end was hastened by two incidents; in one case Pierce behaved dishonorably, and in the other Fanny—her standard of honor was high, it seems to have been the only dishonorable act of her life. She found two unopened letters addressed to Pierce in a familiar hand, opened them and read them; they were, as she had suspected, love letters from a woman—Mrs. X, perhaps, though that affair was probably over by now; whoever the writer may have been she made no practical use of her discovery. Pierce's act was less excusable. A letter from one of the Sedgwicks came for his wife, he told a servant to take it to her; coming from her husband, Fanny supposed that, for some reason, he wished her to read it; she did so, and sent it back to him. He accused her of breaking their compact; she had promised not to read any Sedgwick letters. She retorted that he had laid a trap for her; he denied it, and took advantage of what was at worst a technical error. The family was broken up; the children stayed with their father in the old Butler house in Philadelphia which had been lately put in order, and Fanny moved to a boarding house. A heart-breaking encounter of this time brought the finishing touch. She met Sally in the street; Sally tried to stop, the nurse forbade her to speak to her mother; Sally cried, they walked on. It came to Fanny, as she stood there watching Sally dragged away from her, in tears, that her children were suffering as well as herself. They would be happier without her. It was a dreadful realization, she could not bring herself to act upon it at once. It seems likely that in the end she was helped to go by the removal of her chief anxiety, the governess's guardianship of the children. For scandal had been busy, and Pierce, always sensitive to criticism especially in high places, when he heard, as he did hear, that such oracles as Lady Byron and Lady Lovelace had alluded to his relations with the governess in the plainest terms, would undoubtedly have got rid of the lady and engaged some person of unblemished reputation to look after his children.

Whether or not Fanny had this satisfaction to strengthen her, she did at length nerve herself to the final break. Her friends had of course anticipated it; they were sympathetic, but they could not approve. They saw more clearly than Fanny herself appears to have seen, that if she took any active step, such as leaving Philadelphia, Pierce would make the most of it, and letters of advice came pouring in. Adelaide wrote to Fanny; Edward Sartoris and Charles Greville wrote to Pierce; even Mrs. Charles Sedgwick ventured to send Pierce an affectionate word of counsel. All Philadelphia took sides for and against; Pierce's family tried to patch things up. But it was too late. Fanny was determined to go. But where? She thought of Lenox; a little cottage of her own among the blue Berkshire hills would be a refuge where she might find peace if not happiness. But she had no money of her own and Pierce's allowance, though it had been increased to a thousand a year, was not enough for her to live on. The very smallest farmhouse was beyond her means; and her family foresaw another objection to Lenox, Pierce's "Sedgwick complex" might be intensified. Her father told her to come to him—for a visit—no one could criticize her for coming to her father for a visit; and so it was at length decided.

What that leave-taking meant to her can only be guessed. From childhood she had been accustomed to expressing herself both in prose and verse and to seeing the result in print. She could write of many emotional experiences, of her stage fright and her religious beliefs; of Dall's illness and death, of her mother's death, of her father's financial difficulties; she could describe the sights and sounds of a slave hospital. But there was a barrier she never passed. When, in her reminiscences, she looked back at this time she allowed herself only the vaguest allusions to her married life; Pierce's name is invariably omitted, and of the final break and her last good-bye to Sally and Fan she says nothing. But the underlying agony can be imagined in the bare statement:

"In the Autumn of 1845 I returned to England."

Charles was kind, London did its best for her. Everybody came to call, even the Miss Berrys, very old now and almost ready to drop from the bush; she spent week-ends in the country; she met all her clever agreeable old friends—only Sydney Smith was gone—and made any number of clever agreeable new acquaintances. But London was not what she needed. England was too reminiscent of the past. At Bowood or the Hoo she would see Sally feeding the swans, Fan playing with Lord Dacre's bloodhound; in church she would hear Sally's childish voice singing the psalms so very much too loud, and her father himself was a constant reminder of what she had lost. For Charles missed the children and could not resist talking about them; his lamentations that everything had turned out so badly and the plans he suggested that might heal the breach, bring Pierce to his senses and reunite the family, were almost more than she could bear.

No: London was most certainly not what she needed. She needed sunlight and open spaces and quiet and sleep. She realized she was on the edge of collapse; suicide or insanity seemed possible; but she could not rouse herself to action. When the Sartorises, guessing her condition, urged her to spend a year with them in Italy, she agreed, but reluctantly. She made her preparations without enthusiasm; she would see, what all her life she had most wanted to see, Italy and the Alps, but she would be too unhappy to enjoy the sight; she was too old, too worn out.

A morbid nature would have refused to try Adelaide's prescription for a sore heart, but it was the right medicine for

Fanny and her nature responded with its usual elasticity. Not at once; it was weeks before health returned. Then, as she galloped her horse over the undulating, sweet-scented, many-colored expanse of the Roman campagna she could often forget the past; just as in Georgia, riding along the causeway bordered with coral-colored weeds, she could forget the sorrows of the slaves and laugh with delight as the crabs went scuttling away from her horse's feet.

And Italy had such a wealth of "coral and crabs" to offer! There was more beauty in every yard of Rome than in the whole state of Georgia, more spontaneous gaiety in the Sartorises' household than in all Philadelphia from the time of William Penn on. Edward Sartoris was so kind, Adelaide so affectionate—and the children? Too often the voices and laughter of Adelaide's children as they ran about the garden would break the spell, and Fanny would have given all the camellias and myrtles and roses, the statues and fountains and far-flung view of Adelaide's Roman garden for the small prim flat commonplace green enclosure of Butler Place.

But in spite of such stabbing moments she did achieve a measure of happiness, and before long her interest in writing revived; she set to work on a book. It was merely the story of her Italian experiences; but she found a good name for it, 'A Year of Consolation'; there was good prose in it and a little good poetry, such as the lines written at Frascati commemorating the old garden:

> ". . . Where from a twilight cell
> A Naiad, crowned with tufts of trembling green,
> Sang towards the sunny palace all day long."

The luscious Italian scene inspired her; often her enjoyment was heightened by some association with the past. Of her first sight of Rome—approached, in those pre-railway days, slowly and beautifully from the campagna—she wrote: "I saw the shadowy dome of St. Peter's rising against the sky and felt a tumult of doubt, fear and hope such as I had experienced when I first saw Niagara." The lake at Albano was contrasted with the Stockbridge Bowl, "so much more friendly and humane;" ilex trees reminded her of the live oaks of Georgia, and the Roman market of a similar scene in Philadelphia, "with its great baskets of precious-looking tomatoes, piles of Indian corn like strings of Roman pearls, heaps of purple polished egg plants and downy peaches, interspersed with huge fanlike nosegays of jasmine, magnolias and fragrant tuberoses." She even revised her severest criticism of American manners; in a French steamboat, she wrote: "Oh, my poor dear American fellow-citizens! how humbly I beg your pardon for the reproaches I have levelled against your national diversion of spitting. Spittoons have hitherto been the bane of my life in the United States, but as I sat there in the cabin, surrounded by men hawking and spitting, a spittoon would have been the joy of my heart and the delight of my eyes. How I thought too of the honor and security in which a woman might travel alone from Georgia to Maine as safely as if she were the sister or daughter of every man she meets." Such sentences are significant; in her American journal she spoke of herself as an Englishwoman; in her Italian she acknowledges her American citizenship and turns to America as her home. The poems in 'A Year of Consolation' are shot through with this homesick feeling; sometimes the allusion to her children is direct, as in the 'Lines on a Branch of Flowering Acacia' commemorating Sally's first birthday when the acacias had been in bloom at Butler Place, and the sonnet written after hearing that Sally had burst into tears when someone spoke her mother's name. In almost every poem there is an allusion to the past.

This undercurrent of sadness was inevitable, but courage enabled her to rise above it; she was happy in Italy. With light-hearted Adelaide for a companion she could enjoy carnival time with the enthusiasm of a girl. The summer at Frascati went by like a bright dream; riding, driving, strolling by moonlight, mountain climbing; superlatively good music, superlatively good conversation, in a setting of flawless beauty, the ancient terraced garden with its urns and cypress spires where Pauline Borghese had entertained her lovers. Poets and painters, musicians and philosophers, came and went; every topic under heaven was discussed in that old garden. Often politics crowded out art and literature. 1846 was a momentous year; it brought the death of Gregory XVI and the election of Pius IX. In spite of the heat there was hurrying back and forth between Rome and Frascati that summer, and the Sartorises' friends returning to the villa would find an eager audience . . . The Pope was dying. They said he was dying of starvation; they said his favorite had got tired of taking care of the old man . . . The Pope was dead. It was just as well; he had been most unpopular . . . The Pope was buried, shabbily buried; his catafalque in St. Peter's was only pasteboard . . . The old Pope was forgotten; public interest centred on the conclave. Who would be elected? A long-drawn sigh of thanksgiving—the lot had fallen on Cardinal Mastai; young, handsome, *modern,* a friend of liberty. Rome was safe, the temporal power was safe!

By this time the summer was waning. Fanny wrote sadly:

"The end is come in thunder and wild rain
  Autumn has stormed the golden house of summer."

Then they were back again in the Sartorises' apartment in the Trinità dei Monti. December came; Fanny's holiday was over; she drank for the last time from the fountain of Trevi, and with a sinking heart. In London she would have to decide where and how she was to live. Pierce's allowance was sent too irregularly to be depended upon; her father was old and badly off; she could not expect him to support her or to return the money she had settled on him at the time of her marriage. But there was her Italian journal; if she could sell it, she could get along until she had decided that essential *where* and *how.*

She did sell her book, and for a good price. It was accepted, unread, by Mr. Moxon, and an American edition arranged for with Wiley and Putnam of New York. As usual, she was amazed. Why should anyone want her "rubbish?" Yet she must have known there was good writing in 'A Year of Consolation;' no painter ever wrote more sensitively of the Italian landscape, or Somerville and Ross with more exhilaration of the joy of a good gallop on a good horse on a hunting morning. She had invariably found a publisher ready to take whatever she chose to write; but she was always amazed, always grateful, always dismissed her work as "rubbish."

However, 'A Year of Consolation' was so well received that if she had stayed on in Italy and with the Sartorises, who took for granted that art in some form was the most important thing in life, writing might have become something more than a by-product. As it was, London and her father turned her inevitably to the stage as the surest way of earning a living. She hated the idea. Those prenatal disturbances that, in her girlhood, had welled up from below the threshold to rob her career of pleasure now returned in full force. She fought them down—with that list towards asceticism common in passionate natures whatever she hated most seemed to her, for that reason, safe and right—and prepared reluctantly to resume a life she disliked. In a letter of a later date she tried to explain her mixed feelings towards things theatrical: "How curious it seems to me," she wrote, after reading a biography of Macready the actor, "that he could care, as he did, for his profession, having none of the feeling of dislike for it in *itself* that I had, and then dislike and despise it because he thought it placed him socially in an inferior position to other professional men, or gentlemen of other professions!—that seems to me an incomprehensible thing. I do not think any of my people ever looked at their calling in this fashion."

Fanny was all Kemble when she wrote that; and now, as she made her preparations, her name was the only asset she did not deny. She knew that a theatrical career could not be thrown away and picked up again, twelve years later, as good as ever. She knew she was too old—she was thirty-seven—not for acting, but too old to begin again. She knew she had lost the childlike charm of her Juliet and her Julia and, looking back, she saw herself as merely a clever girl, ignorant and presumptuous. Facing the present, her heart sank; such advantages as she had had were gone.

Characteristically, she told everybody just how she felt, and freely admitted that she wanted to make money, and as soon as she had made enough to buy a farm in America she intended to leave both England and the stage for good. In short, as was her custom, she did her best to alienate a sentimental public, and obstinately refused to profit from the advertising her friends and the press were prepared to give her. It was not her only obstinacy; a showier style of makeup was now being used because of more brilliant stage lighting; Fanny would have none of it. What? smear her neck and arms with cold cream and pearl powder? No indeed! She would rouge, of course—she had always used rouge; but never never would she submit to being whitewashed. Everybody protested; Henry Greville reminded her that Grisi wore white paint as well as red, and hinted that what was good enough for Madame Grisi ought to be good enough for her; Fanny agreed, but remained firm. Henry implored her to let him send her his own *coiffeur,* "a clean, tidy foreigner," she shuddered and vowed that no hands but her own should touch her face; as for pearl powder, if the public did not enjoy seeing her brown they need not come to see her at all. And that was that.

Her friends, knowing Fanny, gave in; they turned their attention to helping her find a house to live in. She finally rented Mrs. Fitzhugh's house, 18 Orchard street, Portman Square, for a year.

CHAPTER XXIII

Hard Work

"My mind was like a conjured spirit that would do mischief if I would not give it employment."

—SWIFT.

HER ITALIAN holiday over Fanny settled down to face two new experiences, solitude and earning her living. London seemed strangely unchanged; streets, shops, friends' faces, ladies' dresses all just the same as a year ago. Lessen the spread of hoopskirts and she could have imagined herself back in the London of three years ago. Let the hoops shrink away altogether and it would have been the London of her girlhood. But a year ago she had been living with her father; three years ago she had had a husband and children; as a girl she had been one of a large high-spirited family. All gone now; her mother dead, Aunt Dall dead, Adelaide in Italy, Henry in Ireland, John retired to a remote country cottage. Even her father had gone; he was living in Brighton and could give her his advice but not much of his society.

It gave a strange unreality to existence to find herself living in the Fitzhughs' house—a house of many pleasant associations —alone. Alone in spirit as well as in body. All her life she had been taken care of and chaperoned. Pierce had never allowed her even the usual semi-freedom of a married woman; her theatrical affairs had been managed by her father; her mother had designed her costumes; Dall had watched over her. Now she had to interview agents; decide places, dates, terms. It was hard work; she made mistakes; now and then someone cheated her. But she had ability and indomitable courage; she learned to manage her affairs and, except for her scorn of advertising, she managed them well. Never, to the

293

end of her days, did she learn how to save money; but she did learn how to make it.

It was not a good theatrical season. What with the political turmoil abroad and the Chartists at home England had neither time nor money for amusement. Worse still, from Fanny's standpoint, Jenny Lind was coming; the shop windows that seventeen years before had displayed cups and saucers, handkerchiefs and fans adorned with Miss Fanny Kemble's smiling face, now showed the blonde head of the new idol—even Rachel was not drawing good houses. A London engagement being impossible, Fanny arranged to act first at Manchester as Julia in 'The Hunchback,' her most popular part, and then make the usual tour of other large towns.

She felt terribly alone when she thought of her opening night, but her friends could do little to help her, for she would not let them; even Harriet was asked not to come. It would be dreary, she admitted, to face an audience of strangers but it would be safer. She wished to preserve the dreamlike atmosphere where she was moving like an automaton, and feared that with the intrusion of any intimate figure of the past she might forget that she was Mrs. Butler, middle-aged and serene, and so identify herself with the child Fanny that when the curtain went up she would burst into tears. However, when Henry Greville insisted on travelling part way with her to Manchester, and promised to be there for the opening night, she was glad. People she loved would be a menace, people she merely liked would be a comfort.

She had been wise; whether because of Henry Greville's sympathetic presence or Harriet's equally sympathetic absence, when the night came Julia stood waiting for the curtain to rise encased in impenetrable self-possession. Of all the first night fears that had haunted her girlhood only one—an echo of the "O.P. Riots"—was left. She had written to Harriet: "I am not very nervous about my plunge; the only thing I dread is the *noise* that may greet me. I wish I could avoid my 'reception,' any loud sound shakes me from head to foot." And she did suffer a few moments of agony when as she entered the house rose clapping and cheering, but her calm soon returned, and Julia moved serenely and competently to the end of the play.

"The theatre here is beautiful," she wrote to Lady Dacre, "the company very fair; the plays are well and carefully got up. The audience were most exceedingly kind and cordial to me, and I have every reason to be thankful and grateful, and more than satisfied." It was a sedate summing-up; no "first, fine careless rapture" such as young Fanny would have poured out from a full heart. Mrs. Butler, safely concentrated on the present, could for the moment forget that young Fanny. Mrs. Butler was *satisfied*.

But often satisfaction was not enough. Often and often she could not forget. How was it possible to forget when her tours took her through the same country that she had traversed in the triumphal progresses of sixteen years ago? Looking out of the window of the railway carriage she seemed to see a cheerful trio—her father, Dall, young Fanny—perched on the top of a high yellow coach, horses' hoofs clattering, whip cracking, horn blowing as they rattled merrily through smiling villages gay with flowers and children. The towns too had their associations. Bath brought back her childhood, Liverpool a more recent past—when she had last stayed at the Adelphi Sally and Fan had been with her! Dublin was sad enough without associations. No rollicking crowds now at the stage door to call for "three cheers for Miss Fanny," no rollicking crowds anywhere in Ireland. 1847 was the year of the famine. She had not wanted to come; it seemed insulting to ask a people wasting away from starvation to spend money on the theatre, and she played to poor houses, except for the night that Lord Bessborough had "bespoke;" but she did not mind, the poor creatures had far better uses for their money.

There was poverty too in Edinburgh—misery and poverty everywhere that year, except in America. The railway had slashed into the beautiful city's heart; Scott's monument was a poor substitute for Sir Walter himself riding down Princes Street on his handsome horse; Mrs. Harry Siddons was dead. But there were lovely grandchildren to play with; Fanny wrote to Harriet: "Lizzie's children are like a troop of angels. The companionship of children is charming to me." During a visit at Carrolside she wrote: "I have been wading in the Leader, and standing on cold rocks by the hour, catching nothing, for the water is so clear the trout see me as well as I see them . . . This morning before breakfast I walked along the banks of the stream, and then knee-deep up its bright waters, and then over the breezy hills, whence I watched its gleaming course between red-colored rocks and cornfields and tufted woods, and felt for an hour as if there were no bitterness in life."

Fanny was still Fanny. She could still enjoy playing with children, and wading in deep clear cold pools in the early morning. And she was as impulsively tender-hearted as ever. Moments of pleasure could alternate with moments of suffering as unexpectedly as in the old days in Georgia. For everywhere she went that year she encountered misery. The unrest of 1832, when ricks had blazed and Manchester operatives shown their hatred of Wellington, had increased; everywhere she met poor creatures in need of help; always she did what she could. She would see a little boy staring at the food in a pastry-cook's window, discover that he was longing for a baked apple to take to a sick brother, buy him what he wanted, follow him home and help the family—though with some irritation, for the mother's chief anxiety was for suitable mourning if the sick boy died. Fanny's benefactions were often mixed with irritation; trying to help a poor girl arrested for sleeping in a London park she came in contact with officials who refused to accept her suggestions, although, as she wrote to Harriet, she "sobbed like a Magdalene and talked like a magpie." Of an instance of the same sort in Hull, she wrote: "As I was walking through the railway station this morning with Mr. Frost I remarked, lying in a corner, what I took at first to be a bundle of rags. On looking again, I perceived there was a live creature in the rags—a boy, crouching on the pavement. I knelt down and asked him what ailed him, he hardly lifted his face from his hands, said 'headache' and, coughing horribly, buried his face again. Mr. Frost began to ask questions; then followed one of those piteous stories that make one smart all over; cruelty from a stepfather, beating, starving, final abandonment. He did not know what had become of his parents, they had gone away 'before snow.' The interrogatory was prolonged; Mr. Frost is cautious, not irresistibly prompted to seize up such an unfortunate in his arms and adopt him for his own. We found that the boy had been in the workhouse, and would be glad to go back there. So I got a cab and put the child in, and with my kind old gentleman carried the small forsaken soul to the workhouse where we got him, with much difficulty, temporarily, received. Would you believe it? We were told that this poor creature had come to the gate the night before begging admittance, but because he had not a certain written order he had been, *of course,* turned away. It seems he had been *sent to prison* several times for being found lying at night on the wharves. I wouldn't be a man for anything! They are so cruel, without even knowing that they are; the habit of seeing sin and suffering is such a heart-hardener— You remember what infinite difficulty I had in rescuing that poor little wretch in Glasgow whose mother drove her out into the streets to sing her starvation in the mud and rain. Well, the boy is safe in the workhouse now and is, according to his own wish, to be sent to sea."

Sometimes it was the hard-heartedness of managers that enraged her. When she wanted to give a benefit for a poor young couple who had acted with her in Norwich their manager made all sorts of difficulties, and in the end meanly insisted on being paid his expenses. Still more annoying was the churlish behavior of her own manager who objected to her taking part in an amateur show that Henry Greville was getting up for the Irish famine fund. However, as the Queen was a patroness, and everybody was helping the Irish—even the Americans; A. T. Stewart, a New York merchant, had chartered a ship and was sending them thousands of dollars worth of provisions—he had to give in, and Fanny was allowed to do her share.

The play was 'Hernani,' Lord Ellesmere's translation acted so long ago at Bridgewater House, preceded by an address written by Lady Dufferin for the occasion which Fanny was to recite. The great night came; the amateurs were in a flutter; Fanny was calm. She stood in the side scenes waiting to go on, laughing and talking with Lord Carlisle who had brought her a bunch of flowers, exclaiming at his dexterity as he stooped and spread out her train for her, amused at his explanation—he had, he said, served a long apprenticeship at court drawing-rooms, where he "had spread out and gathered up oceans of silk and satin, thousands of yards more than a counter-gentleman at Swan and Edgar's." Her train flowing behind her she stepped out on the stage; recited the address, went through one familiar scene after the other. It was over. Everybody said it had been a tremendous success.

But of all her dreamlike repetitions of this time it must have seemed the most unreal, for she was Donna Sol and Augustus Craven was Hernani. As they went through the motions of a romance that was, to them, no longer romantic, when Donna Sol sank dying into Hernani's arms, did Fanny recall that favorite saying of her friend Lady Morley: "There's nothing new, nothing true, and nothing signifies?" Certainly, to both, it must all have seemed as flat as stale champagne. However, flatness, under the circumstances, was safer than effervescence; and the audience was enchanted, and they made lots of money, and Fanny said how nice it was to meet Mr. Craven again, and she hoped his charming wife would come to see her; and they did come, and brought a lovely niece, and they all three tried, without success, to convert Fanny to Roman Catholicism. So everything was as pleasant as possible, and Fanny wrote to Harriet: "Certainly novelists invent nothing more improbable than real life."

It was a year of benefits; after the starving Irish, society turned its attention to buying Shakespeare's birthplace. When Fanny was asked to take part she did not feel that she could refuse, though she wrote to Harriet: "The world seems to me so absolutely Shakespeare's dwelling place that I do not vividly associate him with those four walls between which he first saw the light of an English day . . . He could not have been different from other babies, you know; nor, indeed need be—for a *baby—any* baby—is a more wonderful thing even than Shakespeare . . . If the house he dwelt in in maturity still existed, I should feel considerable emotion in being where his mind had reached its zenith. I have told you how curiously affected I was while standing by his grave; how I was overcome with sleep—my invariable refuge under great emotion—and how I prayed to be allowed to sleep for a little while on the altar steps of the chancel, beside his bones; for his bones *are* there, and above them streamed a warm and brilliant sunbeam, fit emblem of his vivifying spirit . . . They have asked me to act the dying scene of Queen Katherine."

In Fanny's youth Queen Katherine had been beyond her; she was too immature. Now, as it was the part assigned to her in the great memorial celebration, it was evidently considered one of her best. Naturally enough; she had not only grown mentally and spiritually in the years between, she had been forced to study the rôle of discarded wife and bereaved mother from life. She had studied it so closely that 'Henry VIII' would have been a trying play for her at any time. When the last scene of the dying Queen was isolated as on this occasion, it must have been almost unbearably painful, especially Katherine's message to the faithless Henry, speaking of their daughter,

"Beseeching him to give her virtuous breeding,
She is young, and of a noble modest nature."

And the last gasping line:

". . . Although unqueen'd, yet like
A queen, and daughter to a king, inter me.
I can no more,"

on which Katherine exits, must have brought self-control to the breaking point. Add to this, that the benefit was given in Covent Garden—though so altered for opera that Fanny did not consider she was appearing on the stage where she had made her début—and it is not surprising to find her writing to Harriet:

"I have just returned from Covent Garden. At the conclusion of my performance the audience called for me, but I was seized with a nervous terror of going on, and left the house as quickly as possible. I shall incur unpleasant comments for having, as it must appear, ungraciously withdrawn myself from the public call. This does not trouble me very deeply, but I am sorry for it, because I am afraid it will be considered disrespectful, which it was not."

Perhaps Fanny's suffering was evident; there is no mention of her "disrespect" in 'Punch's' account of the Shakespeare Festival, though the absence of royalty was noted and explained with bitter sarcasm; the stoker of the royal train had the influenza, and "to proceed to London under such circumstances—*the* favorite stoker being absent—was out of the question . . . Whilst the Shakespeare Festival was being held, Her Majesty and the Prince took a hand at cribbage." But having disposed of royalty Mr. Punch recovered his good humor, and imagining Shakespeare to have been present made the poet compliment each performer in turn: " 'Very good indeed! Hardly tall enough to be queenly—but very good!' said the Poet, as Queen Katherine died in Mrs. Butler. 'Very good; I shall tell her aunt so, when I go home.' "

'Punch's' estimate of her acting at this time may be taken as typical. Critics and public agreed that she was "very good indeed," but there was no wild enthusiasm; though some realized that Mrs. Butler was a more perfect artist than Miss Kemble, they missed the youth, the naïveté and high spirits that had made her so endearing in the past. Fanny herself knew she had both lost and gained. In a letter to Harriet, speaking of her business difficulties, she wrote: "It is a curious sensation to have a consciousness of power and, at the same time, of helplessness," and after quoting the dying words of Beethoven: " 'Pourtant, Hummel, j'avois du génie,' " added sadly: "Such transcendent genius did not defend him from poverty, and the petty cares of living." It is a suggestive sentence. In her youth she had experienced moments of inspiration; fire from heaven had flashed, through her, to her audience; but it was a mysterious fire, coming and going without her volition. Now she is aware of *power,* a very different thing. The intellectual, Kemble half of her nature was getting the upper hand, teaching her how to control the passionate De Camp inheritance; she was welding the two into a better instrument for her art. But with the sense of power came the sense of frustration; she realized, now when it was too late, that for a perfect welding the intellect must begin to hammer before the fire of youth is growing cold.

On the other hand, the "petty cares of living" soon ceased to trouble her; Macready, the best actor in London, told his manager that he wanted Mrs. Butler for his leading lady at the Princess Theatre. It was a triumph, but it had its drawbacks; Macready was a terrible man to act with. The greenroom reported eyes endangered by his sword, arms dislocated, and heroines emerging half strangled from a demonstration of love or hate. But he assured Fanny that "the devil was not as black as he was painted," and did his best to be kind. Probably he stood a little in awe of her—she was a Kemble—she never had to defend her head with sharp hairpins to prevent his taking it "in chancery" as he had been known to do, and he even apologized for Lear's rough handling of Cordelia. But Fanny wrote despairingly to Harriet: "He growls and prowls and roams and foams around the stage, in every direction, like the tiger in his cage, so that I never know which side of me he means to be, and keeps up a perpetual snarling and grumbling so that I never feel sure that he *has done* and that it is my turn to speak." The smothering scene in 'Othello,' dreaded by all actresses, was an ordeal. Though Macready did not require his Desdemona to imitate Pasta and run wildly around the stage until caught by the hair and strangled, he was "tigerish," and apart from physical exhaustion the scene took on an added grimness at the time because of a recent tragedy in real life, the murder of the Duchess de Praslin by her husband, a crime that, for Fanny, must have had peculiar significance. It was said to have been instigated by the governess, who "had turned the hearts of her pupils against their unfortunate mother, and established her position and authority in the family at the Duchesse's expense," and Fanny knew all there was to know about that sort of governess! (By an odd coincidence, later on, Fanny met this Mademoiselle de Luzzy, acquitted, married to a clergyman and living in Stockbridge, Massachusetts.) But Macready's violence shocked Fanny less than his disregard of dramatic art. The banquet scene in 'Macbeth' should be set with the dining tables at the sides so that Lady Macbeth can rush straight down from the dais at the back. Macready insisted on placing a long table in front of the throne; she pointed out that as this would cramp her freedom it would injure the scene, but he would not give in and she realized that he thought more of his own part than of the artistic whole, an unpardonable sin! When, in answer to his criticism of the part of Desdemona— a poor part, he said, he wondered she was willing to act it— she exclaimed: "It is Shakespeare! I would act Maria in 'Twelfth Night' if I were asked to do so!" he smiled his incredulity; he did not believe her. However, with all his drawbacks Macready could be great in such parts as Rob Roy, and she granted him a painter's feeling for color, grouping and scenic effects. The engagement was a success; she made money and gained in reputation. But her dislike of the stage persisted.

An almost superstitious reverence for Shakespeare added to this dislike; and as she went on acting, attempting the impossible, seeing others attempt and fail, she began to feel that it was a sacrilege. Shakespeare was pre-eminently a dramatic poet; if his plays were to be given merely as vehicles for the triumphs of individual human beings they had better never be acted at all. It was not a point of view calculated to endear her to the profession. To this day, Fanny Kemble is believed by other actors to have "run down her profession." That most discriminating artist George Arliss, in his preface to her essay 'On the Stage,' which he praises as "perhaps the most careful analysis of the actor in juxtaposition to his art that one is likely to find in dramatic literature," he hints that the distinction she makes between "things theatrical and things dramatic" is indicative of professional snobbishness; she despised the stage; an actress who despises the stage is despicable. But Mr. Arliss underrates her reverence for the drama. For her, there was one supreme art, poetic drama, and one true prophet, Shakespeare. It is not despicable to admire the moon more than the baby who cries for it, and that was how Fanny felt about poetic drama.

No doubt the theatrical world of 1848 would have agreed with Mr. Arliss. There must have been some sneering comment when, that spring, as Charles Kemble had finally given up reading in public, Fanny decided to take his place and announced her preference for reading rather than acting Shakespeare. No professional actor would have sympathized; probably it was said that Mrs. Butler talked of retiring merely because readings were the fashion and she could make more money that way.

Nobody could deny that readings were popular and therefore profitable; Fanny's decision met with approval from her

friends. Lady Charlotte Greville offered the drawing-room of
her brand-new London house for a first reading, but Fanny
would not impose on the kindness of even such an old friend
as Lady Charlotte. She even refused to read 'Antigone' for the
Queen at Buckingham Palace; apart from the strain of reading in public for the first time in the presence of royalty, the
Mendelssohn choruses were to be played as an accompaniment and Mendelssohn's recent death had been an overwhelming grief; she was afraid of breaking down. So the
honor was declined and Fanny, quoting Mrs. Siddons's cook,
declared that like that worthy soul she believed "everyone
should stand on their own bottom with fortitude and similar-
ity." When she read in public for the first time in March,
1848, it was at Highgate in a small hall and for a small audience.

As it turned out she needed no help or advertising. Her
genius was immediately acknowledged; managers from all
over England besieged her with offers; the desire to hear Mrs.
Butler read Shakespeare seemed to be universal. This was
gratifying; what was far more important, Fanny herself was
satisfied. Until now, though so sure of herself as a *person—*
not even her matrimonial failure had broken her spirit—she
seldom felt sure of herself as an *artist.* Experience ought to
have told her that she could act, she had it in her to be a
great dancer, she had written three successful books; but she
had set her standard too high and remained dissatisfied. Now
at last she had found the best medium for her genius. She
liked to read Shakespeare. She knew she read well; she hoped
that, through her, the public might learn to love Shakespeare
as she felt he should be loved. Her greatest asset was of course
her beautiful voice; her diction was perfect, Kemble preci-
sion leavened with De Camp flexibility and humor; an ear for
music was another advantage. Alluding to Macready's lack in
this respect, she wrote: "What is called the *natural* style of
speaking blank verse is simply chopping it up into prose;
blank verse demands the same care and method that music

does, and when not uttered with due regard to its artificial
construction and rules of rhythm and measure is precisely as
faulty as music sung out of tune." Her study of Shakespeare
had been profound and continuous; later, speaking of her
debt to him, she wrote: "I have passed a large portion of my
life with the greatest and best English mind and heart, living
almost daily in that world, above the world, into which he
lifted me;" in Philadelphia her talks with Horace Furness,
the Shakespearean scholar, had been one of her few intellectual pleasures. Add personality, charm and a great name and
it is scarcely surprising that for the next twenty years Shakespeare and Fanny Kemble were bracketed in the public mind.

There remains another question; why were readings so
popular at this time? The Kembles and other professionals
had often given readings, but only as a by-product of their
acting. Now, all at once, every celebrity in the United King-
dom seems to have felt drawn to the lecture platform; literary lights such as Dickens and Thackeray read from their own
works; theatrical stars read favorite parts; small fry contented
themselves with "selections." Obviously, a minor amusement
had become a major, for what reason remains a mystery. In
any reconstruction of the past its amusements are less easy to
understand than its afflictions; funerals are still sad and illness
unpleasant. But why should one generation find waltzing de-
liriously exciting and the next tedious? Why should tennis
and golf come in and go out at intervals of a hundred years or
so? Nobody can tell us. So today, when reading is an outworn
form of art, to understand the public's enthusiasm for Fanny
Kemble's interpretations of Shakespeare, one must think, not
of some author who gathers a mildly interested audience
when he reads from his own works, but of a *diseuse,* an artist
such as Yvette Guilbert or Ruth Draper. The latter is probably
the nearest present-day example of the dramatic genius who
works best alone. Like Ruth Draper, Fanny Kemble possessed
the power of evoking a throng of characters without the aid of
costume or scenery, and making them "live and move and

have their being" in the imagination of her audience. No one, not even Ruth Draper, was ever more successful in making her hearers *see*. Fanny Kemble could make them see everything, little and big, that she wanted them to see. They saw not only Rosalind and Celia but the Forest of Arden, the brightness of Elizabeth's christening procession, the darkness of Friar Lawrence's cell. Speaking of this power, Mrs. Augustus Craven wrote in her 'Jeunesse de Fanny Kemble:' *"Elle le fascinait au point de lui faire* VOIR, *jusqúaux paysages dont elle parlait, de lui faire entendre le mugissement de la mer ou le bruit de la tempête ebranlant la forêt"*; and added that she had seen a child in the audience hide her face screaming, afraid she would see Shylock slice the pound of flesh from Antonio's chest.

Fanny, conscious of her fitness for the career she had chosen, was happy in her work, and less lonely for her dream of buying a farm in Lenox began to seem possible. She was making money. Not so much as she might have. She asked a fixed sum for a reading—at first only twenty pounds—and would not take a penny more, no matter how profitable the performance might be. "I have never," she wrote later, "sacrificed my sense of what was due to my work for the sake of what I could make by it," and in accordance with this principle drew up a set of rules that her managers found impracticable and the public absurd. She insisted on reading Shakespeare's plays in a certain order, beginning with 'Lear' and ending with 'The Tempest'—partly because she was afraid of getting stale and wished to preserve a freshness of attack; she would have liked to give each play in its entirety, but as no audience could be expected to listen for more than two hours she used the versions her father had arranged, with some alterations. But this was her utmost concession. Managers might rave and the public complain, Fanny was firm; Shakespeare, being sacred, was not to be trifled with.

And now, travelling about England, she found much to enjoy. Letters to Harriet spoke of many small pleasures; a wall

paper patterned with convolvulus— "You know how subject I
am to the influence of even a ridiculous wall paper;" she
wrote ecstatically of receiving a bunch of Persian lilac and
"two flower-pots full of various mosses so fragrant of earthy
freshness that no perfume ever surpassed it. Flowers are my
'good angels;' " of travelling on May Day, and seeing the engines adorned with branches of hawthorn and laburnum; of a
visit to the nursery gardens at Exeter where she was shown
"the flower tribes of the whole earth, wonderful creatures,
lovely to the eye, delicious to the smell. I was told they have
a flower hunter out in South America and another in India."
Harriet sent her a beautiful Irish setter; now and then she had
a ride on a good horse. Of one morning in a country inn she
wrote: "It poured with rain, so I sent for a pair of battledores
and a shuttlecock, and when Charles Mason appeared I made
him take a good breathing." She saw Rachel act again and
again, and little Maria Taglioni, Taglioni's niece, dance; of
Déjazet, in 'Vert Vert,' a play about a boy brought up as a girl
in a convent, escaping for a week's pleasure in a garrison
town and returning to the convent "with ideas," she wrote:
"My eyes opened wider and wider. I never saw such unflinch-
ing audacity in any male or female, on or off the stage. Mademoiselle Déjazet always wears men's clothes and is seldom
seen without a cigar in her mouth; she carries the town before her, being the least decent actress of the most indecent
pieces I have ever seen."

There were new novels to read and talk over. That spring
she wrote to Harriet: "I had a nice long visit from Thackeray. Have you read his 'Vanity Fair'? It is wonderful." Everyone was discussing 'Jane Eyre' and making wild guesses at the
authorship. Fanny wrote incredulously: "Henry Greville says
his brother Charles is supposed to be the author!" But she
found no impossibility in Jane's hearing her distant lover call
her name: "I have often thought," she told Harriet, "that the
power of love might work such a miracle," and a sonnet written in Italy, "If there were any power in human love," ex-

pressed the same idea; intense love might bring her children
"before her very eyes." The mere sight of youth or beauty
often gave her pleasure; the red-cheeked Eton boys breaking
into ecstasies of merriment whenever in 'The Tempest' "Stephano, your drunken butler," was mentioned, for Stephano
was their nickname for one of the masters, Mr. Stephen Haw-
try; a girl met at Miss Berry's, whose "straight, nymphlike
figure and the sort of chastity that characterized her appearance" fulfilled her ideal of womanly beauty. "The light,
straight-limbed Artemis," she explained, "is lovelier to me
than the round soft sleepy Aphrodite." Sometimes the pleasure would be so small that few would have thought it worth
mentioning, but Fanny wrote at some length of her maid's
having bought her a raspberry tart, still her favorite confec-
tion, during a long wait at a railway station, and ended gratefully, "Was it not kind and courtly of her!"

Often there was the pleasure of good conversation: "What
a delightful thing good talking is," she wrote. "What a delightful thing good writing is. How much delight there is in
the exercise of our faculties. How full a thing, and admirable,
and wonderful, is this nature of ours!" At a dinner party one
night she would meet D'Israeli, Monckton Milnes and Carlyle and be entertained by their discussion of recent St. Pat-
rick's Day disturbances in Ireland; "D'Israeli, said to me," she
told Harriet, "that he couldn't see why Dublin should not be
burned to the ground; that he could understand the use of
London, or even of Paris, but that the *use* of Dublin was a
mystery. I suggested its being the fountain-head of Guin-
ness's stout, but he did not seem to consider porter an equivalent for the ten righteous men that might save a city!" Another evening she would dine at the Greys' and listen with
some surprise to Lord Dacre and Lord Grey talking over the
political situation, for they likened Cobden and Bright to
Danton and Mirabeau, Corn-Law leagues and peace protests
to the first measures of the leaders of the French Revolution,
and predicted a similar end. Her years in America had made

her less conservative than some of her friends; she could not
share the Ellesmeres' horror at allowing Jews in Parliament—
Lord Ellesmere had voted against the measure—or their satisfaction at having convinced Lord Melbourne that Arnold of
Rugby was too unorthodox for a bishopric. She was impatient
with fanatics who objected to "ethereal confinements" as an
effort on the part of women to escape from the curse pronounced in 'Genesis,' and wrote to Harriet: "I hear from
America that Fanny Longfellow has been brought to bed
most prosperously under the beneficent influence of ether,"
and would have agreed with Charles Greville, whose diary
that winter noted: "I went to St. George's hospital to see the
chloroform tried, a boy was to be cut for the stone. He went
to sleep in a minute. It is a privilege to have lived in the times
which saw the production of steam and electricity, but the
chloroform far transcends them in its beneficent operations."
On the other hand she was in some ways too conservative to
keep up with London society; she disapproved of the latest
fashionable craze for "chloroform parties," and was horrified
when Lady Castlereagh admitted with indifference that she
had watched a guinea pig die during a lecture on chloroform;
for she could not understand dissipation, and cruelty to animals seemed to her unforgivable.

Her years of loneliness had helped her to think for herself;
she was working out her own philosophy of life, her own doc-
trines, her own religion. "Place, time, life, death, earth,
heaven," she wrote to Harriet, "are divisions and distinctions
we make, like the imaginary lines we trace upon the surface
of the globe . . . Your theory of partial immortality is abhorrent to me. I would rather disbelieve in the immortality of
my own soul than suppose the boon given to me was withheld
from any of my fellow creatures . . . It is strange that you and
Charles Greville should both be writing to me upon this subject of life after death. He began writing to me with reference
to the rapidly declining health of his and my friend Mary
Berry. His chief regret seems to be for the loss of a person he

cared for and the departure of a remarkable member of society. Whereas, with me, my first feeling at hearing of the death of a good person is one of congratulation; I have a sense of relief, as it were, for such a one, of freer breathing, of expanded powers; of infirmity, pain, sorrow, fleshly hindrance and earthly suffering forever left behind . . . I cannot talk much with Charles Greville, he does not understand a word I say. His *right* always appears to me to be a synonym for expedient, and when I tell him so, he says, 'They are the same thing,' which I do not believe."

Politically too she was building up her own theories. She wrote to Harriet: "The monstrous inequality in the means of existence, more flagrant here than anywhere else on earth, will yet be dealt with by us English. The one revolution which our social system seems to me to need could be effected by legislative action upon the tenure of land, the whole system of proprietorship of the soil, the spread of education and the extension of the franchise . . . At Mrs. Grote's I listened with pleasure to Charles Greville, Mr. Grote and the Italian patriot, Prandi—you know that fond as I am of talking, I like listening better when I can hear what seems to me worth listening to—and I was delighted with their liberal view of the whole state of Europe, especially Italy, so interesting in her half aroused attitude of reviving national vitality."

It was natural that everything connected with Italy should have interested Fanny at this time because of the Sartorises. For the past year they had been talking of returning to England; the Grevilles were urging Edward Sartoris to stand for Parliament, and Henry had been rushing about London for several months trying to find a house that Adelaide would like. Finally a house was rented in Eton Place; Henry had it papered and painted, he had the grates put up; and still the Sartorises delayed their coming. Adelaide wrote that Rome was too exciting to leave; the people had risen *en masse* and marched to the Quirinal, with the Princes Borghese and Corsini at their head, to demand that no ecclesiastic should hold office in the government, and the Pope had consented. Conservatives were horrified; the King of Naples had been so shocked that he had walked up and down the room wringing his hands, and apostrophizing an image of the Virgin with a despairing: *"Madonna mia! Madonna mia! ma che imbroglio che m'ha fatto quel Vicario del figlio tuo!"*

But Italian excitements in that "year of trouble," 1848, were nothing to France's; in February France indulged in a revolution. Fanny wrote to Harriet: "The suddenness of the catastrophe makes it seem like an impossible dream. The streets here are filled with bawling paper-vendors, amidst whose indistinct vociferations the words 'Revolution! Republic! Massacre! Bloodshed!' are alone distinguishable. It is not known where the Duchesse de Nemours is. Her husband has arrived safely here with only one of the children. Of the Duchesse d'Orléans and her two babies nothing is known. Only think of the Princesse Clémentine making her escape on board the same packet with her brother, the Duc de Nemours, and neither of them knowing they were on the same vessel! Guizot and Madame de Lieven, his dear friend and evil genius, arrived separately in London on the same day. Hotels and private houses are thronged. Lady Dufferin is exercising hospitality to the tune of having thirty people in her house in Brook Street . . . Lady Georgiana Fullerton went to Claremont two days ago and says that Louis Philippe's deportment is that of a servant out of place"—she did not add *"pas de bonne maison."* To Theodore Sedgwick Fanny wrote: "The last month in Europe has been like the breathless reading of the most exciting novel. Kings, princes and potentates flying dismayed to the right and left, and nation after nation rising up demanding freedom. Is not the position of the Emperor of Russia awful in its singularity—the solitary despot of the civilized world! Alone of all the thrones in Europe that of our queen stands unshaken . . . Ireland is our weak point."

But though Victoria was in no danger of being forced to join her fellow monarchs now "running about," as Carlyle said, "like a gang of coiners when the police had come among them," England was not to get off without a taste of revolutionary fever. That spring the Chartists renewed their threats. There were riots in London; the windows of Fanny's house were smashed by a mob, there were monster meetings in Trafalgar Square. Fanny was not greatly disturbed. She wrote to Harriet: "Thackeray tells a comical story of having received a letter from his father-in-law in Paris urging him to come there because of the frightful riots in England, which reminds me of the earnest entreaties of my American friends to remove my poor pennies from the guardianship of the Bank of England, and convert them into safe American securities." After the famous Chartist meeting on April tenth she wrote: "I drove from my house in King Street to Westminster Bridge in the morning before the demonstration took place, and though the shops were shut and the streets deserted, everything was quiet and orderly, and nothing indicated the political disturbances, so dreaded that people as far from the Houses of Parliament as Regent's Park had packed up their valuables and prepared for instant flight from London. My friends would hardly believe me when I told them that evening of my peaceful progress down Whitehall."

In the meantime, she was becoming increasingly restless for America. With her usual optimism she told herself that Pierce must have softened during the past two years, and endowing him with her own readiness to forgive and forget—"I seldom," she wrote to Harriet, "waste time in blaming myself and tarry but a brief space in the idle disconsolateness of repentance"—she believed that face to face with her husband they could come to some amicable agreement about the children. But she realized that impatience was her besetting sin; "Uncertainty torments me so," she told Harriet, "that I never endure it, even when the escape from it is by some conclusion I know to be rash;" she forced herself to wait.

Towards spring she saw the way clear, and had been planning to sail in the summer when the European storm broke.

Even the procrastinating Sartorises could procrastinate no longer. To her relief she heard they were leaving Rome; then, after an interval of anxiety, that they were on their way and would be in London the middle of May. This suited Fanny's plans admirably; she was booked for readings six weeks ahead, and that meant clearing over six hundred pounds; she and Adelaide would have a delightful six weeks together, and in July she would sail for America.

Without warning, all her plans were shattered. News came from America. Pierce was suing her for divorce on the ground of desertion.

His action seems to have taken her completely by surprise. Yet she must have known that an absence of two years might be construed as desertion and justify divorce; she must, in her heart, have known that Pierce was too small-minded to be capable of either forgetting or forgiving. She may have trusted to another characteristic of his, respect for public opinion; divorces were not well thought of in Philadelphia society. Anyhow, there can be no question that Fanny was surprised; and she was, of course, indignant. It seemed to her outrageous that Pierce, after driving her out of her home by deliberate persecution, should now have the effrontery to lay the blame at her door. It was too much! She would not submit. She would fight.

If Pierce had believed that his wife would make no defense, he was mistaken. Two days before Adelaide was to arrive in London, Fanny—breaking her professional engagements, forfeiting her precious six hundred pounds—sailed from Liverpool for America.

CHAPTER XXIV

The Valley of Humiliation

"Tymes go by turnes, and chaunces change by course,
From foule to fayre, from better happ to worse."

—FR. ROBERT SOUTHWELL.

IN THE two years of Fanny's absence abroad the gossip over her matrimonial affairs had a good deal died down. When it was rumored that Pierce Butler was suing for divorce on the ground of desertion gossip revived and feeling ran high. By the time the case got into court the newspapers had realized its possibilities and a topic hitherto enjoyed by a small circle of friends became a subject for public discussion in England as well as in America. Naturally so; for apart from Fanny's professional reputation the "documents in the case" were, psychologically, of extraordinary interest. Pierce, until now so anxious to conform to every convention of a most conventional society, having once let himself go seemed determined to tell all there was to tell, to air every grievance, little and big, to leave no stone unturned that he could use as a weapon no matter how many unattractive insects were thus exposed to the eye of day. And his memory was as remarkable as his lack of reticence. His various statements, during and after the hearing, recorded a long list of incidents offered to prove such insubordination on the part of his wife that any judge or jury would realize he had been justified in resorting to measures that might otherwise have been considered extreme. There was of course no need to prove that his wife had left him; to use his own words the question to be decided was "whether a wife is justified in deserting the habitation of her husband and children because she claims a care and control over them which he sees proper to reserve to himself." He

314

was able to cite a very early instance of disrespect; soon after their marriage the proofs of his wife's 'Journal' came for correction, he had offered to assist her, he had crossed out certain indiscreet passages and altered the style of other portions; but instead of accepting these improvements with gratitude she had rejected them with annoyance. Later on, when he took her with him to Georgia she had openly criticized his government of the plantation, thereby setting such a bad example to the slaves that he had been afraid to take her south again. In Philadelphia she had often shown disregard for social conventions, and had once gone so far as to persist in riding on horseback along the waterfront, a locality he had forbidden as unsuitable for a lady to frequent. In London she had not only complained of his conduct to her friends, but, he had reason to believe, she had persuaded a certain Mr. Charles Sedgwick to hire a detective to trail her husband hoping to catch him in some peccadillo—without, it was needless to add, any success whatever. But it was in relation to the children that she showed in the worst light; try as he might he had never been able to convince her that children belonged, not to their mother, but to their father. She was forever interfering with his regulations for his children's welfare, and giving unasked-for advice as to their food, clothes and education, and had capped the climax by venturing to find fault with the governess he had engaged for them, a very nice young lady, daughter of an English admiral. And, mind you, this was no matter of passive resistance to authority, it was open rebellion; when his wife was thwarted she flew into a passion, such "a glare of rage" that she lost all control of herself and scarcely knew what she was doing. Again and again she had run away from him in a fit of temper, once in Georgia and twice in England; each time she had returned in a few days, penitent; each time he had forgiven her and taken her back. But no man could be expected to stand this sort of thing forever; when it came to a desertion of more than two years . . . Pierce's catalogue of grievances ran to many pages of fine print; he painted his wife as a termagant unfit for the care of young children, and himself as a long-suffering husband weary at last of forbearance, asking the law to free him from an intolerable bond. The plea—which recalls Dickens's Rogue Riderhood and his list of "spites, affronts, offenses give and took, dead aggrawations, such like"—makes curious reading for anyone familiar with the facts in the case because of its omissions; naturally, Pierce omitted any allusion to his affairs with other women, to the duel, or to Mrs. X's divorce. Just why he decided to ask for freedom at this time is not clear; he may have wished to marry somebody else; he undoubtedly disliked his wife's return to the stage under the name of Mrs. Butler; probably he had heard she was coming home and wanted to put her in a position that would make it impossible for her to ask inconvenient favors.

Fanny's defense, which included a long "narrative," covers the same ground as Pierce's various statements, and is characterized by similar frankness and similar omissions; she omitted all reference to the duel, or to Mrs. X's divorce; of his infidelities she said nothing except that "early in their married life she had discovered he had been unfaithful," and though she hinted that the governess was not irreproachable in character she did not accuse the girl of being her husband's mistress; probably any attempt to prove his infidelities would have been futile, as she had "condoned" them. Like Pierce, she confined herself principally to the chief question, a mother's rights over her children. She tried to prove that she had been deprived of these rights; she gave instances of her husband's tyranny and of her obedience to his unreasonable demands, such as her signing of the document that gave up all intercourse with the Sedgwick family. She tried to prove that she had been forced most unwillingly to leave her home; forced to take refuge with her father; forced to earn her own living.

She might as well have made no defense at all. Her counsel,

Rufus Choate, did his best for her; his speech arguing that her "narrative" should be admitted is remembered as one of his most brilliant efforts, but the ruling was against him, and the "narrative" was excluded from the case—not, however, from the newspapers; printed at full length it seems to have turned public opinion in her favor. The case dragged on for months, then a compromise was arrived at. Having herself suffered from Pierce's extravagance and turn for speculation, Fanny was desperately anxious to prevent his spending their children's patrimony. Some months previously she had asked her old friend Charles Sumner to look after the children's interests, and he had been doing his best; now, this anxiety swamped all other considerations. There was much discussion; finally she agreed to withdraw her defense and Pierce agreed to tie up some of his property for the benefit of the two children and to insure his wife a small allowance, and to allow Sally and Fan to spend a month with their mother at Lenox that summer.

That month was the one bright spot of a miserable year. The cottage in the Berkshires, so long a dream, was a reality now; soon after her arrival in America Fanny had bought a pretty little place at Lenox with a wide view overlooking the lake—she called it 'The Perch'—and here Sally and Fan came to spend the August of 1849, a happy month for them, almost unbearably happy for their mother. But in September the girls returned to boarding-school, and Fanny had to bid them goodbye knowing that it would be years before she saw them again; for, a few days later, the divorce became an accomplished fact. She was no longer a wife; for all practical purposes, she was no longer a mother; she resumed her maiden name, and henceforth was known as Mrs. Kemble.

What she felt and suffered can only be guessed at; for again there comes a significant gap in her published reminiscences, all her letters of this time to Harriet were omitted. The one allusion to the wretched uncertainty of her future is in a letter to Arthur Malkin and that ends on a fearless note; she knows she has courage, faith and hope; courage, faith and hope will see her through.

So she managed to pull herself together and face the reconstruction of her life sooner than would have been possible to a less buoyant nature. Nor could she afford to waste time in brooding; she had to work if she wished to enjoy more than bare necessities, for the annuity she received from the Butler estate was not any too liberal. Fortunately, Americans were as anxious to hear Fanny Kemble read as they had been to see her act; she had in fact a larger public to draw from, for the back-wash of the evangelical movement was still dampening the ardor of American theatregoers, and Shakespeare readings were considered an agreeable compromise between dangerous worldly amusements and no amusement at all. Wherever she went in the North, East or West—she avoided the South because she would not take money earned by slave labor—she found enthusiastic audiences. The theatrical critic of 'The New York Times' who wrote: "No play can be as well rendered throughout as Mrs. Kemble reads it; we are bored by no miserable creatures in subordinate parts," expressed the sentiments of both the evangelical and the intellectual public.

One of her early successes, a reading of 'Macbeth' at Harvard, had a curious sequel. Two professors had offered to introduce her; she preferred to be introduced by the professor of *belles-lettres*, Mr. Longfellow, rather than by Professor Webster. It was a stimulating audience; she had never read better; faculty, undergraduates and visitors sat in awed silence broken only by one long shuddering groan, let out by "a distinguished member of the bar," that added a nerve-racking touch of realism. Afterwards Fanny went home with the Longfellows who had invited a number of agreeable people to meet her at supper; Mrs. Longfellow—her old friend Fanny Appleton—gave her a bouquet, and the poet presented her with a sonnet,

"Oh, precious evenings! all too swiftly sped . . .
How our hearts glowed and trembled as she read . . ."

and the evening remained flawless in memory. But by a narrow margin. For, very soon after, Harvard's *cause célèbre,* the murder of Professor Parkman by Professor Webster, excited the whole country. Fanny herself was thankful that she had not, as she expressed it, "put her hand in the hand of a murderer," and thus spoiled one of her pleasantest recollections; and the groan now seemed prophetic, for Harvard remembered that not only murderer and victim had been present at the reading of 'Macbeth' but also every important person connected with the trial, the judge and all the lawyers. What, the gossips wondered, had been Webster's thoughts that night, if he were already planning the murder, when that groan broke the silence? What were Parkman's thoughts? Did he experience any premonitory shudder, or feel any satisfaction as he adjusted the new set of false teeth that would lead to the conviction of his murderer? Had the distinguished legal light responsible for the groan, been overcome by a "second-sight" glimpse of the notorious case in which he was soon to be involved? Interesting questions. Boston felt there must be some occult connection between the two murders, Macbeth's and Webster's, though no one could decide just what the connection was.

Another reading in Boston was memorable for a different reason; during an intermission she received a package containing a precious relic, Shakespeare's gloves. They had once belonged to Mrs. Garrick; she had given them to Mrs. Siddons who had left them to her daughter, Cecelia Combe, who bequeathed them to Fanny as the Kemble most worthy to inherit them. As a rule she refused to receive presents—she said herself that she had "an absolute horror of presents"—but she kept the gloves. (Later on, she gave them to Horace Furness as a reward for his 'Variorum'.) Another gift that was not returned was a miniature of her mother as Urania, painted for

Mrs. Fitzgerald, which Edward Fitzgerald sent her when his mother died, and she did consent to accept a jewel from the St. George's Society of New York after a reading she had given for their benefit. The ornament, a replica of the Society's badge in gold suspended from a ruby cross, took her fancy and whenever she read an historical play she was apt to wear her "George" on her bosom, where it looked so like an order that Henry Greville once heard two persons arguing about it. One said "it was an order from the King;" the other that "Mrs. Kemble had never been *ordered* by the King or anybody else"—a statement that Fanny had to admit was only too true.

But she did not need any such decoration to add stateliness to her presence, and her dress, usually of violet velvet and point lace, was magnificent enough without it. She would come stepping out on the stage, bow with grave dignity right and left, seat herself, spread out her flowing skirts, and open her little book; with the first word, an audience would be hers. For three generations of Americans, Fanny Kemble's was a name to conjure with. Parents took their children to her readings, grandparents their grandchildren. Henry James heard her as a very small boy, and Mrs. Kemble's rendering of 'Chevy Chase' at his school was one of Henry Cabot Lodge's earliest recollections. When Louisa Alcott and her sisters acted a play for their Walpole neighbors, Louisa's journal noted as the final touch to their satisfaction: "Fanny Kemble came up." The Longfellows in their Pittsfield house—the house where the forever-never clock stood ticking on the stairs—considered a call from her an honor. Emerson—but a list would be wearisome. It would be hard to find a memoir between 1850 and 1875 that does not mention her, and always with admiration.

In a letter of Edward Everett Hale's, 1850, her name is bracketed with that of a lesser celebrity: "Fanny Kemble was here," he wrote from Worcester, Massachusetts. "I was perfectly fascinated by her. So thoroughly direct, straightforward a woman—who has seen so much of the world, and so hardly—you have hardly seen. Her power is *true expression,* not imitation. And so she strikes you with as much delight and even amazement when she is talking as when she is reading. Then we had Miss Bremer—very short, very plain, but very bright and good natured."

This little lady, Fredrika Bremer, was a Swedish novelist come to America on a voyage of discovery, a simple soul, disconcerted by her popularity. She complained of "the wearisome great dinner parties in New York," of Broadway where "one must fight for life and limb and the most detestable fumes poison the air," of the hot bread that gave her "dispepsy." But she persisted; East and West, North and South, the little lady travelled and those innocent blue eyes of hers missed very little. Her book of travels gives a picture of American life in 1848 as accurate as a colored photograph; one of the best character studies is of Fanny Kemble:

"Jenny Lind's power of impersonation," she wrote, "is nothing to hers. She is best in heroic parts. I shall never forget her glowing, splendid countenance, when she as Henry V incited the army to heroic deeds. And she gave the scene between the enamoured warrior-king and the bashful, elegant, yet naïve French Princess in such a manner as to make one both laugh and cry. When she steps forward before her audience, one immediately sees in her a powerful proud nature, which bows before the public in the consciousness that she will soon have them at her feet. Her figure is strong, her countenance fine without being beautiful, and rich and magnificent in expression. 'In her smiles there are fifty smiles,' said Maria Lowell, and Emerson: 'What an abundance there is in her! She is Miranda, Queen Catherine, and many more at the same time.' He likes strongly-expressed personalities . . . Proud as the proudest Queen, loving pleasure, and expensive in her way of life, she can yet be as simple as a simple peasant; **thus** she often, in the country, dresses in man's attire, and goes ranging through wood and field; and on one occasion she herself drove a cow home to Miss Sedgwick, who had lost hers and who now received this as a present from her 'sublime' Fanny . . . When she took lunch with me, she came fresh from her reading of 'As You Like It,' brimful of life. It so happened that Laura Bridgman had come to call; Fanny Kemble had never before seen the blind, deaf and dumb Laura and she was so struck by the sight of this poor, imprisoned being, that she sat lost in the contemplation of her while large tears streamed down her cheeks. Was it for Laura, for herself, or merely from the contrast between them? I went up to her several times to offer her some refreshment, but she merely answered 'By-and-by,' and continued to gaze at Laura, and tears continued to fall. In a while she became composed and we had an hour's cheerful conversation with the young Lowells . . . As you know Fanny Kemble has been married to a wealthy American and slaveholder, Mr. Butler, and is now separated from him. I have heard her lament the loss of her children in the most heart-rending manner and I cannot conceive how the social spirit in America, in general so favorable to women and to mothers, can permit so great an injustice, when the fault which occasions the separation is on the man's side. In this tragedy of marriage the principals have each their friends and adherents, but the general voice seems to be in her favor. I can well believe that Fanny Kemble would not be the most excellent nor the most tractable of wives. But why then did he so resolutely endeavor to win her? He knew beforehand her temper and her anti-slavery sympathies, for she is too truthful to have concealed anything. Strange to say, this woman, so unfeminine in many respects, exercises a sort of magnetic influence over a great number of men. For my part —to use the words of one of her friends—I am glad there is *one* Fanny Kemble in the world, but I do not wish there should be *two*."

And what did Fanny think of this portrait when Miss Bremer's book came out? If she minded being called unfeminine she bore no malice—in her reminiscences Fredrika

Bremer gets a word of affectionate admiration—partly no doubt because of another character sketch in the book. Fanny must have thrilled with delight when she found her daughter Sally described as "a glorious girl of the New World, richly endowed in soul and body, with that spark of inspired life which is so enchanting; a girl fresh as morning dew, and who sings as I have never heard anyone sing since her who has long since ceased to sing on earth, yet not in my soul. She was Fanny Kemble's pet, and had in her an incomparable instructress in declamation."

Almost as interesting would have been Miss Bremer's descriptions of plantation life. Of a visit to St. Simon's Island she wrote: "The home of Mr. J. Couper is full of gay and youthful countenances, six boys and six girls . . . Mr. Couper regards slavery in America as a school for the children of Africa; he does not think the tropical races can ever amount to anything, though they may arrive at a respectable degree of semi-civilization." Fanny would have agreed with Miss Bremer's moderate summing-up: slaves seemed to be for the most part well treated but everything depended on the individual slave owner, and therefore slavery was wrong in principle. Nor would she have disagreed with another traveller, Sir Charles Lyell, who found much to praise in the South; and she probably read his description of Butler's Island with some pleasure for conditions there had improved since her day; according to Lyell, the negro cabins were "neat and white-washed and floored with wood." For she was far more dispassionate now than in the old days; no longer personally involved she could see plantation life in truer perspective; she could even argue the pros and cons of slavery without losing her temper if the discussion were sufficiently unprejudiced.

Fanatics of either camp irritated her; she could not have read a pamphlet such as 'The Letters of Curtius' and remained calm. "We of the South," Curtius wrote in 1851, "are content with our lot. Let the North enjoy its hireling labor with all its advantages—its pauperism, rowdyism, *émeutes*, and street fights. We do not want it. We are satisfied with our slave labor. It is orderly and efficient. It is the oldest kind of labor—as old, certainly, as the Patriarchs. We like old things —old wine, old books, old friends, old and fixed relations between employer and employed . . . The hirelings of Europe are clamouring for what they term the organization of labor. Slave labor is the only organized labor ever known . . . If the negroes were to be made free, whether peace or war ensued, they would, in time, become extinct." No: Fanny could not have read 'Curtius' with equanimity; on the other hand much of the ranting abolition talk that she heard as she travelled about the United States on her professional tours must have been almost as hard to bear. Slavery was the all-absorbing topic; in every New England country store lean Yankees perched on cracker barrels wagged their chin beards over its pros and cons; on street corners of New York and Boston, shopkeepers argued and loafers wrangled; every wharf on every waterfront from Albany to New Orleans had its muttering, growling group.

It needed some courage—Fanny had plenty—to remain neutral in the keen "Northern" atmosphere of that New England neighborhood during the pre-war years when so many great

Hatred had invaded even the green hills of the Berkshires. When a group of her neighbors gathered in the evening on the porch of Fanny's cottage, watching the moon rise over the tree-tops, talking the idle talk of intimate friends, there would fall a sudden silence; that ominous word *slavery* had been spoken and conversation died. Or, riding on horseback through a leafy lane, she would meet a couple of friends— Emerson and Holmes, perhaps—and know by the stern expression of their faces what it was they were discussing. She tried to keep herself free from partisanship; it was not for her, who had been the wife of a southern planter, to step openly into the opposite camp; she herself wrote: "I was never a thorough-going abolitionist."

men were gathered there that Lenox has been called "a jungle of literary lions." An uncomfortable simile for the colony and its mild inhabitants—Hawthorne, Holmes, G. P. R. James, Catherine Sedgwick—less inappropriate for Herman Melville, busily writing 'Moby Dick' in his old house with its "purple prospect; Greylock, with all his hills about him, like Charlemagne among his peers." But Melville was not yet grown into a lion, and most of Fanny's neighbors were so quiet in their tastes that they found her a trifle alarming. The allusions to Mrs. Kemble in their letters and reminiscences are deprecating, admiration tinged with awe; she was too vivid, a disturbing flash of scarlet across the restrained New England landscape.

For dearly as Fanny loved New England she remained an exotic. Asked to give a reading in Lenox she would suggest that it should be for the benefit of the poor, to be reminded, with a touch of haughtiness, "We have no poor;" worried at seeing the mowers at work in her meadow on a broiling July day she would send out a keg of beer for their refreshment, to be reminded that they were "temperance." Admiration for her fearless riding was tempered with dismay. Ladies seldom rode on horseback in that sedate neighborhood, and never in her flamboyant style; New England could not approve Mrs. Kemble's reckless wish, "The death I should prefer would be to break my neck off the back of my horse at a full gallop on a fine day," or understand her liking for fishing and climbing, and the lure of dangerous cliffs, deep ravines and inaccessible mountain tops; her strange passion for running water became proverbial. A stage driver would point to a foaming mountain torrent, with the remark that "he couldn't of got Mrs. Kemble past that brook, she'd been out the wagon and in the water 'fore the team stopped." Little Julian Hawthorne would describe a terrifying ride with Mrs. Kemble, snatched up, held precariously on the pummel, galloping for miles through the dark woods. But although an echo of Miss Bremer's prim "unfeminine" might occasionally have been discerned, Lenox was proud of its magnificent visitor; she was admired for her radiant personality and her genius, and loved for her abundantly kind heart.

Of any such faint disapprobation Fanny remained unaware. Always, when she liked people, she took for granted that they liked her, and she had a high regard for the Lenox worthies; she loved the Sedgwicks; she was on the friendliest terms with every member of the farming population down to the smallest berry-picker; she gave the village a clock, she helped to found the library; in return, Lenox named a street in her honor. To her mind the only drawback in New England life was its lack of amusement. Boston's inertia puzzled her, just as it had puzzled her when she first stayed there in her youth. She admired Boston's dignity; she would have agreed with Oliver Wendell Holmes's complacent: "We never had a Bohemia in Boston, and we never wanted it;" but she still asked herself why it was that a town crowded with cultivated people had no society in the European sense, and that with so many agreeable husbands there were no wives capable of a *salon*.

But this was New England's one flaw. There was peace in her cottage on the wooded hillside, and some of the best months of her life were spent at 'The Perch' resting after a professional tour, often fatiguing now, for each season took her farther afield. She once ventured into the wilds of Michigan and Wisconsin, and thrilled Milwaukee with her rendering of Shakespeare, thrilling in her turn to hear from a youngish citizen that he could remember the site of the hotel where she was staying as a tangled wilderness crossed by an Indian trail. Even after a month in Italy or Switzerland she would return contentedly to the Berkshires, to enjoy its simple pleasures and watch the circle of the seasons; the tentative northern spring, with its wild flowers "faint and frail"—bloodroot, arbutus, hepatica—yielding so suddenly to the short hot bright summer, that, as suddenly, heightened to the still richer autumn. As she rode on horseback through the mountain trails carpeted with the red and gold of falling leaves—leaves that sometimes fell so softly, letting go their stems, twirling, falling resignedly in the still smoky air of Indian summer, and sometimes swirled in angry eddies about her horse's hoofs driven by a wild October gale—it seemed to her that autumn was the top notch of the American year, perhaps the top notch of any year anywhere. There was beauty too in the New England winter, roads clogged with snow, only the tops of the hemlocks showing in the deep drifted valleys, when, as she said to Longfellow, "The pitiless sky at night is like an armory hung round with steel weapons, and the cracking ice might be the breaking of the great bass strings of a harp."

Then came a winter that must have brought longings for her quiet New England cottage. She had spent the autumn in London with her father, nursing him in his last illness; in November, 1854, he died. She buried him in Kensall Green; accepted the condolences of her friends; read, no doubt with some pleasure, the long poem in 'Punch,' ending:

> "But where shall we now find, upon our scene
> The Gentleman in action, look and word,
> Who wears his wit, as he would wear his sword,
> As polished and as keen?

> "Come all who loved him; 'tis his passing bell;
> Look your last look; cover the brave old face;
> Kindly and gently bear him to his place—
> Charles Kemble, fare thee well!"

and other eulogies; but more than ever harassed by the crowd and noise of London. She was yearning to escape when, just as she felt free to go, another shock came; her brother Henry died. She stayed on, looking after his affairs and making arrangements for the son Henry had left. The summer found her in Switzerland, but not for long; she never stayed very long in one place if she could help it; she was too restless.

For wherever Fanny went, whatever she was doing, during the seven years after her divorce, she was only marking time and waiting impatiently for the spring of 1856 and Sally's birthday. For that birthday would be the twenty-first since the day when the acacias had been in bloom at Butler Place, and Sally's coming-of-age would set her free to return to her mother—if she chose.

1856 came and Sally did choose; from then on, some months of every year were spent with her mother. Pierce Butler seems to have made no objection; probably his financial anxieties helped to reconcile him, for the position of himself and his wife was now reversed; Fanny was rich and he was getting poorer every day. Anyhow, Sally usually spent the summer with her mother at Lenox, and she was allowed to travel with her in the west. Fanny wrote ecstatically of Sally to her English friends; Sally was so handsome and so clever; Sally was, in fact, absolute perfection, except for one small blemish; she was not "savagely disposed." She could not be persuaded to accompany her mother to the Adirondacks, a new region where, in 1858, some Boston men, instigated by Fanny's friend Professor Agassiz, were forming a new kind of club. Agassiz had told Fanny of waterfalls as fine as the Handeck, of primeval forests swarming with game, of lakes alive with trout; she would have given a fortune to be young again. At Sally's age such a country would have been Paradise. But Sally was firm; she said she hated sleeping on hemlock boughs and getting resin in her hair. And, as it turned out, Sally had her reasons; she preferred urban life because she was busy getting engaged to Doctor Owen Wister of Philadelphia. Fanny was delighted. It was a match she could thoroughly approve; she liked the young man and he liked her—men always liked Fanny; she seems to have failed with only one man, her husband. Nor did she miss Sally's companionship as much as she might have, for in the year of Sally's marriage Fan came of age and returned to make her mother's acquaintance.

The sisters did not resemble each other in tastes or political sentiments; Sally was "northern," Fan "southern." But Fan was a charming girl and in her way as satisfactory to her mother; for Fan, unlike Sally, was "savagely disposed." Mother and daughter proved to be congenial companions; Fanny was allowed to take the girl abroad, and in Switzerland discovered, to her joy, that Fan's enthusiasm for mountains, waterfalls and glaciers, an inheritance from their Swiss ancestors, was as intense as her own. So now in her professional tours one or other of her children usually accompanied her; when she returned from abroad, a son-in-law would meet her as well as her girls. The blank in her life was filled; she had a family and a home; and both were in America.

For Sally's marriage had anchored her mother to America. Fanny did not mind being anchored; she had drifted for so long that it was a delight to feel the pull of an anchor. But there was one drawback; no matter how much money she made there never seemed to be enough. For those pre-war years, like other pre-war years, were years of speculation and extravagance. She wrote despairingly to her English friends that she was paying eighty-four dollars a week for three rooms in a New York hotel. 1857 brought a panic—one of the five great panics that have visited the United States; Fanny wrote of her amazement at the financial situation, a great country ruined by extravagance and speculation; or rather, a country that *believed* itself to be ruined. Resources were limitless, but the panic had made cowards of the American people.

The depression continued, and also the extravagance. Ladies' ball dresses must have cost a fortune, judging from the society columns; after a ball in Washington a reporter wrote: "Mrs. Senator Clay wore canary satin covered all over with gorgeous point lace; Mrs. Senator Pugh, in crimson velvet adorned with rubies and crimson pomegranate flowers, rivalled Lady Napier in white brocade and head-dress of scarlet honeysuckle." The panic did not affect the fashions, nor did prices come down. In 1859, Fanny was paying one hundred and forty-seven dollars a week at a Philadelphia boarding house. However, for her the cloud of depression had its silver lining; if Pierce Butler's finances had not been *in extremis,* he might have prevented Fan's seeing so much of her.

Pierce had always been extravagant, his taste for speculation and lack of business ability were notorious. It is scarcely surprising that the panic of 1857 caught him; he lost half a million. Two years later, in March 1859, he was forced to that last most humiliating expedient for a southern planter, his slaves were sold to pay his debts.

It was the largest sale of "human chattels" that had taken place in the South for some years, and one of the greatest slave auctions on record. Four hundred and twenty-nine men, women and children were sold in Savannah at the race course. They were brought there four days previously and kept in rough sheds until the time came; most of them were pure black, there were few mulattoes among them for they all came straight from the remote plantations of St. Simon's and Butler's Island where they had been born and bred and guarded from white intrusion except for an occasional overseer who had happened to exercise *le droit de seigneur.* None of them had been sold before; none of them had ever left their homes until now; they knew they would never see them again. But there was no confusion, no protest, no wild lamentation. For three days they sat about in the mud—it rained steadily—waiting. Prospective buyers strolled up and down, examining the goods, criticizing and chatting. Now and then a colored boy, encouraged by the remark of a possible purchaser, would venture to suggest that if he were bought his sweetheart might be bought too, or a girl would beg to be allowed to remain with her sister. But for the most part they sat and waited in passive silence.

General Cadwalader, Pierce Butler's brother-in-law, was there representing the creditors, and Pierce himself had come to see that the sale was properly conducted. He walked about among his servants, speaking kindly to those he knew, shaking hands with old friends; greeted in return with affectionate respect. They all appeared to be grateful for their master's condescension; if any rancor were felt it was well hidden.

There was no unseemly disturbance during the auction. The rain persisted; the voice of the auctioneer droned on with monotonous and indifferent iteration; the hammer fell; bids came from the audience, now and then a laugh, a word of satisfaction or annoyance from the whites, a whimper from the blacks, instantly suppressed. It was a decorous and orderly performance. There was no unnecessary indecency; the women were of course handled like animals, their lips pulled apart to show their teeth, their bodies closely examined; but that was inevitable; they stood like bronze images, never, by word or smile, attempting to ingratiate themselves. There was no unnecessary harshness; one woman, in spite of protests from the spectators, was allowed to wear a shawl on the auction block because her baby was only two weeks old and the rain drove into the building. Families were kept together; but as a family was supposed to consist of a man, a woman and their children, there were some unavoidable separations. Parents would be parted forever from their married children; grandparents bid goodbye to their grandchildren, and brothers to sisters; sweethearts kissed for the last time.

The receipts were satisfactory. The men, women and children who had worked for Pierce Butler all their lives brought him a total of over three hundred thousand dollars. The highest price paid for a family was for Sally Walker and her progeny, for most of her five children were full grown, and the lot brought six thousand one hundred and eighty dollars. The highest bid for a single man was seventeen hundred for a carpenter named William, and the most expensive woman was Jane, a cotton hand and house servant. Old people did not sell well; a gray-haired couple, Aaron and Violet, were knocked down for only two hundred and fifty dollars apiece.

When it was all satisfactorily over Pierce bade his former slaves a kind farewell and presented each one of them with a dollar in four new twenty-five-cent pieces. The spectators agreed that it had been a very nice auction; no scenes, no rows; nothing, in fact, for northerners to take hold of; no "horrors" for abolitionists to lick their lips over. It was not likely that any newspaper reporters from the North would have ventured to intrude, but if they had, they might have saved themselves the trouble; there would not be much of a story to take home.

And in the main this surmise was correct. One northern reporter did venture to attend the auction, well disguised for he was from the 'New York Tribune,' a paper not allowed through the mails by southern postmasters, and his life would not have been any too safe if he had been recognized. But the story he turned in was matter of fact; he confined himself to a bare recital of events until, at the end, he let his pity emerge:

"That night," he wrote, "not a single steamer left that southern port, not a train of cars sped away from that cruel city, that did not bear each its own sad burden of those unhappy ones, whose only crime is that they are not strong or wise . . . But the stars shone as brightly as if such things had never been."

It was a story that needed no rhetoric, it told itself. Few of the 'Tribune's' subscribers could have read it unmoved, but to none could it have brought such painful memories as to Fanny. She was in Philadelphia at the time, staying at a boarding-house so that she might be near Sally; the past must have come back with sad reality as she read. She saw the lonely rice island, the cotton plantation on St. Simon's, the swarming Negro villages, the neglected hospitals where she had nursed the sick and clothed the naked. All more than twenty years ago now; the children she had played with were middle-aged, the middle-aged were old, the old were dead. House Molly was dead of course, and old Venus. She hoped with all her heart that London the negro preacher was dead— horrible, horrible, to think of that good dignified old man mounted on the auction block to be sold like a bale of cotton. And Headman Frank and his wife Betty would be happier dead, past their prime, now, a gray-haired couple that nobody wanted. What had become of Louisa, who had hidden in the rattlesnake swamp? and of Alec, the clever boy who had learned the alphabet so easily? What about Psyche? poor pretty Psyche . . . Fanny read down the list of names, only a few were given in the 'Tribune'; she came to item 14:

"Sikey, aged forty-three, rice hand, sold for five hundred and twenty dollars." No mention of husband or children; the fate that her mistress had warded off twenty-two years ago had overtaken Psyche at last!

As for Jack—Fanny's own servant with whom she had spent many pleasant hours rowing and fishing on the broad, sun-drenched Altamaha—Jack, Fanny remembered with thankfulness, was safely dead. His masters had brought the boy to the North after an illness, thinking the change might do him good. Unfortunately they had forgotten that, in Philadelphia, he was free; so for fear the abolitionists would get hold of him he had to be kept locked up in an empty house, where Fanny had been allowed to visit him once, on condition that she made no attempt to set him free. But she could do nothing for him, and the "change" was so far from beneficial that he soon pined away and died. As she recalled the incident it seemed to her characteristic of the southern planter's mingling of kindness and cruelty. Characteristic too was that gesture of Pierce's after the auction, presenting each of his former slaves with four bright new twenty-five cent pieces! She could see his condescending smile as he handed out his gifts and bade his old servants goodbye, hear the chorus of "God bless you, master!" that had followed him as he moved away; probably there had not been one dissenting voice in that chorus of benediction. Yet in their hearts some must have cursed. How long could such apathy last? How long before the chorus changed its tune? The South said *never,* the North said *soon.*

And it was soon. Two years after the Butler slave auction at Savannah, the South herself put an end to the old régime. In April 1861 the rebel guns fired on Fort Sumter.

CHAPTER XXV

1861

"The imprisoned winds are let loose. The East, the North and the stormy South combine to throw the whole sea into commotion, to toss its billows to the skies, and disclose its profoundest depths."

—DANIEL WEBSTER.

LIKE ALL thinking people Fanny had long realized that war was inevitable; for five years she had been writing to Henry Greville of her amazement at the political situation in America, and he valued her opinion so highly that many of her letters were preserved in his diary. In 1856 she wrote of the Southerners: "They sit with a sort of stoical despondency on the top of this powder barrel, waiting till it blows up;" and, later, that the South grudged the North its prosperity, but "they neither see nor believe that slavery, and nothing else, is the cause of their inferiority." She spoke of meeting Mr. Olmsted the landscape architect at a dinner party in New York, and repeated Mr. Olmsted's criticism of "back country" Southerners encountered during a ride on horseback of four thousand miles in remote parts of the South; they were, he said, "a collection of children and savages." Of John Brown, she wrote: "The poor wretch is hanged, but from his grave a root of bitterness will spring, the fruit of which at no distant day may be disunion and civil war."

But she had bitter things to say of the vulgar extravagance she often met with at the North. She ridiculed the mixture of adulation and familiarity that greeted the Prince of Wales when he visited the United States in 1859; she laughed at Willy Duncan's "calling to him 'Prince! Prince!' as I address my mocking-bird;" and was just a little shocked by her daughter Fan's lack of respect: "The Prince," Fan said, "seemed to be a nice little fellow and danced well." After staying at

Nahant in the huge wooden barnlike hotel that Paran Stevens had recently built in the hope of turning Nahant into a rival of Newport, Fanny wrote to Henry Greville: "The enormous house is filled with American women, one prettier than the other, who look like fairies, dress like duchesses or *femmes entretenues,* behave like housemaids and scream like peacocks." But though she might dislike the North for its crudeness and ridicule its vulgarity, when the war began she had no doubt as to which side was right.

It had been a strange winter—the winter before the attack on Fort Sumter. For Fanny, outwardly uneventful. She had stayed on in Lenox in spite of the cold—the thermometer that February fell to thirty-two below zero—and often alone except for a couple of convicted thieves whom she had, in her impulsive way, taken in with the hope of reforming their characters. She stayed because, with all its discomforts, country life promised a measure of immunity from the political unrest that infected the towns, and the New England landscape was still peaceful to look at. She could ride on horseback when the roads were clear, or tramp through the drifts if the snow lay deep, happily enough, and often forget the distracted world outside.

But as the winter wore away, and one state after another left the Union, it became increasingly difficult to forget. By the time the first arbutus showed among last year's dead leaves the stars and stripes were blooming out along every village street and from every farmhouse gable in the Berkshires: May twilights brought a sound of drums calling the farmers to drill when their work in the fields was over. Impossible, now, either to forget or to remain aloof. Aloofness was not in Fanny's nature, nor was she in doubt; her sympathies were wholeheartedly with the North. She was not a blind partisan; she complained to her English friends that the North's absorption in money making seemed to her as bad as the selfish egotism of the South; she believed the war had been sent as a punishment to the whole American nation.

States Rights meant nothing to her; if slavery had meant as little she might have hesitated to take an active part. But twenty-two years had not been able to wipe out her memories of Georgia. After the war began, she wrote exultingly to Henry Greville: "When I used to stand in utter despondency listening to the waves breaking on the beach at the river's mouth, and watching the revolving light that warned the vessels from the dangerous bar, not seldom crying with bitter tears, 'How long, O Lord, how long!' I little thought to see the day when Northern vessels would ride along that coast, bringing freedom to the land of bondage." Fanny was as sure as were her country neighbors, the Puritan New England farmers whom she considered the most intelligent men of their class in the world, that the war was being fought to free the slaves, that freedom for the slaves was a magnificent battle-cry, and that the North would win in the end.

So she did her share; she handed out swords and pistols to volunteers in New York and Philadelphia; she gave readings for the benefit of "sanitary fairs;" she tried to keep up her enthusiasm by recalling a conversation with Welcker, the German archeologist, who had insisted that no nation could achieve greatness without "a great heroic war," and hoped and prayed that Welcker was right. But in her heart she hated the war; she was too imaginative and too just. She could not give a sword to some young volunteer whom she remembered as a little boy in a round jacket without a shudder, and both sides boasted unduly of their victories; she was thankful that she was not personally involved, no one near and dear to her could be drawn into the conflict.

She was not, however, to escape being personally involved; her former husband could scarcely be considered *dear,* but because of their children he was still *near.* So it was something of a shock when, in August, 1861, Pierce Butler was arrested at his house in Philadelphia by order of the War Department, and taken off to jail charged with high treason. It was said that he had gone to Georgia just before the attack on Fort Sumter, while there had acted as agent for the South and received large sums of money for the purchase of arms, and on his return to Philadelphia had brought with him rebel cockades and pistols and endeavored to arouse sympathy for the cause of secession. In Fanny's opinion any or all of the charges might be true—she had known of the trip to Georgia at the time; in April, 1861, she wrote to Henry Greville: "Mr. Butler has gone to swear allegiance to the Southern Confederacy, and to establish himself on his plantation again." But her chief anxiety had been for the safety of her daughter, for Pierce had insisted on taking Frances with him, "in spite," Fanny wrote, "of her own and her sister's entreaties and the remonstrances of all his friends," and she had breathed a sigh of relief when Frances got safe home again.

But though she believed that Pierce's arrest was probably justified, it was not pleasant to think of even one's ex-husband being a prisoner, or of Sarah and Frances visiting their father in jail—they had with difficulty secured an order from President Lincoln to go to Governors Island; nor was she sanguine as to the outcome. Pierce had always prided himself on being a Southerner and a slaveholder and he was excessively obstinate; if he refused to take the oath of allegiance to the United States there was every likelihood of his staying in prison until the war was over. So it was a surprise as well as a relief when in September Pierce was released; five weeks in prison had been enough to cool his ardor; he gave a pledge to abstain from any act of hostility against the United States and not to visit the South without a passport.

The affair had however added to the worry of war-time life; the gloom became intolerably depressing as the months dragged on, and as the American public could neither afford nor enjoy Shakespeare readings, in the summer of 1862 Fanny went abroad and took Frances with her.

In America, Fanny had been too aware of the faults on both sides to be greatly elated or disheartened by the victories and defeats of the North. In America, Fanny always felt her-

self entirely British; when after the Mason and Slidell affair
there had been talk of war with England, Fanny was horrified; when Lord Lyndhurst, Chancellor of the Exchequer,
wrote to his Boston relations—he was a son of Copley the portrait painter—telling them what he thought of the conduct
of the United States, Fanny agreed with his sentiments; she
was glad that Lord Lyndhurst's letter had been sent to Mr.
Seward, and she hoped that Mr. Seward would repent and
allow Messrs. Mason and Slidell to proceed on their way . . .
She sailed for Europe in this British mood; sick of the war, of
the miseries and horrors that played havoc with her nerves,
and inclined to feel that it did not matter which side won so
long as the fighting stopped.

During her summer in Switzerland she encountered little
to arouse her partisanship; she and Frances avoided the subject, for Frances remained Southern in her sympathies. It was
not until they returned to England for the winter that Fanny
experienced a change of heart. Her languor vanished; she was
an American now, and enthusiastically for the North. The
North was fighting to free the slaves! What did States Rights
matter? What did bloodshed matter? so long as the iniquity
of slavery was put an end to!

It was, of course, opposition that aroused her. Milder natures than Fanny Kemble's would have been stirred by England's attitude. Fanny was at first puzzled, and then enraged,
by the indifference of her friends. The English upper classes
seemed rather pleased to think that democracy was proved
to be a failure, that the naughty little boys who had behaved
so badly to the mother country were now quarreling among
themselves; England refused to take the war seriously except
as it affected cotton; nobody seemed to care a button whether
or not the slaves were freed so long as cotton came to Manchester. This was bad enough; it was even more enraging to
discover that sympathy, such as it was, was apt to be on the
side of the South. Fanny's friends said that the Southerners
were cultivated gentlemen, the Northerners were boorish

money grubbers; the hands in Northern factories were much
worse off than the slaves on Southern plantations. They
smiled incredulously when she spoke of her own experiences,
and of New England's superiority to Georgia. When she
sneered at the "chivalry of the South" and compared the
Southern planters to "the ignorant, insolent and barbarous
iron-clad robbers of the middle-ages," they could not conceal
their disgust. She talked and explained and implored, but
with exasperatingly little effect; often an argument would
end, to the consternation of her opponent, by Fanny's losing
her temper and bursting into tears. They could not understand why Fanny Kemble felt so strongly about this absurd,
unnecessary and inconvenient war; after all, she was English.
They warned each other that the topic had better be avoided
in her presence; her old friend Mrs. Procter wrote to another
old friend Mrs. Milnes: "Fanny Kemble is here. Should you
encounter her, do not speak of America; she cried so terribly
on Thursday when my husband was speaking of the subject.
She says the women are working during the night at the
harvest, the men all gone as soldiers, and the heat being too
great to work during the day." And Henry Greville's diary
noted: "Fanny Kemble is very unwilling to speak of what is
passing in America; which perhaps is lucky, as she would find
little sympathy with her opinions;" and later: "I dined tête-
à-tête with Fanny Kemble whom I found in great distress at
the disasters of the Federal Army. I think she begins to
despair of success."

It may have been the news of the defeats of 1862 that came
as the last straw; that winter Fanny decided she could no
longer remain passive, she must strike a blow for freedom.
Discouraged by the futility of argument and out of patience
with herself—passionate words and tears had so often ruined
an argument and twisted a recital of tragic facts into improbable melodrama—she turned to writing as a surer way of
convincing England that the North was right. The public appeared to have a superstitious reverence for the printed word:

'Uncle Tom's Cabin' had won more converts than a million abolitionist speeches. She decided to publish the journal she had written in Georgia.

For years her abolitionist friends had been urging her to publish it, but she had felt that for a wife to tell what she had seen on her husband's plantation would be an offense against good taste; the journal, she said, would never be given to the world unless some crisis arose that made its publication necessary. Now, after a quarter of a century, the crisis had arisen. England was getting tired of sitting on the fence, at any moment she might recognize the Southern Confederacy. When Gladstone told an audience that "Jefferson Davis and other leaders of the Confederacy have made an army; they are making, it appears, a navy; and they have made, what is more important than either, they have made a nation," he was cheered to the echo. Fanny decided that it was no time for scruples. The manuscript was rescued from oblivion and, in 1863, 'A Residence on a Georgian Plantation' was published on both sides of the Atlantic; London got it in May, New York in July.

The sensation in England was all that her publishers had hoped for. Her name and reputation would have sold any book; even her juvenile failure 'Francis I' had run into seven editions. Her story of plantation life created a tremendous stir; it carried conviction to every reader except those too prejudiced to be capable of conversion. But the prudish said it was indecent; if Mrs. Kemble had been so unfortunate as to see all those horrid things, she should have kept them to herself. Mothers warned each other not to let their daughters get hold of Mrs. Kemble's improper book and, of course, the more they warned the better the book sold.

Politically, the effect is more difficult to estimate. Extravagant claims have been made for the 'Georgia Journal.' It has been said that the book played a great part in the preservation of England's neutrality; that John Bright quoted Mrs. Kemble in his speeches; that Henry Ward Beecher caused extracts

to be read in the House of Commons; that a copy was presented to every member of Parliament; that Lord Rutland
gave a copy to the Queen who had been much impressed; and
that, in consequence, England had refused to recognize the
Southern Confederacy. Others have said that the book had
no effect whatever, politically. A recent Southern writer has
taken some pains to prove, from contemporary reviews and
John Bright's speeches, that he never quoted from Mrs. Kemble's book, that the critics often postponed reviewing it as if
they did not consider it important, and when they did get
around to a review, were luke-warm, or violently opposed to
her sentiments. But book reviews do not always reflect public
feeling. As a matter of fact, the critics lined up for or against
the 'Georgia Journal' according to the policy of their newspaper or magazine. If the editor were in favor of the North,
they praised the 'Journal'; if he admired the South, they
damned it. An article in the 'Saturday Review' is typical of
the latter point of view; the writer professed to be shocked at
Mrs. Kemble's lack of refinement "in putting such details in
print;" it was unbelievable that any lady could have "attacked
the system she found on her husband's plantation and, after
a lapse of a quarter of a century, enjoyed the double gratifica-
tion of selling her manuscript and denouncing slaveholders."
Some critics hinted that the journal was practically fiction, or
that it had been "doctored."

But, fact or fiction, its worst enemies could not deny that
the horrid story was interesting. No one who began it ever
failed to finish it and to many the book came as a revelation;
Mrs. Kemble's account of plantation life was accepted at its
face value, as the statement of an eyewitness and a dreadful
indictment of slavery. Now, when a pleader of the Southern
cause spoke of happy darkies strumming banjoes and singing
as they picked the cotton, he was apt to be reminded of a less
idyllic side of plantation life. The political influence of this
mass of converts may have been less than has been claimed by
some writers, but it is absurd to suppose that it went for

nothing. The publication of such a book at such a time—a "best seller," read and discussed, with anger and tears, from one end of England to the other—must have affected the opinions of the nation. There is no reason to doubt that Fanny Kemble accomplished what she had hoped to accomplish; she helped to tip the wavering scales in favor of the North by weakening England's admiration for the Confederacy and thus prevented the loan that would have prolonged the war and perhaps destroyed the Union.

In America the 'Georgia Journal' met with the same sharp and divided criticism it had encountered in England. Even in the North, while abolitionists hailed Mrs. Kemble as an apostle of the dawn, Copperheads called her a liar, the prudish deplored her frankness and the fastidious shuddered. But for the most part readers north of Mason and Dixon's line believed in the book's sincerity, felt that the Harpers were justified in advertising it as "the most powerful anti-slavery book yet written," and laid it down with a sigh, agreeing with George William Curtis's summing-up in the 'Atlantic': "A sadder book the human hand never wrote."

'A Residence on a Georgian Plantation' is unquestionably both powerful and sad. Everywhere, North and South, the book was compared to Mrs. Stowe's; many critics assumed that it would rival 'Uncle Tom's Cabin', and, as a statement of fact, would carry more weight. But they were mistaken. Fact is seldom as compelling as fiction; Alfred's cakes, Washington's cherry-tree and Clarence's butt of Malmsey are imperishable stuff. Mrs. Stowe had disguised her moral lesson by wrapping it up in an exciting story, Fanny scorned to offer the public any such palatable emulsion of truth and romance. She would not even condescend to display her material to the best advantage; her book begins and ends with several pages of argument on the question of slavery in the abstract. Being Fanny, she allowed herself an occasional sensitive description of the Southern landscape, and her burning indignation and burning pity flamed out again and again and lit up her

picture of plantation life with lurid distinctness. But romance
was rigorously excluded. Readers hoping for another assort-
ment of Mrs. Stowe's cruel aristocrats and patient feudal re-
tainers were disappointed. Fanny's character sketches were
accurate and she knew how to write; Preacher London,
Psyche and Venus, Jack and Headman Frank are as alive as
any character in Mrs. Stowe's melodrama, but they have long
since been forgotten, while blue-eyed Eva and black-faced
Topsy appear to have achieved immortality.

It was its lack of romance that made Fanny's book so
obnoxious to the South. In Mrs. Stowe's novel the grandeur
of the St. Clares had to some extent made up for the brutality
of a Legree. No Lord of Burleigh could have been more
aware of his birth and breeding than Eva's Papa; her Mamma
had a hard heart but an exquisite taste in dress; the St. Clare
town house with its "fountains, perfumes, silken hangings,
lustres, statuettes and gilding . . . had been arranged to gratify
a picturesque and voluptuous ideality;" at their country
estate the genteel family might lounge gracefully on "light
verandas of bamboo-work," or saunter in "gardens and pleasure grounds fragrant with every picturesque plant and flower
of the tropics," and Mrs. Stowe had been careful to provide
little Eva with a gold vinaigrette studded with diamonds and
a pony of "snowy whiteness," as well as with a Bible.

Unfortunately for Fanny's literary reputation at the South
such opulent establishments were not to be found in her
book. She did indeed explain that her experience had been
limited, that life on a remote sea island must not be taken as
typical of country life in Virginia or Maryland; she spoke of
the graceful ease of Southern manners as compared with the
crude manners of the North, and of having enjoyed the conversation of cultivated and agreeable men such as the Coupers;
she pictured St. Simon's Island as a paradise of flowers and
birds. But this was not enough for Southern readers; that Mr.
Couper had an excellent vegetable garden and a good fowl
house did not make up for his lack of liveried servants and

handsome carriages. Mrs. Kemble described her Georgia neighbors as simple people, living for the most part in careless discomfort in unpretentious houses. This was unforgivable; Southerners could bear being called cruel, they could not bear being called commonplace. They never have forgiven Fanny Kemble and probably never will. Even today, a Southerner writing of plantation life, and obliged to mention the 'Georgia Journal' because it is too important to leave out, always adds a warning: Mrs. Kemble was an actress, divorced from her husband, a passionate, prejudiced, credulous creature, prone to wild exaggeration. One writer will say that "she caused quite a disturbance among the slaves by listening to their small complaints" and another question her veracity by quoting Lyall's description of blossoming orange-groves and wooden-floored cabins, forgetting that six years had elapsed between her residence and his brief visit.

This question, the truth of her narrative, was the only point that Fanny herself considered worth taking up. The 'Georgia Journal' is never mentioned in any of her published letters of the time; she had nothing to say of its literary success, or of its effect on the political situation in England and America. But in her second volume of reminiscences, the letters of 1838 that describe her journey to the South were included and followed by an allusion to the 'Georgia Journal.' After speaking of her extreme unwillingness to publish the book, she said that it never would have been published except for the extraordinary ignorance of her English friends and insisted that it was a true statement of fact, not, as some asserted, "cooked up" for publication but a genuine journal, and quoted Lady Grey who could vouch for its integrity as she had heard the manuscript read aloud, years before, to her grandmother Lady Dacre.

Lee's surrender came in April 1865. Fanny was in England staying with Adelaide in the country when she heard that the war was over, and went up to London so stimulated by the news that in the train she wrote some lines on the fall of

Richmond—sympathetic, beautiful lines—and when she arrived drove straight from the station to the office of the 'Spectator' to give them to the editor, her friend Richard Hutton. There, someone told her that Lincoln had been assassinated. Her cry of horror brought Mr. Hutton hurrying from his room; she was utterly overcome. Writing to Harriet she admitted that she had been near collapse; she could not speak and could scarcely stand.

But that was in a later letter. All her letters to Harriet during the Civil War were destroyed, unpublished. Undoubtedly, they were omitted from her memoirs because they contained too many references to the painful effect of the 'Georgia Journal' on her family. Pierce Butler must have been horrified; her elder daughter, Sarah Wister, may have considered that the gain to the Northern cause made up for the notoriety for the family; but her younger daughter, Frances, most certainly did not. Frances would have hated the book, for she was Southern through and through. She had been in England with her mother when the question of publication first came up; probably she did not hesitate to express herself pretty strongly on the subject, and it may have been her failure to make any impression that took her back to America to range herself resolutely on her father's side of the family disagreement. At any rate, Frances seems to have been willing to accompany her father when, immediately after the war, he decided to return to Georgia to make an attempt to save what was left of the rice plantation by gathering together his former slaves and teaching them to work for wages.

It was an uphill, discouraging business. Pierce's training had not fitted him to deal with the new situation and whatever success he achieved was probably due to his daughter, for Frances had inherited some of her mother's characteristics; she had courage and energy and a strong sense of duty. They made a beginning; there was enough of the old reverence and docile affection for the master left among the Negroes to leaven the lump of inertia and ignorance. But before any real progress could be seen, Pierce Butler died. Within a year of his return to the rice island, in August 1867, he died there, alone—his daughter had gone back to Philadelphia—of fever; procrastinating to the last, he had stayed on after the heat of summer had made the climate unsafe for whites.

CHAPTER XXVI

Retrospect

"It was I who planted all these grounds; mine are the rows, mine the laying out; many also of the trees were planted by my own hand."

—CYRUS THE YOUNGER.

FANNY WAS in England when she heard that Pierce was dead. She had been intending to spend the winter near the Sartorises, either in London or on the Continent; the news put an end to these plans. In the autumn of 1867 her old friend Mrs. Procter wrote to Mrs. Milnes: "Pierce Butler is dead; Mrs. Fanny Kemble sailed—or rather, steamed—for America the very same week the news came."

Except for the sense of excitement and hurry that this sentence gives, one is left in the dark as to Fanny's feelings. Was she thankful that death had broken ties the law had not really broken—she and Pierce had been held together by a common interest in their children—and she could settle down to a surer way of living? Or did the past return too clearly? Chelsea Beach, herself and Pierce galloping their horses along the firm white sand, sitting together on the sun-warmed roof of the fisherman's hut; Trenton Falls where they had crouched on the rocks watching twigs and flowers sucked down into the whirlpool; the day that she and Pierce had gone to Mount Auburn to choose a grave for Dall. Or was she able to stifle all such recollections in other, very bitter, recollections of Philadelphia and Georgia?

But whether her memories were sad or bitter, as Fanny went steaming back to America on the ocean liner so unlike the sailing vessel of her first voyage thirty-five years before, her too vivid imagination would have given her little peace; no doubt she cried her eyes out, lamenting a wasted past and

347

lost happiness. But this is all conjecture; she left no record of
her grief or her relief and all the grown persons who were
intimate with Fanny Kemble at the time Pierce died are long
since dead themselves or too old to remember. Only one
thing seems sure; neither divorce nor death really broke the
bond between Fanny and her husband; with all her passion
and all her impulsiveness she never fell in love with another
man.

Her life did unquestionably become serener. She could stay
in Philadelphia now and see her daughters without running
the risk of an encounter with Pierce. Sarah Wister had a
charming little boy of six named Owen, a clever child, with a
turn for music and an occasional elusive resemblance to his
great-uncle "Glorious John" Kemble. It was pleasant to see
Butler Place in process of rehabilitation after years of neglect,
for Frances had decided to live there for part of the year, and
to know that her banishment was over. Fanny could sleep in
the bedroom where her children had been born, sit on the
veranda where she had sat so often on spring days watching
her two little girls zigzagging about the lawn in their cream-
colored coats; here and there in a garden border she would
discover a clump of iris or a rose-bush, and recall her own
mood, the very look and smell of the day when she had
planted it. The wheel had come full circle, but she who had
once been the center now stood outside looking on; it gave
her a strange sense of unreality; as if she, Pierce's wife, had
been dead and buried all these thirty years and was now
returned, a ghost of the past, to haunt the present. But it was
a pleasant peaceful sort of haunting; she was glad to see the
old place respond gratefully to the ministrations of a new
mistress.

But Frances had other plans much less satisfactory to her
mother. Everyone was horrified when the girl announced an
intention of spending her winters in Georgia to continue
the work of reconstruction that her father had begun on the
rice plantation. It was a daring, even a dangerous plan. Fam-

ily and friends argued and implored; Frances, as obstinate as she was courageous, had made up her mind. She was twenty-nine; thanks to her mother's forethought at the time of the divorce she had some money of her own—though she and her sister were no longer "two of the richest girls in America;" the free Negroes could, she believed, by judicious management be made to work, and the plantation could be made to pay.

The scheme—turning slave labor into hired labor—was exactly what Fanny herself had once longed to attempt. But neither Fanny nor Frances seems to have realized this now. Fanny, as a mother, was thinking too much about her child's safety and happiness to consider any abstract question, and having lost her youthful confidence in Utopian experiments was inclined to feel that the Negroes might better be left to work out their own salvation; Frances's coaxings and coddlings would postpone, not hasten, the day of Negro independence.

But Frances was her mother's daughter, and having enjoyed one flutter as an amateur ministering angel—the part her mother had always wanted to play and never did—she was bound to go on as a professional. The winter of 1868 saw Frances Butler's departure for Georgia; to plant crops, repair dykes, and rebuild ruined cabins; to humor and scold and argue and instruct; in short, to restore the patriarchal past to the best of her ability and at great personal sacrifice.

She lived in the old house where she had lived as a baby; unchaperoned, except by a portrait of General Lee; sometimes with a few guests, often alone; dependent on the black inhabitants of the island, and entirely at their mercy. Some of the Negroes were freed slaves formerly belonging to Mr. John Butler and therefore not sold at the auction, who when the war began had been led into the interior by one of their head men and brought home again when peace came; some were Pierce's people returning from distant places with as little conscious volition as birds to last year's nests. Freedom

had changed their manners, they were less polite and less obe-
dient, but Frances found them the same irresponsible, stupid,
shiftless creatures they had always been and, in her opinion,
always would be. The free Negro was supposed to be a far
more dangerous animal than the slave; but Frances Butler
seems to have lived safely among her black subjects. One
white woman on an island full of blacks, when she happened
to be alone she did take the precaution of sleeping with a
pistol under her pillow but the traditional respect for "young
Missis," combined with her strength of character and physical
courage, was all the protection she needed. There was a good
side as well as a bad to the Negro lack of initiative she so often
complained of.

Her family had hoped that one season would be enough.
But winter after winter, her work on the plantation drew
Frances back to Georgia. Fanny was in constant anxiety, and
letters from the rice island complained of so many afflictions
—floods and fevers, bad crops and poor prices, fleas and mosquitoes—that she could not reconcile herself to her daughter's
sacrifice. Nor did the two think alike about the Negroes;
Fanny in her day had insisted, with bitterness, that every misery of plantation life was due to slavery; Frances insisted, with
bitterness, that every misery was due to emancipation.

Both were prejudiced; but Frances, luckily for her peace of
mind, lacked imagination; she hoped to make the plantation
pay, and she succeeded where a more temperamental woman
would have failed. And, like her mother before her, the
charm of a wild free life remote from civilization consoled
her in discomfort and loneliness. Here Fanny could sympathize; when Frances wrote to her of "sweet smells and sweet
sounds. Magnolia, orange, fig and peach trees in blossom, and
every tree alive with mocking-birds, red-birds, blackbirds and
jays," she must have recalled with satisfaction the hot days so
long ago when she had planted these very trees and shrubs
while the squint-eyed overseer looked on with amused indifference.

On the other hand, the luxuriant beauty of St. Simon's Island was gone, wiped out by the war. The planters had been ruined; most of the old houses had been shelled and burned by Federal gunboats lying in the same harbors where slave ships had once found hiding places. (The last cargo of slaves landed in the United States was put ashore on Jekyl Island from the slaver 'Wanderer' in 1859.) The cotton plantations had for the most part relapsed into wilderness of swamp and forest except for the rude clearings of Negro squatters and poor whites, and as if the desolation of war were not enough, the lumber companies were busy and primeval oaks and pines were crashing down right and left. The natural beauty of St. Simon's had departed and with it the old, easy-going, shabby comfort of its plantation life. Already the legends of past glory that all lost causes seem to need were being compiled. It must have surprised Fanny to hear her daughter repeat the stories she herself had been told of the island's former magnificence; the planters' handsome houses, grounds and gardens; their lavish hospitality, their picnics, hunting excursions and regattas, and always with the implication that this grandeur had been obliterated by the Civil War. For there had been no such magnificent way of living in Fanny's time, 1838; no society whatever in the sophisticated sense of the term; cotton planting was already less profitable and slave labor more expensive, and the planters were already poorer than in the past. (It would seem that whatever magnificence St. Simon's had known must be dated still farther back; not to the time immediately before the Civil War, but to the prosperous years just after the Revolution and the invention of the cotton gin.) It is possible that disbelief in these "before the war" legends had something to do with Fanny's lack of confidence in Frances's enterprise. Anyway, she continued to urge her daughter to give up what seemed to her a hopeless job and was becoming so anxious about her that it was a tremendous relief when Heaven unexpectedly intervened; the island queen acquired a prime minister and a husband.

James Leigh was an English clergyman, son of Lord Leigh of Stoneleigh Abbey, Warwickshire; young, agreeable and cultivated, travelling for pleasure in the United States. As he was a connection of Fanny's old friends the Egertons it was not long before he and Frances met in Philadelphia, and an invitation to Butler's Island followed as a matter of course. His visit there was delightful; a congenial house-party, picturesque setting, rowing and fishing, songs and dances in the Negro quarters, gratifying attention when he preached to the darkies in their little church, followed by a touching welcome from an old Negro moved to recount a dream that had shown him, he said, solemnly, "A lily-white gentleman rise out of the rushes and come to preach to us." But the chief attraction was of course "the fair queen herself," as Mr. Leigh described his hostess, "presiding over her sable subjects and entertaining strangers with royal grace." For the two had much in common. Both were religious. Both were bent on teaching the Negroes to pray as well as work. Mr. Leigh even shared Miss Butler's feeling for the South; later on, he wrote: "I sympathized thoroughly with the Southerners, and considered the North had behaved shamefully to them. They crushed the proud Southerners, conquered them by overwhelming numbers, stole a good deal of property and tried to make the slaves fight against their masters." Obviously, Mr. Leigh and Miss Butler were destined for each other; it is scarcely surprising that in course of time their marriage took place.

Everybody approved, Fanny herself was delighted. In her memoirs James Leigh is often mentioned and always with affection—"My dear Mr. Leigh, my dear James"—although comment on the courtship and description of the wedding were omitted as too intimate for publication. Mr. Leigh was less reticent:

"We were married," he noted in his reminiscences, "at St. Thomas's Church, Portman Square, by my brother-in-law, the Rev. Lord Saye and Sele, my friend Arthur Sullivan presiding at the organ. After a short honeymoon spent at Titsey Place we returned to our parish at Stoneleigh, where a most hearty reception awaited us, arches being erected in the village. The carriage was drawn through the village preceded by the school children accompanied by a drum and fife band. Flowers were strewn in our path and on arriving at the entrance to the vicarage the band struck up the American National Anthem. The company then retired to a large tent in which about five hundred men, women and children partook of tea. A handsome silver inkstand was presented by the parishioners."

With so propitious a beginning Fanny naturally hoped that Frances would soon forget her island. But after plantation life the usual parochial round seemed dull and even silver inkstands could not anchor the Leighs to England. In 1873 they decided to return to Georgia and Fanny, who was in London, decided to accompany them, feeling, she said, that "if they went to the bottom she might as well go too." So they all sailed for New York in the 'Celtic,' and in due time Mr. and Mrs. Leigh arrived at their island.

And there they stayed, off and on, for years, ruling despotically but with benevolence and some material success, for Mr. Leigh turned out to be a good planter as well as a good clergyman. Travelling foreigners—among them Lord Rosebery and Sir Michael Hicks-Beach—often came to stay and had a splendid time shooting ducks and listening to Negro singing. Mr. Leigh urged Sir Arthur Sullivan to come, assuring him that Georgia's Negro melodies would give him material for an oratorio with some such title as the 'Queen of Sheba;' but unfortunately, considering what a libretto Gilbert could have written, Sullivan never found time for the trip.

So the years went by; and what with baptisms and oranges and fine weather life would have been one long idyll, if it had not been for that ever-present annoyance, the laziness and insubordination of the Negroes. The Leighs often thought regretfully of the good old days "before the war" when slaves

were contented and planters rich, but they went on doing the
best they could under present conditions and trials and triumphs alike were duly recorded; for Frances Leigh like her
mother before her kept a diary, that was later made into a
book called 'Ten Years on a Georgia Plantation,' and her husband also published a volume of reminiscences under the title
'Other Days.' Together they give a clear picture of an interesting experiment in post-war reconstruction.

In Frances Leigh's book her mother is seldom mentioned
and her mother's book is pointedly ignored; no reader would
guess that Fanny had ever lived on the plantation, much less
written a book about it. It is a slightly banal record of hard
work and devotion; as a sequel to her mother's drama of plantation life nothing could be stranger. The "set" is the same;
the same black and white figures appear against the same
semi-tropical background; even the words and music, the interspersed songs and dances, are the same; there is the same
comic relief of quaint old darkies and frolicsome pickaninnies. All is alike yet unlike. It is as if the spot-light, managed
by different hands, contrived to brighten every detail that
Fanny had seen in deep shadow and obscure all that she had
made plain. As literature there can be no comparison, and the
same may be said of Mr. Leigh's rambling chronicle. It would
be as absurd to compare the Leighs' nice little books to Fanny
Kemble's powerful and moving narrative, as to compare 'The
Swiss Family Robinson' and 'Wuthering Heights.'

What mother and daughter thought of each other's effusions can only be surmised. Nor is it clear whether Frances
Leigh's book was written with the intention of counteracting
her mother's arraignment of slavery, or whether Fanny modi-
fied her opinions after reading it. There are many affectionate
allusions to the Leighs in Fanny's memoirs; their life on the
plantation seemed to her "both pleasant and good;" but her
daughter's book remained unmentioned. Mother and daughter must have been equally reticent in conversation when it
touched on slavery and reconstruction, for they were happy

together, and James Leigh such a perfect son-in-law that the
two households could even join forces for months at a time.

Fanny had her own house now, York Farm, a small place
on the Butler estate that had been fitted up for her, conveniently near the Wister family who were living in the big
house. Here the Leighs would arrive each spring to stay until the heat became too intense for the baby—they had a small
Alice—when York Farm would be deserted for Newport. Late
summer usually found Fanny in Lenox with the Leighs staying at the inn—her cottage had been sold when York Farm
was acquired—and she was happy there in spite of its discomfort, for she felt at home; she had known the proprietor, William Curtis, ever since his boyhood when she had often hired
him to row her boat and take care of her fishing tackle. Various families of Sedgwicks were still living in the neighborhood; other old friends often turned up at Curtis's, and she
made pleasant new acquaintances. Bret Harte was an occasional visitor; he reminded her of Trelawny. Both were handsome and both, she noted, had "an expression of face which
suggested small success to anyone who indulged in personal
conflict with them." In the evening in her sitting-room Bret
Harte would sometimes talk of his western adventures; one
anecdote seemed to her to have a touch of pathos. Spending
the night in a lonely tavern he had been disturbed by a lynch-
ing party in search of a notorious "bad man;" the landlord assured them their quarry had gone, and they finally departed
grumbling. But when at daybreak Bret Harte was leaving, the
"bad man" emerged from some hidy-hole and joined him,
and the two rode away side by side conversing amicably. But
not about lynchings or future plans to elude capture; the des-
perado had something more interesting to talk about—Dickens's last book!

So what with old friends and new Fanny was as contented
at Curtis's as she could be in any hotel, and she would have
gone there oftener if the journey had not been so long—eight
hours from New York to Lenox—and so expensive. She was

less well off than she had been; her money had been rein-
vested, in safer securities but at six per cent instead of ten,
and two summers had to be spent at York Farm in spite of the
heat. The heat was devastating; day after day the thermometer stood between ninety and a hundred. In a moment of desperation she cut off her long thick hair, and was thankful—
until she looked in the glass! She wrote to Harriet that the
effect was "dreadfully frightful," although brushed straight
back from her forehead and powdered it gave her a look of
her uncle John Kemble, and added that as soon as the
weather moderated she would wear a three-cornered lace
handkerchief draped over her head and tied loosely under the
chin—she had not lost her flair for dress and knew that the
soft lace would set off her handsome old face to great advantage. In the meantime the heat continued. In another
moment of desperation she and her friend Miss Mary Fox
hurried off to Long Branch, found the huge noisy hotel detestable and hurried back again the next day, Fanny to her
small house, Miss Fox to her large country place, Champlost.

Champlost and its chatelaine brought much pleasure into
these years of Fanny's life. A pretty path ran from one house
to the other and only very bad weather could prevent the two
ladies meeting daily for tea and talk. "Dear Champlost," she
wrote in her memoirs, "an unfailing refuge from trouble and
sorrow, a home of liberty and love, of the happiest companionship and the most devoted friendship . . . The only fault
to be found in Mary's supremely luxurious housekeeping is
that the cream from her Alderney cows is too rich to mix well
with the tea!" But of Mary herself Fanny would not say
much; she was too intimate. Nor did she speak of Mary's
brother, Judge Charles Fox, though that witty, somewhat eccentric person must have added piquancy to Champlost's conversation. As it happens, the two appear in another volume of
reminiscences. Jones Wister was only a boy when he knew
Champlost and seems to have dined there rather unwillingly,
for awkward sixteen found a repast, which, to Fanny's sophis-

tication appeared merely elegant, too awe-inspiring for comfort. Miss Fox presided at one end of the handsome table, "gowned," he wrote, "in cream-colored silk, hair sleeked to the head, wearing white gloves, with two men servants in livery, imported from England, standing behind her chair;" while the Judge lounged opposite her, telling funny stories or interrupting his sister's discourse with a contemptuous *damn!* that would send young guests into fits of suppressed laughter. But Fanny was not so easily daunted; she enjoyed both elegance and wit, and the household was one great compensation for her rather dull life at York Farm when the Leighs were not with her.

The other compensation was the nearness of the Wister family. Butler Place was just across the road; she saw her daughter Sarah every day, Dr. Wister often dropped in, and Owen, sixteen now, was old enough to be companionable. When he came back from St. Paul's for the holidays he would read Fanny verses he had written, or play some bit of music of his own composition that seemed to her to give promise of future genius. Together they began an opera; Owen was to write the music, and his grandmother the libretto.

Now and then some figure from the old life in London would appear at York Farm. One year Lord Houghton, travelling in America, came to stay. Fanny had not wanted to invite him, but her children insisted; he was making a stir in American society and they said it would be great fun to have him. Fanny had to admit that she had known Dicky Milnes very well at one time, he had been an intimate friend of her brother John and one of the Cambridge "Apostles;" but that, she said, was a long long time ago, he would have forgotten her by now. Then too he was accustomed to a luxurious way of living, she was not sure that a rheumatic old gentleman could be made comfortable in her cottage. However, her children persisted; and when she was told that Lord Houghton had spoken of her and of his desire to meet her again, she gave in. She bought some more plates and finger-bowls, gave him the best bedroom in the house, and hoped the chimney would not smoke. He arrived and, to her children's amused satisfaction, greeted her with a hearty kiss and called her *Fanny.* The visit went off well enough; Lord Houghton had lost a little of the lively aggressiveness that had earned him his nicknames of "London Assurance" and the "Cool of the evening," but he was still agreeable. They talked about old times; of Fanny's brother John—who had died in 1857—and praised his *magnum opus,* a 'History of the Saxons,' and wished that he had turned his talents to some more profitable pursuit than research. They recalled the dinner party at Mrs. Procter's where they had first met; Browning had been there too, and Henry Reeve; Henry Reeve, who was responsible for a recent scandalous sensation, the publication of Charles Greville's diary. No doubt Lord Houghton felt, as Fanny did, that the diary should have been destroyed or more carefully edited; shocking, shocking, to comment on Queen Adelaide's bad complexion and to allude to King William's sons so rudely as *bastards!*

But Lord Houghton was getting deaf and had lost a good many teeth; conversation was difficult; Fanny thankfully allowed some of the entertaining to be taken off her hands by the family. The Wisters gave him a large dinner party at Butler Farm, and Mr. Leigh asked some interesting men to meet him—Senator Bayard, Sam Ward, and others—at a little dinner at Augustine's where they enjoyed a typical Philadelphia feast of canvasback, terrapin and Madeira. The latter, according to Mr. Leigh's memoirs, was "a very dry old Butler Madeira, called 'Pale Harriet,'" of such superlative excellence that throughout the long drive home to York Farm over rough roads Lord Houghton slept peacefully, except when jolted awake by an unusually deep rut he would murmur "Dear pale Harriet!" and fall asleep again.

So Fanny could bid her guest goodbye with a feeling of duty done, but also with a feeling of sadness; seeing him looking old had made her feel old herself and their talk had in-

creased her desire for England. She wanted to go home, back
to England and to Adelaide, not for a visit but to settle down
for good. The Leighs were always talking about going back
and never going; James Leigh realized that if he were ever to
take up parish work again he must do it soon, but neither he
nor his wife could bear to leave the plantation. Fanny decided that she could not go alone and reconciled herself to
waiting for the Leighs.

In the meantime the days at York Farm went by pleasantly
enough. Routine is a hastener of time, and the routine she
exacted from herself was conventual in its rigidity. Long ago
at Heath Farm, sitting under a tree with a cabbage-leaf of
strawberries, she had alternated Byron's too stirring poetry
with Jeremy Taylor's calm prose; now, her reading was
carefully planned. So was her correspondence; she always
answered letters in the order they came and a long letter received a long answer, a note a short one; interpreting Shakespeare she took the plays in an arbitrary sequence. Stranger
still, in middle age she began wearing her dresses in rotation;
not, as gossips said, wearing a morning dress at night; it was
not so bad as that. But she did number her evening dresses—
what in those days were called "best dresses"—and wear them
one after the other with little regard for occasion or weather,
and would be seen trailing a white embroidered silk over wet
grass at a garden party, or appearing in a plainish frock at a
ball. Only plainish; she still loved pretty clothes, and in London and Paris that numbered row was a long one.

To her contemporaries this streak of rigidity in a passionate nature was unaccountable. But it seems clear that she was
merely attempting to coerce her emotions. She realized that
her life had been ruined by rebellious emotions. Her rules
were fences—Kemble fences built to control De Camp emotions—and all her life she went on building, adding bars, raising them higher. A hopeless business; she never succeeded in
making her fences passion proof!

Even with the help of routine the days often dragged at

York Farm, for just before settling down there she had given up her Shakespeare readings, finding the fatigue and mental strain too great, and after so many years devoted to some form of creative work life seemed empty. Then a chestful of letters arrived from Harriet St. Leger, Fanny's side of their correspondence of fifty years returned because Harriet's failing eyesight prevented her reading them, she could not bear to destroy them and thought it might give Fanny pleasure to look them over. But there was more pain than pleasure to be found in that Pandora's box crammed with the story of a life. As Fanny sat beside the fire, or on her shady veranda, untying the packets, unfolding the yellowing sheets scrawled with faded ink in her own handwriting, the past became too vivid. Even in appearance the letters marked the passing of time; the earliest, large squarish sheets intricately folded, sealed with wax or wafers; then smaller pages enclosed in envelopes wearing one of Sir Roland Young's new-fangled postage-stamps; the latest, the fashionable note paper of the seventies, smooth tinted lilac paper embossed with a purple monogram. Now and then, she laughed as she read and added the letter to a pile beside her; often, she tore the sheet across and across with a gesture of anger or let it drop into the fire reluctantly and sadly. Sometimes she would sit for a long time with an open letter in her lap, staring into the fire or across the lawn seeing, not the red embers or the green grass, but herself—"herself when young." Remembering a long swinging gallop on a frosty morning, snow flakes prickling her cheeks; the rush of water as she waded knee-deep into a trout stream and the sound of the line as it swished and flicked; the look of an ice-capped peak at sunset. Perfect moments, many perfect moments in that story of a life. Outwardly, the girl who had enjoyed them was as dead as if she were lying beside Aunt Dall in Mount Auburn cemetery; inwardly, she was still on fire with passion for adventure. Why, oh why, could not the flesh keep pace with the spirit!

But whether she read with pain or pleasure, as she read she

planned; for she saw that the letters could provide her with what she needed; occupation. Here was material for a volume of most entertaining reminiscences. That girlish self of hers had written recklessly and often foolishly, but she had written well. The editor of the 'Atlantic' would probably take a few chapters, and then perhaps some London publisher would make her memoirs into a book.

She began by destroying every letter that touched on her matrimonial difficulties, and wherever Pierce's name occurred it became a blank; but her literary sense warned her not to omit all personalities or the flavor of her story would vanish, and as she was blessed with a visual memory that covered an extraordinary length of time she was able to present a clearer picture of a longer past than any other reminiscent writer has ever achieved. It is as if Frith's 'Derby Day' and 'Euston Station' were supplemented by a thousand similar scenes, accurate in detail, showing most of the important persons in England and America, and unrolled as a panorama labeled 'The Nineteenth Century.'

Memoirs of this quality could not fail to be successful. They first appeared in the 'Atlantic' as a series of articles called 'Old Woman's Gossip'—she had suggested, with characteristic depreciation of her work, 'Elderly Female Twaddle' as still more appropriate. They proved extremely popular, and as readers never seemed to get tired of Mrs. Kemble's recollections she went on writing. In all she published three volumes: 'Records of a Girlhood,' 'Records of Later Life' and 'Further Records;' they brought her a wider public than even her acting or her Shakespearean readings both in England and America, and royalties soon made up for the recent reduction in her income. She also received the inevitable aftermath of letters; it was pleasant to hear from a very very old lady in New York who had seen Mrs. Siddons as Belvidera; less pleasant to get a complaining letter from her friend Richard Trench, now Archbishop of Dublin, who wrote that his feelings had been hurt by her account of the Torrijos expedition of 1830 in which he and her brother John had been involved. As she had spoken kindly of that quixotic attempt she was puzzled; until, later on, she discovered that as no member of the archbishop's large family knew he had taken part in the "Spanish Crusade," when it all came out in her book they had, naturally, been amused and their father annoyed.

So she wrote busily at York Farm while she was waiting for the Leighs to make up their minds to leave Georgia and was beginning to feel the fatigue when, most opportunely, James Leigh told her of a new invention, a small printing machine "worked by merely striking the keys as one plays a piano." She bought one of these ingenious little contrivances at once, learned to manipulate it and by the autumn of 1875 was dispatching to the 'Atlantic' what must have been one of its earliest typewritten manuscripts.

Thus employed the years of 1875 and 1876 went quietly by. Marked, however, by three occurrences that made them memorable to all Philadelphians. The Colorado beetle appeared in the east; Charley Ross was kidnaped, and American independence was celebrated by the Centennial exhibition. With her detestation of creeping things, she found the potato-bug plague indescribably sickening. As the insect army came marching across the country, roads and garden paths glistened with shiny yellow backs that crunched under foot and every potato patch was reduced to leafless stalks crawling with loathsome pinkish grubs; they gathered so thick on the walls of her house that although they were scraped off into dustpans three times a day they managed to creep into the bedrooms and clothes closet; she never forgot that dreadful potato-bug summer. She was of course deeply stirred by the mysterious tragedy in the family of her neighbors, the Rosses. But the Centennial excitement left her cold. It seemed to her, as to many others, that the United States might better attend to its political and financial difficulties than invite the whole world to visit Philadelphia in the middle of summer. The buildings were hideous, the heat was intense; "as hot as the

Centennial summer," became a saying. One visit was enough. She came away with a confused impression of good-natured crowds gaping at statues made of butter, vases shaped like slippers, fountains that dripped on the tin umbrellas of little terra-cotta boys and girls.

The autumn brought two epidemics. Influenza in the North—Dr. Wister considered it a form of the cattle plague— and an outbreak of yellow fever in the South that at one time threatened to reach Philadelphia and ruin the Centennial. The pestilence was so fatal in Georgia that it probably helped the Leighs to make up their minds to abandon the plantation. Winter found the long-discussed question settled at last. The Leighs reluctantly began their preparations for leaving America early in the new year, and Fanny decided to go with them.

To her surprise, now that she was no longer tied to America she realized there were many places and people she would be sorry never to see again. She was beginning to feel her age —Victorians considered a woman old at sixty-seven; once settled in England, after eighteen voyages across the Atlantic, America, she knew, would seem very far away. So her last look at the blue hills of the Berkshires that autumn, and her last trip to Mount Auburn cemetery where she and Pierce had walked together when they were first engaged and where Dall was buried, were sad with the added sadness of finality. The dull business of packing trunks and finding homes for various possessions became an almost unendurable recapitulation of the past. Mary Fox's greenhouse received a flowering plant of many memories, a Catalonia jasmine that had been Pierce's first present to her after their marriage; she dined at Champlost for the last time. A last Christmas at York Farm came and went; young Owen home for the holidays, a Christmas tree for little Alice, an ice storm that turned paths so glassy that Fanny's present to the elder Owen, a basket of Château Yquem, came near perishing on its way to Butler Place. A last going to church with all her children and grandchildren; a last letter from America to Harriet, so old and blind now that it ended reassuringly "You will never be altered to me. Those that we love never alter, unless we cease to love them, and I am ever *as* ever, your Fanny Kemble, as you will be to the last, ever *as* ever, my Harriet St. Leger." A last night, spent at Butler Place and in her own room there; then off to New York with the Leighs, a large family party; little Alice and her nurse, Fanny's English servants, a colored boy from the plantation, as well as James and Frances Leigh and Fanny herself. Then, all goodbyes said, on board the 'Britannic,' watching New York's skyline dwindle in the distance.

It was cold; Fanny shivered as she stood there on the deck recalling her first sight of America glimmering through the haze of a midsummer morning. August then, January now. But January was no more unlike August than she herself— dignified matron, in feathered bonnet and velvet dolman, sur- rounded by a family—was unlike the laughing girl who had danced away the last night on board ship, full skirts balloon- ing about her ankles in the fashion of 1832. And this huge White Star liner moving solemnly from the pier, how unlike she was to the little sailing vessel that had come tossing to an- chor after that first crossing, a voyage of seven weeks; the 'Britannic,' would make it in seven days. New York too was utterly different. In 1832 Fanny had seen a harbor white with sails, rickety wharfs pricked by hundreds of tall masts; a small town, half wood, half brick, brightly painted, green with trees. Now she saw heavy dark piers, fewer masts, the smoke of many steamships, a higher skyline—architects were plan- ning a building ten stories high—dull in color; a city of brown stone dwellings, dingy warehouses, smoke-stained, hideous (but not altogether Philistine. Olmsted was laying out Central Park, Damrosch founding the Symphony Society, and the Academy of Music on Fourteenth Street was the finest opera house in the world). And New York was typical; the whole country had utterly changed since Fanny's début. Although the first decade had brought the greatest material change— America never again saw such expansion as in the years between 1830 and 1840—a more fundamental change soon became evident. Fanny, always sensitive to the inward and spiritual, had felt it coming. Just after the Civil War she wrote to a friend: "When I first came here the whole country was like some remote part of England that I had never seen before, the people were like *queer* English people. Now there is not a trace of their British origin, except their speech, and they are becoming a real nation."

Now in 1877 her prophecy had come true. The melting pot had gone on filling and boiling; America had ceased to be English; Fanny was glad to be going home.

CHAPTER XXVII

The Delectable Mountains

"Better to breathe at large on this clear height,
Than toil in endless sleep from dream to dream."

—WORDSWORTH.

FORTUNATELY FOR Fanny's peace of mind no such momentous inward change had come about at home. The outward change was disquieting enough. The England of her girlhood—the England of William IV and the Reform Bill—had vanished as completely as the America of Andrew Jackson and nullification. Wellington and Peele had given way to Disraeli and Gladstone, Macaulay and Sydney Smith to Swinburne and Rossetti, Cruikshank to Du Maurier. London was discussing Home Rule and the Pre-Raphaelites; blue china plates had appeared on drawing-room walls and sunflowers in gardens; Oscar Wilde was on his way from Ireland; Victoria had been proclaimed Empress of India. In short, it was the year 1877 and the Victorian era was at the top-notch of its glory.

One suspects that, to Fanny, this gorgeous England seemed a trifle overblown. If American civilization had been too immature for her England, on the other hand, was too sophisticated, too luscious, too sentimental. A taste formed on Racine and Scott, and nourished on Shakespeare, a taste that still preferred Crabbe to any modern poet, would have considered 'The Blessed Damozel' affected and 'The Garden of Proserpine' both cloying and blasphemous. She would have found still less to admire in later eccentricities of the esthetic movement. She would have seen more wickedness than beauty in Aubrey Beardsley's line and little wit in the 'Yellow Book,' and her contempt for Oscar Wilde's costume and literary style would have been expressed with such Old Testament vigor

366

that one regrets her memoirs could not have been carried just a little farther. Fanny's comments on the *fin-de-siècle* type,

> "The greenery-yallery
> Grosvenor Gallery,
> Foot-in the-grave
> Young man,"

would have been worth reading.

But her life, like the century, had entered its last quarter. She had always been intolerant of weakness; she refused to believe that a record of declining years could be of interest to the public. So when her chief link with the past was broken by the death of Harriet St. Leger soon after her return to England, she decided that it was time to stop writing about herself, and except for a few scattered letters to others, none dated later than 1877 were published. From then on, one sees Fanny Kemble only through the eyes of her friends.

Perhaps it is as well. Her own picture of herself would have emphasized the flaws of old age, all the bodily infirmities and restrictions that she found so intolerable; her friends' "portrait of an old lady" is probably a good deal truer to life. And surely no human being ever possessed so many friends and such warm ones, or so many who were able to express their admiration in writing. From her earliest youth Fanny's friendships had been her chief consolation and pleasure; only death could rob her of a real friend; in old age she could still echo Madame du Deffand's, "J'aime l'amitié à la folie!" To the very end, she seems never to have lost her power of attraction; if she chose to make a gesture of friendliness it was eagerly accepted; no one was too young, or too celebrated, or too *blasé* to refuse; the friendship of Fanny Kemble was an honor.

She could charm, *if she chose;* if she did not choose, or if the gesture of friendliness came, not from her but from some intruder who failed to please her fastidious taste, the result was apt to be disastrous. Any hint of pretentiousness or affectation, of meanness or lack of sincerity would antagonize her; and, once antagonized, she could be ruthless. A notable instance was an encounter (some years before her final return to England) with Eliza Lynn-Lynton, the typical strong-minded female of the day, who recorded her impressions of Mrs. Kemble in the waspish style for which she was famous, a diatribe that included a dozen such adjectives as brutal, arbitrary, insolent, inhuman, and ending: "Her assumption of supremacy and cruel strength crushed me flat. The way in which she levelled her black eyes at me, and calmly put her foot on me, gave me a sort of shuddering horror of her such as I fancy a man might feel for one who had flayed him in the market place." Poor Fanny! Obviously she had taken a violent dislike to Mrs. Lynn-Lynton at first sight, a dislike easily understood if 'Punch's' caricature was fair and if the lady's expression was as malignant in real life as in her portraits. One wishes that Fanny too had recorded her impressions—there is no mention of either the flaying or the victim in Fanny's memoirs—or that one could know what she and Mrs. Browning said when they compared notes. For the gentle Elizabeth of Wimpole Street also earned her drop of vitriol; Mrs. Lynn-Lynton wrote: "I used to feel as if I were on a moral dissecting table, when Mrs. Browning probed my thoughts and touched speculative tracts which probably seemed to her hopelessly wrong and corrupt," and this bitterness is understandable in both instances when one remembers that Mrs. Lynn-Lynton, dedicated to the castigation of society, was in the habit of attending to all necessary *flayings* and *probings* herself.

As a rule Fanny's plain speaking was not resented. Her friends had long been accustomed to making allowances, and though they might laugh at her abrupt methods with the boring or impertinent they loved her for her frankness and wit. Now, in her old age, Mrs. Kemble's sharp sayings were treasured and repeated; a caller lucky enough to carry away some anecdote illustrating her "hate of hate and scorn of scorn" could regale his acquaintances as acceptably as if he had brought a special brand of caviare or truffles from abroad. If she had chosen to make the effort she could have been a figure in London society.

But society was the last thing she wanted now. Only a few friends and relations were admitted to her drawing-room, a beautiful room, all violet and purple—violet silk curtains, violet velvet cushions, deeper-colored carpet—fragrant with the mingled scent of flowers and Russia leather that she loved, and gay with singing birds; she herself in her velvet and lace as beautiful as her setting. She had kept her liking for dress, her taste was still exquisite; she had once been the best-dressed actress on the English stage, now she was the best dressed old lady in London. No one was ever bored in that drawing-room so the young came as eagerly as the old. Some member of the younger generation—a nephew or niece, a grandchild, or the child of an old friend—was pretty sure to drop in for tea, or stop on the way home after a new play to regale her with the latest theatrical gossip. Perhaps it would be Harry Kemble, her brother Henry's son, who had taken to the family profession and was nicknamed the "Beetle" by his fellow actors because of the big brown cloak he usually wore, come to describe Irving's last success; he would laugh at his aunt's summing up of the modern drama: "We have archeology," she would remark, "we have ethnology, history, geography, and upholstery; we have, in short, everything but acting, which it seems we cannot have," and then qualify her condemnation, recalling Tom Taylor's prophecy that "Miss Ellen Terry would become a consummate comic actress," and agree that Taylor had been right. Sometimes Harry would persuade her to describe some splendid figure of the past such as Rachel, whom she still considered the greatest dramatic genius she had ever seen except Kean, "and he," she said, "was not greater," ending: "Rachel excelled Ristori as much in tenderness as she did in power, and as for any comparison between Rachel and her successor on the French stage, Mademoiselle Sarah Bernhardt, I do not admit any such for a moment." An allusion to the "Bacon-Shakespeare theory" would bring a burst of righteous anger. She had been intimate, she said, with those great Shakespearean editors and commentators, Harness, Milman, Dyce and Collier, and with many Shakespearean scholars such as Donne, Spedding, Edward Fitzgerald and Horace Furness, and "not one of them ever mentioned the question 'Who wrote Shakespeare?' except as a ludicrous thing to be laughed at."

Other frequent visitors in the London house were the Santleys, Gertrude—Fanny's niece, daughter of John—and her husband, Charles Santley the singer, whom Fanny admired for his delightful voice, and continued to like even after he had told her that she was a conceited old woman. "Nobody ever dared to speak so to me before!" she had flamed out at him; but she had forgiven him, and after that a tirade was apt to soften into, "Although I *am* a conceited old woman, dear!" Perhaps, while the Santleys were still with her, May Gordon, Adelaide's daughter, would rush in, fresh from a Bach concert rehearsal where she had been singing cherubim in the amateur chorus, and more tea would be sent for. Or one of the Leighs would appear hungry and thirsty, and expecting a special sort of tea-cake. Everybody would talk at once; they would rave over Joachim's playing or Leighton's pictures, somebody would speak of the new Gilbert and Sullivan operetta, and May or Charles Santley would be sent to the piano to give Aunt Fanny a taste of 'Pinafore;' the mockingbirds and canaries would sing their heads off, Aunt Fanny would applaud and send for another brew of tea and hotter scones. Everybody would eat more than was good for them and stay until all hours. And the more they ate and the longer they stayed the better she liked it; for she was happier in her present *rôle* of grandmamma and aunt "giving the children a good time," as the Americans would say, than in any of her great successes on the stage.

None of this easy intimacy would have been possible with an earlier generation of young people; Fanny's vivid personality had made them feel insignificant, and she was too unexpected, too alive, too unconventional to be accepted as the perfect aunt or grandmother except by little children— little children always adored her. The young people of twenty years before had been afraid of Mrs. Kemble. It was different now. That awesome tradition in the background gave a piquancy to the present situation. It was as if the splendid fierce exotic bird that one's parents had admired from a distance as it came flashing through the jungle, were now so comfortably domesticated at the Zoo that its feathers could be stroked by the hand of the timidest debutante.

Even young friends of an earlier generation, once afraid of her, had lost their awe now. When Thackeray's daughter, Anne Ritchie, came to see her they would laugh at some incident of the past such as the drive in Rome when the coachman having asked where he should go, Mrs. Kemble's gay answer, "*Andate al Diavalo*—anywhere!" had seemed, to prim sixteen, strange language for a lady; and then, as they drove on and the carriage reached the open flowery spaces of the campagna, the air and the blue of the distant hills had gone to Mrs. Kemble's head, she had burst out singing—a loud passionate song, not the sort of song a lady ought to sing. Amusing to remember, those far off Roman days when young Anne had been so young that she had been alarmed by Mrs. Kemble's exuberance, had had her doubts as to the suitability of Mrs. Kemble's way of dressing; thick soft deep-colored velvets and silks were becoming, she looked much handsomer than Mrs. Browning "dim in her dusky gown," but was such conspicuous richness quite proper for a middle-aged person? Now, here in London, Mrs. Kemble might have worn a djiba, rather than the most perfect old lady costume that Paris could provide, for all her visitor cared. When, later on, Lady Ritchie set down her impressions, though she dwelt on the outward magnificence of her old friend it was far less impor-

tant than Mrs. Kemble's "passionate love of truth and justice," the "gift that she possessed to a rare degree of ennobling
that to which she turned her mind," and her kindness "the
virtue by which she brought us all into subjection."

But charming young friends and relations could not of
course rival friends known since childhood, and of these,
though many had gone, some of the best were still left. One
was Arthur Malkin, son of John's much loved schoolmaster
at Bury St. Edmund's. Fanny's American years had not
broken this friendship for letter writing came easily to people who shared a passion—perhaps the most mysterious of all
primeval passions, overwhelming some natures and leaving
others untouched—a passion for mountain climbing. There
had been no snow mountains in Fanny's youth; heathery
hills, trout streams, the sea, but no peaks, no glaciers or water
falls. In middle-age, just when she most needed help, she discovered the Alps and found there comfort such as she found
nowhere else except in Shakespeare; there was indeed, to her
mind, a kinship between his greatness and the greatness of
the Alps. Her letters written to Arthur Malkin from the
sleepy warm flatness of York Farm had been sick with nostalgia, she had sighed for the icy breath of Swiss water falls and
milk white glacier streams. After receiving a letter from him
even Lenox would seem tame; "I seized my Murray," she
wrote in answer, "I seized my maps, I seized my Bartlett'
Swiss views; I envied you, sore feet, sore face, sore eyes and
all." Even the English seashore failed to satisfy. She might
begin a letter: "I have come in wringing wet with spray
and mist, the wild west wind is driving the big waves of the
Atlantic into the Channel and cramming and piling them on
the shore here, it is a grand sight and makes one wish that
one had the Fribourg organ in one's breast, that one might
sing aloud, 'Glory to God!' " but she would add: "Oh how I
wish I had heard your mountain talk with your climbing
friend!" and end with a revision of her old longing for death
from the back of a galloping horse on a fine day: "Surely if I

had been a man I should have lived on a peak, died in a
crevice, and been buried in an avalanche."

Switzerland once discovered a summer not spent in the
mountains was a summer wasted; there were not many such.
In one of the earliest and happiest she had had her daughter
Frances for a companion; later on, her nephew Harry. Punctually on June first she would arrive, punctually on September first depart. She became a well known figure in Alpine
villages, admired for her courage and her voice—she had
never lost her old trick of singing in any moment of exalta-
tion, glad or sorry. The guides adored her; they had their own
name for her; they called her *"la dame qui va chantant par
les montagnes,"* "the lady who goes singing through the
mountains." Old age was almost upon her when she achieved
her last mountain pass left unexplored, the Stelvio. She remained insatiable. "If it should please God," she wrote to
Arthur, "though I am old, fat and rheumatic, I will, nevertheless, go over certain of those Swiss passes next summer; if
not on my own legs, why, then on mule's legs; and if not on
mule's legs, why, then on men's legs, in a *chaise à porteur*
with sixteen men to carry me, as I had going up Vesuvius."
As long as it was humanly possible she ignored her disabilities;
doing what she could but seeing every summer her mountains receding, forced to content herself with circling lower
and lower around their feet, until the inevitable came and
she could only sit on hotel balconies gazing at her paradise
lost, thinking, perhaps, of that Swiss girl, taken away from
the Alps forever in her youth, the De Camp grandmother,
who had bequeathed her homesick love and longing to her
daughter and her daughter's daughter.

But back in smoky London there were still memories; and
when Arthur Malkin came they would return in spirit to the
Alps; they would discuss outfits and guides, argue about
heights and ascents. Counting up various ascents of the
Shreckhorn she would quote her Lenox friend Professor Agassiz, and they would envy him his ascents, the days and

nights spent on the ice of the Aar glacier, his endurance, his indifference to altitude—Agassiz had smoked a pipe all the way up the Jungfrau! And if, as they talked, she let Arthur guess her hatred of old age, and how cheap she held much that she had lost—it was not the waning of her intellectual powers, nor her charm, nor her good looks, that she most regretted, but the young strong supple active body of her girlhood—it did not matter, for Arthur too was old; he too was a wing-clipped wild duck swimming round and round in a freezing pond, open water dwindling every day. But no regret could hold her long; in an instant she would be off again, to snow fields trimmed with small bright flowers, green setas and the tinkling of cowbells; her "do you remembers?" would piece together forgotten hours and as they reconstructed some day of special beauty and adventure the future could be ignored and the present seem less important than the past.

Another family friend with whom the past—a different and remoter past—could be easily revived, was Edward Fitzgerald, born in the same year as Fanny herself, one of the gifted babies of 1809 (she was to outlive them all except Holmes and Gladstone), she and "Fitz" had kept up a correspondence during her American absences. Their parents had been friends, they had played together as children; he wrote from intimate knowledge when he summed her up: "A more honest, truthful, generous and constant woman I have never known." In these latter London days they saw much of each other. He was a celebrity now; but when he came to call they did not talk of Omar Khayyam or of her stage successes, but of the old days in Paris when she had been a school-girl at Mrs. Rowden's and he a little boy living just around the corner. Together they would reconstruct the street, the Rue d'Angoulême—house on the corner of the Champs Elysées, with ornaments in stone of flowers and fruit, that belonged to Lord Courtenay—a Pépinière over the way—over that, a glimpse of the Temple in the Beaujon Gardens, Parisians ascending and descending in cars—at the end of the street, the

Church of St. Philippe du Roule. Or he would speak of his mother's affection for Fanny's mother; according to Mrs. Fitzgerald, Mrs. Charles Kemble was "by far the most witty, sensible and agreeable woman she knew," and he would please Fanny by noting the likeness between mother and daughter. "When you first came to visit us in 1852," he told her, "I saw your mother in you; that is, I saw her much as I had seen her in a little sixpenny engraving in a cottage bonnet, something such as you wore that day as you stepped out of your chaise at the Crown Inn." Coming down to later times he would recall a dinner party of six at a round table, Mrs. Charles Kemble at the head and Fanny next to him, as "one of the few delightful dinner parties I ever was at," and a dinner Fanny had given for him and the Donnes before taking them to see Wigan in 'Still Waters', a play that interested her because she was responsible for the plot which she had found in a French novel. This would lead to talk of other plays and other friends. When he quoted their friend Spedding as saying that Irving's Hamlet was "simply hideous," and that Ellen Terry's Portia was a *"simply perfect* performance, remembering all the while how fine was Fanny Kemble's" Fanny agreed and was pleased. But it is doubtful if she was entirely in accord with Fitz's criticism of Tennyson: "If he had ever led an active life, as Scott or Shakespeare; or even ridden, shot, drunk and played the Devil like Byron, he would have done much more and talked about it much less," for though she loved most forms of sport she did not think well of playing the Devil. However they were at one again in their laughter when, apropos of his sister Jane, he told Fanny that when he described Jane's husband as

"A Mr. Wilkinson, a clergyman,"

Tennyson had exclaimed, "Why that is verse!" and he and Tennyson had often argued as to which of them was responsible for this, "the worst verse in the English language."

And then one autumn day in 1879 Fitz came, not to laugh and gossip with his old friend, but to sympathize. Adelaide was dead. Adelaide of the golden voice; she whom one admirer described as being *"de la bohème exquise,"* and another, Mrs. Browning, liked best to remember as "singing passionately and talking eloquently," while for Anne Ritchie it was her beauty that was memorable. Lady Ritchie never forgot the day she saw Adelaide Sartoris standing in the drawing-room of her Park Lane house with its high carved cabinets and tapestries, a great golden glass over her head, looking in her brocaded velvet like a picture of Tintoret's, or the day when dressed in gray satin Adelaide sat bent over a golden-headed little boy. Gold—there was always this thread of gold running through Adelaide's web of life. Fanny must have envied her sister's prosperity a little; it is certain that she envied the serenity of Adelaide's family life, but she was never jealous of Adelaide. The sisters were remarkably united, their minds "marched together," they had the same extreme sensitiveness to beauty in nature and art; when Adelaide died, Fanny suffered the last great loss of her life.

Adelaide gone and the Wisters left behind in America, the Leighs became Fanny's closest family tie. They lived at Stratford in an ancient house, Alverston Manor, once a monastery, in such a beautiful setting of elms, broad smooth grass walks where the monks had been used to meditate and fish ponds where they had caught their Friday meals that it consoled the Leighs for having abandoned Georgia. Of all Fanny's family circle of this time James Leigh was perhaps best fitted to understand her. He had known her first in America as a vigorous, handsome, middle-aged woman at the height of her popularity as an interpreter of Shakespeare, but he was also familiar with her English background; he was able to recreate her past and, as he had some psychological insight, account for a few of the many contradictions in her character and even trace them to prenatal sources. He wrote of her: "It was a superabundant dual nature partaking of the extreme characteristics of her parents . . . From her father she inherited a theatrical descent of two generations, but it was from her mother, who was French, that she got that vivid and versatile temperament which was the delight of those remarkable men and women with whom she came in contact."

And just outside the family circle stood another observer as understanding as James Leigh and far better fitted to record his impressions. That "dual nature"—Kemble intellect, De Camp passion—was in Fanny's last years to be studied by a master in the art of analysis and of expression, for whom the intricacies of human nature were the chief interest in life. Henry James's friendship with Fanny Kemble came about through his intimacy with the Leighs, but his memory took him back to a very early day when he, a small child driving in a carriage along an American country road, met a lady on horseback remembered as his "first sight of a living Amazon;" then came two treats of his childhood, her 'Lear' and 'Midsummer Night's Dream'—black velvet for 'Lear,' white satin for the 'Dream'—followed by later occasions when, a young man now, he had heard her read for charity, ending with 'Henry V.' "It was," he wrote later on, "the play she loved best to read . . . It was gallant and martial and intensely English . . . Her splendid tones and her face, lighted like that of a war-goddess, seemed to fill the performance with the hurry of armies and the sound of battle . . . The illusion was that of a multitude and a pageant." There were memories too of Roman days when he got his first near glimpse of the great lady, "still retaining in aspect so much that had made her admirably handsome (including the marked splendor of apparel) as she rolled in the golden sunshine, in her high carriage, through Borghese villas and round Pincian hills."

At length there came a Christmas Day in the late seventies spent with the Leighs at Alverston Manor, a perfect setting for holiday festivities. One of Fanny's last letters to Harriet described the scene in little Alice's immense nursery with its lofty arched roof of oak rafters and cavernous chimney-piece,

the red-cheeked English maids mounted on ladders helping a
Negro boy from the Georgia plantation to hang great wreaths
of laurel and holly, and in the centre a fir tree on an oak table,
where "our dark bearded handsome American friend, Henry
James the author," was busy decorating the branches with
toys and bonbons.

That Christmas brought Fanny an enduring pleasure; her
friendship with Henry James brightened the last fifteen years
of her life. It would be interesting to know what she thought
of him, for she too saw deep into human nature; unfortunately, soon after that Christmas at Alverston Manor she
brought her memoirs to an end. But his record is most satisfying. The monograph in 'Essays in London' * is one of the
best things of the sort ever written, certainly the best written
about Fanny Kemble, and it will never be surpassed for James
is the last who could paint her from life. Moreover, something of her straightforwardness seems to have got into his
style; he wrote of her with simplicity as well as with affection:
"She was one of the rarest of women . . . one of the finest and
most original of talkers . . . She wrote exactly as she talked,
observing, asserting, complaining, confiding, contradicting,
crying out and bounding off, always effectually communicat-
ing . . . A prouder nature never affronted the long humilia-
tion of life . . . The faculty for self-derision was never richer
or droller." As an artist, he valued her power to picture the
past of the London he loved: "She reanimated the old drawing-rooms, relighted the old lamps, retuned the old pianos,"
and he envied her a creative force that, in extreme old age,
could turn to a new form of literature—at eighty she wrote
'Far Away and Long Ago,' a novel with a strange wild plot
but a good setting, the New England country she knew so
well. As a psychologist, her character fascinated him: "She
was composed of contrasts and opposites . . . An extraordinary
mixture of incongruous things, of England and France in her
blood, of America and England in her relationships, of the

* Published by Harper & Brothers. Reprinted by permission.

footlights and the glaciers in her activities, of conformity and contumacy in her character and tragedy and comedy in her talk." Like James Leigh he guessed at remote ancestral causes for these inconsistencies: "She was a reactionary Kemble . . . French rose as quickly and racily to her lips as English and corresponded to the strong strain she owed to the foreignness of her remarkable mother, a person as to whom it was impossible, in her company, not to have a lively curiosity . . . The clever and continental Mrs. Charles Kemble had in advance enlarged the situation, multiplied the elements, contributed space and air." Immediate causes, "the two resounding false notes" that created the discords, were easily discerned: "She detested the stage, to which she had been dedicated while too young to judge," and "the great tempest of her life, her wholly unprosperous marriage, had created waves of feeling which even after long years refused to be stilled, continued to gather and break."

Such understanding is rare enough in any friendship; one may be sure that Fanny was grateful. She was grateful too to her young friend for being young. Not many old ladies of seventy odd could boast of a clever young man—two, in fact, there was Hamilton Aïdé as well, another young novelist— always ready to escort her to plays and concerts, discuss the newest books, or that brand-new adventure in the arts, the Grosvenor Gallery. James or Aïdé—she called them proudly, "my two young men"—or some other young person, was always at her command for there was not only a flattering distinction in being seen with Mrs. Kemble—so celebrated, so handsome and so well dressed—she had her own inimitable way of repaying a companion. Chance allusion could send her back into a past unbelievably remote to the young, and she would return with some priceless, brightly-colored scrap—an anecdote of the Regent, Scott, Byron, the Duke of Wellington— that but for her would have been lost forever. Someone might praise a queer new novel called 'Peter Ibbetson,' a dreamland

story; she would hark back to the days of Sir Thomas Lawrence, recall his theory that in dreams one never became a
child again even in revisiting the scenes of one's childhood;
and then, stepping nearer to the present, recall a story told
her by another old friend, Frederick Maurice, that contradicted Lawrence. Maurice, she said, had once known a woman
lovely in youth, married to a bad man, who had for years led
a double existence. Every night she would dream herself back
into the home of her childhood and the next night take up
her dream again where she had left it; until, deteriorating
under her husband's influence, she gradually lost the trick of
"dreaming true."

No topic, however, could rival the stage as an inspirer of
reminiscence and to take Mrs. Kemble to a play was to make
it memorable. Driving home in her carriage through the
crowded London streets after a French comedy memories
would come to her of Paris holidays sixty years ago, and her
rendering of Poitier's shriek *"Aprochez-vous plus loin!"* as
the scandalized spinster in 'Les Anglaises Pour Rire,' would
reduce her young companion to helpless laughter. Or, if the
performance had been Shakespearean, there would follow,
according to Henry James, "an epilogue that was the real
interest of the evening—a beautiful rally, often an exquisite
protest, of all her own instincts . . . Those who went with her
to the play in the last years of her life will remember the
Juliets, the Beatrices, the Rosalinds whom she could still
make vivid without any accessory except the surrounding
London roar."

So Henry James was grateful too, and the friendship between the clever young man and the clever old woman
ripened through those last years and ended only with her
death. Fanny Kemble died in London at the Leighs' house
in Gloucester Place, January 15th, 1893, aged eighty-three.
James Leigh wrote in his memoirs: "I telegraphed to Henry
James to come at once, which he did, and was of the greatest
assistance interviewing the pressmen who crowded in for in-

formation." She who had all her life "suffered publicity as she suffered bad weather" was, at last, free from both.

But a death notice is a poor cold thing to set at the end of a story such as Fanny Kemble's. In the most commonplace lives there must be best moments, when life reaches its highest perfection or deepest enjoyment. She was an extreme example of what Wordsworth calls "a creature of a fiery heart," the lives of such are crowded with intense moments, and "from the first"—Henry James again—"she had abundantly lived." The top moment may have come in childhood; perhaps with that first startled reading of Byron's,

> "It is the hour when from the boughs
> The nightingale's high note is heard,"

remembered as "a revelation of the power of thought and language." Perhaps it was her first glimpse of Niagara, Trelawny drawing her to the brink of the abyss—"O God, who can describe that sight!" It may have come and gone unrecognized; a gallop on horseback along the sea beach at Nahant, Pierce beside her, neither of them aware that they would never be so happy again; or in Georgia, her small Sally on the saddle-bow, or alone but laughing at the antics of the scuttling crabs and rejoicing in the vivid coral-color of the weeds that bordered the causeway. Anyhow, whenever great moments may have come in her youth one may be sure that they were never connected with any personal triumph; no theatrical success, not even her debut as Juliet; no poem she wrote, or song she sang. As for the middle years, there can be no doubt whatever; she found not only supreme moments but whole hours and days of perfect happiness and release in the Alps. Henry James's picture cannot be bettered: "Those who had not known her in Switzerland never knew what admirable nonsense she could talk, nor with what originality and gaiety she could invite the spirit of mirth, flinging herself, in the joy of high places, on the pianos of mountain inns, joking, punning, botanizing, encouraging the lowly and abasing the proud (that was almost her mission in life) and startling infallibly all primness of propriety."

So it will be fairest to leave Fanny Kemble in the Alps, where she would like best to have been left, remembering her as the Swiss guides remembered her:

"*La dame qui va chantant par les montagnes.*"

THE END